CAMBRIDGE SERIES ON
HUMAN–COMPUTER
INTERACTION 11

Virtual Individuals, Virtual Groups

Cambridge Series on Human–Computer Interaction

Virtual Individuals, Virtual Groups

Human Dimensions of Groupware and Computer Networking

Jo Ann Oravec
Baruch College

CAMBRIDGE
UNIVERSITY PRESS

Published by the Press Syndicate of the University of Cambridge
The Pitt Building, Trumpington Street, Cambridge CB2 1RP
40 West 20th Street, New York, NY 10011-4211, USA
10 Stamford Road, Oakleigh, Melbourne 3166, Australia

First published 1996

Printed in the United States of America

Library of Congress Cataloging-in-Publication Data
Oravec, Jo Ann.
Virtual individuals, virtual groups : human dimensions of
groupware and computer networking / Jo Ann Oravec.
p.   cm. – (Cambridge series on human–computer interaction ;
11) Includes index.
ISBN 0-521-45493-X (hc)
1. Human–computer interaction.   2. Virtual reality.   3. Computer
networks.   I. Title.   II. Series.
QA76.9.H85073   1996
302.3 – dc20   95-31984
                                                             CIP

A catalog record for this book is available from the British Library.

ISBN 0-521-45493-X Hardback

Contents

v

To my father

Overview

We all have had experiences we labeled as successful – perhaps even joyful – workplace or educational collaborations, where joint effort was free-flowing and results obtained were far greater than those any individual could have produced alone. The goal of facilitating such interaction with computer networks raises a number of difficult questions. How do we establish adequate platforms for self-development and self-expression, while providing vehicles for support of productive and efficient collaboration? How do we counterbalance powerful managerial and technological strategies with safeguards for the rights of individuals in their associations? This book takes a first step toward answering these questions.

In Chapter 1, I introduce and develop the notions of the "virtual individual" and "virtual group," and explore how these entities play critical roles in human expression and interpersonal relationships. In this chapter, I also provide background and analysis on the research and application areas of network-based systems, with emphasis on groupware or "computer-supported cooperative work" (CSCW) approaches and linkages of groupware to the Internet and other large-scale networks. Although groupware and other network-based applications are of relatively recent vintage, they have roots that reach far back into the histories of computing, as well as the social and managerial sciences. I consider these applications in light of their many dimensions, in part by developing the notions of "genre" and "narrative" in relation to the growing varieties of computer artifacts and forms of computer-mediated expression.

Chapter 2 provides more discussion of virtual individuals and groups, and explores how people relate to and manage these entities (in effect, how they manage their own and others' portraits, records, profiles, and group contributions). I discuss a number of perspectives on the social construction of individuals and groups, and relate them to current trends in computer networking and virtual reality (VR) applications. I outline current and emerging strategies for construction of groups; for example, "ideal type" models of groups and group pathologies are reflected in many network-based system development initiatives, as well as in efforts of managers to understand and control groups. In Chapter 3, I discuss "collaboration" and "cooperation" in workplace, educational, and research contexts, stressing some of their rhetorical dimensions. Until recently, relatively little attention was given by the social and managerial sciences to the study of collaboration in knowledge work. Groupware and other computer network applications have provided a focus for research in this area, as well as for the day-to-day practices of managers and administrators.

In Chapter 4, I provide an analysis of some artifacts related to or integrated into network-based system applications (including video, design tools, whiteboards and blackboards, desks, filing cabinets, and office environments).

Many themes and issues that have arisen in discourse on computer networking have close counterparts in the history of these related artifacts and associated genres. Network-based computer systems are entering educational and workplace settings that have already been engineered in many ways to reinforce or inhibit certain patterns of group interaction, and to provide various "shared group resources" (resources deemed appropriate for group work purposes). Users have developed a number of informal approaches to resource sharing as well.

Issues of "personality" and "positioning" are emerging as especially salient in the organizational utilization of computer networking. Individuals are being afforded wider ranges for the expression of personal and situational nuances, and they can be positioned (that is, given a "location" in the organization, either physically or in terms of organizational routines) in a greater number of ways. Unfortunately, however, the means that afford these wide ranges of personal and group expression can also be utilized in efforts to distort and commodify the virtual individuals and groups associated with certain persons.

In Chapter 5, I explore the notion of a "cultural object" in depth, and give the cultural objects of dependence and autonomy particular attention. I also examine the cultural object of intellectual augmentation – various aspects of which appear to be growing in influence – with special emphasis on its relation to dependence and autonomy. When individuals are construed as intellectually augmented by the computer systems they use, the character of discourse concerning their levels of dependence on these systems changes. Cultural objects influence the development of technologies: in a reflexive manner, what it means to enhance and augment ourselves (and be either dependent or autonomous) is influenced by availability and use of various forms of computerized support.

In Chapter 6, I discuss the cultural objects of privacy, anonymity, and agency (or surrogacy). I outline some of the privacy implications of network-based computer systems in light of social-psychological perspectives, and develop an approach toward these concerns that links privacy with both social and personal realms. I also examine anonymity and agency in terms of their relation to virtual individual and group concepts, and to such increasingly popular applications as computer "agents." In this chapter, I develop the notion of a "social analogue." Social analogues are system features linked by their designers with specific cultural objects. These relationships are interactive; each element can influence the other.

In the final chapter, I develop an approach for design of network-based systems – "genre-responsive design" – that utilizes the perspectives on the individual and the group outlined in preceding chapters. I discuss the design of collaborative writing and group decision-making tools, both of which provide vehicles for construction of a "group product" (a joint decision or document) from contributions previously associated with individuals. I construe collaborative writing and group decision making as group narrative efforts in which a group character – a "we" – is constructed that plays a role in linking various disparate expressions into coherent sequences.

Herbert Simon attempted to characterize the "sciences of the artificial": in effect, this book frames the "sciences of the constructed," in which users, designers, and various audiences all play critical roles. The social and managerial sciences have often been called upon to develop conceptual frameworks to control some aspects of human interaction, and recent computer networking initiatives are no exception. Many of the applications described in this book – including computer monitoring and group meeting support – present forms of control that merge the considerable pressures involved in group interaction with a new set of technological constraints and affordances. Synergy of these powerful forms of control presents a number of opportunities, as well as threats, to individual and group autonomy and internal integrity. The well-being of the individuals and groups involved should be carefully considered in each stage of design and implementation.

Introduction

The work of a crowd is always inferior, whatever its nature, to that of an isolated individual.

Gustave LeBon (1895/1960, p. 200)

The release of productivity is the product of cooperatively organized intelligence.

Dewey and Tufts (1939, p. 446)

"Collaboration" and "cooperation" among individuals – the harnessing of people's skills and talents to conduct projects, make decisions, and create new ideas – are notions that are both commonplace and elusive. The contradiction between the two epigraphs underscores the fact that controversies concerning the value of collaboration are not new. We have all participated in meetings and team projects, in informal exchanges as well as structured games, but these activities remain only vaguely understood and nearly impossible to predict and control with any precision. Our modes of individual and group expression (our "virtual individuals" and "virtual groups") are intimately linked with the technologies that support group interaction – technologies that have undergone dramatic change in the past decades.

Network-based computer applications designed to support joint efforts ("computer-supported cooperative work," or CSCW, applications) have both staunch supporters and fierce critics. Promoters have characterized these systems as "coaches" and "educators" (Winograd and Flores, 1986); critics, in turn, have labeled the same systems as "oppressors" and "masters" with a "digitized whip" (Dvorak and Seymour, 1988). The terms "groupware" and "workgroup computing" can be found in many computing, management, and social science publications, along with words of high praise, condemnation, or ennui. Virtual reality (VR) applications have been incorporated into some CSCW initiatives, sometimes compounding confusion about the systems and further steepening the learning curve.

There are sensitive ethical and value issues involved in development and use of CSCW applications. Controversies surrounding these systems center on issues of privacy, dependence, trust, and freedom of expression. Discussions about the "real" and the "virtual," about the use of technology to shape our notions of reality, have also been heated. A number of ethical controversies involving these systems have centered on stated intentions of designers; others have been rooted in concerns about the systems' possible unintended effects and implications. Many developers claim that their systems involve efforts to make human interaction more efficient and productive, as well as to modify the quality and structure of group activities in a variety of ways. Critics counter that we know little about how groups (even familiar, face-to-face groups) interact, which makes introduction of these technologies in workplace and educational arenas risky and possibly dangerous. Linkage of groupware to the Internet adds more concerns.

The tailored social universes that are emerging in the era of CSCW–VR linkages have merited special concern. In the worlds of entertainment and education, VR applications can serve to alter our senses of cause and effect, and of the permanence or continuity of objects, in order to thrill us or to reinforce some important educational points. Our commonsense notions of how gravity functions can be readily altered when we don VR equipment or work in environments that have been augmented with VR-related techniques; objects we drop can fall "up" rather than "down," and disappear and reappear periodically. In a related fashion, VR applications can serve to alter our instincts and judgments about social interaction.

Basic assumptions about what it is to interact with others in a team setting can be modified in VR- and CSCW-enhanced workplace and social settings. For example, a certain level of "consistency" is a strong value in everyday social interaction; we generally do not expect the people we are working with in our work groups to alter radically the manner in which they look or talk. However, in the VR–CSCW environment, team members may find that sudden changes in their personal appearances and demeanors are not only socially acceptable, but perhaps required for adequate levels of performance in the group context. Such changes could be used to underscore important points, or to "shake up" an otherwise moribund discussion. Team participants can have a large assortment of images or sounds associated with them; they can also manipulate these images and sounds in ways that are not in keeping with the gender and age stereotypes that participants are normally placed in.

In this book, I develop a framework for discussion of social and ethical dimensions of network-based computer systems, one that can be employed in many aspects of application design and implementation. I begin with an analysis of the evolution of network-based systems, with an emphasis on the emerging genre of CSCW applications. This is followed by a discussion of the self and group: discourse on these notions is an essential component of network-based system design and implementation. Tensions between individual-oriented and group-oriented perspectives are not resolved by technologies, but find new dimensions and outlets in them. I then discuss computer software "genres" and "narratives," and develop the notion of "genre-responsive design" (aspects of the practice of designers and implementers that contribute or relate to a particular genre).

Issues presented in this book are of more than theoretical interest. Many of today's managerial strategies have less to do with the specific direction of employees than with the construction – and sometimes intentional distortion – of virtual individuals and groups. Various traces that individuals and groups produce in their work routines (including keystrokes, voices, and photographs) are often incorporated into their virtual entities, more than occasionally without the knowledge or consent of the persons portrayed. Not all of the construction of virtual entities involves a passive, unaware subject, however. Individuals and groups are often directly instrumental in many aspects of constructing their own virtual individuals and groups, from the letters they pen and pictures they draw to the utilization of such system-supported features as "agents" or "surrogates."

Social and managerial sciences have contributed to the popular and current notions of the individual and the group, as well as to construction and modification of boundaries and relations between and among individuals and groups. International and interdisciplinary discussions aimed toward clarification and development of the basic notions underlying collaborative or cooperative work, and the associated place of the individual in these enterprises, are proceeding at an exciting pace. Some "ideal type" or prototypical cooperative workgroups (from the quality circle to the self-managed team) have become popular topics of discourse. The social and managerial sciences, and the practitioner communities associated with them, are lending insights to network-based system design efforts – and in turn are being influenced in their own directions by the systems.

Technology, the self, and the group

Attention to issues of groups and cooperative enterprise in knowledge work can be traced back several centuries. Francis Bacon used the genre of the novel as a vehicle to impart his vision of cooperative scientific activity. His *New Atlantis* (1879b), first published in 1627, provided a dream and a model for future cooperative scientific enterprise, and reflected a vision that does not deviate greatly from many current perspectives on "computer coordinated," groupware-supported science.

In *New Atlantis,* Bacon describes Solomon's House, on the island of

Bensalem, the objectives of which included obtaining "the knowledge of Causes and the secret motions of things, and the enlarging of the bounds of the Human Empire, to the effecting of all things possible" (p. 480). In the House of Solomon, science is pursued in a cooperative format – with an assembly-line-style division of intellectual labor, made possible by the way science itself is supposedly divided into theory and experiment (a notion Bacon explored in *Novum Organum*).

Bacon was well aware of the notion that groups can limit and manipulate the perspectives of their members, as well as support and extend their members' visions; he warns of how the customs and opinions of others can serve to distort our perceptions. Merton (1973) reflects that Bacon's work is part of a long tradition of scholars who have "emphasized the corrupting influence of group loyalties upon the human understanding" (p. 122). The problem of how team-style, coordinated scientific activity can progress without danger of undue "contamination" by the social world is one that Bacon's intellectual successors are discussing fervently more than 350 years later in the context of CSCW systems.

Today, interest in issues of self and group comparable to those that Bacon tackled is blossoming in a variety of contexts – from managerial and educational circles to "self-help" and "New Age" associations. From the neighborhood bridge club to the surgical team that repairs a heart, we are concerned with the effectiveness and fairness of the relationships that individuals have with the groups they are associated with. Popular works such as Robert Bellah et al.'s (1985) *Habits of the Heart* and Christopher Lasch's (1978) *The Culture of Narcissism* provide a group-oriented approach to issues of the role of human associations and community in personal as well as social spheres. Alternative approaches have emerged, with other emphases and concerns. Wheelis's (1958) *The Quest for Identity* and other volumes influenced by it warn of dangers of conformity that strong identification with community life can engender.

Both the printing press and the computer are linked historically with substantial changes in the way individuals view themselves, and in the way "individuality" itself is constructed. Statements that the advent of the computer will have at least as large and as dramatic an impact on civilization as that of the printing press have become commonplace. Many of the social changes for which the printing press served as a catalyst are chronicled in Elizabeth Eisenstein's (1979) *The Printing Press as an Agent of Change* and in her earlier work (1969). Michel Foucault (1977, 1982) also links literacy, writing, and printing with various stages of the concept of individuality and the development of the notion of self; he contends that many aspects of the self are indeed modern inventions, closely linked to changes in organizations and technologies.

I relate the advent of computer-mediated interpersonal exchange to various permutations of what "selfhood" and "group membership" constitute. Rather than comparing the computer and the printing press, however, I emphasize linkages among genres: for example, I compare the advent of the scientific journal in the 1660s with that of CSCW applications in the 1980s and 1990s. Scientific journals helped to construct "science," as well as the scientist and the scientific community. CSCW and other network-based system genres are today serving similar functions in constructing various social activities and personae in such spheres of life as science, education, entertainment, and business.

Mead's (1934) account of the self does not have strong historical grounding. Unlike the previously described notions, Mead's "self" was not linked with a specific technology such as the printing press. Nevertheless, Mead's ideas have been influential in my work. Mead's *Mind, Self, and Society* has played a pivotal role in both U.S. and European intellectual history, most strongly in development of social psychology and symbolic interactionism. Mead's self is a social product, reflecting and intimately linked with its social surroundings through such constructs as the "generalized other" (an abstract entity that incorporates various social trends as well as moral or religious standards). Through its projection and interaction with a generalized other, the self receives a certain level of guidance as well as a set of social constraints. Projecting these idealized entities helps us make sense of an often-chaotic world.

Individuals deal not only with abstract expectations concerning their behavior, but also with a set of virtual selves – credit reports, photographic traces, educational records, and computer-generated profiles. These virtual entities can be a part of the individual's sense-making efforts in the social realm, and thus serve some of the roles of generalized others. Individuals not only develop biographies and resumes, but have such accounts of their characteristics and interactions with others constructed by managers, bankers, teachers, and others in positions of authority. Many individuals either are now or will soon interact with teammates in groups in which group process and structure are shaped and mediated by network-based computer systems; the virtual groups constructed in these systems are also involved in some of the individuals' own sense-making efforts.

We learn about ourselves, the groups we belong to, and the other human beings around us through interaction with virtual individuals and groups. How we respond to various manipulations of virtual individuals and groups provides clues as to how we construct certain situations. For example, we may respond quite directly and negatively when our names or other markers of identity are removed from a written work we have produced. Manipulation and distortion of virtual individuals and groups have become easier to accomplish with certain kinds of technology (Oravec, in press). With digitized photography, our images can be removed from (or added to) snapshots of family gatherings, making it seem as if we were never present (or that we were indeed present when we weren't). We still have a "mirror" of the group in question, but it is a distorted mirror – and as time passes it may serve to shape our own or others' recollections of the family event.

Our virtual individuals and groups may be used in our job evaluations, for insurance purposes, and in the educational arena. Those who make many of the important decisions concerning our futures may never contact us directly; they may deal only with the virtual entities associated with us. Given the important societal roles of virtual individuals and groups, the proliferation of these entities is a matter of concern. If we lose control over the many, often distorted constructions of ourselves, we indeed lose control over our lives. We may not be able to understand the complex statistics used to construct a certain computer "profile" or analysis of our behavior (one that shows we have tendencies toward underachievement or antisocial behavior), yet we may face prejudice because of that profile. The growing array of virtual groups provides special challenges: we know little about how groups perform their functions, yet powerful tools for their management (groupware) can provide managers with profiles of our groups' operations for purposes of administration and evaluation.

CSCW and other network-based system applications can also afford us heightened levels of control over the virtual individuals and groups we are associated with – including means to construct an assortment of computer-based alter egos and agents. In some VR environments, we are able to move digitized "hands" that can manipulate objects within the environments; some of these environments incorporate technology that simulates touch, allowing us to feel as if we were handling "real" objects (Smith, 1995). The term "avatar" is often associated with entities that are linked with us in VR contexts. Our computer-based agents are also performing such everyday functions as screening electronic mail and news for potentially interesting tidbits for our digestion.

Electronic surrogates may serve a complex assortment of roles in communications for the humans associated with them, as in the following system envisioned by researchers at NASA's Ames Research Center:

The objective [of the Virtual Environment Workstation Project] is to provide a collaborative workspace in which remotely located participants can virtually interact with some of the nuances of face-to-face meetings while also having access to their personal dataspace facilities . . . With full body tracking capability, it will also be possible for each user to be represented in this space by his or her own life-size virtual representation in any chosen form – a kind of electronic persona. (Fisher, 1990, p. 29)

Simpler varieties of these systems (which associate various forms or shapes with team members rather than elaborate personae) are already available for use.

Expansion of means for personal and group expression through electronic surrogates provides exciting (and disturbing) prospects. In the arts and technology journal *Leonardo,* Lentini (1991) projects the "mutation of the individual" in the form of electronic "doubles":

With the anticipated advent of computerized human figures, it will be possible to create doubles of real persons with or without any relation to reality. One will be able to speak with them or manage them and make them do what one wants. I have no doubt that such operations will become within reach of most everyone, from the state to the citizen, in real or deferred time. (Lentini, 1991, p. 335)

Not all forms of virtual representation involve life-sized reconstructions of an individual's physical shape, but the possibility of such expansive forms of computer-mediated expression and interaction opens new ways of thinking about what it is to participate in social activities. If our images can "stand in" for us in certain contexts, then what is it to be fully "present" in an event? Our relationships with these doubles – as well as with other virtual entities linked with printing, computing, or video imaging – have broad social and personal impacts: how we feel about these entities, and whether we draw associations between them and ourselves, help determine the activities they are involved in and the values they reflect. As I discuss in Chapter 2, some of us may become "mirrorless" in some contexts, and lose the tools for self-knowledge and identity management that virtual entities can provide. In contrast, others of us may become "persona entrepreneurs," and attempt to explore and exploit the expanding set of means for development and dissemination of virtual individuals and groups.

VR is adding an assortment of dimensions to these issues. Some kinds of VR applications are stimulating thinking about new varieties of group interaction; for example, new kinds of therapist–client dyads are emerging. Clients and therapists may soon share VR experiences as a mode of communication and mutual discovery in one-on-one sessions. Larijani (1993) explores how "heightened senses of control and safety" possible in VR applications can create a new twist on therapy: "Because a person is engaged in the action and helps determine the course of events, he or she can safely explore issues that hurt or frighten under ordinary circumstances" (p. 90). Extension of these applications to diagnosis and treatment at the level of the small group is likely, as is the development of comparable permutations of the group in workplace and educational settings.

Many mathematicians are proposing that models are better manipulated through interactive graphics – through picking and poking at objects – than through series of equations and diagrams (Brooks, 1988). In comparable ways, we may be able to deepen our understanding of social interactions and structures by manipulating socially significant objects and experimenting with correlates of social forces in VR-enhanced environments. The vehicles we have today for sharing insights about social realms – which include books such as the one you hold now – may soon be supplanted by means through which we can learn through a broad panoply of experiential modes.

I also explore the approaches to management that are emerging from these technological and social innovations. Computer-mediated bibliographic traces and profiles play an important, if not primary, role in some kinds of management and administration. Such basic cultural themes as privacy, dependence, and autonomy are being given a new slant as social and moral theorists attempt to decipher the social trends associated with CSCW applications. The notion of "self as social construct" is becoming incorporated in discourse on informational privacy, as privacy theorists and activists struggle to obtain adequate conceptual tools to aid in understanding the interactions of computers and society (Post, 1989; Oravec, 1993). Related matters involving freedom of human association and interaction in computer-mediated systems are being explored and discussed by civil libertarians as well as technologists.

What is groupware?

Labels that technologies and genres are given, and categories in which they are placed, play an important role in how they are perceived and implemented. For new and complex applications in a growing, changing field such as computing, such labeling takes on even more importance. Even though labels apparently play important roles in discourse, far-reaching policy decisions concerning information and communication technologies are often made on the basis of ill-considered names, rubrics, and categories. By carefully considering the names applied to technology, we can begin to unmask some of the political and social commitments and assumptions associated with the technology (see Rowland, 1984; Opt, 1987).

Precise origins of the buzzword "groupware" are unknown, but are widely attributed to Cal Pava of Harvard and Peter and Trudy Johnson-

Lenz in the early 1980s. The following terms have been associated with groupware efforts in the past decade: "technological support for workgroup collaboration," "workgroup computing," "collaborative computing," "interpersonal computing," "coordination technology," "computer-supported groups," "group process support systems" (see Johansen, 1988, for more). Patricia Seybold's group (which publishes *Office Computing Report: A Guide to Workgroup Computing*) has proposed the following nomenclature:

Groupware is only part of the story – a category of software. It doesn't address the hardware, communications, and sociological issues that are a major part of the new trend toward collaborative work . . . to me, workgroup computing encompasses all of these elements as well as illuminating the concept of the people who make up the group . . . who sit at workstations on the network . . . who use the groupware. The term seems to capture best the human factor . . . which is ultimately the most important. (Marshak, 1990, p. 4)

In a lighter vein, Browning (1990) pinned the name "social lubricants" on CSCW applications in the *Economist*.

The word "groupware" has been used in a restricted sense – to identify multiuser application approaches, approaches that support such group activities as brainstorming, idea organization, and decision making. It has also been used in a broader manner to refer to *any* support tool for groups. Approaches in which the separately generated products of individual users are shared have occasionally been classified in terms of the "single-user application sharing approach," rather than groupware per se (Ohkubo and Ishii, 1990, p. 145; see also Halonen, Horton, Kass, and Scott, 1990).

The fact that the term "groupware" has been openly utilized in academically oriented conferences has lent it some credibility, although how its usage will stabilize is still in question. The CSCW label was reportedly coined by Irene Greif in 1984 (Suchman, 1988a). Discussion of just what the acronym "CSCW" stands for was the topic of a panel session at a 1988 conference of CSCW researchers and developers. Grudin's account of this session provides the following renditions of the acronym:

A brief history of the term was given by Irene Greif, who helped coin it in 1984 in order to concisely identify a group of researchers from different disciplines but with common interests. Mark Stefik suggested several possible expansions of "CSCW," including "Can't Stop Coining Words." Robert Howard focused on the word "supported," noting that in some environments, computers may instead compel collaboration. Several alternatives to "cooperative" were suggested by panelists, including "collaborative" and "coordinated," but Rob Kling suggested "coercive," again touching on ethical issues that are salient to this field but were absent in the conference presentations. (Grudin, 1989b, p. 83)

Labels such as "groupware" can inspire interest, but also create confusion. Lee reports that

although the emergence of the term ["groupware"] has created a stampede of manufacturers who describe their products as groupware, the products do not have a lot in common, except that they are all meant to be used by more than one person, not necessarily at the same time. (Lee 1989, p. 24)

He speculates that the resulting confusion about what groupware consists of may have contributed to the lukewarm acceptance that products with that label have had in some quarters. Suchman, the leader of one of Xerox's current CSCW initiatives, states that she has problems with the theories and technologies currently placed under the label of "groupware": "I have doubts about the extent to which we know what we are talking about – theoretically and empirically" (quoted in Williams, 1990, p. 95).

Categories of products that have been placed under the groupware umbrella include enhanced electronic mail and conferencing systems, schedule coordination aids, collaborative authoring tools and design support, project team coordination aids, group consensus-reaching and decision-making aids, and support for face-to-face meetings. Some of the applications just listed may be considered CSCW application "subgenres" (for lack of a better term) – forms of expression and communication that have identities of their own but that are still closely tied to CSCW-related notions and imagery. I explore several of these subgenres in depth (including collaborative writing tools and group decision-making aids).

Under the general header of "network-based systems" falls a substantial share of computing environments and related applications today. Early experiments in timesharing in the 1960s showed the value of connecting terminals to a powerful, central mainframe. Today, coupling of different types and sizes of computer components occurs with many variations. Network-based systems range from a small number of personal computers (PCs) and peripherals linked together in an office or school computer lab to complex and powerful "client/server networks" that incorporate an assortment of mainframes, workstations, printers, and storage technologies (discussed in Chapter 1). Large-scale networks (including the Internet, AT&T's long-distance network, and IBM's *Global Network*) are being coupled with CSCW applications such as Lotus *Notes* (Cortese, 1995; *Electronic Messaging News,* 1995). Not all computing is network-based, however: for example, computers are found in an increasing number of products, such as cars and microwaves, that are not yet networked into a larger system (but may soon be).

Augmentation, thought transference, and CSCW applications

Norman and Draper (1986) assert that a shift in perspective has occurred recently within the field of human–machine interaction, a shift from concern with the human–machine linkage to exploration of the potential of computers to enhance significantly the "possibilities for communication and collaboration among people" (p. 452). The themes of communication and coordination are playing increasingly large roles in artificial intelligence (AI) as well, as researchers work to design systems consisting of active agents with multiple goals (Bobrow, 1991).

Objectives of controlling, modifying, and enhancing cooperative enterprises have been made more realistic with the advent of powerful and effectively coupled individual workstations. Engelbart (1963) labels these objectives as "intellectual augmentation" and as "bootstrapping" our mental and social capacities. Some CSCW and network-based system efforts have largely been attempts to support the current styles and functions of group activity as they are commonly perceived by managers, administrators, and/or group participants themselves. In contrast, other efforts have consciously developed significant variations on styles of interaction with which we are accustomed and familiar, or have provided some means for reframing current group functions.

Varieties of network-based computer system applications have been proposed and developed for the past several decades, with the work of Douglas Engelbart, Murray Turoff, Starr Roxanne Hiltz, and others providing considerable impetus. CSCW applications, however, have only recently emerged as an identifiable software genre – although the basic notions underpinning CSCW efforts have surfaced in various forms since the 1960s. CSCW applications' (or groupware's) emergence as a genre is significant in itself; it signals increasing levels of interest in the group or team as an organizational and social unit. The continuation (or dissolution) of CSCW applications as a distinguishable, distinct genre will provide clues concerning how individuals and groups, as well as computing technologies, are perceived in this society.

Forecasting the future of CSCW and network-based system applications is a difficult enterprise. Pool (1977) gives an account of early predictions about the telephone, another (and currently a more common) technology for support of human interaction:

The telephone will foster sociability and cooperativeness. These are the words of Herbert Casson; in 1911 he said the telephone "has enabled us to be more social and cooperative. It has literally abolished the isolation of the separate family."

The telephone will foster impersonality. The introduction of phone numbers led to some resentment of the impersonality of telephone relations. There were articles on how to remember telephone numbers. There were also numerous comments on the inadequacies of contacts in which smiles and expressions could not be seen. (Pool, 1977, p. 151)

The telephone has inspired a good deal of thinking and discussion about self, technology, and the nature of human communication. Pool cites a skit put on by some telephone technology proponents in 1913 that portrayed communication 100 years later; the skit forecast that communication in 2013 would be largely through thought transference. Some futurists, writing in the early part of this century, portrayed the telephone as "a stage toward man's ability to communicate by means as yet unknown, perhaps from brain to brain" (p. 153).

Speculations about the future directions and applications of network-based computer systems are similarly lofty and ambitious. Projections of possible CSCW applications include their use as assistants for marriage counseling:

Marriage counselors often draw up lists of problems and opportunities for their clients . . . counselors [can] map these problems and opportunities for their couples in a computer-augmented shared space. Because the shared space can be neutral and cool, it can serve as the medium through which the couple can talk instead of shouting or arguing directly with each other. (Schrage, 1990, p. 195)

In comparably excited tones, the groupware designer Anand Jagannathan contends that groupware should really be considered "all-ware," and extended into the entire organization (quoted in Coursey, 1988, p. 26).

If the Western experience with the inventions of the telephone and the automobile can provide some insight, the permeation of computer network technology and associated applications into U.S. life will be required before the impact of these technologies can be well estimated. Utilization of computer networking is increasing dramatically. Later I will speculate on the future directions of network-based systems by employing insights from studies of technologies related to these systems (for example, video technologies and physical office environments). I attempt to be sensitive to the continuing evolution of these technologies: it is fairly easy to fall into the pattern of treating scientific and technological advances like a "black box" (Whitley, 1972). I examine changes in the technologies themselves, along with the responses they receive in the marketplace and in regulatory arenas (rejections, acceptances, alternate usages, and so on). The term "artifact" (a term with strong anthropological and sociological linkages) is often used in studies of technology to refer to technologies as they are characterized and utilized by society; I often use the term as well.

Considering the human dimensions of network-based systems

The perspective that technology is best viewed in terms of matters other than the purely technical has a long history. In Leonardo da Vinci's notebooks, for example, economic, technical, social, and scientific factors were intertwined; Thomas Edison's notebooks also were such an amalgam. The technocratic movement of the 1920s and 1930s (a movement with broad political and economic ambitions led by Howard Scott) adopted the Monad (a red and silver yin–yang symbol) as a logo in order to underscore their belief that technological, political, and social factors were best viewed as a unified whole. The founders of Stone & Webster (a consulting engineering firm that developed many of the large-scale U.S. engineering projects of the early part of this century) also adopted the triskelion as their advertising logo as a way to emphasize what they perceived as the integrated nature of social and engineering functions (Bijker, Hughes, & Pinch 1987).

Examination of the social and ethical dimensions of network-based system technology is of consequence both for its value in understanding human interaction and for its use in designing and implementing better, more humanistic computing systems. One of the assumptions of my research is that studies and analyses of the ethical problems and issues raised by a technology should be undertaken in its formative years – when the social changes it may induce are most easily discerned and before those changes become faits accomplis, albeit possibly unwanted or unintended. As we become more familiar with the technologies, many problems and issues about them become "resolved" (possibly only rhetorically) – and some of the truly critical questions about them seem to become less relevant.

Consider the now-familiar automated teller machine (ATM). In the middle to late 1970s when ATM networks were expanding, some system designers were worried that people might be confused when interacting with a humanlike ATM. There was also concern about the potential levels of public trust in a mechanical (as opposed to human) money-handling vehicle (Parker, 1979).

Today, public discussion of questions about ATMs is largely limited to complaints about the machines "eating" users' cards. Part of the lack of focus on the machines is due to their relatively high level of accuracy and reliability – although a number of problems still exist, especially for their use by older adults (as described in Adams and Theiben, 1991). Other reasons include consumers' increased comfort level with the devices, and diversion of people's limited attention and interest elsewhere. Even though there are myriad privacy and other public policy issues relating to ATMs and the electronic exchange of funds, the level of discourse on them is low. Network-based system technologies and applications have not yet reached this stage of habituation. Topics of discussion are still wide open and there are many, critically important issues on the table.

A large part of our lives as social and moral entities involves construction and management of the virtual individuals and groups with which we are associated; these construction and management efforts are increasingly being conducted within the scope of the CSCW applications genre. Individuals should be afforded opportunities to see how they are being viewed by others (including their supervisors) in their organization's information system genres, from team-oriented group support tools to applications that monitor and profile a single individual's activities. Providing these opportunities requires more than just opening access to files, however; individuals must be assisted in understanding the context of the utilization and dissemination of the virtual individuals and groups with which they are associated.

It is indeed difficult to separate "social" from "technical" concerns when one is dealing with systems expressly designed to affect the attitudes and behavior of individuals in groups. I characterize research and development in the area of network-based systems as forms of social engineering and experimentation not to be alarmist, but to underscore that what designers, marketers, implementers, and users are doing is not ethically and politically neutral. Insights and techniques that psychologists, policy analysts, sociologists, and anthropologists have gleaned from long experience in handing matters of experimentation in the social realm (in informing subjects of their rights, for example, and in providing experimental "debriefings") should be drawn on by network-based system developers, implementers, and users.

Whether or not CSCW and related applications survive as a distinct computer genre, discussion of the use of computers to enhance human interaction in groups (a discussion taking place in conferences, journal articles, and trade magazines, and via CSCW systems themselves) will undoubtedly have a great impact on computing, as well as on how other social technologies (for example, managerial systems and group methodologies) are viewed and utilized. Even technological failures (artifacts that go out of circulation or cease to retain their separate identities) can have considerable social impact – although that impact may be fully appreciated only by historians and philosophers of technology.

One of the individuals who predicts the disappearance of groupware as an identifiable genre is Johansen (1988), who projects that CSCW capabilities will soon become integrated, effectively invisible aspects of computer networks, networks that will be an integral part of our daily lives. The possibility that Johansen may be right provides all the more reason why, during the formative years of the technology, we should be sensitizing ourselves to what CSCW technology can do for us and to us – how it can both enhance and limit the social dimensions of our schools and workplaces, public forums and social gatherings.

1

Evolution of computer application genres: Groupware and other network-based system applications

The word "genre" (originally from French, meaning "type") is largely associated with the realm of literature. In that context it is usually employed to refer to generic varieties of written material, such as novels, poems, and short stories. Viewing a set of computer applications as a genre emphasizes commonalities and family resemblances among set members (although genres can occasionally include loosely knit, heterogeneous compilations, held together for reasons that are largely accidental and historical). Questions about the range of expression that genres afford, and of individuals' rationales in their choices of genres, occupy the attention of many literary critics (for example, Banta, 1978; Todorov, 1990), media specialists, and active as well as prospective consumers of the genres.

Discourse on genre plays an important role in genre construction. Genre-related notions can be powerful tools for understanding a variety of phenomena associated with human expression. The document you have in your hands right now conforms to a certain set of standards for presentation. Some are set by the American Psychological Society (APA), whose *Publication Manual* is the generally accepted style book for many written works. Writing standards may seem arbitrary, a trivial nuisance one must put up with in one's journey toward self-expression and group expression. However, these standards serve considerable functions in the development and maintenance of academic disciplines. For example, the adherence to uniform standards of citation that the APA requires bolsters the prestige of psychology as both a profession and a research area, supporting the notion that authors are indeed building on the work of others and adding to the growing stock of knowledge of the discipline as a whole (Bazerman, 1987b). The word "discipline" is indeed an appropriate label for academic disciplines, referring to the almost punishing rigor with which the various areas of knowledge are established and distinguished from each other (Foucault, 1977).

Certain features of the document you are currently reading (its length, tone, and number of citations) signal why it was written and provide information about the individuals who wrote, reviewed, edited, and published it, as well as those to whom it is targeted (its consumers, or audience). The genre it best fits into – the academic publication – is one that has some major differences from other, more popular book genres, such as mystery novels and science fiction. Academic books are filled with (sometimes annoying) citations and cross-references, while novels and science fiction generally are not.

Genres involve more than form or features, however. A network of relationships is reflected in the document you are currently engaged in reading. Its chapter topics reflect my disciplinary allegiances. Its careful phrasing reflects the intense scrutiny that academic books undergo by those responsible for their quality control. The unfortunate features of academic books make for laborious reading, but serve an assortment of purposes related to their various roles. Remaining within the boundaries of this genre while reflecting the turbulence and multidimensional character of current discussions involving collaboration and its support is not an easy feat, and demonstrates the power of a genre's constraints, however they are transmitted or understood. Genres facilitate and encourage a certain range of expression, but can also make other kinds of expression seem obscure – and efforts to achieve them clumsy.

Genres are complex amalgams of rhetorical styles and matters of form and linguistics. They also reflect critical aspects of the relationships among individuals, groups, and organizations. How can the academic book, groupware, or any other genre be characterized? It is generally much easier to distinguish deviations from established genres than to characterize the genres themselves. Blanchot (1969, 1982) and Todorov (1990) explore the role of deviation in defining a genre's limits from a literary perspective:

The fact that a work "disobeys" its genre does not mean that the genre does not exist . . . in order to exist as such, the transgression requires a law – precisely the one to be violated. We might go even further and observe that the norm becomes visible – comes into existence – owing only to its transgressions. (Todorov, 1990, p. 14)

Blanchot argues that James Joyce's novelistic transgressions demonstrate that the genre "lives only through its alterations" (1982, p. 133). Genres are modes in which we construct our own (as well as our group and organizational) realities: metalanguages for genre construction and modification are difficult to develop.

If this book would suddenly change certain critical aspects (such as sentence length or style of citation), its identity as an academic book might come into question – although characterizing fully what an academic book involves would be nearly impossible. However, some deviations are acceptable, if not required, for achieving certain kinds of expression. For example, this lengthy, self-referencing (possibly recursive) section may have stretched the boundaries of the academic book genre somewhat, but has facilitated my discussion of the notion of genre.

The scientific journal as a genre

The scientific or research journal is one example of a genre that has played a substantial role in the development of modern science (as well as research and academics in general). Most of us are aware of how journal publication influences promotion decisions in many disciplines; however, the power of this genre has been underrated.

Ziman (1976) describes the scientific journal as an "invention," in much the same sense as that of the light bulb – it was a "quite novel invention of the late seventeenth century" (p. 99). A noted chemist has compared maintaining journal standards with keeping rules of etiquette, characterizing the editors and referees of scientific journals as "the main defenders of scientific 'good taste.' " The number of scientific journals has increased at a tremendous rate since the 1660s (nearly doubling every 15 years since the seventeenth century), creating massive problems for libraries that need to obtain and store them (de Solla Price, 1963).

The first scientific journal in the English language was founded in 1665 by Henry Oldenburg, then secretary of the Royal Society of London. The journal, *Philosophical Transactions of the Royal Society of London,* was carefully edited by Oldenburg to emphasize not only the similarities among the various experimental agendas of journal contributors, but also their differences (Bazerman, 1987a). Oldenburg's motives in starting the journal included using it for personal income; the ultimate impact of the journal extended far beyond personal gain, however, as it placed Oldenburg at the focal point of the scientific communications of his age. Correspondence with the *Transactions* increased twofold within its first year of existence, and increased threefold again by the end of the 1660s.

The theme of coordinated scientific activity – scientific teamwork – was intimately linked with the founding of the Royal Society. In the *History of the Royal Society* (published in 1667, just 5 years after the Royal Society was founded), Sprat describes the ideal of scientists who "work and think in company, and confer their help to each others' Inventions." Sprat justifies the use of coordinative devices for scientific endeavor in terms of scientific productivity: "how much progress may be made by a form'd and Regular Assembly" that synchronizes "the joynt force of many men" (Sprat, 1667; Gross, 1989). The *Transactions* supported the Society's face-to-face meetings by documenting what transpired, as well as by publishing descriptions of discoveries and other scientific activities – correspondence that subsequently evolved into formal academic "articles."

In the early days of modern science, public demonstrations of certain scientific outcomes were often feasible, and in some sectors very popular. Seeing, in effect, was believing. Britain's Royal Society sponsored many demonstrations of this sort in the 1600s. The *Transactions* then produced a published record of these demonstrations' outcome. Letters describing scientific experiments in depth were also excerpted and published in this vehicle; these letters became increasingly formalized in their tone and detail. The scientific journal served to establish a new set of tools for portraying the initiatives and contributions of individual scientists and their associations. As a genre, it also reflects deep tensions between a form of activity ("doing science") that is empirical, and kinds of language and presentation that can be evocative as well as sometimes clumsy. Scientific journals extended the audience for science and expanded the kinds of accounts that could be included under the rubric of "science"; however, in being composed of accounts of past activity and speculation, journals cast scientific activity in a different light than actual demonstration does.

Genres such as the scientific journal affirm and support certain values and themes associated with their creators and users. These values and themes are often seen most clearly in the early stages of genre development – when those who develop and use them are actively and aggressively justifying the genres' existences. Oldenburg reflected on the purpose of written scientific exchange to Huygens. "There is no doubt at all that, if we press forward at a steady pace, maintaining a frank and regular correspondence for our mutual benefit, we shall in time see regular progress in every branch of science" (Oldenburg, 1966, vol. V, p. 583). In *The Structure of Scientific Revolutions,* Kuhn (1970) identifies establishment of scientific journals in a field as a signal of group focus and maturity in scientific undertakings.

Considerations relating to genres and artifacts are tightly interwoven. Access to printing made production and distribution of the *Transactions* feasible. You are now reading a bound book (not a loose-leaf notebook). The permanence and finality of an artifact such as a bound book in comparison with many other forms of written text relate to the standing of certain forms of academic communication in our society. Genres cannot be fully examined without considering the physical artifact (or artifacts) with which they are associated, as well as the means of production of those artifacts. Discussion of the computer as an artifact is especially critical in understanding the human dimensions of computer networking.

We are, as a society, heavily engaged in exploring the potential of computers and computer-related artifacts – an activity that is consuming a substantial amount of our society's resources, both monetary and attentional.

The notion that an easy conversion of genres from one artifact to another is possible without any change in the social impact of the genres has stirred considerable controversy. Thousands of historical documents (such as books, leaflets, maps, and newspapers) are being either transferred to microfiche or transformed into some sort of digitized medium – and the originals destroyed – primarily for lack of storage space. Our knowledge of these works as a whole (what it felt like to hold them, how the maps were folded, what the works' sizes and shapes were) is thus severely reduced. Unfortunately, many of those who hold the purse strings at some of our major museums and institutions of higher learning feel that nothing has been lost through such transference.

Some of the destruction is inevitable; paper deteriorates and the original documents are not immortal. Much of it is being done merely to save room on curators' shelves, however. (Many of the losses may be especially tragic since the paper involved may indeed be readable for hundreds more years, whereas the electronic media to which its notations have been transferred have yet to prove their longevity.) Some librarians and curators have campaigned for a renewed interest in gleaning the insights that the physical document of a book or map may lend to scholars – insights not only about the "author" of the document itself, but also about the complex web of relationships among editors, publishers, book binders, and marketers that each document reflects.

Computer software and the genre notion: "Genresizing" the computer

We take for granted such literary genres as the novel: in most cases, we could recognize one and would have a set of expectations for its contents. Many of us are already comfortable with such computer software genres as spreadsheets and word-processing packages. The plasticity of the computer affords an incredible range of expression and an infinite scope of potential application. Genres serve as organizing and sense-making tools, shaping our expectations for experiences with computing technology.

"Genresizing" involves increases in the availability of readily recognized genres associated with certain technologies. It makes technologies more widely understandable and approachable, and brings them more fully into societal discourse. For example, in the early days of printing, such genres as "how to" books and travel chronicles were quickly distinguished. Television broadcasting of the 1940s was limited to a few genres largely borrowed from theater and vaudeville; these have expanded in the intervening decades to include sitcoms, miniseries, infomercials, and a host of others. The genresizing of the personal computer began with spreadsheets and word processing packages in the 1970s, and shows few signs of abatement. Genre theorists sometimes refer to genres as ways that society "talks to itself" – the ways it structures its modes of expression and interaction. As societal discourse on computing intensifies, so does the proliferation of computer genres.

Evolution of computer software genres reflects a number of strong societal currents that extend over the last half-century. Development of a workable computer in the mid-1940s is associated with such early prototypes as ENIAC (United States) and Colossus (Great Britain). The crafting of a set of commonly recognizable computer software genres has occurred in the intervening years. With early computers, users "programmed" by wiring boards and flipping switches. Machine language coding followed – a laborious process that still required substantial knowledge of the workings of the computer. Widespread availability of user-ready, producer-categorized software "packages" on the market (packages that often fell into recognizable genre categories) is an even more recent phenomenon.

In the mid-1950s and early 1960s, applications-oriented programming available for computers was still fairly limited. Many programmers swapped subroutines and various units of computer code that performed limited functions (for example, doing square roots and matrix operations). Computer users were well advised to become proficient in computer programming in order to employ computer capabilities to fulfill a specific purpose. Applications-oriented programming available at the time often required extensive customizing by expert programmers to suit specific needs.

As the number of users increased, so did markets for ready-to-use computer packages, and the need for individuals to be proficient programmers (or to hire such people) decreased. The notion of "computer literacy" was expanded to include an awareness of available genres of computer software and knowledge of how to approach a user's manual or other paper-bound documentation associated with the software. Among today's readily recognizable packaged software genres are spreadsheets (recent variations of which are described in Markoff, 1989, and Antonoff, 1990), expert system "shells" (discussed in Oravec, 1988b, 1992), and word processing packages (characterized in Heim, 1987). Although the first in this series is primarily associated with numeric projections, the second with the organization and preservation of experts' "rules of thumb," and the last with the production and manipulation of the written word, all three are adaptable for a variety of purposes.

Steady demands for descriptions of available genres and associated packages, as well as for advice concerning their alternative uses, have stimulated the growth of a large class of periodicals and newspapers. Computer industry trade press and consumer-oriented computer publications have become a sizable market and reach a large and influential audience of readers. *Computerworld,* for example, has a circulation of more than 135,000. *PC Week* (self-labeled as the "National Newspaper of Corporate Microcomputing") has a circulation of nearly 200,000. *The Wall Street Journal, New York Times,* and other nationally distributed print publications similarly carry columns and stories on available and emerging kinds of computing packages – a kind of discourse that could well be labeled "genre talk."

Most people have had some exposure to at least a few of the various computer genres. In many cases this familiarity has had a dramatic influence on the way work activities are constructed. The late John Kemeny (formerly president of Dartmouth) noted with dismay that "word processing mania" siphoned off interest in other forms of computing in administration and education. He described the effect of word processing on his department in the following terms:

As chairman of the math department at Dartmouth I was proud to have built up a very able secretarial staff to take routine chores off the shoulders of the faculty. Then, in 1969, I left to serve as president of the college. When I returned twelve years later, I found that faculty members were again typing their own papers. They were even typing routine notices. Why? Because they had fallen in love with their word processors. A notice that a meeting had been postponed would look like an illuminated manuscript! (Kemeny, 1990, p. 46)

Kemeny's observation that the word processing genre was a dominant factor in acceptance and eventual popularity of personal computing has a great deal of support. For instance, Koohang and Honeycutt (1990) report that among a group of PC users in companies within the Research Triangle Park in North Carolina, word processing was by far the genre they were most familiar with (that is, had a "working knowledge" of); spreadsheet and database management tools ran second and third, respectively. *The New York Times* has found as "fit to print" many stories about the ongoing debates as to which spreadsheet package is the most popular (Markoff, 1989). The phrase "word processing" captured the tensions that many of us who work with words feel: we must move and manipulate often-recalcitrant words and phrases to produce a finished, polished product on paper or screen.

Many of the scholars who have attempted to capture the notion of genre from a literary perspective have used concepts and images with strong linkages to biology: when we classify the vast number of literary works according to some principle of coherence, we can better understand their functions and structures. The skills of taxonomy and classification practiced on animal species by Steven Jay Gould (1981) are often reflected in the work of genre theorists such as Tzvetan Todorov (1990). Genre categories are structured and shaped, but are seldom "invented" by those who study genres, however (just as Gould does not invent new categories of animals, but borrows heavily from observation as well as reflection).

The study of genre development is more than classification, however. Genres can reflect contradictions and conflicts among societal themes or large-scale shifts in social values; the resultant societal tension draws increased attention to the genres. We as audience or producers become participants not just in our own, isolated enterprises, but also in broader societal functions. An example is the audience-participation talk show (such as *Phil Donahue* and *Oprah Winfrey*) in which the "public" and the "private" are conjoined: intimate secrets are revealed and confidences shared, all in the public setting of nationwide broadcasting. Similarly, CSCW applications in the U.S. reflect the deeply rooted tension between the individual and the group in organizational settings, a theme that often emerges in the history of managerial thought and practice. Individuals must be good team players and contribute to the welfare of the group as a whole. However, in most organizations evaluation is still at the individual level; it is the individual who is promoted (or demoted). Many groupware initiatives support the team in some aspects of their functions and rhetoric, yet can be used to monitor the individual's own performance. VR applications reflect a disquiet as well, one about the nexuses between "action" and "thought," or reality and fantasy.

The question of how specific computer system genres are generated and evolve also opens issues relating to the entire computing experience. Operating systems such as *Windows* and *OS/2* organize the linkages of packages with each other and orchestrate the overall coherence of the activity of working with a computer. These systems support the development of genres and subgenres, and organize the flow between and interactions among genres; they influence the experience of people using computers. Operating systems thus serve as "genre environments," providing a set of constraints and affordances for the genres associated with them. In the same way that a human host for a television show or a moderator for a discussion organizes the proceedings and increases their comprehensibility, genre environments provide a backdrop to events involving human–computer, and human–computer–human, interaction.

The biological themes of "variation" and "selection" are also applied to genre approaches. Development of a species of plant or animal life is seldom well described in linear terms; similarly, the developmental process of a technological artifact and associated genres is best characterized as an alternation of variation and selection. Eliminating the assumption of progressive, step-by-step development of genres opens the way to richer descriptions of how they are refined (or rejected) by users. The genres discussed in this book are still in early stages of development, with a number of variations in circulation and a good deal of attention being paid to the processes of selection among them.

An approach to the characterization of CSCW applications

Research and development in computer-supported cooperative work (CSCW) is an amalgam of technical and managerial initiatives. Determining just what this multifaceted area constitutes has been labeled as akin to "squeezing jello" (Buerger, 1993). A large variety of organizations and institutions have had an impact on (and, in turn, have been affected by) CSCW applications; these groups have varying perspectives on and interests in CSCW, and have contributed different themes to the discourse.

Genre-related arguments and controversies (for instance, discussion of the questions "What are 'CSCW applications'?" "Can this computer software package be considered 'groupware'?"; "How should we consider intellectual property rights – originally designed for certain text-oriented media – in regard to groupware-mediated products?") have played a major role in formation of an image and identity for the CSCW genre, and have served to influence research in this area. Since the field of computer systems is growing rapidly and changes occur so quickly, a clustering around identifiable (and readily grasped) themes and imagery is often required for software ideas to be digested and ultimately adopted. This thematic clustering is also influential in organization of collaborative efforts and funding of research in CSCW-related fields, as well as in development of specific CSCW products.

What is a genre? How are genres distinguished from each other? Todorov's notions are often used as catalysts for discussions of genre. He links genres with speech acts; a genre, Todorov argues, is "nothing more than the codification of discursive properties" (1990, p. 18). He outlines three possibilities for the development of genres (p. 21):

1. The genre codifies discursive properties as any other speech act would, like a sonnet.

2. The genre coincides with a speech act that has a nonliterary existence, like prayer.
3. The genre derives from a speech act by way of a certain number of transformations or amplifications, like the novel (which is based on the act of "telling").

To encompass more fully the emerging set of electronic and interactive technologies, I expand the notion of genre to include forms of expression that are rarely considered utterances – such as one's physical appearance in a video portrait or one's motion (or lack thereof) in a VR configuration. Genres can thus be seen as codifying and coinciding with various forms of "constructive expression" (although that phrase can be viewed as redundant), rather than just with speech acts. Constructive expression involves the full range of ways we make our presence known in the setting of a particular genre – the way we present ourselves or are presented in the context of interaction with others.

My primary focus is thus not how the CSCW application genre affords certain ranges of utterances: rather, I focus on what kinds of virtual entities emerge in the context of the genres. One of Todorov's examples is the written genre of prayer (as reflected in a prayer book); it is linked to a specific speech act. In my formulation, I am concerned with the character of the individual who "prays" as it emerges in the genre, as well as with the production of the prayer (the "event"). I am also concerned with how current and potential audiences are constructed in the context of the genre. If I had been dealing with multimedia prayers (as in the setting of a music-filled gospel church) I would also be concerned with synergies among various genres and artifacts represented. Genres can be rooted in images, sound, smells, and tactile sensations; combination of these modes can be used to create especially rich forms of expression.

Given the wide (and growing) range of ways in which we express ourselves and are characterized by others, we should indeed direct our attention to expression considered more broadly than speech acts; we should consider modes of expression whether or not specific attempts to "communicate" something to someone else are involved in that expression. For example, silences can serve strategic, communicative roles, sending signals of disagreement; they can, however, simply serve to accompany an individual's or group's state of calm and quiescence. I may move my hand in a VR environment either as a conscious gesture of goodwill or as an instinctive reaction to surprising stimuli. I may consciously pose for the camera or be characterized by a photographer in a portrait in ways (camera angle, range of light or color) that I do not fully appreciate. Yet all of the ways just described involve some aspect of constructive expression; they are aspects of the way we are presented to society, and the way we are reflected to ourselves.

Genres and their related artifacts have the potential for affecting the network of relationships among individuals, and influencing in profound ways how individuals and groups themselves are constructed. For example, boundaries between self and group – what is properly considered one's own (one's own space, one's own expression) and what belongs to the group – can be said to shift as the genres used for expression and exchange shift. The virtual individuals and groups associated with us are developed in the context of specific genres (as discussed in the next chapter).

In the early stage of genre development, strong images and themes are often associated with genres, images that serve to stimulate and inspire genre-related activity; in later stages, these early themes and images are more carefully dissected. For example, as a society we have been familiar with the genre of the late-night television talk show for a number of decades; in the past few years, however, the myths and conventions of the genre have undergone widespread analysis and scrutiny (as well as satire). The early stage of a genre's development could be considered a "projection period," one in which the genre is associated with especially powerful and evocative (though ill-formed) notions, and in which there are only limited examples that demonstrate what the genre can indeed do for us in terms of its capacities. The early images of VR were powerful (and often shocking); today, many who deal with VR applications have gone beyond these early visions to the critical consideration of existing applications and specific research initiatives.

The effects that debates and discussions concerning one technology have on other, related technologies (including the "social technologies" of management and administration) are influential in genre delineation. CSCW applications are still in very early stages of development; some of the discussion and concern now being generated concerning this technology relate either to "vaporware" (products that have been announced but that have yet to be made available to the public for purchase) or to the CSCW-related concepts and notions introduced in the research and popular literatures. Discourse on themes underpinning CSCW initiatives (or CSCW genre) influences the development of a variety of aspects of computer systems by underscoring the dimensions or potential dimensions related to collaboration and group process. For example, linkages between CSCW and VR were drawn quite early in the evolution of these genres and have been helpful in providing inspiration for, and expanding research directions in, both areas (Wexelblat, 1993).

CSCW research (along with some AI initiatives) can be readily characterized as "generative" (that is, rich in concepts and images that can be readily infused into other, related technological approaches). Some of the researchers associated with CSCW system development have already predicted its demise – that is, its incorporation into other computing approaches and its disappearance as a distinct topic for research (see Johansen, 1988; Holt, 1989a; Winograd, 1989).

The concepts of a technological "problem" and its "solution" as utilized in this book are sometimes at variance with approaches that link the emergence and solution of unique problems with specific groups of individuals, or "actors"; a number of groupware-related problems and issues are only loosely associated with specific actor groups. Rather, many of the problems addressed in genre-development efforts reflect and extend broad cultural themes (such as privacy, dependence, and other issues involving the individual's relation to the group). The solution or resolution of these themes is sometimes manifested in a change in the technology itself; such resolution can also occur, however, through political and social changes, or when society (for whatever reason) moves on to other problems and concerns. End-user advocates have powerful roles in the framing of and interpretations given to genres, particularly in their early stages of development. Advocates include self-appointed consumer watchdogs, members of the trade press, professional group leaders, and academics.

Genre development is heavily sensitive to context, having many relationships with cultural themes. The emphasis of most of this book is on the U.S. response to the groupware genre, although some international perspectives are certainly relevant. For example, large European audiences for U.S. software have a substantial influence on the success of the U.S. computer industry. Lotus *Notes* (a widely marketed CSCW product) met with an early, enthusiastic reception in Germany, which kept Lotus's hopes alive for a large financial return for the product in the early days of commercial groupware (*Information Week*, 1990b).

Examples of cross-cultural differences in how a computer genre is presented are provided by Schneider (1982). In her study of advertising strategies promoting office automation in the United States and Scandinavia, she found significant variations among the nations. For example, a particular word processing system was marketed in the United States in terms that emphasized cost efficiency and ease of learning (and subsequent reductions in training costs). In Scandinavian countries, the same product was sold with an emphasis on creating a better work environment, reducing routine work, and creating more challenging jobs. The impact of an artifact (how it is perceived, how it fares in the marketplace, and how it is used) obviously depends on factors beyond the purely technical. Another cross-cultural effort in this area is Allwood and Wang's (1990) examination of differences in perceptions of computers in Sweden and Singapore.

Genre-talk: Look for the "groupware" label

The CSCW software genre traces its roots to the 1960s and the work of Douglas C. Engelbart at the Stanford Research Institute, now SRI International. Engelbart's notions of the "augmentation" of the human intellect, and of the enhancement of the productivity of individuals working in teams, can be found in many of the current CSCW design perspectives.

In his research, Engelbart (along with such collaborators as William C. English, Charles Irby, Jeff Rulifson, William Duval, and William Paxton) attempted to distill some general principles and methodologies to aid researchers in their understanding of the process of and potential for augmentation (see Engelbart, 1963). The research effort at Stanford attempted to develop an interactive computing environment that incorporated means for individuals and groups to conceptualize and organize materials more adequately. The issue of whether or not Engelbart and his collaborators delineated an adequate notion of augmentation (rather than just support) has been raised (Mahmood, 1989) – but Engelbart's work is still widely acknowledged as developing many of the seminal concepts for today's efforts to enhance group work activity.

Engelbart's notion of the "knowledge workshop" served as a framework for some of his early efforts (Engelbart, 1988). The knowledge workshop is the "specially provided environment in which knowledge workers do their knowledge work." (Engelbart relates that he borrowed the terms "knowledge worker" and "knowledge society" from Drucker, 1966, using them to point out the growing level and importance of information-related work in our society.) Engelbart predicted the direction in which knowledge communities would grow, one that is consonant with many current CSCW research and application initiatives:

With the probable increase in the amount and intensity of distributed collaboration within the Community, "committee work" would become more widespread, dynamic, and important. Thus there would be greater dependence on better techniques for inter-communication and management within the committee-like structures by which a Community goes about its composite business. Harnessing these new techniques will lead to very different ways in which they can go about their business. (Engelbart, 1988, p. 6)

Importance of funding considerations for research work is underscored by the history of Engelbart's research efforts. His project group (which expanded to 18 members at one point) had trouble receiving sustained funding. In 1977, Engelbart moved to Tymshare, Inc.; when McDonnell-Douglas bought Tymshare in 1984, Engelbart reports that many of his ideas seemed to take on renewed relevance because of the "very heavy knowledge work involved" in the aerospace firm. Another possible influence for the acceptance of Engelbart's research strategies in 1984 was the advent of the CSCW movement – described shortly – which crystalized at about that time. Engelbart's work in support of "multi-disciplinary, multi-corporate collaboration" continued in his Project Bootstrap. The expressive image of bootstrapping has linkages both with a strategy for pulling up one's own boots and with an approach to restarting a computer system: Engelbart declares that organizations can "boost their own effectiveness" by the appropriate combination of computer tools, work methods, and organizational structure.

Other pioneering efforts include those of Rand Corporation's Olaf Helmer and Norman Dalkey to computerize Delphi group conference techniques. Delphi was developed in the 1950s as a paper-and-pencil methodology to assist in the exchange of opinions among experts in an area. Delphi group conference methodology is one of several, originally non-computer-based methodologies that have been adapted for CSCW applications; others include nominal group technique (NGT) and brainstorming. A CSCW effort involving the former is described in Archer (1990).

Starr Roxanne Hiltz and Murray Turoff's research at the New Jersey Institute of Technology on computer support for group interaction was instrumental in developing some of the major approaches in design and evaluation of computer conferencing and related technologies. Many of their research tangents originated in Turoff's work at the U.S. Office of Emergency Preparedness in the late 1960s. Turoff states that the "single long term design goal" for his efforts involving computer-mediated communications is that of "collective intelligence," which Turoff claims is a "measurable" commodity. Turoff, like Engelbart, occasionally uses the phrase "group augmentation" in his discussions of this goal. "Collective intelligence" involves "the question as to whether a group utilizing an appropriate communication technology and support tools can reach a better result than any individual in the group acting alone" (Turoff, 1989, p. 120). Although Turoff was one of the first to do design work that could be classified as groupware, he has recently stated considerable opposition to current groupware efforts. He labels them "victims of commercialization" and "solutions seeking problems" (1989, p. 111). Turoff criticizes

many of today's CSCW designers for developing highly tailored, specialized systems for specific tasks and for losing sight of CSCW's roots in the
more broadly based efforts of the 1960s and 1970s. Turoff states that
"the long term result is absurd. Users will not tolerate using a different
communication system for each type of communication task."

In the 1970s, the Institute of the Future (with a team that included
Jacques Vallee, Kathleen Vian, and Robert Johansen) conducted pioneering explorations of group communications through computers, emphasizing collaborative efforts in the scientific community (Johansen, 1988).
Most of the field tests involved groups of scientists (many of whom were
separated geographically) who performed joint tasks. Reflecting on these
studies and their more current efforts, Vian and Johansen express concern
about the term "computer conferencing," noting that it has "already become inadequate to describe current applications, and is likely to become
even more so" (1983, p. 494).

The 1980s brought a new research agenda (and new research tools) to
this area, as well as a new identity – that of CSCW, or groupware.
Although the pioneering work of the individuals described in the preceding paragraphs is still recognized in its historical context, the notion of
groupware is often presented as radically new. In the 1980s, infrastructure
for group work applications became more refined as the capabilities of
workstations continued to increase, along with their connectivity. The
speed of the Intel 80286–based workstations available in the 1980s was
greater than that of the IBM 365 mainframes that sustained the activities
of large governments in the 1970s. This increased power stimulated new
thinking about how computing could be utilized in organizations. Many of
the groundbreaking efforts just described were rooted in timesharing systems and mainframe technology – systems that were shared by a number
of different computing functions but for which access was often limited.

The technological underpinnings required for many CSCW systems (for
example, network file systems and distributed computing) became more
common in workplaces in the latter half of the 1980s. However, changes in
technological capabilities alone are insufficient to describe how groupware
emerged. Managerial demands for higher levels of productivity in white-
collar, administrative, and professional settings also increased during this
period, and instigated efforts to make the work done by teams more
efficient and effective. By the end of the 1980s, some CSCW products
became mass marketed, and the buzzword "groupware" became popular
in computer industry trade magazines.

A number of large companies are considering or already have made
sizable investments in groupware research and development. Gordon
Bridge of AT&T Computer Systems is quoted as stating that "the work-

place is no longer defined by the four walls of an individual's office" and that AT&T's early network-based software product *Rhapsody* "will let [workers] act as a team, coordinating and completing collaborative work efficiently and effectively" (Keller, 1990a). Pioneering vendors of groupware include Action Technologies (Emeryville, California), with the product *The Coordinator,* and Coordination Technology, Inc. (Trumbull, Connecticut), with the product *Together.* Neither of these corporations is currently selling these breakthrough products. The groupware market has proven, for many developers, to be a difficult one to interpret and thrive in. Although most new technologies present steep learning curves to those who wish to develop and disseminate them, groupware's status as a somewhat mysterious yet inviting genre is also somewhat to blame.

Structure of a software revolution: The growth of interest in CSCW applications and research

People, events, and organizations are strong forces in the emergence and shaping of technologies, as well as their associated genres and research agendas. The Royal Society's activities and publications shaped science and firmed up the growing scientific community in the 1660s. Today, conference activities, funding initiatives, and market data are often invaluable in identifying the important "actors" and "actor networks" in the development of a technology. Other groups that can be involved in a technology's actor network – the loosely coupled set of interest groups and associations that affect a technology – include regulatory officials, product distributors, and users.

Establishment and maintenance of a conference series send signals that a field is becoming mature. The 1980s version of the CSCW research community began to take form with a meeting (arranged by Irene Greif of MIT and Paul Cashman of Digital Equipment Corporation) in the summer of 1984 at MIT. Another important milestone for CSCW efforts was the CSCW-86: Conference on Computer-Supported Cooperative Work. CSCW-86 was jointly supported by the Microelectronics and Computer Technology Corporation's Software Technology Program, the Association for Computing Machinery's Special Interest Group on Software Engineering (SIGSOFT), and the Software Psychology Society of the Institute of Management Studies (TIMS). Over half of the approximately 300 attendees were from industry research labs. The conference had an interdisciplinary emphasis, and thus helped to shape the eclectic nature of current CSCW research agendas.

Scientific and business research organizations were both represented in early CSCW initiatives. The National Science Foundation (NSF) provided a stimulus for the interdisciplinary bent of CSCW research. The first NSF funding programs specifically relating to CSCW-related topics (started in 1988) required an interdisciplinary team, even though demanding such team formation might have encouraged the formation of less organized, hastily formed research groups. Interest in CSCW-related research by schools of business was demonstrated in a 1987 meeting at the Graduate School of Business at NYU (the Symposium on Technological Support for Work Group Collaboration). The funding initiatives and conferences just described were instrumental in identifying the active players in CSCW research, and in jelling CSCW research and development communities.

Despite the apparent success of these groundbreaking conferences in stimulating interest in CSCW work (Suchman, 1988a, reports that CSCW-88 had 125 submitted papers), conferences in the CSCW series are held every other year. One rationale for this schedule is that CSCW advances take time to materialize (for example, they involve development of new systems and studies of organizational impacts), and, given the present level of activity in CSCW, an annual meeting is not yet warranted (Greif, 1988a). European interest in CSCW was demonstrated by the formation of EC-CSCW'89, the First European Conference on Computer Supported Cooperative Work. EC-CSCW'89 was billed as "a multi-disciplinary forum for exchange of ideas and information on the use of computers to support collaborative working." It organized opportunities for matching people with similar interests in CSCW-related projects and provided workshops on the interface of CSCW with such topics as AI, organizational forms, education, and medicine. Subsequent EC-CSCW conferences have been held every two years.

Some of the better-established computer societies have also taken part in CSCW-related initiatives. The Association for Computing Machinery's (ACM) Special Interest Group on Office Automation Systems (SIGOIS) has assumed a leading role in CSCW-related activities. SIGOIS spokespersons have expressed the need to broaden SIGOIS membership and functions to include CSCW interests (*ACM Member Net,* 1990, p. 4); SIGOIS published a special issue devoted to CSCW subjects relating to privacy (Clement, 1993). Journals such as *CSCW* (inaugurated in 1992) and *Human-Computer Interaction* (begun in 1989) have also provided forums for CSCW research results and discussions of social issues. (It is perhaps ironic that paper-based journals and face-to-face conference sessions have been so influential in development of the CSCW applications genre.) An assortment of newsgroups on the Internet and World Wide Web pages feature discussions and updates on groupware-related topics.

Individuals and groups that comprise the markets targeted by designers and developers for groupware products are also key actors in the CSCW technology picture. Some of the commercially available groupware products on the market are being framed for consideration by higher-level administrators and managers. This is in contrast to the bulk of the other software purchased for networks and PCs, which research shows is generally purchased by PC support personnel, including mid-level information center staff (Bartholomae, 1990). Sall (of Lotus Corporation) reports: "[*Notes*] changes the way an organization communicates, and that's a decision that belongs to the people high up in the organization. So we're selling *Notes* to chief information officers and, in some cases, CEO's" (Ambrosio, 1990a, p. 24). As groupware prices fall, and as networks become a better-known and more widely accepted part of the organization, a broader range of managers has become responsible for groupware-related purchase and implementation decisions.

Early announcements of some groupware products have triggered claims that vaporware was being described. CSCW applications are often viewed as having a relatively long (six- to nine-month) sales cycle (it often takes that long for an organization to make the decision to purchase groupware). This has supposedly made early declaration of a product's existence a business necessity (Ambrosio, 1990b). Fogarty (1994) reports that "Lotus Development Corp., Microsoft Corp. and IBM have whetted the appetites of users for new technology by promising next-generation [groupware] products, but they will not deliver on those promises for three to nine months" (p. 4). One product that was announced long before its actual availability was Coordination Technology's *Together,* largely rooted in Anatol Holt's theoretical work in "coordination mechanics."

Holt relates that Coordination Technology was organized "to turn linked computers into coordination engines by turning coordination mechanics into technology and technology into product" (1988, p. 110). *Together* was announced in June 1990, even though its designers said it would not be available for purchase for more than a year. Coordination Technology's vice-president of sales and marketing gave the following rationale for this decision: "Groupware is hot right now, and we wanted to throw our hat into the ring" (Ambrosio, 1990b, p. 35), although the product had not at the time entered beta (on-site) testing.

Concern over the fact that groupware has not been as successful as some forecasts had projected has stimulated a number of analyses and discussions. Nagasundsram, in an article in the *Bulletin* of the Special Interest Group on Computer–Human Interaction of the Association for Computing Machinery (ACM-SIGCHI), argues that groupware designers should first look to the felt needs of potential users and design "middle-range" (MR) applications:

An MR application for a given new technology is defined as one for which a serious need is felt but which currently available technologies or techniques do not address. A low-range (LR) application is one which could be handled by the new technology but for which this technology is not perceived to deliver any significant incremental value over the technology currently utilized. A high-range (HR) application is one which could be handled by more powerful versions of MR technology but little or no need is currently felt for the application itself. (Nagasundsram, 1990a, p. 24)

Nagasundsram contends that groupware developers should address the MR needs of organization managers, rather than trying to design high-range applications for needs that may never be felt. Nagasundsram's commentary underscores the linkages between groupware designers and practicing managers, linkages that he hopes will be reinforced by the relatively conservative approach of projecting today's managers' current needs.

Developments in technology are often related (if only in image and rhetoric) to the perception of certain "problems" on the part of relevant actors. One of the reasons for increased interest in linking workstations and PCs into effective, controllable networks relates to managerial problems caused by the often-unexpected popularity of freestanding PCs and workstations. Kemeny (1990) noted with dismay that although his predictions about the future of computers were always "far-out" and optimistic, he failed to predict the advent of PCs: "I always talked about time-sharing systems and access through terminals, but I could not conceive of buying a computer comparable in power to the mainframes of those days that would sit on my desk" (p. 44). Kemeny described his PC as being more powerful than the time-sharing system he helped launch at Dartmouth more than 25 years previously. Since there were few accurate projections of the PC's potential, organizational participants were not alerted to changes over the horizon.

Extent of PC proliferation varies across different industrialized nations, so the historical account in this section is circumscribed by the American experience. In the United States, computer center managers and other information systems personnel were dramatically affected by the PC revolution. Some lost their jobs. Those remaining had to retrain (LaPlante, 1990, provides a case study). Individuals who survived these transitions were often called on to support and maintain a variety of PCs and workstations with a full range of different applications, machines, and programs – technology often not acquired with their oversight. The control that these managers once had of the organization's use of computer technology – when a limited number of mainframes were available in a centralized location – quickly dissipated. Nontechnical middle-level managers were faced with similar problems concerning the lack of control over information-related functions. Organizational participants only mildly conversant with computer technology were often utilizing PCs for sensitive organizational tasks, sometimes with unfortunate consequences in terms of security and reliability of information resources.

Although many people were unsettled by what transpired, others were euphoric. A number of computer industry figures have voiced their opinion that the "PC era" became the "era of the network," and have been especially vociferous in their satisfaction with that result. Johansen begins his book on groupware (one of the first widely distributed volumes specifically on CSCW systems) with the line "The personal computer is often too personal." Terdoslavich (1990) similarly declares that the "personal computer is becoming less personal every day" (p. 33), referring to increases in networking. Kemeny (1990) related that "for several years, we lived in a solipsistic universe: just me and my computer" (p. 46). He lamented that before the current networking initiatives, computers were isolated and not as useful as they could be. Anderson (quoted in *Information Week,* 1990a) declares that "as the PC leverages the individual, groupware will leverage the organization." An ad for Lotus *Notes* declares that because of this product "the COMMITTEE is dead; long live the TEAM" (*PC Computing,* 1994).

The rapid series of changes in computing technology has thus provided management with problems as well as opportunities:

Briefly stated, the problem that faces management is the re-establishment of control of the information resource (where this has been lost through the use of PCs) without losing the flexibility, user enthusiasm, and productivity that PCs have generated. Control needs to be re-established, in general, wherever dispersed PCs contain information of significant operational, managerial, or strategic value to the organization. For personal, rather than corporate, PC use, control may be much more relaxed. However, personal systems often grow and develop in importance to an enterprise, so that a periodic audit of uncontrolled systems is necessary. Some would argue that all PC use within an organization involves corporate data and should therefore be controlled. (Haywood and Tate, 1986, p. 5)

To achieve control over the increasingly distributed computing function, management needed to introduce both control-oriented practices and such technologies as communication networks, distributed databases, and data dictionaries (all of which require a certain amount of coordination among users).

Many network-based computer systems provide explicit mechanisms for controlling PC proliferation and use in organizations, including the

capacity for the monitoring of users' system utilization and ways to centralize mechanisms for the access and updating of certain files. With its
emphasis on the generally unobjectionable notions of cooperation and
collaboration (as well as sharing computer files and other resources), the
CSCW applications genre introduces the issue of PC control in a way that
is not readily seen as offensive by much of the American workforce.
Although the notion of groupware appears to incorporate some considerable control-related dimensions, its emphasis is indeed on cooperation –
something that comes from within an individual (rather than being externally imposed). Thus, groupware, with its positive, upbeat associations,
was added to the tool kit of the centralized information function of many
organizations.

The promise of client/server computing has become another of these
lures. The term "client/server computing" became popular in the early
1990s in referring to networked configurations in which one or more main
computer units (server platforms) hold widely used data and handle major,
"back-end" processing. Workstations, PCs, and smaller networks are
networked to the server platforms and do "front-end" processing. One of
the notable features of the client/server approach is that the server platforms can be of different kinds and makes, and can include mainframes as
well. This flexibility allows an assortment of PCs, workstations, and
networks to be tied into the client/server system; users can thus access
the varied equipment they already have and are familiar with, while taking
advantage of the power of networking. The use of the term "client" in
"client/server" may be significant, for it has associations with professionalism and service orientation, whatever its technical meaning.

An advertising insert funded by Businessland, Inc. (a supplement to
The *Wall Street Journal* in November 1990) heralded the new era of client/
server computing as one of increased management control:

In the rush toward personal computer productivity during the 1980's, many companies leapt from the proven security of centralized time-sharing to the relative
chaos of early PC networks. In this explosive environment, technologies and
standards evolved quickly. Unfortunately, this runaway evolution of diverse
computers on divergent LANs [local area networks] created a technological
Tower of Babel. (*Businessland*, 1990, p. 6)

The advertising copy presents the client/server approach as a solution to
both technological and managerial problems, increasing the control of
management over the organizational information function.

These computer system transitions have not been without difficulty.
John Dinkle, vice-president of WorkGroup Technologies, Inc., reports

that users of client/server arrangements wish to have the same access and ease of use with the new configurations that they had in working with a centralized mainframe: "[The users'] concern is if they off-load the information down to the server, whether they can secure it in the ways they are used to in the mainframe or midrange environment" (Smith, 1990, p. 18). Today, problems of dealing with a vital, shared resource in an age of rapidly changing technologies have directed a good deal of attention across organizational levels to such information-related concerns as security, access, and privacy. In the past decade, computer and information activities have attracted high levels of interest as new configurations have been considered, been implemented, and become out of date within a few years; an increasing number of new, less technically literate participants in development of computer application genres have emerged.

In many quarters, association of the PC with autonomy on the part of organizational participants was short-lived; the age of "solipsism . . . just me and my computer" that John Kemeny described passed quickly as workstations and PCs came under centralized managerial control. Changes in the workplace have been more than merely technical. The PC's isolation also provided a measure of individual freedom for many. Fano (1985) labels the PC as a "personal working tool," providing "the ability to isolate oneself while retaining the ability to share information and communicate with others at the appropriate time . . . close to an operational definition of 'privacy.' " Fano's ideal is at variance with the emerging office environment, where workstations and PCs are connected, monitored, and supervised by centralized authority, and the individual is not in control of many of the aspects of the computer technology he or she uses.

The path from the isolated PC to the network is a rocky one and has still not been traversed by a number of organizations. Many CSCW applications and related software require substantial network capabilities, so CSCW acceptance may hinge on the success of solutions to networking problems. Assemblers of networks face a number of intimidating problems on the way to network installation and use, involving such basic issues as purchase and installation of connective wire, whether plain copper, coaxial, or fiber optic. Wireless networks offer new potentials in terms of connectivity (they would allow networked computers to be moved from room to room without wire-related concerns), but also have an intimidating array of technical problems. Other issues in installing networks involve the lack of industry-wide networking standards. Without a stable standard, customers for networks have good reason for concern that their chosen network could become quickly obsolete. Uncertainty about the directions that the Internet and large-scale private networks are taking is also causing concern. Many organizations want to be able to link their own networks to the Internet (Arnst, 1995).

The power and adaptability of spreadsheets provided the impetus for many organizations to purchase PCs. Similarly, the groupware genre and its products may provide rationales for organizations to attempt to overcome the many and varied technical hurdles associated with networking; groupware development may thus be of interest to organizations with commercial stakes in selling and maintaining network-related technologies. Price Waterhouse's national director for information and technology, Sheldon Laube, claims that Lotus *Notes* (Lotus Corporation's major groupware initiative, and probably the most popular groupware product to date) had "taken off beyond our wildest expectations." He claims that users demanded access to computer networks just to be able to run it (McPartlin, 1990b). *Notes* has undergone a series of modifications and extensions as network capabilities have expanded, along with users' awarenesses of what is feasible in a network-based environment. A *Notes* variation provides the means for users to exchange video segments as well as other kinds of files. Other *Notes* variations make it suitable for sharing information over the Internet or large-scale private networks (Cortese, 1995). Partly as a result of the success of *Notes*, Lotus Corporation was acquired by IBM in 1995.

Dream teams: Shared virtual reality applications

Statements of how the tools and approaches of VR can be adapted for use in group work contexts and other settings for collaboration have often been euphoric: Larijani (1993) writes that "VR systems make it possible for decision makers themselves to define and create environments or problems in clear, graphically explicit images" (p. 153). The images of being able to "fly through" shared data files and be "present" at meetings held at distant locations have stoked interest in VR–CSCW linkages.

Limitations of current VR technologies have often dampened enthusiasm for specific projects, however. VR is generally associated today with sets of often-restrictive and clunky head-mounted devices and data gloves, though less restrictive VR environments are under development, inspired by the work of Krueger (1991). Early head-mounted VR displays with graphics components that were responsive to user movements were designed by Ivan Sutherland in the 1960s. The Virtual Visual Environment Display (VIVED) was introduced in 1984 by McGreevy and Humphries as a tool for astronauts; it was a heavy, monochrome, head-mounted display. In 1985, VPL Research began to commercialize VR products, primarily serving to stimulate interest in such VR applications as research and entertainment. Along with producing *DataGloves* and *EyePhones,* it marketed software for support of VR applications development. *Swivel 3-D,* a vehicle for creating three-dimensional environments, became a popular product for the *Macintosh* PC. VPL also pioneered the development of some of the basic notions behind shared virtual environments. Other commercial development efforts are underway internationally (in such corporations as Sense8 and W Industries); a good share of this activity is being undertaken in small start-up companies with incorporation dates after 1990.

Some VR–CSCW developers have drawn linkages between their applications and the social science simulation game initiatives popular in the 1960s and 1970s. In social science gaming (as in shared VR), participants interact directly with a model that provides various forms of feedback and affords continuous, dynamic interaction. However, there are some differences between gaming and VR, as developers note. Today's VR environments do not have the same room for spectators and explicit pedagogical direction that many kinds of social science gaming affords; VR feedback is also more direct and immediate than the kind gaming produces. The history of simulation gaming provides an inescapable backdrop for VR development efforts, though, however different the associated technological artifacts; VR and gaming are linked by the strong identification that individuals have with their roles as created in these genres, and by the strength of their basic models and images in capturing the imagination of participants.

Shared VR application initiatives have also been linked with the development of flight, spacecraft, and other vehicle simulators (which has several decades of history to draw from); in keeping with this linkage, the term "cybernaut" has often been used to describe the VR user. Many vehicle simulators are designed for use by individuals working alone, or by an individual with a single human trainer. However, a growing number have facilities for team interaction, mirroring the team maneuvers required in piloting large aircraft or space vehicles. With the images of flight simulators to guide them, many VR developers have been inspired to incorporate immersion (where individuals become "part of the simulated world"), real-time interaction, three-dimensional graphics, and force-feedback into their applications.

Shared VR applications also have a number of tangents to cinema and other modes of entertainment that are large-scale and communal. However, to create involving roles for spectators in multiparticipant VR environments is problematic, and guiding images are just beginning to emerge. A number of specially designed buildings are being constructed for shared

VR entertainment experiences, most of which will combine possibilities for being "spectators" and watching the activity of others, as well as being direct participants. Whether the role of spectator can be made interesting (or at least comprehensible) in a VR environment is still in question. The high level of "immersion" involved in VR (or "the subjective experience of presence," according to Heeter, 1992) is difficult to obtain using a projection screen or comparable vehicle.

Development of VR applications for design collaboration has been an area of special attention, given designers' first-hand acquaintance with collaborative design problems and possibilities. Technical hurdles have been especially frustrating here, given the ideal of many developers that "all participants would be identically equipped [with VR gear] and able to feed their ideas into a common system" (Larijani, 1993); some designers have developed modifications of this ideal while attempting to retain the spirit of VR. Multiparticipant VR applications that aspire to create the compelling effect of immersion in a three-dimensional world have proved difficult to design as well as costly; multipurpose applications (ones that users can readily modify themselves) have been especially challenging. Such design tools could attract substantial, lucrative markets to VR, including those in construction and engineering, so attention to their development continues.

Reaching a decision: Group decision support systems and collective support systems

A thread of research and application efforts that has run parallel to that of CSCW activities is that of "group decision support systems" (GDSS). GDSS research has close ties with decision support systems (DSS) research and application efforts. DSS has a much longer history, with a number of initiatives in the 1970s, whereas GDSS research is much more recent (with concentrated efforts beginning in the early 1980s). DSS initiatives aim to support the individual decision maker using methodologies and techniques generated from decision theory, cognitive psychology, and industrial engineering. GDSS efforts generally integrate group process notions with strategies and perspectives linked with decision theory and related fields.

Dennis, George, Jessup, Nunamaker, & Vogel (1988) compare and contrast GDSS and CSCW systems in terms of the primary type of group support they are designed to provide. They assert that GDSS are generally task-oriented (GDSS provide a means for groups to work on specific tasks such as decision making and planning). Huber (1984) describes the early

GDSS designs as tailored for the needs of one kind of group performing one kind of task. Dennis et al. state that CSCW systems, in contrast, are more driven by the "communication needs" of the group (for instance, needs to critique or create a document jointly), and are less closely tied to an individual task or tasks.

The prospect for GDSS use received some general discussion in the management and industrial engineering literatures since Keen and Scott Morton (1978) described and publicized GDSS-related notions. In the early 1980s, Paul Gray's "decision room" ideas (Gray, 1981) and G. P. Wagner's (EXECUCOM Corporation) GDSS efforts (Kull, 1982) provided some of the first extensive applications research in the area. Few of the GDSS systems developed and distributed in the 1980s met with market success, or even gained general awareness (Kraemer and King, 1988); partly because of these market failures, GDSS is apparently losing its individual identity in the spectrum of computer software genres and is blending into the groupware field. An example of labeling shifts in this area is the classification of the University of Minnesota's SAMM system (Software Aided Meeting Management) as groupware – thus emphasizing its group process and coordination aspects – rather than as a GDSS system – thus emphasizing its ties to the DSS field (Halonen et al., 1990). The system had previously been classified as GDSS by designers.

Another kind of application that has tangents to groupware is the "collective support system." Collective support systems (as defined by the Center for Innovation and Co-operative Technology of the University of Amsterdam) are attempts to meet the demands of externally structured societal problems, problems arising when "an indefinite number of actors try to increase their competence for action, at or about the same time, in about the same environment." Examples of computer systems for collective support include the various forms of e-mail and problem-solving environments that can assist users in large-scale emergencies (such as floods and earthquakes), in social advice and casework, and in community development. The problems that collective support systems are applied to can change unpredictably and chaotically as the number and kinds of people utilizing the systems vary and as the environment changes.

The study of the social and ethical implications of network-based systems

Another in the set of actors to consider in the study of the CSCW applications genre (and other software genres) includes theorists, researchers, and social "watchdogs" who attempt to understand the impact of computing technology on society. Attention to the social and ethical dimensions

of computing systems has often closely followed the technological advances in this area (although voices of concern have sometimes been
muted for long periods).

Even when access to computers was limited to a few universities,
military installations, and businesses, Norbert Wiener (1954/1967) warned
of dangers that could be faced by society from the growth and development of automation. In the case of VR and some aspects of AI applications, it is apparent that social analyses and expressed concern have
preceded the widespread utilization of the technologies; this is not surprising, given the importance of the "projection period" of genre development
described earlier (the time early on in genre development when strong,
though unclear, images are linked with the genre). Social and ethical
analyses have disseminated general information about these innovations
to the public, as well as delivered their intended warnings.

Writers in widely distributed computing magazines serve major roles as
watchdogs in the field of computing, introducing and characterizing new
programs and products before users have had the chance to see them in
action in the workplace, and often before the products are made commercially available (recall the earlier discussion of vaporware). Research
conferences also sound alarms: calls for raising the standards of advanced
computer technologies have been delivered at academic and technical
gatherings. One example is Bundy and Clutterbuck's (1985) plea for maintaining the "credibility" of AI products at the Ninth International Joint
Conference on Artificial Intelligence. Computer Professionals for Social
Responsibility (CPSR) – originally modeled somewhat on the Physicians
for Social Responsibility – has often assumed leadership in issues relating
to computers and society (for example, computer-enhanced weaponry,
privacy, and workplace issues). Another group associated with the movement to examine critically the functions of computing in society is the
Association for Computing Machinery's Special Interest Group on Computers and Society (SIGCAS).

One of the major (and most influential) research themes on organizations and computing focuses on the direction of the effect of computerization: will computerization lead to organizational centralization or decentralization? Several major studies of the impact of computing applications
on distribution of power in organizations show that introduction of such
technology generally ends up supporting the status quo (see, for example,
Danziger and Kraemer, 1986). One interpretation of these studies is that
users view the technology and its potential applications in light of their
existing preconceptions of the organizational balance of power. Most of
the studies on this theme have been conducted in large organizations,

however – organizations in which the structures of hierarchy and authority are relatively well determined; studies of smaller, less calcified organizations may reveal different insights on how new technologies can shape organizational power structures. Many recent studies on the impact of computing on organizations target specific computer system applications and uses, rather than the effects of computerization per se. An emerging common theme is that computing systems are malleable tools suitable for a variety of organizational applications, and that they have a wide assortment of social effects (rather than a few, consistent ones).

Kling (1990, p. 21) predicts that research in social and ethical consequences of computing systems is likely to increase through the 1990s because of a number of factors, including the following:

1. The steady stream of computing innovations.
2. The drive by academic computer science departments and funding agencies such as NSF [National Science Foundation] and DARPA [Defense Advanced Research Projects Agency] to justify large expenditures on computing research.
3. Justifications for major national computerization programs, such as the High Performance Computing Initiative; and
4. [The production of] articles examining life and technology in the 21st century.

Kling emphasizes the important role that literature on social aspects of computerization plays on the developments in computing technology. A good share of this literature utilizes psychological and sociological concepts and methodologies. The journal *Computing in the Human Sciences* presents a broad sampling of these approaches. Turkle's (1984) characterization of the computer as the "first psychological machine," and her chronicles of the impact of the computer on the psychological self-awareness of individuals, followed closely on the heels of the PC revolution (that is, the period in the early 1980s when PCs became widely distributed) and helped to strengthen associations between the social and technical realms of computing.

Turkle claims that by utilizing machines that have intellectual capabilities strongly similar to our own, we are stimulated to reflect on our own modes of thought and feeling. Similarly, the use of CSCW and other network-based system applications as tools of coordination and communication could earn for these systems the label "socio-psychological machines" (Oravec, 1989b). Reification of group structure, roles, and interaction patterns that some CSCW applications provide could stimulate users to reconsider (and perhaps alter) the way they deal with others in tasks not supported by computing (as well as the way they conceptualize group activity in general).

Typical of the ethical and social concerns raised about CSCW systems in recent literature are those of Howard, Grudin, Opper, and Garson. Howard's (1987) article was one of the first to tackle CSCW-related social issues; the piece was an outgrowth of a speech given at CSCW-86. Howard predicts dilution of individual responsibility and accountability for CSCW-related decisions, documents, and designs, and projects that personal identification with CSCW-assisted activities is likely to be low. There is thus some concern as to whether decisions of ethical and social consequence should be made with the use of CSCW systems.

Grudin (1988) and Opper (1988) (in articles in the widely distributed PC magazine *Byte*) both note that cooperation among individuals interacting through the medium of a CSCW system is a crucial factor in success of the system. For example, a group calendar management system will fail dismally if group members do not regularly and conscientiously update their individual calendars; if use of the system does not reinforce individuals enough to elicit their voluntary cooperation, the required behavior may be enforced by managerial pressure. Grudin (1989a) explores ethical issues of fairness involved when installation and implementation of a CSCW system results in the expectation of increased effort from (with little commensurate benefit to) lower-status individuals. *Electronic Sweatshop* (Garson, 1988) explored a number of issues related to computer monitoring and other network functions, and helped to popularize the phrase in its title as a description of working conditions in computer-mediated organizations. Garson characterizes problems involving computers in the workplace as directly affecting the quality of working life for middle-level management and professionals, as well as clerical workers.

Vehicles for discussion of the social implications of VR have spanned from the *Economist* to *Christianity Today*. A TV situation comedy, *Mad About You,* explored the changes in a marriage that occurred after one member of the couple engaged in VR-supported interaction with a fashion model. Negroponte (1995) explores such "socially responsible" applications of VR as its use in driving schools, in which VR "allows one to experience a situation *with one's own body*" (p. 117). VR technology has had broad cultural exposure, as further described in upcoming chapters.

Some conclusions and reflections

Genres do not appear full blown, with their dimensions, social implications, and relationships with other genres obvious. This chapter introduces the nascent genre of CSCW applications and discusses some of the relevant groups and markets influencing its development. Genre research has special relevance to computer networking: with the wide expansion of access to networking and related technologies across our society, an increase in the number and variety of network-based system genres (and subgenres) can be expected in the near future.

Genres reflect important societal tensions and themes: for example, tragedies portray the failure of heroes and heroines despite the best efforts of these characters, capturing a basic disquiet at the very core of our existence. The scientific journal has conflict at its very root: it provides static snapshots and limited slices of a very active and very empirical enterprise. Despite its inherent limitations and frustrations, involvement in genres and genre creation activity makes us participants in our societies in a broader sense than does less focused human expression. Our efforts become part of the larger struggle for societal definition and awareness. In CSCW applications, long-standing conflicts and compatibilities between individual and group, self and collective, find new outlets.

Delineations between CSCW systems and other network-based systems have been somewhat loose, in part reflecting the volatility of these research and development areas. Characterizations of ongoing societal debates and discussions related to genre issues may indeed be more useful than completed maps of the terrain. CSCW applications development began to take on an identity distinct from other currents of network-based system initiatives in the 1980s. CSCW applications R&D provides a potentially stable amalgam of a number of specialized disciplines (including human–computer interaction, group dynamics, intraorganizational communications, and decision support research). Growing numbers of subgenres, including collaborative writing and design tools, meeting support applications, various Internet linkages, and group calendaring and scheduling programs, are also emerging under the CSCW umbrella.

As a source for marketable products, many kinds of network-based systems applications are potentially fruitful, especially the ones associated with managerial control functions. Managers who were taken aback by the popularity of the PC are beginning to view networking and groupware as solutions for their perceived need for control and integration of information-related functions in their organizations. Commercial software developers who want to profit from the proliferation of powerful workstations and enhanced network capabilities in organizations are seeing new markets and new opportunities in groupware. Designers and system developers are envisioning innovative applications for computing in the CSCW applications genre, as well as obtaining inspiration for new modes of doing information-related work. Developers of educational and entertainment packages are seeing new prospects in the linkages between VR and CSCW, and new varieties of games and cooperative learning tools are evolving; uses of VR–CSCW applications to enhance workgroup interaction are also being explored.

Advocates for the end user are reflecting on the quality and usefulness of specific groupware products and are attempting to characterize the groupware genre itself. In contrast with the positive appraisals of some other industry observers, Dvorak has produced the following assessment of groupware:

> The [computer] business has finally matured into nothing more than a marketing war game and innovation is the first casualty . . . Groupware – software for groups of workers. This is turning into the biggest pile of baloney I've ever seen in the industry. (Dvorak, 1988, p. 71)

Expanding communities of computer science researchers and other professionals concerned with the impact of computing on society are also generating discussion and providing new perspectives on groupware and network-based computing themes.

Meanwhile, end users (professionals, secretarial staff, scientists, educators) are beginning to use groupware and are reflecting on their own experiences. Some users are ecstatically heralding the dawn of a new computer age, as reflected in the remarks of James Christie, a groupware user at an IBM-sponsored *TeamFocus* electronic meeting room site in Chicago, Illinois:

> It would have taken us an entire day of brainstorming, and we still couldn't have come up with so many ideas or thoughts. You just get worn out after a couple of hours, listening to other people talk and trying to hold on to your own idea. Without the technology, it would have taken us at least five times longer, and I'm not sure we would have produced the same quality [ideas] that we did with this method. (Van, 1990, p. 4)

The societal endeavor of constructing and characterizing a new kind of computer system and its associated concepts is not an obtuse intellectual exercise. Identification and crystalization of sets of computing capabilities into readily recognizable concepts and application packages have important implications for the management of information-related activities, as well as for the well-being of individuals who conduct or are affected by those functions (which includes just about all of us). CSCW and groupware notions are, as yet, partly shaped, their implications hazy. However, their introduction into discourse on computing in organizations has already underscored a number of critically important themes.

2
On the infinite variety of virtual entities

> *Let us hope . . . that in the years ahead we can construct a society
> that is less in need of suffering and a self that is less a sacrifice to the
> nihilistic economics and politics of our time.*
>
> *Philip Cushman (1990, pp. 608–609)*

This book is about virtual individuals and virtual groups. It is also about a specific set of computer system applications – groupware and other network-based systems – and the way we employ them in construction, dissemination, and manipulation of these virtual entities. To an increasing extent, management in organizational contexts has become the management of virtual individuals and groups. These virtual entities are employed in establishing the patterns and setting the standards by which we are evaluated and with which we often must conform.

Virtuality has become a common theme in American life, taking on connotations of the "imaginary," as well as the "designed" or "engineered": "virtual corporations" are created when corporations design sets of linkages with each other and with critical environmental factors, thus extending their effective spheres of influence (Davidow and Malone, 1992). Instead of tales about lonely teens and their imaginary companions, stories about an engineered "virtual girl" are consumed in the mass market (Thomson, 1993).

A virtual individual is a selection or compilation of various traces, records, imprints, photographs, profiles, and statistical information that pertain (or could reasonably be said to pertain) to an individual – along with writing done, images produced, sounds associated with, and impressions managed by the individual. The amalgam that results (whatever its components) is associated with the individual in the context of particular genres and artifacts. Certain kinds of virtual individuals emerge in relation to the genre of biography; others may become fictionalized and emerge in the novel. Others are produced in the context of CSCW applications. The individual may be highly aware of a number of the virtual individuals associated with him or her. We may be very conscious of how our writing is conveyed in an everyday electronic mail exchange or telephone call, for example (that is, how our expressions appear to others in the exchange). We may also be very watchful of the various images that are associated with us as a part of our own or our group's activities.

Many aspects of the virtual individuals associated with us may be unknown to us, however. For example, we may not be aware of what statistics and profiles are being constructed from data collected in the computer monitoring of our workplace activities. (We may not even be cognizant of the extent or even the existence of the monitoring, in some cases.) Some virtual individuals may be constructed by others with little concern for correctness or consistency. Even if we take great pains to keep track of them, or tailor them to certain situations, the virtual individuals we are associated with may be distorted in a variety of ways: they may not appear to others the way we believe or intend that they appear. Such distortion may make management of our virtual individuals difficult, if not impossible. Some of the virtual individuals composed of traces of our activities may lose their ties with us entirely. They may cease to be associated with us as individuals, as do expressions we coin that another people appropriate. Others may become "composite" virtual individuals (as in the profiles constructed by marketers of an "average" community member) and gain traits of others as well as ourselves.

The notion of a virtual individual, as developed in this book, is quite broad in its formulation. It reflects the many traces that can be associated with individuals and the wide variety of modes for personal expression that are available. My signature can be a virtual individual, standing in for me in certain contexts, and also supposedly "revealing" personal insights about me when interpreted by an expert in handwriting analysis. Virtual individuals can also include the multimedia, full-body electronic surrogates that we may soon control as we participate in meetings with others located many miles away. When the traces associated with a virtual individual have ties with an individual that are strongly reinforced by legal, cultural, and professional authorities, that virtual entity can have considerable functions in society.

Virtual groups are composed of transmissions of group interaction (technology-mediated and unmediated), records of group interaction (tape recordings, transcripts, and minutes), decisions and products associated with the group, articulated impressions and imagery associated with the group, and statistics linked with levels of group performance. As social and managerial scientists devise more varied and intricate indices of group performance and structure, and these are incorporated into organizational strategies, the complexity and number of virtual groups increase. An assortment of new virtual groups can also emerge in the context of user interaction. CSCW applications have also served to expand the variety of virtual groups. For example, face-to-face meetings generally have minutes, taken by a human recorder or secretary; some of the "meetings" held in the context of CSCW applications involve videos that are accessible in terms of various computer-supported indexing schemes.

Traces of individual and group traits and behavior that are employed in construction of virtual individuals and groups are removed from their initial connections with a time frame (that associated with their production and collection) and adopt a different set of time orientations. These orientations can indeed be closely associated with reconstructions and recollections of "what happened" at a particular time or in a particular context. However, these orientations are also tightly coupled with the traces' storage, retention, and/or potential review by others. Linkages that such traces had with the contexts of their production are in large part severed, and the traces take on an independent existence as "facts," "records," "meeting minutes," or "videotape recordings."

Group interaction takes on an added set of dimensions when aspects of time and pacing are considered. Words travel quickly, and people who are just about to view a transcript, computer-based record, or videotape of a meeting may already know much more than any of the original participants about what the meeting's "results" were (even if that transcript is provided seconds after the interaction in question); they may have picked information up by word of mouth, made an inference from the length of the meeting, or obtained some other background information. Viewpoints and subsequent evaluations and accounts of events pertaining to the group are conditioned by "application sequencing" (a critical element in many considerations involving complex vehicles for group support, such as CSCW applications). For example, responses to CSCW application-supported group proceedings are made in relation to what individuals already know about the interaction in question (and interactions that may be in the offing), and about how available transcripts or records are constructed (or put into sequence) in the context of a particular application.

Perspectives about application sequencing that other meeting participants may have are also relevant. Time is often less of a factor than sequence in these matters: notions and rumors as to "what preceded what" in the perceptions of group members, rather than specific time frames, provide rich clues for interpretation of group interaction. Various aspects of the applications involved serve as "hooks" or frameworks for the construction of sequence, linking events into a series that makes sense for participants and audiences. There may be a variety of accounts or transcripts of group interaction, each produced from different perspectives, analyzed in different ways, or rendered in various media.

Perceptions of the degree and context of application sequencing aid in determining who considers him- or herself (and is considered by others) as a legitimate "meeting participant" or "group member." These perceptions can also be a major factor in allocating responsibility for group activity. Piecing together a convoluted trail of "who knew what when" (for attributing either reward or blame) is a complex matter when various forms of asynchronous interaction and account construction are involved. (Matters involving application sequencing in the context of CSCW applications are taken up again in Chapter 7.)

Although there may be some general consensus as to the forms that construction may take, virtual individuals and groups are given different nuances by the various parties associated with them. A given profile or record admits of a variety of interpretations and emphases. However, the parties will generally talk as if they are relating to a central, shared "object," that of the virtual individual or group (although constructions of the shared object may differ widely among these parties). Many of the parties may adopt the "standard" interpretations lent to the object by professionals, system designers, and others associated with the object's collection, retention, or analysis. Others may be more creative and explore the outer reaches of character construction (and reconstruction).

Virtual reality and custom "social universes"

The word "virtual" has been readily adopted by computer science and applications communities for a variety of purposes. In those camps, it has taken on a number of technical associations (for example, "virtual memory"). The term has also been used frequently within education and training realms: Hiltz and Turoff (1990) employ the phrase "virtual classroom" to refer to their computer-mediated efforts in education (see also Hiltz, 1986), and a number of VR applications for health care and military training have been developed. The first presentations of VR notions are often credited to Ivan Sutherland. In his 1965 talk to the International Federation of Information Processing Societies (IFIPS), he proposed an "ultimate display" at which individuals could have the sense of being in control of their own movement through an environment simulated by the computer (Sutherland, 1965; 1968). Interest in VR is international in scope: Japan's Ministry of International Trade and Industry (MITI) has directed attention to it (Zachary, 1990), and several international conferences of VR designers have been held in Montpellier.

Entertainment-oriented applications of VR are many and varied, gaining the serious consideration of art critics as well as the attention of video game aficionados. The terms "virtual" and "artificial reality" (the latter associated with the work of Myron Krueger, 1983, 1991) are often associated with stimulating descriptions:

Enter artificial reality, the ability to program a custom universe into a computer. Throw on a high-tech bodysuit that senses body motions and feeds them into a computer that interprets movements as commands. See through video-display goggles that reflect the commands and experience the newly-created world. (Nash, 1990, p. 20)

Participants in VR utilize skills developed in previously experienced environments and develop other sets of skills as they encounter unexpected situations in the VR setting. VR notions have already been employed in medical and psychological research as a means for exploring aspects of human perceptual and cognitive functioning (Tart, 1990). VR-related issues have become a welcomed part of human factors conferences and research initiatives. Computer scientists, educators, psychologists, and others have demonstrated great concern about the impacts of VR on the individuals who participate in it. In the first annual conference on the topic held in December 1990 (where Krueger presented the keynote address entitled "Shaping Cultural Consciousness with Artificial Reality"), dystopian images were described and their implications debated: individuals exposed to artificial reality could "lose their moorings" and not recover their senses of what is "real." Individuals trained with VR tools (for example, as pilots, physicians, and soldiers) could respond adequately to VR situations yet fail to recognize significant factors when confronted with real-world jets, patients, or opposing military forces.

With the mechanisms involved in creation and support of virtual individuals and groups we can similarly design custom "social universes" for various purposes, as well as open up a large set of social and moral issues concerning the nature of "reality." Computerized simulations or models of society are already a standard part of training in the social sciences, and the development of policy in the social and political spheres. Virtual individual and group perspectives shift the notions involved with simulations to a more intimate level – the level of specific or composite individuals and groups. They also force individuals to deal with such issues of image manipulation and distortion on an immediate and personal basis, as participants immersed in fast-moving interaction. Development of other kinds of virtual entities (including varieties of subgroups, communities, and institutions) is accompanying the implementation of CSCW and other network-based applications, and is adding layers of complexity to an already-overwhelming set of social constructs. Conceptualization of a virtual entity does not ensure that it will play an active role in society: for a virtual entity to be assimilated into society, it requires an assortment of linkages (albeit tentative) to past or presently existing genres, cultural objects, and modes of human interaction.

Individuals and groups are generally at least vaguely aware of how some of the virtual individuals and groups they are associated with are constructed, and are often able to manage their behavior in response to them. They may also participate in construction of virtual individuals and groups by providing alternative constructions, such as metaphors descriptive of their groups, or by introducing various cultural themes as being relevant. The reflexive nature of this interaction provides complexities not found with many simulations – where some reflexivity may be involved, but where the bridges in time, distance, and context between constructs and the constructees are generally much longer.

Much of the effort of the research and design communities that are constructing VR tools is focused toward developing means for the creation of "faces." These faces can be controlled through a number of means (including *DataGloves* and other hand-controlled computer interfaces) and utilized for a variety of expression by both users and animators. The choice of the face as a focus for VR designers reflects the considerable societal attention placed on the face as a conduit for expression and information display. Simply put, in this society we generally look at each others' faces when we want to find out what is going on (as opposed to looking at hands, feet, or other bodily parts). The CSCW application *TeamWorkStation* supports this custom by allowing two collaborators to see what expressions are on their counterparts' faces when they work (Ishii and Miyake, 1991). According to its developers, these facial expressions go beyond verbal reports to enhance communication and task focus. Touching and other physical expression are also involved in human interaction, and VR developers are including full-body components in VR gear that provide vibration and other forms of physical stimulation.

VR applications have been linked with a variety of dystopian and utopian images. Utopian images associated with custom "social universes" of virtual individuals and groups include the following prospect: benign group leaders and participants will draw from virtual individual and group constructions effective tools for the support of group members' expression and exchange. One of the dystopian images that arises is that of an administrator, project leader, or educator sitting at a computer terminal and managing a (perhaps geographically dispersed) group – that has only vague resemblances with the group as its participants view it. The computer-based tools that are used only capture aspects of group interaction that serve to further certain, limited aims; the administrator in the dystopian setting may simply have no other, more adequate tools with which to view the group.

Virtual or artificial persons of various sorts are not unique to the computing environment. From the perspective of the American legal system, the social system is comprised of persons, both natural and juristic. Juristic persons are described in the following terms by Coleman:

"Juristic persons" are intangible entities which none of us natural persons has ever seen. They include what we commonly think of as corporations, along with many other entities: churches, certain clubs, trade associations, labor unions, professional associations, towns, and others . . . they cannot be physically imprisoned (although they can be punished in other ways, including death, a sentence not infrequently imposed by judges), they have no intrinsic capability of acting, and so must act through agents in the form of natural persons. (Coleman, 1974, p. 14)

The way juristic persons are constructed in a society provides some perspective on virtual individuals and groups. A group of legal theorists are working on new perspectives as to how society constructs and relates to such persons: "The social reality of a legal person is to be found in the collectivity: the socially binding self-description of identity and action" (Teubner, 1989, p. 728). Earlier in this century, Max Weber also proposed a perspective for viewing juristic persons:

These concepts of collective entities . . . have a meaning in the minds of individual persons, partly as something actually existing, partly as something with normative authority . . . Actors thus in part orient their action to them, and in this role such ideas have a powerful, often a decisive, causal influence on the course of action of real individuals. (Weber, 1956/1978, p. 14)

Although juristic persons are not "real" in the sense that flesh-and-blood persons are, our actions give them levels of existence that afford them major roles in many societal contexts. In comparable ways, the virtual individuals and groups associated with us are acted upon in ways that give them value in themselves (even apart from any value they have in the context of direct association with us as individuals and groups). Our records indeed speak for us in many ways, but they also speak for themselves, taking on a level of existence that is supported by the professions and industries dealing with information and the processing of individuals.

The play's the thing: The dramaturgical perspective and ensemble characters

How does the individual relate to virtual individuals and virtual groups, the constructions of self and group with whom he or she is intimately linked? To a large extent we view ourselves and each other in terms of how we manage (for example, how we relate or respond to threats or changes involving) the virtual individuals and groups with which we are associated. How do we respond to changes in our educational records, or relate to statistics concerning our work behavior? Do we consider the norms or standards of our group or community in evaluating this information? Do we change our behavior or attitude as part of our response to this information?

One way that we manage our identity in relation to the virtual individuals and groups we are associated with is by relating to such cultural objects as "consistency," "integration," or "balance" in the manner in which we organize the personal histories in our resumes and job applications, and in our explanations of our pasts to others (as well as to ourselves). The notion of the "dramatic" as a model for how individuals and groups manage their expressions and presentations in interactions or in personal expression is also useful for tackling some of the questions outlined in the preceding paragraph. Goffman (1974) utilizes dramaturgical imagery to characterize how people develop the textual accounts they create about themselves. He argues that in self-descriptions and autobiographical stories an individual presents "not himself but a story containing a protagonist who may happen also to be himself" (p. 541). In many contexts (whether computer-mediated or not), a wide assortment of virtual individuals can be associated with a single individual. This presents opportunities for developing "ensemble characters," in which synergies and conflicts among these virtual individuals provide vehicles for personal expression.

Origins of the dramaturgical perspective on selves and groups are often linked with the writings of the literary critic Kenneth Burke (1937, 1945, 1955, 1966). Hugh Duncan's (1962) *Communication and Social Order* was one of the vehicles through which Burke's dramaturgical perspective was introduced into social psychology. Duncan portrays Burke as claiming that human relations can best be seen in the light of dramaturgy: "Men enact roles. They change roles. They participate. They develop modes of social appeal. People are not animals, or machines . . . They relate as actors playing roles to achieve satisfactions which only other human actors can give them" (Duncan, 1962, p. 112).

Burke's "pentad" (the five basic elements he argues are needed to describe social life) was originally developed as a tool for the analysis of literature. The pentad involves an account of the relationships among (1) act (what is actually done), (2) agent (who is doing it), (3) agency (how it is being done), (4) scene (where it is being done), and (5) purpose (why it is being done). Burke omitted from the pentad – but many of his followers and critics, including Edgely and Turner (1975) incorporated – considerations involving the audience, that is, how what is being done is received and responded to by others.

In an approach similar to Burke's, Goffman (1959, 1961) describes construction of the self as accomplished in the context of a performance:

> A correctly staged and performed scene leads the audience to impute a self to a performed character, but this imputation – this self – is a product of a scene that comes off, and is not a cause of it. The self, then, as a performed character, is not an organic thing that has a specific location . . . it is a dramatic effect arising diffusely from a scene. (Goffman, 1959, p. 252–253)

After a performance, the critical questions raised by the audience are whether or not the self who is the product of the scene is considered creditable or discreditable (or mentally healthy or mentally ill).

The notion that human beings are best described as actors has often been met with vehement objection. Cuzzort (1969) asserts that Goffman's dramaturgical framework "forms the foundation for a view of mankind more disenchanting than that emanating from Darwin's theory of evolution or from Freud's conception of man as an impulsive animal held in an uneasy state of control by society" (pp. 174–175). Cuzzort objects that Goffman leaves humans "with practically nothing [and] appears to divest us of our sanctity by suggesting that we are all incorrigible 'con' artists – and that we have no choice. Moreover, the same tricks that make a con game work are basically the devices used in the act of being human" (p. 175). Hewitt (1989) describes Goffman's "disturbing, seemingly cynical" view of the self as being strenuously rejected by many (p. 58).

Cuzzort links morality with aspects of an individual's self-presentation – an individual is capable of morality only if he or she is not hiding behind a mask. The virtual individual perspective outlined in this book tightly links individuals and their masks, although individuals often have a good amount of control over how these masks are presented and interpreted by others. There are a variety of moral dimensions to these linkages, which relate to the tools that individuals are afforded and the leeway they are given in their efforts to manage their identities. Other observers have construed Goffman's approach as being decidely amoral, and declare that dramaturgy offers straightforward descriptions in comparison with many of those found in social psychology (see Edgely and Turner, 1975).

The usefulness of the dramaturgical perspective in considerations of the virtual individual and group includes its focus on the quality of the "performance" individuals conduct and on their relative successes and failures in managing their personal identities. There are indeed a number of social events that have special ramifications for self-construction (including job interviews, customs clearances, and educational admissions): individuals openly declare aspects of themselves. The metaphor of drama reinforces the notion that the self is indeed being constructed in the context of performances and not directly in relation to some hidden qualities or mechanisms, and the notion of an "audience" adds other important considerations addressed often in this book. The dramaturgical perspective also has limitations for our purposes, however: in our viewpoint, performances presented by individuals or groups are often not associated with a particular space and time, and may have aspects that the individuals are not consciously aware of (as in the collection of traces through computer monitoring). A particular performance may be pieced together through a variety of analytic and procedural means, as in construction of computer profiles. It may also involve efforts by the individual to balance or set into conflict various virtual individuals, so as to create the appearance of consistency or conflict in the ensemble or composite character associated with him- or herself.

Genres of the self

Writing, speaking, and choosing images and sounds with which to surround oneself, and other forms of personal expression, are tightly coupled with the self. Political displays in voting and polling are yet another kind of personal expression. Not too long ago, people were advised to "write a letter to Congress" concerning their opinions on an issue. Today, public opinion polls have largely eroded the effectiveness of that prerogative of citizenship. However, the virtual entity of the "average citizen" has obtained voice through the organized polling efforts of various media and political associations.

Choice of vehicles for writing, art, music, and dance provides another opportunity for self-expression. Holland discusses George Bernard Shaw's choice of the expressive vehicle of the play and his apparent search for a natural expression for his own "personal myth" or identity (one that involved the need for control):

Shaw submitted to and became that overwhelming but emotionless parent he was forever trying to find and not find his independence from. In doing so, he achieved his own unique style of playwriting. He turned the conventional plots and wisdom of his day inside out, giving his characters arias of paradox and inversion . . . Where other dramatists submerged their personalities into their characters', he exhibited himself throughout his plays as if he had to insist, I am still here. (Holland, 1978, p. 455)

Expression through the written and spoken word is often linked with images of self and notions of self-efficacy. The popular writer Joan Didion (1976) proclaims that "I write entirely to find out what I'm thinking, what I'm looking at, what I see and what it means." Discussion of how much identity should be revealed in written works has occupied artists and critics for some time. T. S. Eliot warned poets not to flaunt their personalities, stating that the true poet should aim for the "extinction" of personality; Barrett (1987) counters that Eliot's work speaks to us in an unmistakable "individual voice." (One should add here, however, that Eliot's collaboration with Ezra Pound was pivotal in formulation of that "individual voice.") Perelman (1986) observes that writing conventions in the context of institutional life often reduce means for expression of self to the projection of standard, institutionally sanctioned roles: "In institution-based discourse both speaker and hearer exist largely as projections of institutional roles rather than as idiosyncratic individuals" (p. 474). University education often follows this pattern, Perelman argues, thus lessening its ability to facilitate self-development on the part of students. The leeway that individuals are afforded to create virtual individuals in this context is therefore minimized.

Vehicles of expression and communication of various sorts have been linked to the construction of self. Clothing can be seen as one kind of vehicle, as in this description of how the veil worn by Algerian women affects their self images:

The body of the young Algerian woman, in traditional society, is revealed to her by its coming to maturity and by the veil. The veil covers the body and disciplines it, tempers it, at the very time it experiences its phase of greatest effervescence. The veil protects, reassures, isolates . . . Without the veil she has an impression of her body being cut up into bits, put adrift; the limbs seem to lengthen indefinitely. When the Algerian woman has to cross the street, for a long time she commits errors of judgment as to the exact distance to be negotiated. (Fanon, 1965, pp. 58–59)

Many discussions of the relation of personal expression and interaction to self and group apparently center on verbal expression (for example, the speech acts theory of Winograd and Flores, 1986, and Searle, 1969), and can thus miss the nuances associated with other forms of expression (such as those linked to the visual and tactile senses, or with the range of modalities associated with clothing, as in the example in the preceding paragraph). The fact that computing is not yet able to convey with ease a sense of the tactile, for example, may serve to warrant this exclusion. As more of our human senses are brought into experiences associated with computing, more inclusive explanatory efforts will most likely be developed.

Artifacts and their associated genres are linked tightly to forms of expression of the self. An unfamiliar artifact, or rapid switches between genres, can engender personal and societal disequilibrium. Even the avowed technological optimist Pamela McCorduck (1985) has stated her despair at what word processing has done to her penmanship, the pen once being her primary artifact of communication and personal expression: "I pen a letter and am appalled at my handwriting. The keyboard, through which thousands of my words pour each day, is obliterating this sign – this signature – of myself" (p. 54).

Some researchers have questioned the capacity of computer-mediated vehicles to reflect a range of expression adequate for construction of self. For example, Bjorn-Andersen (1988) states his doubts about the capacity of computer-mediated exchanges to reflect subtle shades of irony and innuendo. Partly in response to these concerns, a number of observers of the electronic realm have produced statements, similar to the following one by Strassman, which assert how the full spectrum of personal expression can indeed be reflected in the vehicle of a computer-mediated message:

> In actual use, an electronic message expresses a great deal about the character, the idiosyncracies, and the interests of the person who generated it. It is a delight to see how messages convey a person's involvement in his [or her] work, and how bored handlers of office routines suddenly blossom forth to become motivated contributors. The electronic medium thrives on ideas and suggestions about how to improve the quality of services. (Strassman, 1985, p. 229–230)

Strassman asserts that computer-mediated expression is even superior to the nonmediated, being able to trigger renewed interest in the routine communications related to office work.

Much of identity construction involves the management of aspects that cannot be readily changed (such as height and weight); we dress to look shorter or taller, depending on our gender and the circumstances of an engagement. Construction of identity can also incorporate the management of voluntary aspects of one's existence as well, as is involved in the choice of a name or nickname. There are relatively few circumstances in which name-related choices are made in this society. Conventions associated with citizen's band (CB) "handles" (names that are used to identify individuals during CB radio communications) provide adults with a mechanism through which they can choose how to present themselves to others and thus manage their identities (Smith, 1980). The fact that many people readily take advantage of the opportunity to coin an especially expressive CB handle attests to the pleasure often received through certain aspects of self-management of virtual individuals. Opportunities for such self-management certainly abound in many kinds of network-based applications, where individuals are afforded means to create and modify online personae through choice of names, images, and narratives. However, in other kinds of applications (such as computer monitoring), there are often major restrictions on the kinds of traces associated with individuals, and individuals are given little control over how and when these traces are collected.

Group expression and virtual groups

As with virtual individuals, development of virtual groups requires conceptual mechanisms with which groups can be constructed and vehicles through which groups can express themselves. There is still only a limited range of available models for cooperative work groups, though these models are growing in number and variety (the following chapter has a section devoted to their description and analysis). Genres that expressly afford group-level expression are still relatively limited in some contexts. For example, writing is still constructed largely as an individual-level activity, although co-authors, critics, editors, book publishers, and the reading audience are linked in the effort to turn out a published document.

A group's relation to its virtual groups can also be constructed in dramaturgical terms. Goffman (1959) provides a number of descriptions of how groups work as teams to manage the impressions non–group members receive of them. The "frontstage" behavior of the group (the behavior of group members who are constructing a certain situation for outsiders) can be contrasted with its "backstage" behavior (the group members' behavior when they are no longer being observed or are suddenly shifted to a different context, such as an emergency or fire drill). Department store clerks conspire to present a flawless performance to shoppers even during a hectic noon hour; waitpersons assist each other in the effort to construct a peaceful, harmonious setting for their diners despite the obvious obstacles and demands associated with busy restaurants.

As with individuals, groups orchestrate their performances to create virtual groups that are in consonance with relevant cultural objects (for example, consistency, coherence, and harmony). (The notion of "cultural object" is explored in depth in an upcoming chapter.) When a video camera is on, when a meeting is being taped or recorded, or when formal minutes are being taken, groups can often conspire either to present a united front or to temper their performances so that their conflicts and oppositions have a structured flow. Even outbursts from angry

or seemingly disenfranchised individuals can be related to the performance's overall progression, as references to relevant cultural objects
(for example, tolerance) may be introduced to counterbalance the disruption.

In many formal meetings and other group situations, the bulk of the
"work" of the group is conducted backstage (out of earshot of the audience) so that the frontstage performance of the group can appear to be an
organized one. For example, much of the effort involved in decision
making in Japanese organizations (and in some of their American imita-
tors) is reportedly conducted backstage (that is, before formal meeting
procedures are involved);

When an important decision needs to be made in a Japanese organization, everyone who will feel its impact is involved . . . In the case of a decision where to
put a new plant, . . . that will often mean sixty to eighty people directly involved
in making the decision. A team of three will be assigned the duty of talking to all
sixty to eighty people, and, each time a significant modification arises, con-
tacting all the people involved again. (Ouchi, 1981, p. 37)

Ouchi asserts that before the formal meeting associated with the decision
is convened, the group's "decision" has largely been made. Implications
of this division of activities between frontstage and backstage for development of meeting support applications are many and varied: means for
the vast number of backstage interactions should be provided, and the
ceremonial functions of approval must also be given some support.

Meyrowitz (1985), in *No Sense of Place* (an expanded discussion of
the frontstage–backstage dichotomy), argues that modern communication
media have served to erode rigid separations between frontstage and
backstage regions, and thus that many individuals have "no sense of
place" (no sense of where they stand in relation to their communities,
their institutions, and each other). Meyrowitz provides as an example the
fact that television programs deliver revealing "inside" pictures of places
and scenes formerly inaccessible to all but a few, privileged individuals.
Other information technologies can similarly be construed as eroding
barriers of place (a lower-level employee can occasionally reach an administrator several levels higher through e-mail, for instance). Some managerial theorists have applauded the electronic erosion of these barriers (including Peters, 1992), declaring that top-heavy managerial hierarchies
serve little purpose in a fast-moving society.

Explicit forms of frontstage–backstage separation have been integrated
in some CSCW application arrangements, providing an interesting twist
to this dichotomy. Ellis, Rein, and Jarvenpaa (1989) describe the "Project

Nick" electronic meeting room environment, a computer-mediated vehicle that makes subchannels, as well as the "primary" channel, of interaction available to participants. With these subchannels, participants are afforded "an easy way to send anonymous, social/emotional, electronic messages to other participants." Using Goffman's terminology, frontstage interaction (the formal course of the meeting, in which individuals are identified and during which rules of turn taking are enforced) is rigorously separated from backstage interaction (the interaction that goes on through subchannels, in which individuals may remain anonymous).

Nick subchannels include (1) talk requests (broadcast to all participants), (2) leader messages (directed only to the leader), and (3) comment messages (broadcast to all participants). The subchannel messaging facility is described by its designers as a means for participants to gain equality in, and to influence the direction of, meetings even if they are not currently "on the floor" (that is, when they are not the current frontstage speaker). Ellis et al. provide the following commentaries from Nick meeting participants about the subchannel and its potential to enhance the business meeting environment:

Several participants remarked that the "communication subchannel has powerful, interesting possibilities" and said that it was "very intriguing and useful." Some participants considered the subchannel a more polite way to interrupt, while others thought that it was just as rude as a verbal interruption. (Ellis et al., 1989, p. 21)

In Goffman's account, boundaries between frontstage and backstage interaction are negotiated constantly by participants, and tend to be porous. In contrast, Nick segregates a frontstage and a backstage channel electronically, automatically framing for participants what is to be considered frontstage and backstage, although some individuals may work to supercede these application-rooted distinctions.

Many forms of collaborative writing incorporate an implicit frontstage–backstage dichotomy. Backstage discussions and deliberations are hinted at but not fully reflected in the frontstage text. For example, task force reports are often written in a careful manner that sidesteps areas of disagreement and emphasizes areas of accord, and may clearly state where consensus was wrought on a tough issue. In contrast, other collaborative writing vehicles openly link specific individuals with their opinions – whether divergent, convergent, or off the topic (some hypertext-based applications are designed with this capability in mind).

Inventing virtual entities: Constructing self, group, and community in computer-supported cooperative work applications

Descartes's dream in November of 1619 set him on the search for the differences between self and world, and between self and physical body. His exercises in *Discourse on Method* and the *Meditations* (1965) portrayed a solitary and self-conscious figure whose plan for a philosophy was to begin with a self (an "I") with no apparent tethers to group and community. In his *Meditations,* Descartes did not directly address questions of the nexus and boundaries between self and group – an omission that played a role in the choices of many Western scholars through the centuries to overlook these questions, especially when considering matters of cognition. Descartes's "Cogito ergo sum" translates as "I think, therefore I am," not "We think, therefore we are" (or "I interact, therefore I am"), and cognitive science, with ties to Cartesian philosophical roots, has likewise followed suit.

Following these Cartesian influences, many of the philosophical problems (and practical design questions) engendered by the advent of the computer have centered on similarities and differences between human and machine intelligence, rather than on questions of how machine intelligence is involved in construction of self and group. In this perspective, "human" intelligence is associated with the individual human being; more specifically, the functioning of the human brain is very much the center of concern. The brain is considered the locus of intelligence, the scratch pad on which knowledge is somehow directly encoded. Group-level or collective intelligence (intelligence that requires for its very conceptualization such units as groups and communities, and such functions as interaction and communication) is generally downplayed or ignored.

Some of the questions that have arisen in the current, mainstream philosophical treatments of computing and AI include the following: Can computers have humanlike emotions? Can computers be programmed with humanlike "common sense"? These questions seem to require some relation with and ability to construct social context. What is considered common sense, for example, in many cases involves the ability to construct notions of how other human beings and their societies function, or how to interpret what others are doing in a social situation. However, philosophers and computer science researchers have largely centered their efforts on how individual mentality, construed as largely autonomous and "self-contained," can be modeled or replicated in the computer (see Sloman, 1978), not on how computers fit into or can be made part of the larger social framework, a framework that intelligence is just one aspect of. (See the collection edited by Gilbert and Heath, 1985, for approaches that reflect the latter perspective.) Questions that deal with social framework are generally considered sociological – and thus not within the parlance of philosophy and AI – whereas questions from the perspective of individual mentality (which might analogously be considered as belonging within the psychological realm) are not excluded from consideration.

Constructions of self and group are pivotal in our legal and economic allocations of intellectual property rights; they are crucial for management science constructs; they are an element in our construction of scientific knowledge; and they are central to literary criticism and perhaps our very notions of "literacy" itself. In our research initiatives and in our daily lives, we must deftly navigate the shifting boundaries between self and group. Issues concerning self and group arise constantly in academic and workplace pursuits. Is an idea or document "mine," or is it more properly attributed to the group I work closely with? How far should we go as scholars in citing the influences of others' thought in our published works? How should we distinguish and identify an individual and his or her contributions – through psychological profiles, group evaluations, or number of keystrokes entered into a word processor? Should I accept a decision that the group has agreed upon or take my own course of action on a certain issue? Understanding and accommodating the changing constructions of self and group is a difficult task, but (however we evaluate its necessity or morality) it is vital to being a competent scholar, employee, and citizen.

Failure to distinguish correctly the boundaries between self and group can precipitate serious consequences. We hold in contempt those who plagiarize, who monopolize group resources, who fail to make an adequate contribution (or who contribute too much), or who are otherwise not considered team players in a group intellectual endeavor. However, we also hold in contempt those who do not have the self-esteem to recognize when they have themselves made a substantial contribution to a group. Gender, age, economic, and racial variables play a role in where these boundaries are in any context and for any individual.

There is growing interest on the part of many of us in the way individuals and their associations are viewed and constructed, particularly in organizational contexts. Movements that champion self-awareness have proliferated, precipitating new popular interest in literature about the self – a trend that disturbs some social observers, who believe our attention is better directed elsewhere. Schur offers the following advice:

Self awareness is the new panacea. Across the country, Americans are frantically trying to "get in touch" with themselves, to learn how to "relate" better, and to stave off outer turmoil by achieving inner peace . . . While the movement provides middle-class consumers with an attractive new product, attention is diverted away from the more serious problems that plague our society – poverty, racism, environmental decay, crime, widespread corporate and governmental fraud. (Schur, 1976, pp. 1, 8)

A casual flip through a stack of recent magazines and newspapers, or a few twists of the television dial provide a number of calls to be "ourselves" and to be "genuine"; there are also images and verbiage that place human activities and expressions squarely in a group or team framework. Managers and administrators applaud both the work group for its cohesion and the individual worker for his or her personal incentive. We are called on to explain our behavior in terms of our own, internal motivations, and in terms of our effects on and influences from other individuals and groups.

Genres provide platforms for both individual and group construction. CSCW applications will undoubtedly have critical implications for the boundaries between self and group. These applications serve to frame individuals' contributions, shape group interaction, direct the attention of group members to various aspects of group process, and provide repertories of group-related activities. Some CSCW application designers and researchers state their intention to reinforce in individuals the notion that the groups and organizations to which they belong are best seen as "networks of commitments," commitments that properly bind the individual's range of action (Flores, Graves, Hartfield, & Winograd 1988). Others are working toward the creation of electronic alter egos by individuals, entities that will serve to express and enact the individuals' ideas and strategies. What an individual is, what a group is, and how the boundaries between them are constructed are all being profoundly influenced by CSCW applications.

Creation of various other kinds of virtual entities follows some of the patterns observed in the construction of virtual individuals and groups, including the development of institutional "characters." "Virtual shopping," as lampooned in the cartoon strip *Doonesbury* through much of 1993, has become a reality through the efforts of *CommunityCommerce*:

When *CommunityCommerce* opens for business this summer [1995], it will operate as an electronic mall, with virtual tenants such as Naturally Fresh Co., a gourmet food producer, and the Durham (N.C.) Bulls, a minor league baseball team. Just "outside" the mall on another screen will be electronic banking offerings from First Union. Banks "have always been been a central part of a community." (Holland, 1995, p. 101)

Designers of virtual shopping services, who so far have borrowed heavily from the characters of today's stores and the modes of interaction in today's shopping experiences, can be expected to expand these as familiarity with the virtual services increases. In many parts of the United States, shopping malls have become a kind of community center; various aspects of "community life" are taking root in network-based applications, as will be described later.

Composing ourselves (and our groups)

The social sciences have played an important role in modern constructions of the individual and the group. A large share of research and application development in the CSCW area has had an interdisciplinary social science flavor, although there have been repeated calls to make CSCW efforts reflect even more directly a social science–technology linkage. For example, Galegher and Kraut (1990), in their introduction to one of the first major anthologies of academic literature on the topic of intellectual teamwork, assert that some CSCW designs "fail to reflect what we know about social interaction in groups and organizations" (p. 6). A tighter association between social scientists and technologists, they claim, is required for better CSCW initiatives to be generated and for substantial progress to be made in the area.

Social science has often been utilized to generate sets of concepts and perspectives for the support of certain forms of social control and managerial functions (Graebner, 1987; Yates, 1989; Smith, 1990). As workplaces, research organizations, and educational environments have changed – often due to changes in technology – the social sciences (including sociology, education, social psychology, managerial science, psychology, and anthropology) have worked to reframe the categories in which human beings are placed and the concepts with which their institutions are considered. The advent of CSCW applications is no exception.

Some of the historical examples of the role of social science in construction of individuals and groups should make any of the social scientists who wish to contribute to the formulation of a conceptual structure for CSCW application design hesitate, however. Foucault, Rose, Gould, Yates, Graebner, and Smith describe the uses of the social sciences in political and social realms as powerful – and often oppressive – ones. It may be some consolation that these uses are often moderated in practice by a number of factors, including the generic problems involved with disseminating and applying ideas, along with the common sense of those who consume social science.

This book's approach on matters concerning virtual individuals and groups has some intellectual roots in social constructionism. Gergen (1985) describes social constructionism as inviting us to challenge the "objective basis" of conventional knowledge:

Social constructionist inquiry is principally concerned with explicating the processes by which people come to describe, explain, or otherwise account for the world (including themselves) in which they live. It attempts to articulate common forms of understanding as they now exist, as they have existed in prior historical periods, and as they might exist should creative direction be so directed. (Gergen, 1985, p. 266)

Social constructionism has been applied to such areas as scientific rhetoric (Simons, 1989), notions of the self (Hewitt, 1989), and the discipline of psychology (Danzinger, 1990). These perspectives can be readily extended beyond the "description, explanation, or account" (Gergen's phrase) of worlds and individuals: we as individuals develop a variety of relationships with these constructions and accounts, in how we live with, talk about, relate to, and feel toward virtual individuals and groups. We make meaning out of the profiles and portraits created of us and others in the computer applications we use, and out of the way we involve the applications in our personal and group-oriented expression. A primary means we employ to learn about ourselves and each other is by observing how we each relate to and respond to events pertaining to various virtual individuals and groups.

Another of the perspectives that can aid us in our efforts stems from the nascent field of "narratology" (Young, 1989; Todorov, 1990). Recent studies of narrative have extended beyond literature to cinema (Whittock, 1990) and social science discourse (Gergen and Gergen, 1986, p. 20); a feminist approach has been presented by Smith (1990). Narratologists examine how individuals use stories and various linkages to account for human actions and traces across time. Approaches on narratology can be readily expanded in efforts to explore the construction of group identity, along with the current and potential uses of CSCW applications as a vehicle for narrative. Responses, interpretations, and resistances that individuals form to their virtual individual and group constructions are highly relevant in our efforts to understand these constructions.

The social construction of individuality has deep roots in intellectual history; in recent literature it is often associated with Foucault (1977). Foucault describes the employment of "disciplinary methods" (systems for drawing distinctions, with our academic disciplines as examples) in individuation:

For a long time ordinary individuality – the everyday individuality of everybody – remained below the threshold of description. To be looked at, observed, described in detail, followed from day to day by an uninterrupted writing was a privilege. The chronicle of a man, the account of his life, his historiography, written as he lived out his life formed part of the rituals of his power. The disciplin-

ary methods reversed this relation, lowered the threshold of describable individuality, and made of this description a means of control and a method of
domination. (Foucault, 1977, p. 191)

The record produced through application of disciplinary methods is
utilized in constructing the individual as a distinct societal entity: the
individual becomes publicly known. My health record captures the details
of what is considered important about my health; my educational record
portrays my intellectual life; my credit record conveys a history of my
financial dealings. My health, intellect, and character are constructed in
ways that involve these documents and their associated social and technical apparatus. The individuation processes that Foucault describes are
much more precise and detailed than many of those involved in creation
of virtual individuals and groups; much of the creation of virtual entities
can be only thinly related to specific disciplines, and is fairly sloppy in
terms of procedure, serving largely the organization's own temporary
purposes (if they relate to any purpose at all).

In his analysis of individuation, Foucault emphasizes the significance of
the power relations that support and take advantage of it. Foucault asserts
that "the disciplines show, first, according to artificially clear and de-
canted systems, the manner in which systems of objective finality and
systems of communication and power can be welded together" (1982, p.
788). He emphasizes that power relations require a specific discourse
(which, in the case of individuation, involves varieties of medical and
educational examinations and associated record keeping):

In a society such as ours, but basically in any society, there are manifold relations of power which permeate, characterise, and constitute the social body, and
these relations of power cannot themselves be established, consolidated, nor implemented without the production, accumulation, circulation, and functioning of
a discourse. (Foucault, 1980, p. 93)

Foucault also describes the importance of the "contract" as a tool for
individuation, a specifically tailored relationship enforced by the state that
identifies the individual as a unit in relation both to other individuals and
to the community (see also Dreyfus and Rabinow, 1983). The contract
notion has been given heavy emphasis in social thinking, from the "social
contract" of Lockean philosophy to our various economic and legal systems. As discussed later in this chapter, some CSCW applications have
contractual aspects, in which understandings and agreements as to an
individual's or group's commitments to an organization are wrought.
Foucault asserts that the "chronicles" of a person's life were once the
individual's own prerogative to produce and distribute; the power to

define him- or herself was once in the individual's own hands. Expanding Foucault slightly here, matters involving virtual individuals could be said to have once been more solidly in the hands of individuals and their immediate relations and acquaintances to negotiate and establish.

Utilization of computer networks and CSCW applications for monitoring employees has increased the available forms of individuation. Nussbaum describes with anger an advertisement in *PC Week* for *Close-Up LAN,* a work group computing product that enables certain parties in a networked configuration to view what is currently visible on others' computer screens:

[It] boasts to management that "*Close-Up LAN* brings you to a level of control never before possible. It connects PCs on your network giving you the versatility to instantly share screens and keyboards . . . You decide to look in on Sue's computer screen . . . Sue won't even know you are there! All from the comfort of your chair. (Nussbaum, 1989, p. 3)

The impact of these products extends beyond the business community: *Close-Up LAN* and similar monitoring tools have been employed in the K–12 educational environment, as well as in workplace settings.

The National Association of Working Women ("9to5"), which Nussbaum once directed, has collected accounts from employees pertaining to contexts of their computer-monitored work situations and how they feel about monitoring:

A secretary from Florida told us that the thing she found most offensive about her generally abusive boss in her small office was that he calls up on his VDT the work she's doing when she's doing it. (Nussbaum, 1989, p. 3)

In light of the information collected by 9to5, Nussbaum asserts that "there's a resurgence of management control today – almost a fetish – with managers attributing the need for it to rising competition and falling productivity" (1989, p. 2).

In its examination of computer monitoring, the Office of Technology Assessment (OTA) of the U.S. Congress places monitoring among a number of other individuation approaches, many of which are computer mediated:

Electronic monitoring is only one of a range of technologies used in today's workplace to gather information about the work process or to predict work quality based on the personal characteristics of the workers. Many applications of technology, including polygraph testing, drug testing, genetic screening, and possibly, brain wave testing, illustrate the tension between employers' rights to manage their enterprise, reduce costs, and reduce liability, and the employee's rights to preserve individual liberty and autonomy. (OTA, 1987, p. 12)

"Direct" monitoring of an individual's work activities involves the immediate, computer-assisted surveillance of what he or she is doing. Detailed statistics and records of an individual's computer-mediated activity produced through direct (and other, more indirect forms of surveillance) are often pieced together to provide elaborate portraits (or "profiles") of his or her work-related behavior.

Modern profiling techniques have also enlarged the scope of individuation enormously. Profiling of individuals involves fitting the information associated with an individual to a roster of characteristics and associated statistical norms linked with a particular construct or constructs. OTA (1986) defines computer profiling as "the search of a record system for a specified combination of characteristics of interest to an agency" and outlines how profiles can assist agencies in various investigations (for instance, how the Internal Revenue Service applies profiling techniques to identify potential income tax evaders). Marx and Reichman (1984) state that the "very idea" of profiling relates to statistical reasoning and group comparisons, and is thus prone to error in individual cases. In some of its applications, institutional profiling methods may also incorporate the assumption that an individual is "guilty before proven innocent" – that because an individual fits a certain profile, he or she will be treated as a "suspect" before having done anything to merit that treatment. A student or employee whose associated records fall into a certain statistical profile could be classified and treated as a member of a certain group (for example, as an "underachiever" or "suspected white-collar criminal"), whatever behavior the individual engages in.

Profiling is an especially intense means through which individuals become subjects for investigation and research. Motivations behind profiling extend beyond individuation, however. Profiling is often used to "create" subjects – composites that have only tangential connections to specific individuals. Profilers are often interested in obtaining correspondence in the aggregate so that direct marketers and others interested in targeting a certain group can obtain pools of potential consumers. Existence of a real individual or set of individuals attached to the composite is not the primary consideration.

Sets of profiles can be conjoined to obtain a reading on such abstractions as a neighborhood's "television viewing habits" or "average viewer." Cost in dollar terms of collection and verification of data on individual consumers is for some purposes too high – or the information in question not legally available. Profiling can provide statistically formulated composites (which may be just as effective for some kinds of marketing efforts as precise information on individuals) at a fairly low price. Combining those composites can provide even more abstract constructions, such as neighborhood or peer group trends.

Profiling techniques are used extensively in marketing research to design portraits of composite individuals – fictional beings that reside in a certain community or even a certain block. These portraits encapsulate the buying habits and other trends associated with these composite individuals. When specific information is desired but not available on individuals, it can be "inferred" from the composites that the individuals are associated with. Individuals seldom participate directly in the profiling of their own characteristics (and may not be aware that they are being profiled), although they may respond to the "side effects" of profiles constructed of them by others (for example, telephone and mail solicitations) in a number of different ways.

Many of the tools of individuation, vehicles through which individuals are systematically distinguished from other individuals and entities, are applied by individuals themselves. Constructions of biography through the resume and curriculum vitae (constructions often tailored for particular audiences) are one example of voluntary individuation. Broadhead (1980) describes how applications for medical school are shaped by non-traditional students (including women with children) in ways that applicants hope are in consonance with values and biases of reviewers. Producing voluntary "confessions" of our inner life is another tool of individuation, one that plays an especially large role in the construction of sexuality (as our nationwide craving for talk shows and revealing autobiographies supports), as well as in religious practices (as in the confessional).

Foucault creates a history of the different modes by which "human beings are made subjects" (1982, p. 777); construction of individuals as subjects is one of the means through which virtual entities are created. CSCW and related network-based applications can be involved in creating such virtual individuals, and can also be a part of how groups are made subjects as well, amounting to an overall increase in the potential for institutional control. In making an individual or a group a "subject," institutions formalize aspects of the mechanisms through which individual or group identity is constructed, and thus appropriate a large portion of control over the individual's or group's means for identity management.

Social scientists have played a large role in individuation in their research efforts to codify aspects of human individuality, such as "intelligence" and "personality." This research has helped to fulfill the requirements of large-scale institutions for systematic ways to construct differences among individuals. In historical perspective, Rose (1989) describes the systematization of files, records, and case histories as being "contemporaneous with the transformations in the organization of asylums, prisons, hospitals, and schools in the nineteenth century" (pp. 125–126).

In the past hundred years, size and complexity of social institutions have expanded enormously: for instance, groups of isolated, one-room school houses became large, well-organized school districts. The tools of individuation – techniques that place individuals in relation to statistical norms and other comparative measures – became refined as the power and influence of large-scale social institutions increased in the nineteenth and twentieth centuries. Business, education, and the military required that large numbers of individuals be distinguished, categorized, and otherwise processed. The weight of these institutions was placed behind specific tools for individuation, and often served to bolster those institutions' credibility. In turn, the individuation process often increased the appearance of institutional efficiency and effectiveness. As a function of the individual's participation in these large-scale institutions (a participation that is often involuntary), he or she must submit to individuation. In the educational sphere, standardized tests for college admissions (the SAT and ACT) stand out as examples: to become college freshmen, high school students must pay for and submit to a battery of multiple choice examinations, results of which will be used to judge their places in relation to national norms.

Institutional reinforcement of individuation techniques is a powerful mechanism, but does not ensure the continued existence of any specific technique. Techniques of individuation pass in and out of vogue for various reasons. Gould (1981) traces an account of the "mismeasure of man," the attempts to measure intelligence by calibrating brain size and other physical features. He describes how having such "useful," readily applicable measures served to support certain political and societal goals. Political value of the measures in supporting the construction of the "inferiority" of certain sectors of the population buttressed their sagging scientific credibility, although the scientific community itself eventually assisted in their discreditation.

Examination scores, records, measurements, and other traces utilized in individuation are not without some connection to the individuals with whom they are associated. Some sets of traces have more credibility than others and a stronger linkage to the individual; credibility is possibly related to some combination of historical precedent, connections to science, psychological validity (the fact that the trace appears on the surface to be relevant), and other factors. Popularity of the use of certain traces gains momentum as industries form around the traces (such as the lucrative psychological testing industry), and as various professional groups adopt them as their own and attempt to ensure their proper utilization (as the medical industry has for various health-related measures).

A trace associated with an individual can gain "factual" status as institutions and professions focus on it and orient themselves to it. To convey this orientation process, Smith uses the analogy of wolves focusing on a caribou:

> Notice, next time you see that movie of wolves hunting caribou, how they attend to each other through the medium of their object. Each is oriented to that caribou and through that to each other. Thus they coordinate the hunt. A fact is such an object; it is the caribou that coordinates the activities of members of a discourse, a bureaucracy, a management, a profession. A fact is construed to be external to the particular intersubjectivities of the knowers. (Smith, 1990, p. 69)

When considered as a fact, a trace often becomes dissociated from the context of its collection. For example, a psychological test score or IQ measurement quickly loses some of its connections with the specific event of an individual taking a test, as many educators and psychologists assert a level of facticity to the test score beyond any association with a specific testing situation.

Not all social scientists join Rose, Gould, and Smith in their critiques of the codification of individuality; in fact, tools for individuation remain a fixture of a good share of social science approaches. For example, Miller (1980) strongly supports the use of standardized mental testing and other tools of individuation, and attacks the "belief that we can simply wish away social deviance, mental handicaps, and the bottom half of the normal distribution curve of ability" (p. 79). Norm-referenced tests are still a standard feature in educational research, although (according to Miller) "one finds oneself apologizing for suggesting" their use (p. 79).

Norm-referenced tests and other tools of individuation serve both to separate and distinguish individuals, and to place them into certain approved categories or groups for ready treatment by institutions. "Underachievers," identified by their test scores and aptitude scores, may be segregated in an educational context for certain kinds of remedial treatment. These groups are not formed by voluntary efforts on the part of individual subjects – although individuals can, to some extent, position themselves to be included in the groups (for example, by managing their appearances, behavior, and records so as to be considered "underachievers"). Manipulation of individuation processes by individuals requires some knowledge of how membership in the target group is determined, or at least the observation of some sample group members (individuals previously labeled as underachievers, in the current example). It also requires substantial knowledge of the virtual individuals and groups associated with the individuals (for instance, how they are constructed within various artifacts and genres).

Many of today's institutions have only a marginal concern for the precision used in constructing virtual individuals. Foucault projects a world in which the individual's activities are precisely captured and documented; today's institutional needs often require no more than approximations and averages. For example, many marketers need only have approximate data about a community's consumption patterns; precise or correct records about a specific individual are not required, and the extra cost to maintain accuracy can be outweighed by overall efficiency. Individuals themselves must contact the institutions and go through the relevant procedures if errors or omissions are found that have some significant impact on them; the burden of proof is on the individual to show the error and why it should be corrected.

Perspectives on self and group: The "strong" notion of individualism and the "mental health" approach

There is a ready market in both the academic and lay communities for literature and theoretical work concerning the relationships of self and personal identity to the group and community, whether or not those relationships are somehow mediated by computers. A resurgence of interest in the philosophy and social psychology of George Herbert Mead (Collins, 1989) is one signal of such concern. Recent discussions in the social psychology literature on self and self-identity have taken on a sense of urgency. Sampson (1988) uses strong language to support his own position: "An indigenous psychology of ensembled individualism may better realize central cultural values of freedom, responsibility, and achievement than the currently dominant self-contained form of individualism" (p. 21); Cushman's quotation in this chapter's epigraph is another example.

Roots of intellectual concern about self and group run deep. In the early part of this century, Durkheim painted a portrait of the individual as a group-oriented entity – one requiring some form of solidarity with others. Durkheim underscores the double-edged sword of group life: it can be "coercive" to the individual, yet the individual prefers it to structureless, anarchic life:

Common life is attractive as well as coercive . . . when individuals who are found to have common interests associate, it is not only to defend their interests, it is to associate, that is, not to feel lost among adversaries, to have the pleasure of community, to make one out of many, which is to say, finally, to lead the same moral life together. (Durkheim, 1947, p. 15)

Talcott Parsons (1937) notes a shift in Durkheim's thought concerning the tethers between the individual and the group; recognition and expansion of this shift by Parsons and others played an important role in social thinking in the 1930s and 1940s. In his early work, Durkheim describes society as employing the tool of sanctions and other lawlike apparatuses as a way of controlling the individual. In his later work, Durkheim describes social rules as "enter[ing] directly into the constitution of the actors' ends themselves" rather than serving as external regulators or environmental obstacles (Parsons, 1937, p. 382). We come to own, and self-enforce, these sanctions.

Discussions of individuals, groups, and internalized norms cross disciplinary boundaries, and particularly rattle the nerves of those who wish to maintain firm distinctions between psychology and sociology. This discourse breaches issues concerning "human nature" (Wrong, 1961) – issues that some sociologists would rather not involve themselves with for fear of trespassing on psychologists' turf, and that many psychologists and philosophers claim should be the province of sociology. The notion that individuals "internalize" norms has been interpreted to mean that norms become part of the psychic structure of the individual (in Freud's terminology, becoming part of the superego). Another psychologically oriented account of norm internalization involves individual needs. For instance, a 1960 sociology textbook links norm internalization with a felt need for conformity: "Conformity to institutionalized norms is, of course, 'normal.' The actor, having internalized the norms, feels something like a need to conform. His conscience would bother him if he did not" (Johnson, 1960, p. 22).

In a strategy analogous to Parsons's, the notion that individuals are categorized and differentiated by the tools of individuation by institutions for various purposes, and that they internalize (or otherwise are in relationship with) the mechanisms and results of individuation, will be distinguished for our study of virtual individuals. In this book, I explore the various relationships that individuals can have with their individuated profiles, traces, and records, relationships that can include forms of internalization, as well as rejection, exploitation, distortion, and acceptance. Do I, as an individual, actively seek out information concerning my credit history and change my spending habits in ways I believe will make me appear more worthy of credit? Or, rather, do I try to avoid the use of credit, and thus attempt to minimize the role that the credit record plays in my life?

Do I try to ignore the existence of the record entirely – or, rather, display openly my credit worthiness (for example, by flashing my Gold Card at important dinner engagements, reserving my less distinguished plastic for mundane purchases)? Some orientations toward credit records appear to reflect economic concerns, others reflect linkages of credit worthiness to status, personal responsibility, and even morality. Our patterns of accommodation to individuation reflect deeply rooted constructions of self and group. Do I assume responsibility for the record and attempt to manage my identity in relation to it? Do I consider all financial concerns as family-related and think only in terms of the "family budget," whatever the records about me as an individual reflect? Or, rather, do I employ other maxims and strategies in managing my financial identity (for example, "save your pennies") and hope that whatever records are kept about me will reflect positively upon me? Our relationships with our virtual individuals and groups influence our day-to-day activities, as well as our long-range life goals and strategies.

In recent years, argumentation on the theme of the self–group nexus has often been composed of alternating critiques and support of the "strong notion of individualism," the notion of a self-contained and integrated self. Anthropologist Clifford Geertz (1979) provides a capsule characterization of strong individualism, in which individuals are seen in terms of their integration and boundedness:

. . . a bounded, unique, more or less integrated motivational and cognitive universe, a dynamic center of awareness, emotion, judgment, and action organized into a distinctive whole and set contrastively against other such wholes and against a social and natural backround. (Geertz, 1979), p. 229)

In similar terms, psychologist Robert D. Romanyshyn (1989) describes our Western sense of self as "a solitary, singular atom of individuality, that self which is more or less experienced as an interior reality on this side of our skin somewhere more or less behind the eyes gazing out upon the world" (p. 65).

In her Presidential Address to the American Psychological Association, Janet Spence (1985) defined individualism as "the belief that each of us is an entity separate from every other and from the group," a belief that "leads to a sense of self with a sharp boundary that stops at one's skin and clearly demarks self from nonself" (p. 1288). Psychologist Edward Sampson (1988) coined the term "self-contained self" to refer to the integrated, Western notion of self, a notion that has had a strong hold on the fields of psychology and sociology. He asserts that resurgence in the past two decades of the ideal of "androgyny" relates to the powerful hold that the notion of the integrated, self-contained individual has on our society. To be truly "self-sufficient," Sampson argues, many Westerners assume that they must internalize both female and male aspects and characteristics; they cannot rely on members of their family or community to supplement their own apparent "deficiencies."

Critiques of the "strong" notion of individualism – the notion that the ideal or healthy self is self-contained and integrated – have come from a number of quarters, reflecting wildly varying perspectives. From the pragmatist camp, William James (1892) portrays the self as a several-layered entity, the layers often being inconsistent or in conflict. Philosopher and religious figure Thomas Merton (1960), who spent many of his years in solitary contemplation and prayer, argues that his solitude convinced him that individuals are deeply and inextricably tied to other individuals, a condition that affects their very essence. He asserts that "true solitude is not mere separateness. It tends only to unity" (p. 172).

One of the most popular recent works presenting the notion that the way the self is constructed in Western society is problematic is *Habits of the Heart* (Bellah et al., 1985). *Habits* takes a stand against "utilitarian individualism," a perspective that views the self in reference to the pursuit of economic objectives. Bellah and his associates claim that although utilitarian individualism apparently supports the individual self, it largely serves to diminish the self by defining it primarily in terms of its economically oriented accomplishments and relations. "Expressive individualism," the alternative proposed in *Habits,* encourages individuals to seek fulfillment through personal expression and self-development, with the assumption that this noneconomic orientation will draw individuals closer to family and community. In a manner reminiscent of *Habits,* Cushman (1990) presents the thesis that the self in today's Western society is constructed as "empty," needing to be filled up with socially sanctioned experiences and consumer items of various sorts: Cushman decries the fact that the social sciences have "worked to the advantage of the state" by helping to construct selves that are the subjects of control.

Means through which selves are constructed include the labeling of certain patterns of conduct toward self and others as "pathological" – reflecting systematic, abnormal variations from a sound and healthy condition. Goffman describes how the infringement of "involvement rules" (generalizations concerning how individuals should conduct themselves in a social situation) is often labeled as pathological and indicative of mental illness even though the rules are ambiguous (or even contradictory) and the situations involved can be constructed in a variety of ways:

Even a loosely defined social gathering is still a tight little room; and there are more doors leading out of it and more psychologically normal reasons for stepping through them than are dreamt of by those who are always loyal to situational society. (Goffman, 1963, p. 24)

Szasz and others have also questioned the "myth of mental illness" (the title of Szasz's 1961 work). Szasz outlines various ways that constructs associated with the notion of mental illness are formulated to reinforce positions and attitudes of dominant sectors of society.

In a manner I label the "mental health" approach, the self is constructed in relation to models of both healthy and pathological functioning. These models can be imparted in terms familiar to academics (with a set of constructs and their relations), or in terms of accounts or examples (by stories, parables, biographies, autobiographies, or designated exemplars). The form of analysis associated with this approach does not deny the existence of real pain and suffering on the part of individuals in relation to these concerns. Rather, the approach's focus is on construction and labeling of these conditions.

There are a number of common themes reflected in the efforts to characterize the "healthy" human being, including consistency and integration. In some of the stages of life that are constructed, themes of growth and development are emphasized; in others stability or decline are favored. In contrast, pathologies are often associated with themes of dysfunction and imbalance. Often, pathologies are linked with various treatments or "fixes" (drugs, electric shock, confinement, education, and others). Generally, these fixes are applied to the individual subject, although in some recent approaches, pathologies once associated with the individual (for example, alcoholism or infidelity) are assigned to the entire family or group, and more than one individual involved in treatment (Kerr, 1988).

A good deal of attention is now being focused on supplying sets of models, accounts, and exemplars of healthy and pathological *group* functioning, in a manner similar to that which is applied to the individual. The extension to the group level forces researchers to include aspects of context and interrelation often omitted or downplayed when the individual is singled out for categorization. Technological and managerial treatments or fixes of various sorts for group-level pathologies are being devised as well. (The next chapter provides a history, taxonomy, and analysis of these attempts.) Themes of internal harmony, balance, coordination, and integration are common in the models and accounts being devised. For example, some CSCW application designers have as their stated goals the facilitation of harmonious adjustment toward a common objective (Singh, 1988) and of balance among team members' styles (Parker, 1990).

Virtual individuals and their community connections

Social scientists have often looked beyond the level of the individual for clues to individual functioning. The notion of a "true" community – an "organic" community – has been linked by a number of sociologists and psychologists over the past four decades to the attainment of individuality: to be a fully realized individual, a person must be in relationship with a true community, group, or association. The strong emphasis of many recent social observers and commentators on development of humane "virtual communities" in the era of computer-supported communications thus has considerable precedent. Stein (1960) asserts that "it almost seems as if community in the anthropological sense is necessary before human maturity or individuation can be achieved, while this same maturity is, in turn, a prerequisite for community" (p. 248). In the social psychology text *Individual in Society,* Krech presents the group as an essential support of personal freedom:

The paradox of modern man is that only as the individual joins with his fellows in groups and organizations can he hope to control the political, economic, and social forces which threaten his individual freedom . . . Only as the individual in society struggles to preserve his individuality in common cause with his fellows can he hope to remain an individual. (Krech, 1962, p. 529)

In attempts to address this self–community linkage, a number of social scientists chronicled the failures of community life to support development of healthy individuals, placing the pathologies of individual functioning squarely on the shoulders of the collective. Problems that individuals suffered – lack of fulfillment, loneliness – were related to a community incapable of encouraging individuals' growth and development. Newman's "futilitarian society" is one example:

In the desert of the suburb, community life has lost whatever vestiges of meaning it ever had for Americans; if any community life exists at all, it exists frantically at the synthetic level of the club and church; it has a tinny quality betraying a lack of conviction on the part of all concerned. Nowhere is there more consciousness of the need for community; nowhere does this consciousness of need reveal more clearly its hopelessness. (Newman, 1961, p. 355)

Other themes emerge in the social science literature on the self–community nexus: one is the linkage of the individual's responses to community influence with various degrees of conformity and self-expression. In Riesman's *The Lonely Crowd* (1961) and previous work (Riesman & Glazer,

1951) he develops a continuum from "other-directedness" (overresponsiveness to community influence) to "inner-directedness" (direction that comes from "internal" factors):

This awareness, this radar-like sensitivity to how one is navigating in the social world, and this tendency to make that navigation into an end of life as well as a means – this seems to me to be characteristic of the psychological type I have termed other-directed. (Riesman, 1961, p. 138).

Riesman asserts that the inner-directed person has incorporated at an early developmental stage a "psychic gyroscope" that regulates his or her activity despite pressures from outside (p. 24).

The notion that the self not only is influenced by others and by community (as described by Riesman and Newman), but is – at least in part – the reflected "other" has been a thread in American social thinking from the turn of the century. Charles Cooley (1902) provides one of the first sociological examinations of the influence of the other on the self, using the analogy of the individual as a piece of clay and of others as potters. Mead's (1934) account of the individual as a social entity provided inspiration for many of the previously described varieties of criticism of the self-contained self. Mead flatly states that "it is impossible to conceive of a self as arising outside of social experience" (p. 140). Mead proposes that the ability to role-take is a feature of the human condition that distinguishes it from animal life. Role taking (assuming the attitude of the other) is essential for human cooperation:

The control of the action of the individual in a co-operative process can take place in the conduct of the individual himself if he can take the role of the other. It is this control of the response of the individual himself through taking the role of the other that leads to the value of this type of communication from the point of view of the organization of the conduct in the group. It carries the process of co-operative activity farther than it can be carried in the herd as such, or in the insect society. (Mead, 1934, pp. 254–255)

Mead describes in detail the functions of the individual's reflection of significant others (family members, people in positions of authority) as well as reflection of constructed "others." "Generalized others" are composites of the perspectives that an individual attributes to a community or group:

It is in the form of the generalized other that the social process influences the behavior of the individuals involved in it and carrying it on, i.e., that the community exercises control over its individual members; for it is in this form that the social process or community enters as a determining factor into the individual's thinking. (Mead, 1934, p. 155)

Individuals role-take the attitude of the generalized other, an activity that is critical to socialization as well as to establishment of a system of common meanings and discourse. Mead goes so far as to say that only by taking the attitude of the generalized other can an individual "think" at all (p. 156).

The reflection of others by the self is not unproblematic. Mead underscores the essential tensions between self and others as well as their interactions. Mead's self is inextricably bound to the groups and larger community to which it belongs: what the self *is* by its very nature is reflected in its group affiliations. On the other hand, he emphasizes that individuals can influence groups and communities. "Persons of great mind and great character have strikingly changed the communities to which they have responded" (1934, p. 216).

How can such a profoundly social entity as the individual play an active role in influencing (if not changing the directions of) his or her communities? Mead's dichotomy of the "I" and the "me" (which is often overlooked by scholars who associate him with the "self as reflected other" notion) is central to his explanation of this seeming contradiction. Mead describes the eminently social me, one part of the self, in the following terms:

The "me" is essentially a member of a social group, and represents, therefore, the value of the group, that sort of experience which the group makes possible. Its values are the values that belong to society. (Mead, 1934, p. 214)

In contrast, the I is reflective and can react against the situation in which the I finds itself. Mead states that the values of the I are values that can be found in "the immediate attitude of the artist, the inventor, the scientist in his discovery" (p. 214). In Mead's perspective, a community or group can thus change by the event of an individual becoming part of the community or expressing him- or herself in that community. The critical and creative perspective of the I can be reflected in others and influence their direction and evolution.

Other social theorists became intensely concerned with the community and its influence on the self in the 1930s and 1940s. MacIver characterized individuals in communities as being tightly intertwined with multiple associations and group affiliations:

The relation of man to the many groups and forms of organization to which he is . . . attached is not solved by making one of these, whether the state or any

other, the sole or exclusive object of his devotion, the one social focus of his being. There are other forms of order than the simple uni-centered order. (MacIver,
1947/1970, p. 421)

The context of MacIver's work was a political milieu in which it was
difficult to understand joint loyalties. How could one be a Pole, a Jew, or
an Arab, yet be fully integrated into the "American way of life"?

Many social scientists since Mead have sought to characterize individuals in terms of their reflection of their communities and societies. Dreitzel
links the condition of modern individuals to their internal reflection of
various, often conflicting, societal images: "The symbolic structures of
this society are like a broken mirror: man sees himself reflected in his
many identity-fragments yet he does not recognize himself as whole"
(Dreitzel, 1981, p. 220). Dreitzel underscores the pathologies associated
with the "broken mirror," pathologies linked with a lack of coherence
and integration.

Virtual individuals and groups have some functional similarities with
the significant other or generalized other, and serve important roles in the
construction of a unified self (and thus in the solution to the broken mirror
dilemma). The rootedness and stability that connections and associations
in the community once afforded the individual is not available to many of
us. In this mobile society, credit, medical, employment, and educational
records (and traces produced in the context of CSCW applications) serve
to anchor our existences and provide continuing reflections of our selves.
Whatever other purposes they serve, the "broken looking glass" that
Dreitzel describes is given some unification – at least temporarily – in
many of these reflections. Our social, economic, and personal dependence
on the reflections and mechanisms through which they are created may
thus be reinforced as a result.

Many of the developers of computer applications and large-scale networking projects have been fairly conscious of the need to "create community" in the context of their efforts (see Schuler, 1994, for an example
of this effort). Many of the more traditional means for creating community
are not available to these designers. There is no physical town square or
meeting room in virtual communities, for example (though designers can
make computer access available in public meeting spaces, such as libraries and shopping malls). Efforts to construct social analogues of functions
currently linked to communities ("social analogues" referring to system
features that are accepted by users as serving certain social functions)
have occupied much of the time of these developers. Coate (1992), associated with the Whole Earth 'Lectronic Link (WELL) network, compares
the job of maintaining the WELL with that of an innkeeper – facilitating

interaction and keeping order among patrons. It is an ongoing assumption of many network designers that if electronic networks are to serve as communities for participants, they must embody (or replace with adequate substitutes) some functions of community life that parallel those currently provided by "traditional" communities.

The self-contained individual and responsibility for decision making

Despite widespread recognition of the individual's relationships with groups and communities, the notion that the individual is ideally autonomous is a predominant theme in many societal contexts. One often-presented support of the construct of the self-contained individual is that we require such a notion to make sense of personal "agency." When we find that some individuals do not have such a coherent self-conception, we cannot legally hold them responsible for their actions (for example, their crimes against the state or their contracts with other individuals). The coupling of the notion of a self-contained, individual agent with our Western model of decision making is a tight one. In Western discourse, individuals are said to frame decisions, consider alternatives, and make choices. This decision-making process changes the course of future events for the individuals and their organizations. The role of the individual as a conscious decision-making agent is essential to the current structure and process of our legal systems.

Harre (1981) contrasts Islamic and Western constructions of decision making, as well as their associated notions of the individual. In the Islamic model, "God determines in advance the proper path; man succeeds and fails to move along it" (p. 92). The Western model (in its modern formulation) places the individual at a decision point from which two or more options flow. The individual is considered "autonomous" because he or she can make without any direction or assistance (in a "self-contained" manner) a movement that can be constructed as a "choice" among the options. Noddings (1984) defends the notion that self-containment of the kind that proponents of strong individualism posit is not required for social responsibility and personal agency. She defines "caring" and maps its linkages to responsibility and agency in terms of a definition of individuals as "self-in-relation." The individual is defined in terms of his or her relations with others, including the caring relationship.

The perspective that a self-contained individual is required for decision making is linked to means through which individuals can be controlled in an organizational context. If this viewpoint is adopted, a single individual can be assigned blame for the consequences of unfortunate decision making when organizational problems occur, thus relieving other organizational participants (at least temporarily) from the need to reexamine the organization and its procedures. Decision making can be constructed with groups or with individuals as primary figures. The former involves a set of transformations from choices made by individuals to the product of a group decision. Various activities and sequences related to decision making are linked together in narrative accounts. Some narrative accounts of decision making are generally accepted in our society and some are not; which are and which aren't reveals a great deal about current Western perspectives on personal and social responsibility, as well as on cognition.

Many modern perspectives on the self appear to downplay consideration of one of the most critical aspects of our current society: the self is intimately and inextricably involved with biographical traces that it does not directly and immediately construct, and that it may have a restricted range of control over (and, often, incomplete knowledge of). Credit reports, educational biographies, medical histories, employment records, and criminal records are all entities that the self must deal with as a function of his or her very existence in modern society. Contrast the notion of a "birth" as it is presented in the official records of a city and the birth as it is experienced by mother, father, infant, and friends:

The demographer's stripped version, a "mere birth," is not birth as it is in the experience and practices of the child's mother, father, kinfolk, and friends. The construction of a birth as merely a birth is the product of a specialized organizational practice of reporting . . . The recording agency is concerned only to set up a certified and permanent link between the birth of a particular individual (an actual event), a name, and certain social coordinates essential to locating that individual – the names of her parents, where she was born, and so forth. (Smith, 1990, pp. 86–87)

In situations in which aspects of an individual's work are monitored electronically, minute traces can be collected, and highly intricate and detailed biographies may be constructed.

For the individual, the management of biography – which includes efforts to frame life transitions in a way in which overall coherence and integration are achieved – is a major, ongoing task. This management may be direct (individuals may rewrite their resumes, possibly eliminating certain references) or more indirect (individuals may seek certain opportunities to make their biographies appear more consistent). Mead (1934) uses the term "knife-edged present" to signify the way time is best described in the life of the self; however, much of the process of identity management has a largely retrospective nature, as individuals attempt to manage the traces that past activities may have left. Groups, similarly, are associated with biographies and are often faced with the task of making appropriate nods to the notions of coherence and integration.

Erikson (1976) asserts that major "cultural ideas" (such as coherence and integration) are complex and must be viewed in terms of their contradictions and negations, as well as their positive assertions: "The identifying motifs of a culture are not just the core values to which people pay homage but also the lines of point and counterpoint along which they diverge" (p. 82). Hewitt (1989) employs the label "cultural objects" for these themes and ideas: "Culture does provide objects and visible paths for moving toward them, and in this sense it 'provides' models of conduct" (p. 71). Along with Erikson, Hewitt asserts that cultural objects are complex, and the array of objects provided by a culture is far from consistent. The American cultural idea or object of "unity" cannot be fully understood without considering the notion of "diversity," which is also a cultural object of critical importance. In later chapters, the cultural objects of "privacy," "efficiency," and "dependence" will be explored in the context of CSCW applications.

Arts and sciences of group construction: Basic assumptions and metaphors of groups

Groups and the group–individual nexus can be seen as socially constructed in relation to cultural themes and images in much the same way as individuals themselves are constructed. The group is perhaps more apparently a social construct than is the individual, not having the obvious physical boundaries that the individual human body provides. Artifacts such as team uniforms, filing cabinets, oblong tables in seminar rooms, blackboards, and computer networks help to define groups and delimit their membership.

As well as being influenced by imagery, rhetoric, or argumentation to consider the group as a unitary entity, individuals can be said to have some internal motivation to do so. The assumption that individuals have internal needs to get into emotional contact with the groups with which they are associated has been posited by some modern psychologists and sociologists. Bion (1961) states that group members attempt to establish such contact by imagining a group entity that is rooted in several basic assumptions: (a) fight–flight (the assumption that group problems should be confronted through fight or flight); (b) dependency (the assumption that the leader has the needed answers and/or is the only one who can ultimately resolve problems); and (c) pairing (the assumption that a chosen pair of group members will be able to solve group problems through their interaction).

Bion's basic assumptions (which might be seen as being akin to the cultural objects or themes that individuals relate to in constructing their biographies) are outlined as being powerful forces in the group. Perspectives that run counter to the assumptions can often be transformed in ways that confirm the assumptions. For example, obvious displays of resistance on the part of members to the current basic assumption can be construed as support for the importance of the assumption. Bion and others describe how basic assumptions can work to dampen group creativity, since group members' modes of expression are limited by the assumptions – with new approaches or strategies often being ignored.

Bion's insights stimulated a number of theoretical and empirical efforts related to issues of how or to what extent groups employ metaphors and assumptions in their interaction. The stated motivation behind this research is that examination of the group's adoption of metaphors can assist in understanding the "tacit awareness" of the group while it is interacting (Polanyi, 1959; Srivastva and Barrett, 1988). Srivastva and Barrett describe the "generative" function of metaphor in a group, a function that "facilitates contact between group members and in this way supports the growth and development of the group" (p. 32).

Winnicott (1951/1974) in *Playing and Reality* explores the possibility that the group is neither "self" nor "other" – but somewhere in between. Winnicott posits that groups are "transitional phenomena," existing in the "area of illusion." The notion of the group as a transitional phenomenon hinges on the assumption that this area of illusion continues to play an important psychological and social role. Winnicott (1971) notes that there is a "direct development from transitional phenomena to playing, and from playing to shared playing, and from this to cultural experiences" (p. 60). Groups can serve as the "location of cultural experience" and harbor various forms of creative expression.

Many groups are intentionally organized, with their membership well aware that they are forming a group; however, we also form a number of associations in our day-to-day lives without such conscious consideration (as the Winnicott reflections allude to). Intentionally formed groups can be defined and their activities organized through a large number of vehicles. Some groups are formed with decision making as a focus; one of the anticipated outcomes of group functioning is a decision or decisions. Procedural mechanisms for group decision making are one of the means through which decision-oriented groups are defined and shaped, and are a familiar part of institutional settings of all kinds. A number of common, popular technologies and systems are associated with these mechanisms (many CSCW applications incorporate variations of such procedural mechanisms). Importance of procedural mechanisms in our society looms especially large in environments for decision making in which (a) social implications are important, (b) members initially possess disparate decision preferences, (c) potential conflict accompanies the search for agreement, and (d) member concern about outcomes is substantial (Davis, Kameda, Parks, Stasson, & Zimmerman, 1989, p. 1000). Examples of such environments include resource allocation panels, town councils, and state commissions.

Employment of procedural mechanisms is found in many attempts to "educate" and "socialize" individuals as well: Boy Scouts and Girl Scouts, high school councils, retirement community groups, and other groups are shaped by the use of procedural mechanisms. (Graebner, 1987, provides a historical progression of such groups.) Sometimes general standards such as Robert's Rules of Order are utilized, although particular, tailored sets of standards are also readily observable (such as those established for courtrooms and governmental administrative bodies). Procedural decision mechanisms provide the means for constructing a single, unified group decision from a set of decisions made by individuals. This transition can be problematic in a number of ways: one or more individuals can disavow the group's decision as not being truly reflective of the group's will, for example. Explanations of how the transition can "fail" are often rooted in the distinction between "procedural" and "substantive" aspects; they may relate to a set of unstated policies or tacit understandings dealing with how procedural mechanisms are to be acted out, to matters of "content," or to concerns that procedural and content-related matters have been confused with each other. Bedau (1984, p. 118) describes one possible set of tacit group policies, where the members of the group

a. agree upon procedures whereby substantive decisions of the group are to be reached, and abide by those procedures and the results reached by using them;
b. seek to increase opportunity for all group members to participate in the deliberations; and
c. treat the views expressed during deliberation seriously and with respect.

Developers of nominal group technique (NGT) (Delbecq, Van de Ven, and Gustafson, 1975) and of NGT's related implementations in CSCW applications (Archer, 1990) state their intent to reduce the potential for the domination of certain individuals in a group discussion context, which may occur because some members are more articulate or outgoing, or hold higher organizational positions, than other group members. NGT places constraints on the quality and kind of interaction that groups engage in, restricting the group to a set sequence including round-robin suggestion of ideas, discussion, and voting. In a similar strategy, a number of CSCW researchers have stated their intent to limit "social" aspects of group interaction as a way of enhancing the purely "information-related" aspects. Siegel, Dubrovsky, Kiesler, and McGuire (1986) present the premise that the reduction of social context cues that occurs with computer-mediated communication will "reduce normative influence relative to informational influence. This should reduce the impact of implicit reference group norms and of group members' social approval of each other, and increase the importance of arguments and decision proposals." Distinctions between the social and the information-related aspects of interaction reflect a common theme in much of current social science, that of the need to remove "context" from "facts" in order to achieve some level of "clarity."

Along with decision-making groups, many intentionally formed groups are linked with the stated goal of producing some sort of entity, a product "owned" by the group as a whole. A task force report falls into this category, as well as a PBS documentary, a budget for a project, and a grant application. Groups often shift from viewing these entities as produced through efforts of individual workers (that is, as a piecemeal compilation of individual efforts) to constructing them as entities produced by the group as a whole. A number of difficulties arise in this transition, and occasionally, groups do not survive to see the transition through to a satisfactory completion.

Management and administration of virtual individuals and groups

All "management" (except the most arbitrary and random varieties) is to some extent management of virtual individuals and groups: the very conceptualization of individuals and groups involves various combinations and permutations of the traces and expressions associated with them. As more workplace and educational interaction becomes mediated (through computer networks, video, or other means), day-to-day management and administration become ever more tightly coupled with the genres associated with this mediation. For example, as techniques for developing the statistical profiles attached to individuals and groups are refined along with constructs and associated norms for self and group, management has become more dependent on the conceptual structures designed with social science–inspired techniques and less on notions associated with commonsense management.

What social science, managerial, and related technological strategies and applications have provided is a set of constructs and a way of looking at and responding to individuals and groups. In these strategies, properly constructed groups have been characterized as "important agencies of social adjustment" (Graebner, 1987), "tools required to achieve wholesale involvement by everyone" (Peters, 1987), and as vehicles for the conveyance of such managerial themes as "efficiency" and "productivity." In creating a need for the application of new social science constructs and approaches, current managerial strategies are often construed as deficient in various respects. A case must be developed for the adoption of the innovative approaches. Graebner (1987) asserts that democratic social engineering approaches convey the notion that "interactive skills have become the province of experts" and that "knowledge of social skills has been appropriated by scientists." In other words, to know how to relate to each other properly, we must acquiesce to the authority of experts.

However, social science does not have complete leeway in the development of "knowledge of social skills." Unless social science and managerial notions and theories are framed in ways that individuals can understand and thus can manage their identities in relation to, they have a small likelihood of being incorporated into organizational routines. One of the major problems with the early adoption of the CSCW application called *The Coordinator* is that individuals found it difficult to understand a new language and incorporate it into their activities (Dvorak and Seymour, 1988; Reder and Schwab, 1988; Erikson, 1989; and Oravec, 1989b); subsequent versions of the application made many of its novel linguistic aspects optional (Dowie, 1990).

There are a number of competing voices and perspectives that attempt to furnish explanations about self and group. Many of these have been outlined in preceding sections, including psychological explanations relating to inner needs and sociological explanations involving such constructs as social structure. Which ones do we generally listen to? What kinds of explanations do we accept? Ease of use and acceptability of various CSCW applications (along with their success in the marketplace) may indeed reinforce social perspectives associated with those applications. Just as the microscope encouraged certain approaches to biological science, CSCW-related artifacts support certain sets of assumptions about self and group.

Conscious development of managerial perspectives toward self and group has a long history. Scientific Management (or Taylorism) helped to establish many of the vehicles for construction of self in organizational contexts that are still present today. Many social critics have decried the Taylorization (or "rationalization") of work and educational life (Braverman, 1974; Shaiken, 1986), a phenomenon with close historical and philosophical links to computerization. Some have labeled certain efforts to streamline and rationalize white-collar and professional work as akin to turning intellectual laborers into "assembly line" workers (see Kraft, 1977; Oravec, 1982; Perrolle, 1987). Work rationalization has largely adopted an "individualistic" orientation: it is the individual worker, not the work team, that is the relevant unit of consideration.

Frederick Taylor's *Scientific Management* (1911/1947) provided a theme that guided the approaches of many managers and sculpted much of the organizational thought of the twentieth century: "It becomes the duty and also the pleasure of those who are engaged in the management not only to develop laws to replace rule-of-thumb, but also to teach impartially all of the workmen who are under them the quickest ways of working" (p. 104). Taylor was aware that the rule-of-thumb knowledge of workers, knowledge of the job that was acquired by actually performing the job, gave the workers a powerful tool: "Foremen and superintendents know, better than anyone else, that their own knowledge and personal skill fall far short of the combined knowledge and dexterity of all the workmen under them" (p. 32).

By establishing "one best way" to do a certain task, Taylor sought to place in management (rather than labor) the largest share of skill-related knowledge. The work group (either constructed by management or informally assembled by workers themselves) was considered by Taylor as being largely detrimental to managerial efforts:

Loss of ambition and initiative . . . takes place in workmen when they are herded into gangs instead of being treated as separate individuals. A careful analysis had demonstrated the fact that when workmen are herded together in gangs, each man in the gang becomes far less efficient than when his personal ambition is stimulated; that when men work in gangs, their individual efficiency falls almost invariably down to or below the level of the worst man in the gang; and that they are all pulled down instead of elevated by being herded together. (Taylor, 1911/1947, pp. 72–73)

Scientific Management methods were designed to provide alternatives and remedies for deficiencies of group work, which Taylor characterizes pejoratively as "herding." Two of his proposed remedies were the construction of the individual as the relevant unit of concern and the engineering of the individual's relationships with others and with the organization – themes that still travel with many modern management efforts. In Scientific Management, individuals' largest loyalty was to be with their supervisor, with whom they were to gain "intimate, friendly cooperation" (p. 96). Taylor reinforced the importance of intimacy in manager–worker relationships by stating that "close, intimate, personal cooperation between the management and the men is the essence of modern scientific or task management" (p. 26).

Taylorism had a ready audience in the world of education in the early part of this century, as well as in the industrial realm:

The appeal [of Taylorism] to a science of education was not only an attempt to establish more effective modes of teaching, but was also a way of justifying the profession of education at a time when the expert was achieving more and more expertise. (Feinberg, 1975, p. 62)

Taylorism took on connotations of "expertise" and "science," and was often used to support the claims and strategy of proponents of such individuation strategies as standardized testing and evaluation of students. Similarly reinforcing a scientific and engineering perspective in management, industrial psychologist Lillian Gilbreth (1914/1973) asserted that Scientific Management gives each worker "a chance to be an entity rather than one of an undiscriminated gang" (p. 36). She devoted a chapter to individuality in her well-known textbook *The Psychology of Management*.

Harry Braverman's account and criticisms of Taylorism were highly successful in reattracting the attention of sociological, political, and ethical thinkers to Scientific Management and its modern forerunners. Some sociologists have characterized as "Bravermania" the large impact of Braverman's work on sociological thought in the 1970s and 1980s. Braverman's *Labor and Monopoly Capital* (1974) describes the legacy of Taylorism as reflected in modern office automation efforts as the elimination to the largest extent possible of lost labor time, even the time "lost" through casual interaction.

Braverman identified as work "routinization" the view of the human laborer and his or her work as a component or mechanism in the production process. With work routinization, the manager divides the overall work process into task units for individual laborers to perform, without regard for the meaningfulness of the units from the laborer's perspective. Max Weber (1958) described as "rationalization" the social dynamic associated with routinization and similar strategies. Rationalization refers to the ways observed phenomena are selected and processed so as to conform to a set of "rational" considerations, often without regard to their meaningfulness and wholeness. Weber's (1956/1978) ideal type bureaucratic organizations (described in *Economy and Society*) successfully eliminate "all purely personal, irrational, and emotional elements."

Taylor's Scientific Management principles have been viewed as one solution to the problem of coordinating human beings. In his evaluation of Scientific Management, Green adopts a Kantian perspective and argues that Taylorism can be seen as removing the individual from the role of agent to that of an observer. He argues that the shift from active moral agent to observer can take place in subtle forms (see also Baier, 1965). Observers can be contrasted with agents in dramaturgical terms:

One can endeavor to understand what has already happened, and one can be surprised at what is actually happening. In any case, the observer is conceived of as passive in respect to what is happening when it is happening . . . In contrast to the observer, the agent is a participant or performer who makes things happen. (Green, 1986, p. 165)

Although the agent can be seen as choosing among various "scripts" for action, he or she is still a participant or performer who "makes things happen." Observers, in contrast, are passive viewers and thus are not given the opportunity to exhibit moral agency – and thus are disabled in that aspect of their humanity.

Taylorism has been criticized in recent years in terms of both its morality and its effectiveness. Shaiken describes the "two critical limits" of Taylorism's effectiveness, social and technical:

The social limit stems from the distaste workers quickly develop for highly routinized and regimented jobs. The technical limit arises from the impossibility of fully eliminating skill and control from many occupations through the organization of work alone. (Shaiken, 1986, p. 26)

Inability of management to apply Tayloristic techniques in many technical- and information-oriented activities was instrumental in precipitating its displacement as a managerial approach, although much of its imagery and perspective remain in managerial literature and strategies to this day.

McLuhan and Nevitt (1972) write that Taylorism and its assumptions (1) that there is one best way to do a job and (2) that individuals should be assigned separate functions became obsolete when the computer was shown to be able to extend simultaneously its "chords, harmonies, and controls" into a number of diverse areas of operation:

This is at a great remove from the "hardware" days of specialist functions assigned to quite separate organizations and individuals. The old pattern had been for everyone to mind his own business and to keep out of everyone else's way as much as possible. In the new harmonic scale of the computer console, choral togetherness and harmony will supplant the old separate notes of separate voices. (McLuhan and Nevitt, 1972, p. 256)

In their criticism of Taylorism, McLuhan and Nevitt foreshadow some of the rhetoric associated with CSCW applications: "togetherness" and "harmony" are characterized as being orchestrated with the assistance of the computer.

Even the staunchest critics of Taylorism admit that it has had a tremendous influence during the twentieth century, one extending far beyond the realm of management. According to Kennedy (1989), Taylorism "seemed immanently consistent with a broad social dynamic that, from a modern perspective, could be observed throughout human history," a dynamic that often takes on the label of "Progress" (p. 146). Beniger traces the roots of Taylorism and similar approaches in his history of the nineteenth and twentieth centuries. He focused on the development of various technologies (including information technology) as mechanisms of managerial control:

Foremost among the technological solutions to the crisis of control – in that it served most other control technologies – was the rapid growth in the late nineteenth century of formal bureaucracy and rationalization. The latter includes what computer scientists call preprocessing, a complement to the control exercised by bureaucracy through information processing, increasingly using computers and microprocessors. (Beniger, 1986, p. 15)

Beniger labels as "preprocessing" the codification of information about processes, individuals, resources, and other organizational aspects. This codification was later required for many forms of computer-assisted work and for the construction of virtual individuals and selves, although preprocessing efforts began long before the invention of the computer.

Harnessing the group: The Human Relations school and the informal group

Despite Taylorism (and in some cases, in direct reaction to it), recognition of the importance of group work in organizations increased in the twentieth century. Mayo (1937, 1945) and others associated with what is commonly known as the Human Relations school responded to problems involving the Taylor-inspired rationalization of work by positing that workers should be stimulated to join and relate to a small "primary group." Primary group activities would assist them in obtaining a feeling of "belonging":

It may be described as a profound need to live in anything continuous in life as a relationship with other persons. It is a species of fictional kinship which emerges to perpetuate and develop any sufficiently happy situation of collaborative human endeavor. If the organizers of human activities cannot contrive to get the support of this fictional kinship they will find to their regret that it is moving against them. (Mayo, 1937, p. 697)

Mayo and Taylor were thus both intensely involved in the "engineering" of human relationships in the workplace, Mayo attempting to build certain kinds of group relationships and Taylor focusing on relationships between individuals and their immediate supervisors.

Mayo argued that large-scale institutions (which were dramatically growing in number and size in the first half of the century) were fostering psychological pathologies. He labeled as "obsessive" the predominant pathology that emerged, one that he asserted was becoming increasingly common as large-scale institutions flourished. Obsessives were unable to perform social-oriented functions, including those functions related to work and citizenship in a democratic society. Mayo theorized that individuals in large organizations were deprived of the opportunity to interact and form close bonds with others in a social setting, a deprivation that triggered the obsessive condition. Thus, Mayo proposed a "fix" for obsessiveness – the encouragement of small-group bonding by organizational participants.

Mary Parker Follett, whose early associations were with social work, also had a tremendous influence on managerial thought in the 1920s and early 1930s. She posited that conflict in the workplace could be avoided if individuals could only see the "order" that was present in every situation; with a vision of this order, solutions could be found in which "neither side has . . . to sacrifice anything" (Parker Follett, 1941, p. 32; Graebner, 1987). Parker Follett's description of the potential for organization-wide sharing and coordination has a close parallel in the recent efforts of managerial theorist Shoshana Zuboff (1988), whose self-characterized "vision of a concentric organization" is one that "rel[ies] upon metaphors of wholeness – interdependency, fluidity, and homogeneity" (p. 399).

The "informal organization" – networks of worker-established groups and ties – became popular in sociology and management science in the late 1940s and 1950s as a way of characterizing aspects of the organization that affected (either positively or negatively) the affiliations of workers, but that were not formally organized by management. The growth of unionization during this period provided considerable stimuli for management scientists: among factors that served as catalysts for informal organizations, they sought to identify those that were either benign or neutral to management concerns, as opposed to those that fostered undesired union activity. For Mayo, the most beneficial form of association was a "spontaneous" collaboration – one that is very much in contrast with the organized union (Graebner, 1987).

In the late 1930s, the Hawthorne studies (conducted and analyzed by Roethlisberger, Dickson, Mayo, and others) set the stage for a number of subsequent management approaches to the group, linking worker productivity with informal group structure:

It is well to recognize that informal organizations are not "bad," as they are sometimes assumed to be. Informal social organization exists in every plant, and can be said to be a necessary prerequisite for effective collaboration. (Roethlisberger and Dickson, 1939, p. 559)

The studies were large-scale efforts that were given the imprimatur of "scientific truth," as well as a good deal of popular attention in the decades that followed. The studies' support of the importance of the group level for productivity considerations was a boost to the managerial scientists who built their research agendas and their careers on that unit.

Chester Barnard (1938/1968), in the influential *Functions of the Executive,* makes attempts to separate the "organization" and the "individuals" associated with it in logical terms. Barnard posits the "superlative degree to which logical processes must and can characterize organization action as contrasted with individual action" (p. 186). For Barnard, organizations are composed of processes through which social action is accomplished:

With all the thought that has been turned upon the unrest in the present day in the literature on social reform, one finds practically no reference to formal organization as the concrete social process by which social action is largely accomplished. (Barnard, 1938, p. 1)

Barnard characterizes the formal organization in relation to its "forces," and in terms of the "nonpersonal" (p. 77; Perrow, 1979). The rhetorical trend toward considering organizations and organizational settings as composed of forces and structures continues in the CSCW-related literature, with Winograd and Flores's (1986) notion that organizations are "networks of commitments" and Holt's (1988) characterization of organizational "work arenas" as "organization machines . . . physically organized utilitarian structures" (p. 111).

Preceding Mayo's, Parker Follett's, and Barnard's work were a number of efforts to develop and disseminate certain notions of "group effort" both among both workers and young people. Beginning in 1917, the YMCA sponsored "foremen's classes," organized meetings of foremen designed to inculcate them with proper attitudes concerning their subordinates and their organizations. Graebner (1987) reports a 1921 YMCA study that asserts "a group of men working together, in the companionship which comes from common working problems, can swing work through with a capacity that is impossible in the lone individual" (p. 83). YMCA foremen's classes inspired other, similar associations, such as the Foremen's Clubs of the National Association of Foremen (clubs that flourished in the 1920s and 1930s).

Some management theorists sought to harness the informal organization for the benefit of management; others recommended that managerial energies be expended to dismantle informal organizational structures. An example of the former is Wilbert Moore (1951) in *Industrial Relations*. He outlines the informal organization's role as a force for moderating the exclusive concern for competitive performance. Such a concern, Moore claims, is "not only destructive of group morale, but may actually subvert the general ends of the cooperative system by destroying the basis for joint activity" (p. 291). Homans describes the increasing institutionalization of all forms of interaction in the organization, an institutionalization that increases the complexity of the organization, its distance from the individual worker, and the worker's alienation:

> The increased complexity seems to take two main forms which are themselves related to one another. First, a particular activity gets to be maintained not just by what I call natural or primary reward but also by other, contrived rewards, particularly by generalized reinforcers like money and social approval. For instance, a man cuts wood, not because he needs it for his fire, but because a firm will pay him for cutting it. Second, the process of exchange by which an activity gets rewarded comes to be roundabout rather than direct . . . What the two processes have in common, compared with elementary social behavior, is an increased reliance on explicitly stated norms and orders (Homans, 1961, p. 380)

Like Mayo and Moore, Homans sought to reduce this formalization of interaction by encouraging informal organization assemblages.

The relationship that management has had with the group (whether the formally composed workgroup or the groups associated with the informal organization) has undergone dramatic shifts in the past century. Bramel and Friend (1987) present the case that the power relationship between workers and management, the "amount of leverage each can exert on the other," is a major factor in these shifts.

Explicit introduction of the cultural object of "democracy" into management strategies was one attempt to place the power balance between workers and management in a new light. Workers were afforded opportunities to engage in self-management in selected, limited spheres through mechanisms that had the imprimatur of "democracy"; democratic theories related to managerial concerns were developed by 1940 by Kurt Lewin and others. An example of how Lewinian techniques were applied in practice is provided in the extensive accounts of Lewin's and his protégé

Marrow's efforts at Harwood Manufacturing in the early 1940s. Harwood's pajama factory initiated the institution of "team captains" with the following, democratic procedures:

Marrow and French organized a whole factory so that each of the 20 departments would elect a representative to a weekly group meeting with the personnel officer. These representatives discussed such issues as weekly prayer meetings and backround music – issues that, according to the authors, were not of central importance to management. (Bramel and Friend, 1987, p. 243)

Harwood is described as actively repelling attempts to unionize in that period; team captains are portrayed by Marrow as performing some of the functions of unions.

The assumption that information-related work was somehow special and required support different from the kinds given to industrial labor was strongly supported by the management theorist Drucker (1966) and others in the 1960s. Efforts to control and support information-oriented operations predated Drucker, however. As early as the beginning of this century, businesses began to seek vehicles through which information-related work could transcend the individual, leading to the design of systems for coordination and message transmission. The notion that correspondence and accounts should be put in writing and made available to a central authority served as underpinnings for efforts to make information work less individual-centered and more group-oriented. Henry Metcalef (1886) outlined a system for taking record keeping out of the hands of the individual:

The proposed system of shop accounts is based on two compensating principles:

1. The radiating from a central source, let us say the office, of all authority for expenditure of labor or material.
2. The conveying toward the office from all circumferential points of independent records of work done and expenses made by virtue of that authority. (cited in Yates, 1989, p. 14)

Managers were increasingly becoming convinced that information handling and exchange required some group work – some interaction among individuals – and that appropriate vehicles were required for this exchange.

The "committee meeting" was one of these vehicles. As explained by Galloway, an administrative theorist, in *Organization and Management,* divisional meetings served several purposes: they encouraged esprit de corps and responsibility for group product, and elicited information from plant foremen:

The primary idea is to enlist the cooperation of the [fore]men in the shop in form-ing plans and offering suggestions for the good of the company. By frequent meetings and a thorough airing of opinions, an esprit de corps and a feeling of re-sponsibility for the success of the business as a whole is established. In its method this system is the opposite of the military system of management. (Gallo-way, 1914, pp. 170–171)

Designated "meeting rooms" soon became popular, places segregated from the normal working environment in which meetings could be con-ducted without interruption.

Fear that individuals in group sessions (such as the one just described) would no longer be accountable for their behavior was commonly ex-pressed, and managerial researchers sought means to control individuals despite their apparent anonymity in the meeting room. In the early 1900s, the recording of committee meetings by stenographers was one of the means suggested by management theorists to circumvent possible prob-lems. Also suggested as a control device in this period was a folding blackboard on which could be written the various agreements and associ-ated deadlines. It was recommended that the blackboard be brought out and examined at each meeting (Yates, 1989), thus also providing some semblance of continuity among meetings.

From the early part of this century, blackboards, meeting rooms, and other group-tailored tools served as visible physical support for the emerg-ing constructs associated with the workgroup; they provided tangible symbols of unity, order, and shared purpose. Most of these vehicles are still present in some form in organizations. The quest to devise even more effective tools to shape groups has continued in the late twentieth century with development of CSCW applications.

Groups, control, and CSCW applications

A number of observers of computing practices in organizations have noted that managerial interest in CSCW applications often centers on their potential for controlling individuals (see, for example, Howard, 1987; Dvorak and Seymour, 1988; Oravec, 1989b). In Beniger's *Control Revolu-tion* (1986), control is defined as "purposeful influence toward a predeter-mined goal" (p. 7). Edwards (1979) defines "control" as "the ability of capitalists and/or managers to obtain desired work behavior from work-ers" (p. 17). One popular definition of "control" is provided by Kanter (1977): "the ability to get things done, to mobilize resources, to get and use whatever it is that a person needs for the goals he or she is attempting to meet" (p. 166).

Most recent discussions of control (such as Beniger's, Edwards's, and Kanter's) link it with movement toward some preexisting goal – whether that goal is the capitalist's, the manager's, or just any organizational participant's (as in Kanter's account). Control over an individual's behavior in this framework thus involves ensuring that he or she behaves in ways that support, or at least are not in direct conflict with, the goal.

The recent literature on the general topic of computers and control in organizations provides some contradictory results about the effectiveness of computers for control purposes, results that should be taken into account when considering the social and ethical dimensions of groupware and other computer-based systems. Braverman (1974), Garson (1988), and others support the notion that computers are indeed of use in controlling workers; these results are countered by studies reported in Kraemer, King, Dunkle, and Lane (1989) and Danzinger and Kraemer (1986) that show that computing may be of far less use in control efforts.

One of the ways in which these apparently contradictory results concerning computers and control have been explained is found in Thompson, Sarbough-McCall, and Norris (1989). They propose a "non-zero sum" perspective on computers and control in organizations. They follow the work of Tannenbaum (1962) and Kanter (1977) in positing that increases in the control exercised by nonmanagers in an organization (for example, professionals, staff members, and subordinates) need not entail overall decreases in managerial control. Control can expand (or contract) within an organization, leading to a larger (or smaller) control commodity, which can be divided among a number of groups in the organization.

One way that control has expanded is by the development of mechanisms encouraging "self-control." Foucault (1977) describes the changes in prison systems in the past 200 years and the transition to self-control from the application of external restraints. Emergency measures initiated to curb the spread of the plague led to a prison system in which the separation of guards and prisoners was of the essence. Jeremy Bentham (1791) suggested the "Panopticon" as an appropriate incarceration device in this situation:

Bentham's Panopticon is the architectural figure of this composition. We know the principle on which it is based: at the periphery, an annular building; at the centre, a tower; this tower is pierced with wide windows that open onto the inner side of the ring; the peripheric building is divided into cells, each of which extends the whole width of the building; they have two windows, one on the inside, corresponding to the windows of the tower; the other, on the outside, allows the light to cross the cell from one end to the other. All that is needed, then, is to place a supervisor in a central tower and to shut up in each cell a madman, a patient, a condemned man, a worker, or a schoolboy. (Foucault, 1977, p. 200)

In Panopticon-like environments, the prisoner (or worker, or schoolboy) never knows when he or she is being observed. According to Foucault, this creates " a state of conscious and permanent visibility that assures the automatic functioning of power" (p. 201). This type of power is rooted in the individual's self-subjugation: the prisoner need not be under the direct influence of the guard, but only believe that the guard is watching.

Power, Foucault asserts, is only exercised over "free" people (non-slaves), people who are "faced with a field of possibilities in which several ways of behaving, several reactions and diverse comportments, may be realized" (p. 790). Winner, Zuboff (1988), and others have described computer monitoring and surveillance in terms of an "electronic Panopticon":

It appears that we may now be building an electronic Panopticon, a system of seemingly benign electronic data gathering that creates conditions of universal surveillance. The danger here extends beyond the private spheres to affect the political freedoms upon which our privacy depends. Unless we take steps to prevent it, we could see a society filled with all-seeing data banks used to monitor an increasingly compliant, passive populace no longer willing to risk activities supposedly protected by civil liberties. (Winner in *IEEE Spectrum,* 1983, p. 116)

In Herbert Simon's *Reason in Human Affairs* (1983), the propensity to respond in a socially approved manner is labeled as "docility," a form of behavior that can be seen as similar to the compliance and passivity Winner predicts.

As previously described, some CSCW applications include the capability of analyzing and closely monitoring employees' work efforts and interaction patterns. Enable Software's package *Higgins* includes this capability. A technician working with corporations installing *Higgins* has observed, "We are finding that among customer sites with more than 1,000 *Higgins* users, management wants more centralized control in *Higgins* software for monitoring purposes" (quoted in Williams, 1990, p. 95).

Observers and critics of modern management and administration have sought ways to characterize the systems of control associated with advanced information technology: the term "technocracy" has been widely applied to the current amalgam of work methods and technological strategies. Burris (1989) asserts that organizational control structures have evolved from highly personalized forms of domination to increasingly abstract, formalized, and impersonal forms of technocratic control. These technocratic control structures are blended into the design of advanced technology, general societal ideology, and various dimensions of the organization.

Notions of virtual individual and virtual group developed in this book can be employed in characterizations of many current managerial practices, as well as in practices associated with computing systems. The kind of control that stems from their managerial application involves the placement of individuals in a situation where they are somehow compelled to relate to the virtual individual or group associated with them. (To obtain schooling, individuals must contend with a set of educational records, for instance.) Individuals must somehow manage their identities in relation to those records – whether or not they are clear about the audiences for whom they are performing this management, or sure about what precisely is incorporated in their virtual individuals or groups. The result is a relationship more precisely characterized by Franz Kafka (1969) of an individual who was confronted with records associated with him that he could not remember or relate to, than by Jeremy Bentham's prisoner, who was not directly called on to explain, defend, reconstruct, put into context, or otherwise manage specific aspects of his or her identity and personal expression in relation to a guard or other observer.

The basic assumption that individuals are indeed responsible for their reputations and other images of themselves is an especially intense element in current American socialization, and plays a role in the widespread acceptance (or "docility" toward) many virtual individual–related practices. Benefits of unblemished criminal records and acceptable educational records are recited to schoolchildren. Adults are reminded by many quarters that many aspects of their "adultness" indeed depend on their demonstrated responsibility in record management: driver's records must be managed, for example. Issues involving the management of medical records have played an especially important role in individuals' and their employers' decision making, as recent trends in the use of results of genetic screening tests and AIDS-related records demonstrate:

Spiraling health care costs are forcing insurers to look for more and more ways to exclude people who are most likely to use medical services in the future. People with suspect genes are a natural target . . . Dr. [Paul] Billings [a medical ethicist] said. "If employers can identify prospective workers who are not currently disabled but who may later develop illnesses, they can save themselves anticipated health insurance and other costs by refusing employment to the worker." (Blakeslee, 1990, p. B6)

Employees (and potential employees) are often evaluated in terms of their likelihood of engaging in certain conduct or of suffering from an ailment at some time in the future.

Although many mental health labels have lost some of the stigma they had in decades past, questions about whether individuals should receive psychological counseling or psychiatric care still often center on whether the placement of information concerning this treatment on one's health records will be construed negatively by future employers or (in the case of politicians) the public at large. Many individuals still turn to members of the clergy for advice and counseling rather than to the medical profession for this reason.

In the management system that involves virtual individuals and groups, the precise definition of how real individuals should behave is not involved. In fact, managers may not be clear themselves as to what they want or how, conceivably, a certain result can be obtained. Sets of standards are often associated with virtual individuals and groups; these serve to provide a general description of the desired ends of behavior (that is, the record that should result if one behaves in an manner acceptable to a certain audience). Much self-subjugation is involved in this system, as in the Panopticon described by Bentham, Foucault, Winner, and Zuboff. It is largely up to individuals themselves (or to teams of individuals, as in the case of virtual groups) to figure out how to manage their records or characterize their accounts so as to fall within the bounds of acceptability. It is up to individuals to ascertain the critical cultural objects with which to relate, and to decipher the genres with which their virtual individuals are to be interpreted.

To glean the information needed to perform this management, individuals often exchange information about their own identity management strategies, and about the effect of various virtual individual characteristics on job or promotion prospects, success in obtaining credit, or educational outcomes. Many of the mechanisms involved with the manipulation of virtual individuals and groups for larger organizational ends discourage such sharing of strategies, however – since standards for such management are often set in relation to one's peer group (and one is thus given little incentive to improve others' performance in this regard).

One of the ways that virtual individuals and groups can be utilized for control purposes is through shifts (or potential shifts) in whether individual- or group-oriented constructs and standards are being emphasized. To serve its purposes, management can shift from one to the other, with little indication of what is happening. CSCW applications such as *The Coordinator* provide the potential for these managerial shifts. The design philosophy expressed by the application's developers reinforces the linkage of the system with the maintenance of the "networks of commitments" that comprise the organization:

Communicative competence means the capacity to express one's intentions and take responsibilities in the networks of commitments that utterances and their interpretations bring to the world. In their day-to-day being, people are not generally aware of what they are doing . . . Consequently, there exists a domain for education in communicative competence: the fundamental relationships between language and successful action. (Winograd and Flores, 1986, p. 162)

The Coordinator is rooted in the assumption that "there are a surprisingly few basic conversational building-blocks (such as request/promise, offer/acceptance, and report/acknowledgement) that frequently occur in conversations for action" (Winograd and Flores, 1986, p. 159). As individuals use the system, they build a set of requests and promises: "The request or promise you make in the conversation sets in motion a conversational structure and a structure for observing your conversation that is defined by the linguistic move you have made" (Flores et al., 1988, p. 164). Winograd and Flores describe what transpires in terms of speech act theory (with roots in Austin, 1962; and Searle, 1969):

An individual performs a speech act using a system such as *The Coordinator* by: selecting the illocutionary force from a small set of alternatives . . . indicating the propositional content in text; and explicitly entering temporal relationships to other (past and anticipated) acts. By specifying directly, for example, that a particular utterance is a "request" with a specific date for satisfaction, the listening is constrained to a much greater degree than it is for an English sentence such as "Would you be able to . . ." (Winograd and Flores, 1986, p. 159)

Are the requests, promises, offers, and acceptances to be construed in terms of individual contracts (the binding of an individual with an agreement of some sort) or as a kind of glue that holds the organization together (as in the interpretation provided by Winograd and Flores)? The first interpretation may lead to individuals establishing their priorities in order best to manage the impressions of themselves that others (including their immediate superior) may receive; the latter interpretation places overall benefit to the organization as the leading criterion in establishment of priorities. For an individual in a demanding job, the difference between the two interpretations could in practice be considerable. Informal hints about which interpretation would be more helpful to the individual (the kinds of hints often gleaned in face-to-face interaction) are not available within the scope of the CSCW application. Managers could use the ambiguity of this situation to increase control over employees.

Another control-related aspect of virtual individuals and groups relates to the number and kinds of records of interaction: How, when, and by whom will these records be analyzed (or otherwise utilized)? Many CSCW applications provide copious, multifaceted records of interaction. For example, the Capture Lab employs the videotaping of individuals in group interactions, as well as an associated computer log; both are time-stamped so that one can serve as the index to the other (Horton, Elwart-Keys, & Kass, 1989). Management and disposition of these application-produced records are often not major topics of discussion among designers (although Capture Lab designers and other application developers have indeed struggled with the issue). Opposition to the collection of these data is often labeled as "user resistance" (Harrison, Minneman, Stults, & Weber, 1990).

Control of individuals' behavior often incorporates the establishment and maintenance of "roles." The social agendas of some designers and implementers of CSCW applications include efforts to construct the individual's "position" (or role) in the system; opportunities to use social skill in negotiating the scope and limits of one's role with others are thus reduced in number and effectiveness. For example, Fish, Kraut, Leland, and Cohen (1988) discuss the mechanisms of their Quilt system, a tool for cooperative writing, for "defining, changing, and enforcing . . . social roles and their associated rights and responsibilities." Roles are allocated and potential conformity with them is enhanced through the mechanisms provided by this application. Dimensions that these role manipulations will take are slowly emerging, as linkages between the social and managerial sciences and CSCW application development increase.

Some conclusions and reflections: On mirrorless persons and persona entrepreneurs

The strong hold that the self-contained individual has had on Western society is possibly one of the factors that makes virtual individual and group considerations seem foreign and perhaps puzzling. The idea that the records, profiles, and traces that pertain to us play substantial roles in how we view ourselves and each other, and that our thinking and personal expression are influenced by the scope and dimensions of the genres that are available to us, is indeed hard to swallow. There is also a good deal of negative sentiment toward characterizations of human beings as entities that hide behind masks, as well as concern that manipulating impressions of ourselves demotes us to the level of con artists.

The notions of virtual individuals and groups place in relief some concerns that are often omitted in discussions of computer ethics. To manage impressions of themselves, individuals must be able to learn about the virtual individuals and groups with which they are associated – how they are constructed and disseminated. Without this knowledge, individuals lose something akin to moral agency: the ability to participate fully in the construction of their selfhood or their group's identity. Characters associated with individuals in a certain context may best be described as often-contradictory "ensemble characters," which require a good deal of information and cultural background to understand and manage.

Without the ability to manage our identities, we become disconnected from the decisions that are made in our names and the contributions associated with us; we are disconnected from the virtual individuals with which we are tightly associated. As secondary and tertiary uses of personal information by commercial, educational, and medical institutions increase, so do concerns about the extent to which this disconnection occurs. Distortion or manipulation of virtual individuals and groups is akin to removing from the individuals associated with them opportunities to fulfull the requirements of moral agency and selfhood.

In *Asylums,* Goffman (1961) relates how even "total institutions" such as asylums and prisons afford individuals the mechanisms through which they can effect personal identity management. Although the prisoner is stripped bare and given prison garb to wear, some tools of personal expression are still available. Goffman describes how the process of negotiating personal identity is a reciprocal one. All of the parties involved (in this case, prisoner and guard) have something at stake: both prisoner and guard are involved in the "performance." When virtual individuals and groups are "overdetermined" – when there is little room for negotiation of roles, and where some of the parties involved have little investment in the process – the performance can become a sham, and the outcome may rob all of the parties involved of aspects of their humanity.

Such overdetermination can engender apathy. The phenomenon of the "mirrorless person" may emerge, an individual who has abrogated a good share of responsibility, to others and to institutions, for the management of the virtual individuals and groups associated with him or her. The mirrors that these entities would have provided for the individual are no longer available. Today, interest in and concern about our images, appearances, names, and characters are still rather intense; we employ these vehicles to learn about how others are responding to us. However, as the flood of organizationally produced and societally sanctioned virtual individuals and groups increases, and potentials for distortion and manipulation expand, these vehicles may be of less value to us as mirrors. Individuals may thus disengage and place far less effort in keeping track of them. We may try to shake off responsibilities for our own personae and images, and thus for some aspects of our selves.

However, some of us will face this situation not with apathy, but rather with adventurism. An experimental attitude toward constructing one's own and others' virtual individuals and groups could lend some interesting dimensions to issues involving these virtual entities. Stewart Home (1989) could be described as a "persona entrepreneur," one who has explored the mass production of his own and others' personae with open disregard for considerations of plagiarism and the rigors of maintaining personal identity. For example, he and fellow artists have put on shows in which all of the pieces displayed are associated with a mythical person; the "artist" whose work was celebrated in the show did not exist.

Entrepreneurs in the realm of the virtual could explore organizational and societal mechanisms that relate to virtual individuals and groups through various social experiments (mass production of these virtual entities, for instance). Law school students who blanket the country with resumes or authors who distribute hundreds of copies of manuscripts in hopes of interesting a publisher have displayed a kind of entrepreneurism in terms of the written material associated with them. These strategies and others can be extended to the full, increasingly expanding range of virtual individuals and groups, with facilities added for tailoring and doctoring the virtual entities. It also can be expected that advisors and experts on these matters will seek profit from advising others on these concerns.

In developing mechanisms for creating increasingly complex virtual groups, social scientists are helping to provide yet another, important arena for institutional control. Coupled with the virtual individual, the virtual group becomes an especially powerful set of constructs. As managerial attention shifts from one to another – from virtual group to virtual individual, and back again – individuals may not have a sense of where their energies are best spent and their involvement best placed. Should I manage the presentation of my individual contributions, or place my energies in the images or products associated with the group? If so, what are these group-level images or products, and how are my contributions related to them? Uncertainties involved are not only discomforting; they provide opportunities for undue control and manipulation.

Issues of who sees the videotape of my contributions to the group, for example, or who else is online in our computer conference are also placed in a different light by the notions of virtual individuals and groups. Effective management of identity requires some notion of audience. Affording individuals information about what is happening to the virtual individuals and groups associated with them helps them obtain a realistic sense of audience, and thus increases their capabilities to manage their identities.

The self is a construct that has emerged relatively recently in our human existence. Words for "self" and "identity" reportedly began to circulate at the end of the sixteenth and beginning of the seventeenth centuries (according to the *Oxford English Dictionary*). CSCW applications are elements in various new genres for human expression, genres that serve to alter the prevailing set of constructions of self and group. Insights and clarifications that philosophers and social theorists, computer application designers and ethicists, users and citizens can afford will be critical in their development.

3
The shape of groups to come:
Efforts to define, label, explain, and model collaborative activity

"Committee Coma"
The meeting's so dull
That when there's a lull,
It's hard not to notice or mention
That eyelids are lifting
On those who are drifting
And everyone snaps to attention.

D'Amico, 1990

Picture a modern office setting, perhaps an insurance company headquarters. Some people are writing on sheets of paper. Others are looking into computer screens, entering numbers into a spreadsheet. Still others are conversing. Which of these individuals are working individually, and which are engaging in cooperative work? And which of the individuals engaging in cooperative activity are participating in healthy, well-working groups? Some of these issues might appear to be riddles or trick questions. Whether there are "riddles" (or linguistic puzzles) involved, the issue of how best to construe cooperative work activity is one of the most salient focal points of research and theory in CSCW applications.

In much the same manner as healthy and unhealthy forms of individual behavior have been constructed by social scientists, today's administrative theorists, network-based system developers, and CSCW researchers are attempting to construct notions of "functional" and "dysfunctional" collaborative behavior. Several of the theorists whose work is described in this chapter are attempting to segregate some kinds of work as "cooperative" and give them special forms of support. Others want to transform existing forms of work from their current, supposedly noncooperative form into cooperative work. Still others label all work as cooperative and want us to see work itself in a new light. Many have identified "right" ways of thinking about and engaging in cooperative activity, their conclusions bolstered with theoretical scaffolding, empirical research, and appeals to common sense.

Efforts to get work done in a group context have received much bad press (an example is provided in the chapter's epigraph). The poem addresses the point that meetings are often considered by their participants as insufferably dull and boring. The apparent lack of productivity in meetings is often attributed to their labor intensiveness (Volonino, 1989); the assumption that as many people as conceivably required (and then some) should be included in a meeting is commonplace in some organizational settings. Although most administrators spend a substantial share of their working days in meetings (the figure 30% to 70% is often cited by management researchers), the very notion of a meeting is strongly linked with a break in normal working routine and being removed from one's own office and working tools.

The assumption that computer technology can provide a "technological fix" for the problems involving meetings and other group work is a popular theme in discussions of CSCW applications. With the fix that these technologies will provide, we will supposedly become able to mesh our intellects and energies more completely, and misunderstandings will be minimized. Anatole Gershman of Andersen Consulting describes how an electronic meeting room provided a remedy for small-group pathologies:

Recently, I was part of a small group that met in our meeting room with those computers, but we didn't use them. We just talked, each of us taking notes, and then reached agreement. We thought. But when the report was written, it wasn't what we thought we agreed to. That was a week's work wasted. If we had written out on the computer screen so everyone could see and agree, there would be no misunderstandings. (Van, 1990, p. 4)

The apparent ambiguity of a set of oral agreements produced in a meeting is here taken to be an aspect of group work pathology. The possible benefits that ambiguous agreements might afford – allowing individuals a larger range of action or creative leeway, for instance – are often minimized in favor of more tightly constructed agreements.

In the preceding chapter, I discussed the use of mental illness constructs as instruments of social control. Many social theorists, including Goffman (1961) and Szasz (1961), describe the social utility of assigning the label "pathological" to behavior seen as having the potential to disrupt the established order. If we apply the mental health model to social science approaches to group work, we can predict that some group work pathologies will be identified and that "healthy" team and individual approaches to cooperative activity will be constructed – along with the development and application of appropriate technological fixes. We can also project from the mental health model that sets of conceptual tools will be developed by social scientists to frame and convey the notions of group work health and pathology, tools that are generally designed to be intellectually accessible to administrators, managers, and workers, as well as suitable for the needs of researchers. Tools constructed by social scientists to address group work pathologies are incorporated in some CSCW applications. Identification of healthy and pathological approaches to cooperative activity are important elements in constructing virtual groups. Such identification can provide benchmarks and categories with which to make sense of group activity; they can also be restrictive in their use, however, overly constraining the evolution of groups.

In the next sections, I discuss many of the recent efforts to interpret "collaboration," "cooperation," "teamwork," and related notions. The approaches I highlight include (1) development of accounts of teamwork in various fields and contexts; (2) construction of various teamwork pathologies, including the labeling of individualism as "pathological"; (3) development of labels for cooperative work efforts, and mapping of research strategies to approach cooperative work; (4) cognitive science–inspired searches for formal "coordination processes" (in the form of either laws or heuristics); (5) attempts to distill "norms" for various forms of cooperative work activity; (6) categorization of certain kinds of work as "ideal types" of cooperative work; and (7) efforts to place cooperative work teams in relation to other, mainstream organizational functions. Identifying groupwork pathologies, categorizing ideal type groups, and other intellectual undertakings are major parts of research efforts to design network-based computer systems and frame their various features for relevant actor groups.

There are considerable gaps in the social science literature on the treatment of group work. These gaps can be largely attributed to the individual-oriented focus of much of the research that has been done on work and educational activity, a focus with linkages to Taylorism and other perspectives that are centered on the individual worker. Much of the impetus for recent initiatives to frame the notion of collaboration (and related concepts) comes from managerial and administrative pressures for increased productivity in, and more powerful control strategies for, "team-oriented" efforts; the effectiveness and efficiency of office and other white-collar work are similarly receiving attention. The theme of "control" is rooted in much of the material I discuss. For example, Rothenburg's (1993) article entitled "*TeamAgenda* Keeps Groups in Line" reflects strong levels of interest in using CSCW applications such as schedule management packages for managerial control.

The 1980s and early 1990s brought demands for higher levels of productivity in the white-collar and administrative workplace (Peters, 1987; Savage, 1990), demands that have triggered efforts to make the activities of individuals working as teams more efficient and effective. Part of the incentive to develop computerized tools for the support of white-collar workers has been managerial awareness of growth in the ranks of white-collar workers. In the years between 1978 and 1986, annual growth in white-collar employment in the United States was about five times that of production workers (Browning, 1990). Despite increases in the perceived importance of white-collar and administrative work, investment in capital for its support lagged far below that of blue-collar work through the 1980s – a situation that many developers of network-based computer systems have been eager to remedy.

Accounts of the individual and the group in American intellectual and social life

The linkages between notions of workplace cooperation and collaboration can be viewed in better perspective with some background on American cultural currents involving the individual and the group. Sampson (1977) argues that American values concerning the individual may be responsible for many social situations being framed without consideration of the group level. Tjosvold reflects on the outcomes of these values for the social and organizational sciences:

The individual is celebrated in folklore; the individual is studied in the social sciences; the individual is seen as the building block of organizations. Values concerning the virtues of rugged individualists and the decrying of the "organizational man" all reinforce the emphasis on the individual. (Tjosvold, 1986, p. 518)

Historical accounts of early American intellectual life often reflect this individualistic spirit. In a speech delivered at Harvard on August 31, 1837, Ralph Waldo Emerson emphasized the "new importance given to the single person" and called for scholars to reflect renewed importance in declaring their personal intellectual freedom:

If the single man plant himself indomitably on his instincts and there abide, the huge world will come round to him . . . We will walk on our own feet; we will work with our own hands; we will speak our own minds. (Emerson, 1971, pp. 69–70)

Emerson calls not only for the independence of the individual, but also for an intellectual freedom from the constraints of books themselves: "I had better never see a book than to be warped by its attraction clean out of my own orbit, and made a satellite instead of a system" (p. 57). Nearly a century after Emerson's address, individual-oriented constructions of academic life were still popular in the United States. In his comparative study of university systems, Abraham Flexner (1930) asserts that the scholarly individual was the productive core of the American university –

although "individuals and organizations are in everlasting conflict." Flexner warns that the university "cannot flourish unless it is elastic enough to supply the different conditions that different productive individuals find congenial" (p. 25).

In the classic treatise *Excellence,* John Gardner (1961) underscores the benefits of a "moderate" emphasis on individual achievement: "No feature of our own society is more treasured today than the opportunity for every man to realize the promise that is in him, and to achieve status in terms of his own performance" (p. 16). Gardner also outlines the dangers of an "extreme" individualism (which he claims we have come close to as a society): "The let-the-best-man-win philosophy can lead to something close to the law of the jungle: let those who can, survive; let others go under" (p. 20).

The notion of "rugged individualism" (expressed in poetic terms by Emerson as an abhorrence to individuals being "satellites" rather than "systems") is linked to images of the exploration of the American frontier, as well as the ideals of self-reliance ascribed to early pioneers. The label of individualism (as applied in a number of literary and social writings of the nineteenth and early twentieth centuries) is most often associated with doctrines and theories that stress the independence and freedom of movement of the individual, independence that has the self-contained frontier individual as a symbol (Baum, 1977). In a paper delivered in 1893, historian Frederick Jackson Turner framed American social and institutional life in terms of its relation to the frontier and placed American emphasis on the individual at the center of social life:

Western democracy through the whole of its earlier period tended to the production of a society of which the most distinctive fact was the freedom of the individual to rise under conditions of social mobility. (Turner, 1920)

Theories of American life that focused on the frontier emerged at approximately the same time as the theoretical foundations for a legal right to privacy (foundations outlined in Warren and Brandeis's 1890 *Harvard Law Review* article championing the "right to be let alone"). This cotemporality signals close linkages among American views concerning privacy, the self, and the frontier (linkages traced in Copple, 1989).

Many recent Western cultural traditions also reflect a concern with individualism, although the individualistic bent is often seen as a detriment, rather than an enhancement. Hewitt (1989) claims that American social critics (including many social scientists) generally regard individualism as "the most significant problem of American culture." For example, the social scientist Homans (1961) writes that the loss of human intimacy associated with American industrial society is creating a "dust heap" of individuals without connections to each other.

The American cultural picture is a complex one, and proclaiming "individualism" the dominant paradigm leaves out important dimensions. In a sports-hungry American society, the team provides a strong model of cooperation and unified effort. There are also a number of other countervailing tendencies to the individual-centered trend, tendencies that emphasize or idealize "communitarian" forms of life. For example, ideologically united and well-organized groups are often portrayed as essential for countering attacking forces or weathering life-threatening conditions on the frontier. These tendencies can be seen as moderating or counterbalancing the individualistic ethic – or even providing an ethic parallel to individualism – but they are apparently not yet strong enough to move individualism from center stage on the American scene.

American cultural biases toward individualism (as constructed through accounts of historians and social scientists) contrast with many other national cultural traditions and values concerning the interdependence of the individual with groups and with society as a whole. Shenkar and Ronen's (1987) account of Chinese interpersonal norms relates that tenets of harmony, deference to a hierarchical system, development of one's moral potential, and maintenance of kinship affiliation (values rooted in Confucian philosophy) permeate Chinese organizational and social life. Similarly, Scandinavian attitudes toward self and group life that favor a collective-oriented, rather than individual-oriented, approach to education and worklife (described in Ehn, 1988) have been characterized as having a substantial interaction with forms of organization in Scandinavia – as well as their approaches to the design of computer systems (including network-based ones).

The image of the American professional is also linked with the expression of individual-oriented values, values that are being called into question as organizational demands for group-based activity increase. As professional work becomes more complex, fewer professionals can be considered "independent":

We may be moving beyond the era of the individual professional as the complexity of professional practice forces individuals into teams and groups. As we enter the knowledge economy, managers in many settings will need to organize such professionals as engineers, scientists, accountants, and market researchers so that "intelligence," the firm's intellectual capital, can be pooled and systematically deployed. As managers help create professional teams they may find that they cannot rely on the traditional norms of professional life to link the work of one professional to another. (Hirschhorn, 1989, p. 252)

In Hirschhorn's investigation of the interaction of professionals in a law firm, he describes the "ideology of collegiality" as providing a thin veil for aggression and ill-will within the group. He calls for creating "new values, norms, and processes" in professional arenas in the attempt to encourage effective and satisfying group life.

The emphasis of social scientists in studying the professions has been largely placed on relationships between individuals and their professional groups, rather than on aspects of professionalization that support team-work among professional peers. Part of this deficiency may be based on the selection of the "ideal" professions generally utilized to develop models of professionalism; law and medicine have the potential for individual-centered practice, and the images associated with such professions focus substantially on the individual practitioner. Professionals have been observed to support each other against malpractice suits (Zuckerman, 1984), and have banded together for various service and charitable functions related to their professional status. However, the call for increased attention to the group work dimension of professions (delivered by Hirschhorn and others) is not a surprising development, countering a tradition of professionalism that is apparently centered on the model of the independent individual professional.

Collaboration as the exception, not the rule

One of the difficulties that CSCW researchers face in developing readily accessible and powerful notions of intellectual teamwork is the lack of available models and images of collaboration (although a few fields of endeavor serve as exceptions). The myth of the isolated and autonomous writer has not yet been replaced or supplemented by collaboration-oriented myths. Orson Wells is quoted as stating, "Any production in any medium is a one-man production" (Carringer, 1982), although he had often outlined how others had contributed to his own work. Creative writers are often described as asocial and individualistic:

A writer exists because he puts into words what has never been put before. He exists only as he separates himself from everyone else who has ever written. Even though much of his work depends on that of his predecessors and contemporaries and will last only as it becomes a part of his successors, his stories and poems count because they are original . . . Although he usually writes about society, his life as a writer is not social. (Stern, 1986, p. 4)

In keeping with the individual-oriented model of the creative writer, James M. Barrie (1890) – the creator of Peter Pan – remarked that "collaboration in fiction, indeed, is a mistake, for the reason that two men cannot combine so as to be one" (p. 54). Stern's and Barrie's comments fail to reflect the considerable tradition of collaboration among writers and other creative individuals, especially among those of the late nineteenth and early twentieth centuries (Koestenbaum, 1989), a tradition often hidden because of linkages to lesbianism and male homosexuality. For instance, "Michael Field" (the pen name of Katherine Bradley and Edith Cooper) is associated with more than two dozen well-received plays and many poems.

Collaboration among writers has apparently been a powerful literary force, although its influence has generally been minimized in studies of literature. We recognize the name Robert Louis Stevenson, but not those of his influential female and male literary collaborators. Issues of collaboration have preoccupied many writers: Henry James offered to collaborate with H. G. Wells on a joint novel about Mars, but was rebuked by Wells, who often characterized collaboration in distinctly negative terms.

In 1893, James wrote the short story "Collaboration" – a picture of joint writing practices among British literary figures. H. G. Wells warned one member of a collaborative team (Joseph Conrad, who often collaborated with Ford Madox Ford) of the sexual connotations of joint writing and of the possibly unfortunate ramifications of such efforts upon writing style: "Style is as delicate as clockwork and you'll only ruin it by sticking your fingers in it." However, Wells himself conducted writing projects with others, including his wife (Koestenbaum, 1989). An early group writing effort, initiated by Oscar Wilde, was designed in part to elude the stigma of homosexuality through anonymity. The novel *Teleny, or the Reverse of the Medal, a Psychological Romance of Today* was a relatively successful group writing endeavor. Writers would leave the manuscript at a bookshop; the proprietor would pass it on to a friend.

Questions of how to label collaborations in writing and creative work have puzzled some biographers and literary critics. Andy Warhol's methods of creative production have been especially problematic in this regard:

> For a decade, he was rarely without a tape recorder and was notorious for taping everything his friends said. He loved the way the machine transformed the verbal flow by isolating it, perpetuating it, dignifying it. "The acquisition of my tape recorder," he said, "really finished whatever emotional life I might have had, but I was glad to see it go. Nothing was ever a problem again, because a problem just meant a good tape." (Rose, 1989, p. 22)

Warhol's tapes were then edited and condensed by Pat Hackett. Rose asks whether this "oral, indirect" process can be considered as "creative activity," or whether the heavy mediation of Warhol's work has somehow changed its character.

Although many single-medium efforts (such as writing) are constructed as individual-oriented, collaboration is an explicit and accepted aspect of many multimedia efforts – ranging from Gilbert and Sullivan's words and music to the February 15, 1991, performance of "The World Upside Down" (a large-scale performance billed as a collaboration of architects and choreographers, composers and lighting designers held at the City Center in Manhattan). However, in many multimedia efforts, one party – generally the individual labeled the "director" – is credited as the controlling agent in the collaboration, thus superimposing an individual-oriented perspective on these activities.

Team science: Accounts of collaboration in research

There are a large number of biographical and autobiographical accounts of the lives and work of individual scientists and technologists (for example, Hilts, 1984, on the "temperaments" of scientists). These writings are generally designed with the individual as a focal point. There are relatively few extensive accounts of the process of scientific and research teamwork, even though some of the accounts that are in current circulation have drawn large and enthusiastic audiences. The story of the collaborative efforts of one of Data General's R&D teams in *The Soul of A New Machine* captured the imagination of the readers of both technologically oriented and adventure-oriented literature (Kidder, 1981). Kidder's work has often been cited in managerial and computing literatures as an example of successful team operation.

Two decades before Kidder's work, James Watson's (1968) description of the search for a powerful and useful model for DNA in *The Double Helix* provided a participant's perspective on what scientific teamwork constitutes; Sayre's (1975) history of Rosalind Franklin's contributions to the project adds additional dimensions and complexities. *Lawrence and Oppenheimer* (Davis, 1968) examines the creation of the atomic bomb in terms of the teamwork and conflicts among the scientists involved. Nobel laureate Arno Penzias's (1989) popular exploration of the development and application of information technology at Bell Labs *(Ideas and Information)* emphasizes themes relating to research teamwork; Penzias claims that "complex information work often calls for collaborative efforts" (p. 21), although he underscores that some of today's bureaucratic controls have frustrated group endeavors.

Biographical and autobiographical accounts of organizational life such as those just listed serve a variety of prescriptive functions: they provide fleshed-out (and occasionally mythological) accounts of how individuals, groups, and organizations supposedly should function in times of tension, stress, and change. Many of the available accounts of organizational life are either portraits of the "great figures" associated with the institution or historical accounts of the organization's progress. The relative dearth of rich accounts of group work may be one factor in the difficulty many organizations have in fostering successful and rewarding team activity.

Debate on the proper role of teamwork in scientific activity (and in creative and intellectual enterprises in general) has on occasion been passionate. A major thrust in this discussion has been the labeling of various forms of individualism as pathological, a tack that deviates from the individual-centered accounts described elsewhere in this chapter. In a philosophical defense of a team-oriented perspective on science and intellectual undertakings, Feyerabend (1987) reminds us of the attitude of fifteenth-century Renaissance artists: "They worked in teams, they were paid craftsmen, they accepted the guidance of their lay employers" (p. 711). The artists' lack of individual recognition, in Feyerabend's account, apparently did not detract from the beauty and creative value of their artistic expression, nor from their own level of motivation. Feyerabend warns that an individual-oriented view on creative output and a lack of recognition of teamwork can lead to dire consequences:

The conceited view that some human beings, having the divine gift of creativity, can rebuild creation to fit their fantasies without consulting nature and without asking the rest of us, has not only led to tremendous social, ecological, and personal problems, it also has very doubtful credentials, scientifically speaking. (Feyerabend, 1987, p. 711)

Feyerabend presents the example of Bell Laboratories and the development of the transistor to demonstrate that teamwork "already plays an important role in the sciences." He calls for scientists to restore their "efficiency," "modesty," and "humanity" by making various changes in their perspectives and modi operandi.

In the influential *Greening of America,* Charles Reich presents reasoning similar to that of Feyerabend:

The peasants of a medieval manor, or the anonymous craftsmen who worked on a great cathedral, must have had a feeling akin to "together." It seems doubtful that they felt a need for our society's individual egocentric recognition and separation of individual work from that of the group. Art and workmanship came out of a cultural tradition, not an act of "individual genius." (Reich, 1970, p. 421)

Both Reich and Feyerabend link creativity and artistic production with the group rather than the individual; they both harken back to a "golden age" of selfless dedication to a common goal. Reich's and Feyerabend's general messages are strongly stated, but some of the specifics of their diagnoses and prescriptions seem to be missing. A healthy approach to teamwork for the pair would involve recognition of the social influences on an individual's work; questions of how these social influences can or should be expressed or manifested (other than by a general change in attitude) are left open, however.

Hettinger also presents the notion that all intellectual products (whether accomplished by individuals working in a collaborative group or by individuals working alone) are best seen as social rather than purely individual creations – thus presenting the team approach to intellect as a "natural" state of mind:

Invention, writing, and thought in general do not operate in a vacuum; intellectual activity is not creation ex nihilo. Given this vital dependence of a person's thoughts on the ideas of those who came before her, intellectual products are fundamentally social products. Thus even if one assumes that the value of these products is entirely the result of human labor, this value is not entirely attributable to any particular laborer (or small group of laborers). (Hettinger, 1989, p. 38)

Hettinger provides some specifics as to the ramifications of shifts from individual- to social-oriented perspectives. He asserts that repudiation of an individual-oriented analysis of the production of ideas leads to much-needed changes in the notion of intellectual property:

A person who relies on intellectual history and makes a small modification to produce something of great value should no more receive what the market will bear [than] should the last person needed to lift a car receive full credit for lifting it. (Hettinger, 1989, p. 38)

Hettinger is not specific, though, as to how credit for intellectual accomplishment should be allocated (if at all), and intellectual property determined; however, his essay is a bold first step in addressing some of the more practical consequences of a social-oriented perspective toward intellectual production.

Expressions of linkage to others' work and associated debts are common in science and intellectual work as a whole. Scientific "humility" – the expression of modesty about one's place in the scientific enterprise – has a long tradition, a fact that in some ways counters Feyerabend's,

Reich's, and Hettinger's concerns about individualistic attitudes. Merton (1973) has a long roster of scientists who have professed such humility, one of the most famous of whom is Isaac Newton:

I do not know what I may appear to the world, but to myself I seem to have been only a boy playing on the seashore, and diverting myself in now and then finding a smoother pebble or a prettier shell than ordinary, whilst the great ocean of truth lay all undiscovered before me. (quoted in Brewster, 1855, chap. 27)

Popularity of Newton's remarks and similar confessions of modesty among many members of the scientific community signal some determination to separate that community from individualistic ideology and imagery. Vehicles for drawing further away from an individual-oriented perspective – in providing the means to express more adequately the richness of the interactions among members of the scientific community, for example – are currently in development; much of the effort of CSCW research and development communities is directed toward the support and enhancement of scientific undertakings.

Kohn (1986), in *No Contest,* charts the benefits of having some readily available models of cooperative activity even in a competitive, individualistic society:

Even in a mercilessly competitive society, there are pockets of cooperative activity – enough, at least, so that each of us knows what it is to work with others to paint a room, prepare a report, cook a meal. To remember such experiences is to know that cooperation encourages us to view our competitors favorably; it is to understand how cooperation teaches us, more broadly, the value of relationship. (Kohn, 1986, p. 149)

Benefits of cooperation for Kohn are construed in terms of efficiency and effectiveness (reaching certain goals with a minimum of wasted effort), but they are also considered in terms of other basic values, those not having to do with production. Kohn asserts that cooperative efforts give individuals the opportunity to share experiences with other human beings in a positive, supportive atmosphere. This sharing is considered by Kohn to be a benefit in itself. The healthy or well-functioning group for Kohn is one that allows the "irresistable inducement" of positive, constructive interactions with others to flourish, and has affinity of individuals with fellow members as a driving force.

Message salad and other pathologies of group work

Social scientists have been faced with the problem of how to construct the group as an entity for analysis. The notion that groups meeting face-to-face have a great deal in common – across various contexts and content areas – has been often expressed by social scientists in the past half century. Sproull and Kiesler assert:

For good or bad, the dynamics of face-to-face meetings usually are predictable and similar across groups. The dynamics of electronic group meetings, however, differ from those of face-to-face meetings and are less predictable. (Sproull and Kiesler, 1991, p. 58)

These cross-group commonalities are generally attributed to the groups themselves, with little recognition of the roles of the measuring devices and conceptual structures used to make these generalizations. Some theorists have asserted that with increased experience with electronic group meeting contexts, computer-mediated groups will also have a large degree of cross-group commonality (Chesebro and Bonsall, 1989). Constructing members of the set of "groups" to be similar in many major respects is a useful and powerful assumption, allowing for a level of generalization not possible if every group were considered as having critically important idiosyncrasies.

A number of researchers have attempted to construct group work pathologies – to identify dysfunctional approaches to group work. Anatole Holt links the functionality or dysfunctionality of groups to how well they perform certain activities and engage in "coordination efforts." Holt (1989) states that coordination is the "greatest common denominator" of group activities (p. 202). He asserts that, despite its importance, coordination is an "odd category" of activity because (1) it has no direct product; (2) it often cannot be performed alone; and (3) much of it is not even performed consciously. Holt argues that since coordination is "odd" in these respects, it receives less than its due share of management's attention (although it consumes a large share of organizational resources) and has not as yet obtained adequate academic and research treatment. Malone and Crowston (1990) similarly construct coordination as an activity in itself, akin to an "overhead" involved when more than one individual pursues a given objective.

Many designers consider the greatest common denominator of group activity to be the passing of information objects from person to person. In an effort to counter this limited notion of group activity, Holt (1989a) includes as coordination efforts such activities as "waiting, collecting, checking, organizing, monitoring, and responding to the unforeseen" (p. 202). Holt claims that poorly designed systems can precipitate group work pathologies, either by not taking advantage of already available group work regimens or by overemphasizing one kind of group activity over other, equally critical ones. A concentration on passing information objects, for example, can lead to the production of "message salad" (a cleverly characterized group work pathology).

One of the most famous discussions of group work pathologies is found in Brooks (1967, 1982, 1971). Brooks cites many project group failures as stemming from the "man–month" conception, the notion that the number of individuals assigned to a project per month is an appropriate way of determining its dimensions:

Men and months are interchangeable commodities only when a task can be partitioned among many workers with no communication among them. This is true of reaping wheat or picking cotton: it is not even approximately true of systems programming. (Brooks, 1971, p. 19)

Brooks argues that much knowledge work has a sequential component, and adding more people at a particular juncture will not increase (and may actually decrease) its quality and the speed with which it is done. Group work pathologies thus develop when the number of individuals assigned to projects is not appropriate.

Brooks attempted to demonstrate through anecdote and argumentation something that many managers declared was counterintuitive: having more people working on a project in some stages can actually lengthen the time the project takes to complete (partly since communication and training efforts involved in connecting the various parties are themselves time consuming). Brooks's book *The Mythical Man–Month* (1967/1982) popularized discussion of the "project team" as a separate unit and triggered concern as to how this entity should be conceptualized and managed.

Parker (1990) considers most group work pathologies to be largely a function of team composition. He argues that most managers or leaders who form teams concentrate on obtaining technical diversity and overlook the need to balance team-player styles. The team-player styles identified by Parker include the "contributor" (who is task-oriented and focuses on performance), the "collaborator" (who sees the accomplishment of team goals as paramount, and who will sacrifice personal recognition for team success), the "communicator" (who is process-oriented and skilled in conflict resolution), and the "challenger" (who encourages risk taking on the part of team members and who questions team methods and goals). Parker claims that teams that have all four styles represented evenly are more productive than those that are imbalanced. Overrepresentation of any one style (or "style overload") can lead to team pathology. Style overload is a common phenomenon, Parker asserts, because group leaders and managers seldom have adequate notions of team roles and functioning.

The "group cohesion" notion has undergone a large amount of theoretical and empirical scrutiny; a number of group work pathologies related to cohesion have been outlined. The literature on cohesion in small groups is abundant (compare Kellerman, 1981; Wolfe and Box, 1988). "Cohesiveness" has been defined in terms of the extent to which the group holds an attraction to its individual members and the level of desire with which individual members want to remain in the group (Eddy, 1965). Festinger et al. (Festinger, Pepitone, and Newcomb, 1952; Festinger, Schachter, and Riecken, 1956) defines cohesion as "forces which are acting on the members to stay in the group." Shaw (1981) informally defines cohesion as the way in which the group as a unit "hangs together."

Sundstrom and Sundstrom (1986) outline how an environmental arrangement can influence group cohesion:

A dozen factory workers are placed in a segregated work area, where they assemble automobile engines as a team. Their physical separation from other workers makes it inconvenient to seek social stimulation from outside the work area, and close proximity during the performance of work creates opportunities for conversation. Their common work area also helps define them as a group. As they work and talk together, they eventually develop into a cohesive team . . . The process underlying group formation is face-to-face conversation, made convenient by the physical environment. (Sundstrom and Sundstrom, 1986, p. 5)

Some researchers have targeted cohesion for technology-mediated support (Short, Williams, & Christie, 1976), as well as rhetorical and symbolic encouragement.

Consensus has been lacking in management and administration communities as to whether group cohesion should be considered as healthy or, rather, as pathological – whether it is a functional or dysfunctional element in group work. Group cohesion has been viewed as binding group members to each other rather than to the organization and its goals, triggering managerial attempts to weaken workgroup cohesion (Bramel and Friend, 1987). Group cohesion has also been construed as functional for both the group and the organization, helping to circumvent obvious sources of intragroup tension and disruption, as indicated in the following statement by administrative theorist Peter Blau (1967): "Group cohesion promotes the development of consensus on normative standards and the effective enforcement of these shared norms . . . Cohesion, therefore, increases social control and coordination" (p. 60).

Identification of overt resource and environmental barriers to teamwork provides another angle on the construction of teamwork pathologies. Lerner contends that teams must overcome such obstacles as the following on their way to healthy functioning:

The most obvious difficulty with team research is getting the persons involved to believe they are a team and act like one. There is no tradition of teamwork in social research. Rewards in power, cash, and glory – such as they are in academic life – are distributed to individuals. Hence, the attractions of semi-anonymous participation in team research are low, except to young persons who are just getting started in their academic careers. (Lerner, 1952, p. 14)

A barrier to group work that was identified by CSCW researchers Ahuja, Ensor, and Horn is the "isolation" of group members that results when group work is conducted in today's meeting rooms and other group settings. One of the purposes of their Rapport multimedia conferencing system is the following:

We want to be able to hold discussions with our colleagues from our own offices, thus our vision is to move the necessary features of the meeting room into our offices . . . We believe that holding meetings in which the participants can stay in their offices will reduce the isolation of present meetings by allowing more information in the offices to be used, and by making the participants more accessible to others. (Ahuja, Ensor, and Horn, 1988)

Ahuja, Ensor, and Horn thus construe as dysfunctional some aspects of group work considered vital to others. Their strategy of affording means for group members to participate in groups from their own office environments runs counter to many other group work trends: removing individuals from their home environments to a centralized place where they can focus on group activities (for example, a conference room) has been a critical feature of a number of group work efforts. Attempts to remedy the pathology of isolation may open the door to other kinds of problems (for example, those involving group members' levels of concentration on group activities as opposed to the demands imposed on them in their individual office settings).

Other teamwork barriers have been identified in training and education, most notably in Ph.D. and other professional programs that reportedly direct individuals to be independent and not team-oriented. Ziman asserts that the "headstrong" and individualistic attitudes associated with Ph.D.-level training can subvert group work efforts:

The aim of a good Ph.D. course is to produce men and women with well-founded confidence in their own intellectual independence: the more science grows, the less room it may have for people with this quality of mind. (Ziman, 1976, p. 350)

Social science researchers often frame the basic problems with group work in terms of the trade-offs involved in efforts to remove group work barriers. In attempts to overcome obstacles to productive group activity (such as those outlined earlier), administrators and managers can also precipitate an assortment of new teamwork pathologies. For example, by instituting tight bureaucratic controls over the recalcitrant professionals and scientists described by Ziman, management can thwart the creative efforts it desires. The establishment of a reward system that encourages team efforts (designed to counter the group work barrier outlined by Lerner) may decrease the quality or quantity of contributions by individuals. Meetings could be conducted while individuals are each in their own offices (to counteract the isolation described by Ahjua, Ensor, and Horn), but one implication is that the individuals involved are not able to meet, and share pleasantries, face to face.

In efforts to map group pathologies and explain why healthy groups work as well as they do, a literature and set of research agendas that focus directly on topics involved in collaboration – among peers in particular – have developed. Although there had been some expressions of concern about a lack of research in collaboration, relatively little research output was produced in this area before the 1980s; anecdotal pieces, analysis of coauthorship patterns, and autobiographical accounts constituted the primary sources of information on this topic. Three notable exceptions to this lack of research are Latour and Woolgar (1979), a description of the day-to-day conduct of research entitled *Laboratory Life: The Construction of Scientific Facts;* Brooks (1967/1982) *Mythical Man–Month,* discussed earlier in the chapter; and Bennis (1956), "Some Barriers to Teamwork in Social Research," described later.

Until recently, research on collaboration in the scientific and technological fields largely centered on the master–disciple nexus, rather than on collaboration among equals. Over attempted to increase the pool of research in this area by calling on fellow psychologists to engage in field research on topics relating to scientific collaboration:

The study of scientists as they engage in collaboration offers an ecologically valid setting for investigation of small group processes such as affiliation, trust, cooperation, competition, and conflict that have received detailed attention within the laboratory. (Over, 1982, p. 1000)

In a pioneering effort, Bennis (1956) describes the state of collaboration among interdisciplinary social science research teams of the 1950s. He characterizes a tension between norms of academic "professionalism" (individual-centered academic production and adherence to a single discipline) and then-emerging academic "teamwork" norms (including identification with a common group task); these tensions are still present in many organizational and professional contexts. Bennis (1956, p. 233) personified these conflicts in the following five roles:

a. The Articulator: . . . an individual capable of maintaining a liaison be-
    tween two or more disciplines, one who could speak the language of
    several styles of research.
b. The Innovator: . . . the individual who set[s] out to devise a new form
    of interdisciplinary cooperation – usually quite unique to the particular
    group or individual using it.
c. The Ritualist: . . . individuals who evidenced deep misgivings about
    teamwork and yet attempted to "play the game" . . . the ritualists pub-
    licly accepted yet privately rejected the teamwork effort.
d. The Isolate: . . . not only rejected the cultural goal but was determined
    to stay cloistered both socially and intellectually. For this adaptive role
    there was no "group," no common task.
e. The Rebel: . . . rebels rejected the institutional means of teamwork by
    strong adherence to their professional imperatives . . . here the cultural
    goal of interdisciplinary cooperation was replaced by traditional profes-
    sionalism.

Bennis's subjects (all academics of high standing) are portrayed as seldom
being "neutral" with respect to teamwork issues, signaling a good deal of
concern. Some of the pathologies that result from having members of the
last three types in team work situations are still often noted in accounts of
group work. Williams (1992) advises managers and group leaders to "come
to grips with non-teamplayers," pinpointing them early and giving them
guidance in their adjustments to group life.
    A major theme in early social science research in this area was quanti-
fication of the advantages and disadvantages of joint activities. Some of
this research focused on the efficiency and effectiveness of group versus
individual effort, often with results that did not reflect well on cooperation. At the turn of the century, Ringelmann devised an experiment in
which the amount of strength individuals exerted to pull on a rope when
others are pulling as well (as in a "tug of war") was measured. Ringlemann
found that individual performance gets worse as more pullers are added.
Groups of two pulled at about 90% of their individual scores, groups of
three at 85%, and groups of eight at less than 50% (Sanders, 1990). Triplett
(1898) stimulated a slightly different, but related, thread of research activity, identifying and centering on what have become the common social-
psychological issues of "social facilitation." Such group-related factors as
rivalry among groups and emulation of group members of each other were
described by Triplett as having some positive value in terms of individual-
level productivity. These early experiments in cooperative work generally
involved physical labor or memorization tasks. Decades later, "intellec-

tual labor" and "knowledge work" (Drucker, 1966) were targeted for such examination.

Theoretical and experimental work on the "public goods problem" (the problem of getting individuals to contribute to joint effort or to the joint pooling of resources when their individual contribution is not in itself critical) has pointed to dilemmas in inspiring and maintaining individual contributions to collaborative effort from the perspective of economics (Yamgishi and Sato, 1986). The public goods problem and other, related problems in economics posit the "individual" as a self-contained and self-interested unit, with no direct obligations or tethers to groups or communities other than those that can be imposed through coercion. New models of cooperation, rooted in assumptions of individuals as altruistic and team-oriented, can be expected as research in groups expands beyond a narrowly construed economic perspective.

Constructing group work by labeling: What are "collaborative" and "cooperative" work?

Labelings of certain kinds of work as "cooperative" or "collaborative" have been a focus of management science community efforts to characterize group work, and of the development of CSCW genres. Burke (1966) argues that labels serve as "terministic screens" and that "whatever terms we use, they necessarily constitute a corresponding kind of screen; and any screen necessarily directs the attention to one field rather than another" (p. 50). Brown (1981) underscores the importance of naming by contending that "as names for an entity shift, so do some extent our perceptions of it" (p. 371). Application of the label "cooperative work" can call attention to a change in the way researchers, system designers, and implementers want us to view certain kinds of work.

Sorgaard (1987) defines "cooperative" work as being a less general term than "collaborative" work: "To collaborate is to work together or with someone else, and to cooperate is to work or act together for a shared purpose" (p. 3). He asserts that his distinction is motivated by *Roget's Thesaurus*. It links the term "collaborator" with "co-worker" and "teammate," whereas the term "cooperation" is grouped with "coagency," "symbiosis," "duet," and "clannishness."

Discussion of what cooperative work involves has fueled a number of controversies among developers and critics of CSCW applications. Ehn (quoted in Grudin, 1989b) asserts that "all work is cooperative work" (that is, all of the work performed in an organization must be seen in relation to the overall goals and objectives of the organization, and is thus in some senses cooperative. Kreifelts (1993), of the COMIC Project (Computer-Based Mechanisms of Cooperative Work), seeks to understand the "natural conditions" and features of cooperative work, pointing to nonmediated cooperation as constituting that "natural" state. Holt (1989a) states that cooperative work relationships and patterns can be distinguished and defined, and should be used to drive the design of computer networks: "It must become possible to express a network of work relationships among people so as to control a network of machines" (p. 8). Gibbons, in contrast, makes the claim that the notions that people work in groups (and that software can serve to facilitate group work) are "erroneous":

People don't work in groups; they communicate in groups. Each person works on individual tasks and shares the results of those tasks with his or her co-workers. That is why I think groupware will go the way of the commune; it is a fictitious software category. (Gibbons, 1989, p. 8)

"Coordination" is another term closely associated with CSCW-related activities. The laboratory at MIT dedicated to research in and development of CSCW applications and related topics is called the Center for Coordination Science. Much of the work done in the CSCW area is placed under the rubric "coordination theory." A standard definition of the verb "to coordinate" is "to place or arrange in proper position relatively to each other and to the system of which they form parts; to bring into proper combined order as parts of a whole" (*Oxford English Dictionary*). One of the rationales for the existence of organizations involves such a variety of coordination, one in which the "proper" order of parts helps ensure the maximization of productivity (Brunsson, 1989).

The "coordination problem" identified by Ellis, Gibbs, and Rein (1991) is the "integration and harmonious adjustment of individual work efforts toward the accomplishment of a larger goal" (p. 43). A shared goal is an element in a number of constructions of both coordination and cooperation (see Tjosvold and McNeely, 1988). The notion of a "shared goal" is itself generally taken to be unproblematic, even though an adequate specification of it is difficult to come by. As an example of difficulties in characterizing shared goals, imagine that we might all want a snack at the end of a lecture, and one of us proposes, "Let's go get a snack." However, "a snack" is not a complete specification of our common goal. We want a snack, but none of us would want to knock over a sleeping man at the lunch counter to get the snack. None of us would want to steal the snack. However, one of us may be frugal and intends to haggle the price for the snack, while another may want to pay whatever it takes to get an adequate snack (as long as it is served up quickly). And what would constitute an adequate snack? For you, it might be a hamburger; for me, a salad.

As we differ on various points in our snack-related discussions and activities, or as circumstances disturb the understandings we have already achieved, when does our shared goal stop becoming shared? The notion of a shared goal is deceptively simple and disguises the fact that a large variety of understandings and constructions are involved in any form of human interaction and in each joint endeavor. The ambiguity in the statement "Let's go get a snack" helps to circumvent lengthy, possibly endless negotiations.

With a decidedly different slant toward the "coordination problem," Weick (1979) argues that many collaborators "discover" similar goals after their compatibility has been established and their work efforts have progressed to a certain point. Weick thus counters those theorists who posit that shared goals are a prerequisite for cooperative activity. Attainment of common goals among work group members might thus be seen as a by-product of their joint efforts, and not as an essential element of them. Extending Weick's analysis here, as collaborators work together the narratives they produce about their intents and objectives coincide as they interact and share resources over a period of time.

CSCW researchers are exploring the possibility that individuals have access to a number of "coordination heuristics" of various sorts, ways of solving the coordination problem or resolving other concerns related to joint effort. Holt (1989a) asserts that individuals already have "ancient skills and understandings" about coordination that have helped them utilize and navigate the coordination systems of the past (p. 206), although he does not state whether these are learned rules-of-thumb or deeply engrained (perhaps innate) heuristics. He declares that these understandings can be drawn upon in design and implementation of CSCW applications.

Some organizational theorists have attempted to distill the processes of coordination into a comprehensible sequence. For example, in *Administrative Behavior*, Herbert Simon (1957) outlines three elements of formal coordination processes: (1) development of a plan of action, (2) communication of the plan to the parties involved, and (3) acceptance and adoption of the plan by the parties. Simon's elements require a large degree of openness and explicitness on the parts of all relevant parties. Other organizational theorists have illustrated the theoretical shortcomings of such explicit coordination processes, including the requirements for large amounts of information (Devons, 1970), as well as for the existence of a "community of interests" among the parties involved (Seidman, 1980).

Until recent years, cognitive scientists made little effort toward understanding the processes through which groups attempt to reach a collective goal. Some of today's cognitive science approaches on this issue posit that there are no "general algorithms" to dictate optimal cooperation; rather, an increasingly common assumption is that expertise involving cooperation takes the form of a broad range of heuristic rules (or strategies). From a cognitive science perspective, Durfee, Lesser, and Corkill (1989) speculate that reasoning about coordination is a "fundamental aspect of intelligent behavior," claiming that we judge the intelligence of entities by how they interact with us and whether we can coordinate our efforts with theirs (and vice versa). However, most research in AI has overlooked problems concerning coordination among intelligent entities, focusing rather on the epistemology of individual, self-contained "intelligences."

The question of whether a formal set of coordination processes can be constructed, or a number of coordination heuristics identified, has significant ramifications for design of CSCW applications. Such a set of coordination processes could be used in modeling groups and in building design features that would facilitate or encourage coordination (or at least not subvert coordination efforts on the part of groups). Some of the studies that have sought coordination processes or heuristics have had both experimental and theoretical aspects. Most of these efforts have been rooted in the assumption that the individuals being coordinated are self-contained and self-interested (nonaltruistic), which somewhat limits the scope of the coordination processes or heuristics projected.

One of the themes of research on these issues is the exploration of parallels between human organizations (including small groups) and computer systems. This research is often placed under the label "coordination theory"; the parallels being drawn are incorporated both in computer design efforts and in design of groups. Some emerging models of organizations draw heavily from computer-related themes, imageries, structures, and processes. In turn, computer systems are being designed that use such notions from organizational life as negotiation, agents, and strategic interaction.

Analogies between the "group mind" and an individual mind have also been recently employed to build theoretical frameworks for the design of various kinds of groupware and decision support systems. Thordsen and Klein (1989) outline a model of a "team mind," which they utilize to view team decision-making performance:

The model of a team mind treats the team as an emergent entity. The crew of a Boeing 727 can be considered to consist of four entities: the Captain, the First Officer, the Flight Engineer, and the team of all three together. The model of a team mind attempts to describe the nature of this fourth entity. (Thordsen and Klein, 1989, p. 46)

Thordsen and Klein's model has five postulates: (1) the mind of a team can be treated as analogous to the mind of a person; (2) the mind has three aspects – cognitive behavior, collective unconscious, and subconsciousness; (3) the team is embodied in the actions taken; (4) the conscious part of the team mind is whatever is said out loud for all to hear; and (5) part of the team mind is subconscious (p. 47). Thordsen and Klein utilize the model to generate hypotheses about team decision performance.

Thordsen and Klein's approach has some tempting dimensions for social scientists: strong parallels in structure and function between individual and group minds would allow those doing research on cooperative work to utilize the insights of individual-oriented cognitive psychology in their efforts. Designers of group support systems of various kinds would also be able to borrow models directly from the kinds of support that work adequately in individual-centered situations. If workable and plausible parallels could be constructed either between the group mind and the individual mind, or between the computer and the group, researchers would have a number of research leads and a full set of experimental tangents. Such parallels would also draw into the study of coordination more researchers from the computer science and cognitive psychology communities (individuals who would have an even greater influence in shaping research agendas for the nascent CSCW field). The 1989 report of the NSF's group on coordination theory suggests that these parallels may have little more than marginal aesthetic appeal. However, the plasticity of groups, and their abilities to incorporate various metaphors, labels, and imageries into their processes and structures, signal that many computer–group parallels may indeed prove to be fruitful if only in inspiring new modes of group interaction.

Some "ideal types" of collaborative and cooperative work

A good number of managerial approaches to collaborative work have modeled or segregated certain kinds of work as being collaborative or cooperative, in efforts to create "ideal types" of collaborative or cooperative activity. Reconstructing and relabeling previously popular models of work activity are common strategies in the development of these ideal types. Designers of ideal type models seldom spell out intricate details of what the models involve in practice (which obviously would be a difficult undertaking). Often, exemplars of ideal group structure and behavior are provided in the form of scenarios and vignettes. Rhetoric and imagery play critical roles in the endeavor to create ideal types, with types that are relatively "successful" (in terms of longevity) often being associated with picturesque labels with strong associations (for example, "skunkworks" and "quality circles"). Such ideal types can play powerful roles in shaping group behavior and in communicating the group's products to current and potential audiences.

Organizational and management science communities are placing increased emphasis on development of workgroup concepts and strategies. Sundstrom, DeMeuse, and Furtrell (1990) note that the terms "work team" and "work group" (defined as "small groups of interdependent individuals who share responsibility for outcomes for their organizations") are appearing with greater frequency in the organizational and management literatures. Peters attempts to steer administrators and managers away from the use of the supposedly mundane phrase "work group," preferring "business teams":

The team focus at Livonia GM Cadillac engine plant meant that every person in the organization became part of a group of eight to fifteen people. Importantly – and appropriately – the groups came to be called, not work groups, but business teams. The "business team" is a highly autonomous group (especially by prior standards), responsible for scheduling, training, problem solving, and many other activities. (Peters, 1987, p. 299)

The term "business team" apparently emphasizes the group's role in the organization's overall business plan, in contrast with work group (which merely relates the fact that productive labor is going on).

Distinguishing and labeling certain activities in terms of cooperation, collaboration, and group activity (that is, directing attention to the group level and underscoring the element of social interaction) provide a framework for the interpretation of these activities and can have a reflexive effect on how the activities proceed. Johansen (1988), for example, notes the large difference in the effect of two common rubrics: "Committees are bureaucratic and slow, but task forces cut through the red tape" (p. xi). The name "quality circle" similarly appears to reflect certain assumptions about the activities the groups it refers to will undertake.

One of the most picturesque labels for a kind of group is "buzz group." Consider Thelen's description of the origins of buzz group methodology:

The technique of "buzz groups" appears to have been invented by Dr. Donald Phillips at Michigan State University. The "Phillips 66" technique is one of breaking the large audience into small groups of six members each, having them introduce themselves to each other, and then talk for six minutes to find answers to some questions assigned to the whole audience. One of six people acts as chairman and another as recorder; the latter reports back to the total group the deliberations of his buzz group. (Thelen, 1954, p. 201)

Many of the groups given the "buzz group" label in the 1950s and 1960s were not as well structured as Phillips 66 groups. However, they did share the general model of subgroups breaking off from a major group so that discussion could be conducted on a specific set of ideas in a more intimate setting. Although the label is less often used today, the buzz group did serve for a period of time as a recognizable, purposeful kind of group, one associated with the exchange of ideas. Ideal types can have strong connections to a certain era (as buzz groups have with the 1960s), linkages that can serve to date them and perhaps limit their future effectiveness.

Attempts to develop and popularize workable and understandable ideal types of cooperative activity were in full force from the middle 1970s through the 1980s, with the quality circle being a prime example. The quality circle has been heralded as one of the major managerial innovations of the past decade, with 90% of Fortune 500 companies utilizing them at some point in the 1980s (Lawler and Mohrman, 1985). Part of the circle's popularity is linked with its similarities with Japanese team-oriented organizational structures.

Quality circles are groups that meet to discuss strategies for enhancing workplace productivity and quality. They may be coextensive with the organization's regular workgroups, or they may be a specially constituted group of workers (Daft, 1992). In some organizations, quality circles have been effectively coupled with various participatory managerial strategies to enhance the power and status of workers. Other organizations have apparently followed a less empowering strategy, however:

Quality Circles can effectively collect ideas of the individual closest to the work. If management has no interest in shifting its management style towards participation or in creating an elaborate structure, it can create quality circles, capture the ideas they produce, and then stop them. (Lawler and Mohrman, 1985, p. 69)

Use of quality circles by many managers for obtaining information from individuals without affording them fuller participation in decision making ties in closely with the themes of Taylorism outlined earlier. Information and the control it affords are moved out of the sphere of the worker (or in the case of the quality circle, the workgroup) and into managerial hands. The disappointing performance of the quality circle vehicle in making deep and lasting changes in American organizations (a statement supported by the fact that they have been discontinued at a number of sites) may be located in part in the transparency of these Tayloristic strategies.

The "focus group" is another ideal type group that became popular in the late 1970s and has had enduring recognition. It is generally not considered a workgroup because of the associations it has with information collection in marketing research. The term "focus" reflects the very limited range of topics that its participants' attention is directed toward. It is often used to elicit research and evaluation information, for information exchange in personnel-related concerns, and for public health information collection and delivery. An example of a focus group setting is:

In one end of a standard seminar room there are four or five persons comfortably seated around a low, circular coffee table . . . hanging down over the center of the table is a microphone. In the other end of the room, the two researchers are seated at a separate table. At the beginning of the session, and again after a brief break in the middle, the researchers give instructions to the participants. (Morgan and Spanish, 1984, p. 256)

Focus groups are generally small (less than 12 participants, excluding researchers) and unmoderated (after a topic or issue is introduced, discussion generally proceeds without a large amount of explicit direction by a leader).

Focus groups are often employed to collect data for research purposes or to deliver information on specialized topics (such as how to deal with the aftermath of a heart attack). One of the assumptions that focus group conveners often make is that information exchanges in a group setting are qualitatively different from those conducted when individuals are interviewed separately. Morgan and Spanish (1984) argue that the major advantage of the groups is that they give researchers "the chance to observe participants engaging in interaction that is concentrated on the attitudes and experiences which are of interest" (p. 259), with the interaction itself being of value to researchers. In terms of efficiency of information production, focus groups have not been highly rated by some social scientists, however: Fern (1982) studied the efficiency of the groups in producing ideas, finding that as group size doubled from four to eight, the number of ideas generated did not increase proportionately.

Among the most famous ideal types of cooperative workgroups is the skunkworks – not very attractive imagery to be sure, but apparently an effective way to characterize a closely knit, task-driven team. The first application of the "skunkworks" label to groups is generally credited to Lockheed Advanced Development Company (a research division of Lockheed Corporation). Skunk Works was the appelation given to this unit in the 1940s, a reference to the fugitive alcohol operations in the comic strip *Li'l Abner*. Lockheed Skunk Works is still in operation, with one of its most recent products being the F-117A Stealth Fighter.

The notion of skunkworks has a renegade, antiestablishment flavor, although linkage of skunkworks with such establishment-approved goals as efficiency and high productivity is also strong. Formation of a skunkworks allows certain groups of individuals the ability to break many long-standing organizational rules and cut red tape in order to accomplish certain management-approved goals; direct managerial interference (or micromanagement) is intentionally limited. The high-energy atmosphere associated with skunkworks reportedly stimulates innovation and promotes group cohesion. Management consultants Tom Peters and Robert Waterman helped to make the word "skunkworks" a familiar managerial term in *In Search of Excellence* (1982). Peters continued the popularization of the concept with creation of Skunkwork Camps, intense gatherings of business leaders who are encouraged to explore "what works" to enhance organizational performance – even if what works breaks time-honored organizational tradition. Skunkworks-style operations were portrayed in the popular book *Soul of a New Machine* (Kidder, 1981), in which a team's heroic and sometimes nonconformist efforts to design a workstation were documented.

Robert Reich labels his ideal type "collective entrepreneurship," a hybrid of the self-reliance themes associated with entrepreneurship and notions of cooperation:

If we are to compete in today's world, we must begin to celebrate collective entrepreneurship, endeavors in which the whole of the effort is greater than the sum of individual contributions. We need to honor our teams more, our aggressive leaders and mavericks less. (Reich, 1987, p. 78)

Reich's collective entrepreneurship approach has close parallels to the skunkworks notion, stressing the effectiveness of team-based motivation and underscoring a certain renegade group status. An article in which Reich outlines his collective entrepreneurship ideas, published in *Harvard Business Review,* is entitled "The Team as Hero." Reich states his intention to counter the emphasis on the individual "star" worker or manager, and replace it with concentration on the team as a whole. His call for focus on the team level is linked directly to his supposition that managerial attention to teams (for example, building team structures, evaluating the performance of teams) will lead to increased organizational productivity. In an example of the battles that can accompany discussions of ideal types, Peters (1992) declares that Reich's collective entrepreneurship notion capitalizes the "C" in collective and not the "E" in entrepreneur, and reflects a dangerous disrespect for individual initiative.

"Self-directed" groups are yet another ideal type group that emerged in the managerial literature of the 1990s. Holpp (1992) describes them as small, autonomous, functionally focused work units. Carr (1992) uses the labels of "self-managed" and "empowered" teams to characterize these groups, but warns that higher-level management should provide the teams with clear focuses and goals to ensure their success. Horton (1992) discusses how such teams can "boost the morale" of employees by making them feel more in control of their destinies. Using the word "self" in the label "self-directed" underscores the initiative of team members, although managerial advice concerning these groups generally includes ways to rein them in and ensure some control.

Rosabeth Moss Kanter's (1983) ideal workgroup model is the "participative team." She asserts that a balance between emphases on the individual and on the team is an essential part of successful teamwork:

> "Individual" or "team" are not contradictory concepts in the innovating organization. Teams – whether in formal incarnations or as an implied emphasis on coalition formation and peer cooperation – are one of the integrative vehicles that keep power tools (information, resources, and support) accessible. (Kanter, 1983, p. 34)

Kanter's progressive "integrative" (or "innovating") organizations are described as allowing both individuals and teams requisite headroom. In contrast, "segmentalist" companies (organizations with a style of thought that involves "compartmentalizing actions, events, and problems and keeping each piece isolated from the others"; p. 28) stifle team activity and thus precipitate various workgroup pathologies.

Kanter attempts to counter managerial cynicism about groups or teams by claiming that it is largely the "old-school" organizations that cannot benefit from group-level activities:

> Participative teams are not equivalent to "groupthink," or inaction without consensus, or management by committee – three negatives to many American managers. They are action bodies that develop better systems, methods, products, or policies than would result from unilateral action by one responsible segment, or even from each of the team members working in isolation. The results are likely to be more innovative and more easily used. (Kanter, 1983, pp. 34–35)

Kanter describes how innovating, integrative organizations have managed to establish climates in which groups can flourish and increase organizational productivity. She relates that participative teams are "action bodies" that have been given sufficent resources and rein to act in their organizations.

Sorgaard (1987) is fairly specific (and almost severe) in his ideal type characterization, and also attempts to work out its ramifications for network-based computer system applications. He outlines four criteria for how a workplace or other group-oriented situation can become "cooperative": (1) individuals must work together due to the nature of the task (that is, due to the intrinsic characteristics of the work process); (2) individuals share goals and do not compete (one of these shared goals is the fulfillment of their shared task); (3) the work that individuals do is performed in an informal, normally flat organization (cooperative work is not hierarchically organized, and the organization has an informal character); and (4) the work performed is relatively autonomous (external planning and control of the work reduces the cooperative nature of the work). Sorgaard admits that these criteria are strict and define an "ideal" or "prototypical" situation; he asserts that "pure cooperative work is hard to find" (p. 3).

Sorgaard observes that despite obstacles imposed by the technology, cooperative work can and does go on; he provides as an example the production of a large project proposal by his technical group at Aarhus University in Denmark. The computer systems involved produced situations that could be labeled "computer-disrupted cooperative work": files were exchanged from hand to hand, various versions and updates were lost, and so forth. (Winograd, 1989, labels this kind of quasi-computerized cooperative work system "sneakerware.") Partly from his observations of how work can be disrupted, Sorgaard contends that cooperative work is coordinated in two distinct ways: (1) through explicit coordination, and (2) through the manipulation of shared material. He deemphasizes or omits the coordination potential of other, less explicit coordination vehicles, such as standard group routines; knowledge of the patterns, biases, and habits of individual team members; and rhetoric and imagery.

Another ideal type of group work, one that has been explored in the management literature, is the "clan." Ouchi (1981), following Durkheim (1933/1964), describes the clan form of human organization as consisting of "intimate associations of people engaged in economic activity but tied together through a variety of bonds" (p. 70). Ciborra and Olsen (1988) speculate about the implications of the ideal type clan for CSCW applications in their discussion of the "electronic clan."

Ouchi's "clansperson" is an individual in whom the position and the person are united. The artifact of the "position" (as separate and distinct from the position holder) has been at the core of much of modern organizational structure (Coleman, 1974). A project director's position is constructed separate from the director as an individual, for example. In past centuries, there was a much tighter linkage between person and position; individuals and their positions (or "callings") were considered inseparable units. In similar ways, clanspeople identify strongly with their organizational roles and functions.

The clan approach is rooted in the transaction costs perspective, which has been used as a tool of analysis in organization theory and economics. In this perspective, the primary goal of information technology is to reduce transaction costs through improving information handling and communication. Arrangements that do not match these conditions are not excluded in theory; the transaction costs approach merely states that if the arrangement does not meet the conditions outlined, the organization will have to "pay" (in terms of additional resources expended) for this mismatch (Ciborra and Olsen, 1988). Once a clan is established, exchanges among clan members can be fairly economical (depending on the context). Other types of transaction arrangements besides the clan include the "hierarchy" (organization chart–style exchange, in which information is conveyed according to hierarchical position) and the "market" (a form of exchange mechanism that mimics the free enterprise system).

Why is the clan considered a powerful organizational structure by Ouchi? In the clan, the socialization of members to some common goal is so complete that members can be trusted to do that which is in the "common good" (Ouchi, 1981). Professional training and experiences associated with professionalism can provide such socialization. In a classic study, Kaufman (1963) portrays the training of forest rangers – individuals who are called on to maintain consistent standards of work conduct despite isolation – as involving a high level of professional socialization. In the clan form of organization, the individual's own selfish ends interleave almost completely with the organization's goals. The monk, the Marine, and the Japanese auto worker are examples that illustrate high levels of socialization for Ouchi.

With intense socialization, certain economies for the organization can emerge. Layers of management once required to monitor, discipline, and otherwise control workers may be obviated. If self-direction can replace hierarchical direction, some cost economies can be reached. However, the overhead costs of indoctrinating workers in clan ideology and practice in a particular occupation can be extraordinarily high (if such indoctrination is possible at all in that context). Ouchi argues that clans can be cost effective when there is high task uncertainty (that is, no one really knows what is going on, so hierarchy is not an effective organizational strategy) and high goal congruence (in which the organization's members are tightly focused on joint goals).

Ciborra and Olsen provide the following analysis of the socialization requirements an organization incurred when a new subgroup was formed 400 miles away from the central research facilities:

A particularly difficult problem was instilling in group members, especially new ones, a sense of what were the most appropriate problems to work on and how to spend their time. Modes of appropriate behavior needed to be provided and reinforced across a distance. Therefore, the tools the group migrated toward were video-based; they established an interactive audio and video link between the two sites. In essence they tried to broaden the communications channel between the two sites as much as they could, so that all kinds of information, much of it behavioral cues rather than specific requests or commitments, could be transmitted. (Ciborra and Olsen, 1988, p. 98)

Ciborra and Olsen assert that the organization just described (Xerox PARC) has high task uncertainty because its projects and directions are constantly redefined through discovery. The organization also has relatively high goal congruence, according to their analysis. This combination of organizational characteristics supposedly makes the establishment of an electronic clan feasible.

Ciborra and Olsen describe video links ("broad communication channels") as being suitable vehicles for support of clans. Wellens and Ergener (1988) present results from a simulation game experiment that bolster Ciborra and Olsen's assumptions; these results suggest that some increase in the "richness" (or breadth) of communication channels linking game participants working as team members on common problems increases their feelings of "teamness." However, additional channel richness did not significantly enhance team performance or increase situation awareness.

Trust is another critical aspect of the clan. Ouchi claims that many clans function largely on the basis of trust, and presents an analogy from neighbor-to-neighbor relations:

"For instance, in most societies it is considered rude to rush over to repay a neighbor for a favor just received . . . the leaving of many debts between people amounts to evidence of their trust of one other, and the evidence of trust in turn serves as the oil that lubricates future social transactions." (Ouchi, 1981, p. 74)

Trust of this sort, trust that is constructed among individuals through various activities, takes on a different dimension in the electronic clan, however. Accounts of group member behavior are accessible (at least in principle) through monitoring and profiling mechanisms, replacing the need for trust with the ability to "verify." The tight interweavings of group members' goals that are characteristic of clans can also be stimulated through construction of virtual groups (virtual entities that are framed and labeled in terms of desired group goals). Control of individuals is increasingly possible in network-supported and monitored group activity, making the electronic clan ever more feasible (although some aspects of its palatability are still very much in question).

The ideal types of cooperative workgroups just outlined, from the quality circle to the electronic clan, have a number of similarities: all are explicit as well as management approved, and can serve to designate and label smaller groups within larger organizations. All are designed to build some solidarity or team spirit among the individuals working as a group. Skunkworks attempt to nurture solidarity through a renegade mode of operation, the clan through various forms of socialization, Reich's collective entrepreneurship group through eliciting a spirit of team-oriented enterprise, and the quality circle through collective pride in group product.

None of the ideal types has the notion of a "leader" (a member who is given special organizational responsibility and authority for group activity) as an integral element. However, all of the types could incorporate leadership as a major dimension, and most skunkworks do in practice. All of the groups have some definite focus or identity, whether completing a project, solving a quality-control problem, or initiating some enterprise. The image of the management-sponsored, peer-centered, and project-focused group exhibiting team spirit and solidarity without "leadership" being a major factor thus emerges from the ideal type groups of the 1980s. The focus group was included in the set of ideal type groups to emphasize that the quality of interaction among workers is increasingly of interest to management. Managers can elicit survey data from employees or deliver information about a health plan without convening a group; a portrait of the interaction among employees in the context of a certain problem is sought when a focus group is formed. The notion that interaction changes the character and quality of information exchange (for example, that the "group's contribution" is somehow different than the sum of individually delivered member contributions) emerges in research about and implementation of most of the ideal type groups discussed in this chapter.

Proliferation of ideal type groups shows little sign of abatement. We should indeed expect development of a variety of ideal groups (many directly associated with CSCW applications) in decades to come. Some, possibly, will be designed out of a negative reaction to forms of group work that are seen as overly "mechanized" and influenced by computer applications; more "natural" forms of group work may indeed be projected. Other ideal types will reflect and underscore aspects of group interaction that are especially enhanced by or related to utilization of CSCW applications.

Constructing "normal" mechanics of collaboration: Initiating and developing a collaboration

How and why are collaborations initiated? A number of social scientists and CSCW researchers are attempting to provide some sense of how collaborations are normally started. In many research and professional collaborations, the original impetus for joint effort initiates from outside the collaborative team. One of the most striking examples of such an impetus was the September 1987 meeting funded by Citicorp that linked 10 physical scientists (including Nobel laureate Philip Anderson) and 10 economists (including Nobel laureate Kenneth Arrow). The purpose of the meeting was to trade ideas on how to deal with complex economic systems (Pool, 1989). In more mundane contexts as well, a good deal of direction is generally provided by administrators, group leaders, and other organizational "matchmakers" as to who should team up with whom.

Many other collaborations, especially in academe, are initiated by the efforts of one or more potential team members. In their interviews of 50 pairs of researchers in social psychology, management science, and computer science, Kraut, Galegher, and Egido (1988) obtained the following rationales for collaboration: (1) to combine resources to accomplish a project (including both intellectual and material resources), (2) to change the process of research in desirable ways (for example, working with others was considered "more fun" than working alone), (3) to maintain preestablished personal relationships (especially ones that are threatened by physical separation, as researchers leave for other institutions); and (4) for career-oriented purposes (often based on belief that "working with a particular person or being in a collaborative relationship per se was valuable for their careers") (p. 35). These and other research results may serve to "normalize" and support the heavy personal and informal component involved in group activities. Many of the reasons for collaboration described earlier have less to do with concrete research plans than simple "good feelings" about working together with another person.

The labeling, packaging, and subsequent dissemination of products created through team research efforts and other collaborative activities comprise a substantial portion of the time and energies of many groups. The "marketing" of scholarship (for example, attempts to increase the probability that a paper will be published or a proposal approved) may include providing elements of information to influential parties that are extraneous to the document. Silverman (1982) describes how editors of refereed journals receive and make use of such added information, although the peer review system (which evaluates works of scholarship in conditions where the identities of and other information about the authors are supposedly rendered irrelevant) prohibits its use in any substantive fashion. The identity of the research "team" can thus be a nontrivial aspect of the evaluation of its research.

Information about the research environment in which academic and research work is conducted apparently plays a role in how the work is evaluated. For example, a study of the peer review system in psychology showed that scientific papers were accepted on the basis of the institutional affiliation of the authors, although the norms applying to peer review prohibited such a practice (Ceci and Peters, 1984); many of the published commentaries on the study revealed that the practice described by Peters and Ceci was indeed widespread. The practices may signal the existence of some "normal," socially approved, yet undeclared ways to consider team and institutional affiliation in peer review procedures.

Increased incidence of coauthorship in academic and research papers is often used to indicate a trend toward the open recognition and support of collaboration in academic, research, and professional arenas. Coauthorship citations rarely, if ever, provide direct information as to who did what in a project – that is, who came up with what ideas, who wrote what sections of the paper, and who disagreed with what conclusions. Rather, they primarily serve to convey some association of specific individuals with an overall product (the report, book, public address, or paper in question).

Explicitly recognized coauthorship has been widely acknowledged as a kind of index for the extent of collaboration in a discipline or research field – although its use as such an index can be problematic (as will be discussed). In a similar study, Over (1982) examines changes in authorship practices in the journals published in the years 1949, 1959, 1969, and 1979 by the American Psychological Association. The mean number of authors for papers published in the journals increased from 1.47 (in 1949) to 1.72 (1959), to 1.88 (1969), to 2.19 in 1979. Economics and management science reflect similar trends: Schweser (1983) describes the increased incidence of coauthorship in the academic field of business finance, and Barnett, Ault, and Koserman (1988) document similar trends in economics.

The National Science Board's *1989 Science and Engineering Indicators* outlines that the proportion of scientific and engineering papers with multiple authors has increased sharply. Concern about these and similar trends in the medical research community stimulated the creation of authorship guidelines at Harvard Medical School and at a National Institutes of Health (NIH) conference on scientific authorship (Culliton, 1990). The Harvard guidelines directly tackle the issue of the dilution of individual responsibility for collaborative team product. They state that authors should be held responsible for the research papers on which their names are placed; also, for a name to be included in the list of authors "the only reasonable criterion should be that a co-author has made a significant practical or intellectual contribution" to the research effort.

Several researchers have considered the coauthorship patterns just outlined and asked what has caused the apparent increase in the practice of coauthorship. McDowell and Melvin (1983) argue that the increase in specialization on the part of academic professionals has made it more necessary to combine the skills of a team of scholars in the conduct of projects. As such specialization continues, McDowell and Melvin predict, the incidence of coauthorship will increase as well.

Barnett et al. (1988) argue that an increase in the emphasis placed on research output has put a premium on the time of colleagues, time that would have otherwise been put to use in informal review and in assessing ideas. They posit that more individuals are demanding coauthorship as "payment" for their time. The point of Barnett et al. is well taken: the possibility that many colleagues are no longer satisfied with a "thank you" or a mention in the acknowledgments for a return on their investment of time – and thus demand coauthorship status – does not entail an increase in the overall level of research and academic cooperation. However, various trends in multiauthorship practices, along with other factors supporting "big science" and "big scholarship" (including trends in research funding), do seem to point to the "rise of group science" (Norman, 1990) at least in some research areas.

With coauthorship comes the problem of name order on various published documents. Zuckerman describes the mechanics of name-ordering practices in the published rosters of authors' names:

Intrinsically, it seems trivial or humiliating to be concerned with the order in which the names of authors appear; for scientists to be as interested in the order of their billing as actors or business partners. But, symbolically, name ordering is an adaptive device that facilitates the allocation of responsibility and credit among co-workers in otherwise ambiguous situations induced by the new structures of scientific research. (Zuckerman, 1968, p. 277)

By "new structures of scientific research," Zuckerman is referring to the increase in the size and complexity of the organizational infrastructure required by "big science" projects. Although the previously mentioned norms involving scientific humility may prohibit direct bickering over name order, this should not be taken to imply that name ordering is unimportant; the economic and social impacts of name order on academic careers are critical in many contexts.

Kraut et al. (1988) note that some professions have norms that govern allocation of authorship credit. They provide accounts of norms in computer science that make authorship strictly a matter of alphabetic sequence; in psychology and management science, they state that the highest authorship credit goes to the member who supposedly made the greatest contribution. Many of the collaborators they interviewed also report using explicit rules in the credit-allocation process:

Ownership of the original ideas seemed to be the strongest determinant, as long as the initial ideas had not been modified too extensively by the second member of the team. No other kind of work is valued as highly as the intellectual work involved in the initial formulation of the research plan. The ability to formulate interesting research questions and translate them into research plans is the sine qua non of being a scientist; those who contribute to the execution of a project in this way are generally seen as project leaders . . . despite the fact that they may be totally reliant on others to carry out the plan. (Kraut et al., 1988, p. 49)

Some of the authorship-recognition practices that have been proposed or instituted include the following:

1. Eliminating name-order rosters entirely: Since the allocation of credit to individual researchers can be problematic, give credit to the research group as a whole instead of the individual. Research groups could be organized into teams with names such as "The Harvard–MIT Yankees" (Weston, 1962).
2. Playing with name-order sequences: Use of the last name in a sequence of coauthors for recognition of the "senior" person in a team is a way to acknowledge a particular sort of contribution (of the laboratory director or other distinguished individual, for instance). Employing forward or reverse (or rotating) alphabetical sequences can also mitigate some name-order concerns. Use of alphabetical order may openly demonstrate the team's reluctance to allocate differential credit; it may also be a system imposed by the research institution or professional group.
3. Instituting a "two tier" system: The NIH's conference on scientific authorship produced the suggestion that a set of authorship categories be established that recognizes the particular roles individuals play in conducting research and producing a manuscript. For example, primary authorship would be assigned to individuals who "actually contribute to the conception, generation of data, or analysis and interpretation of data"; a second roster of authors would be comprised of individuals who "fit the 'with the assistance of' or 'in collaboration with' description" (Culliton, 1990, p. 525).

These changes in name-order protocols may mitigate some problems and eliminate some injustices, but other concerns remain. Lapidus provides a strikingly frank discussion of the ethics of acknowledging the contributions of individual scientists in large-scale, "big science" projects.

He observes that Nobel Prizes have been awarded for experiments in which dozens of scientists have been active participants; many of the scientists involved, however, have remained anonymous while one or two project leaders are credited with a "discovery" and receive large-scale media attention as well:

Perhaps scientific papers will be formally "authored" by superstars but will actually be produced like "handbooks" or "instruction manuals," created by anonymous scientific writers sitting in cubicles in the publications offices of major industrial corporations. (Lapidus, 1989, p. 144)

The dystopia presented by Lapidus may stun our sensibilities, but the shock approach may be required: the fairness issues he presents are indeed often overlooked. The majority of those concerned about authorship rosters generally center their attention on making sure that those who have managed (through whatever means) to get their names on the roster consider themselves accountable for the product in question, and not on matters of unfairness.

Simply put, institutions require that someone be held accountable for the report, study, journal article, or the like: the fear that authorship rosters reflect political strength rather than accountability and responsibility for scientific products has ramifications for the quality of intellectual output (as well as for the careers of the anonymous many described by Lapidus). Construction of many genres – including the academic article – as having easily identifiable authorship relates to long-standing traditions concerning intellectual property and accountability for how ideas are expressed. A simple authorship roster also makes classification and storage of knowledge "units" possible, no small feat in an age when the number of publications is increasing at almost an exponential level. Although some researchers estimate that nearly 45% of the articles in top-level science journals are never referred to again in the academic literature (Begeley, 1991), having ready handles for access to the building blocks of knowledge is an important factor to consider.

Name-ordering practices can be said to reflect the "strategic uses of ambiguity"; Zuckerman (1968) argues that "ambiguity in the meaning of name orders reduces the stress of collaboration" (p. 290). Zuckerman's use of the term "strategic" is problematic: there is little data concerning researchers' and academics' awareness of their field's "normal" name-ordering practices and possible alternatives, and thus to their strategic application. Carl Sindermann, in the popular *Winning the Games Scientists Play,* makes the following appeal for the conscious removal of any ambiguity in these matters:

A critical, never-to-be-overlooked aspect of joint authorship must be early and unanimous decision, even before any collaborative research is started, about first authorship and even about the sequence of authors on the published paper. (Sindermann, 1982, p. 13)

Sindermann asserts that rather than being a trivial side issue, the authorship decision is itself of critical importance: "More dissension, unhappiness, bitterness, hostilities, and long-standing enmities have been created by failure to observe this basic rule than by almost any other issue in science" (p. 13).

Ambiguity in name-order practices may simply be a product of the fact that most research communities are still limited enough in size that the real story behind who did what in a research effort is accessible to interested individuals with a few phone calls. As research communities expand, however, exchanges among groups become more formal, and the economic and social values associated with name order increase, leading to calls for clarity in the practices.

Name-order problems have been considered to be some of the most important issues concerning intellectual collaboration; institutions (including Harvard Medical School and the NIH), professional groups, and individual academics themselves are mobilizing to address them. However, few critics and commentators on name-order issues have questioned the basic structure of the name-order situation – the fact that a linear roster of names is attached to a single, apparently integrated, document. Modifications to this structure (including the development of alternative genres for expression of group work) will be developed along with new technologies for supporting cooperative work. New and more complex means for associating team members with team-produced intellectual products will certainly precipitate a new set of problems and concerns for academic and research organizations, but they may forestall the spread of dystopias of the type Lapidus describes – where anonymous legions of researchers bask in the reflected glory of a few acknowledged authors.

Another attempt to shape the growth and development of groups involves identifying group work stages and sequences. If groups – like other human relationships – are considered as having a beginning and an end, how do they proceed from the one to the other? Tuckman (1965) identifies a unitary sequence of workgroup development:

1. Forming: initial efforts to establish group identity and cohesion begin.
2. Storming: conflicts begin among members, often involving personality disputes.
3. Norming: standards and compromise areas of agreement emerge.
4. Performing: the group accomplishes its task and evaluates its success.

Tuckman and Jensen (1977) altered this model by adding the fifth and final stage of "adjourning" (which, unfortunately, muddies Tuckman's otherwise-impressive alliteration).

Several social scientists have countered Tuckman's notion that work-groups proceed in a linear fashion. Their approach has shifted from that of distilling discrete stages (building a stage model) to analyzing the rhythms of the working patterns of collaborative groups. Poole (1983a, 1983b) finds that decision-making groups proceed in multiple (as opposed to unitary) sequences, a manner that is more cyclical than linear. Gersick (1988) also describes the behavior patterns of teams as "alternating inertia and revolution in the behaviors and themes through which they approached their work" (p. 9).

Gersick developed the notion of "punctuated equilibrium" to describe the rhythms she charted. In Phase 1 of a group's existence (roughly the first half of its life) a group constructs a stable "framework of behavioral patterns and assumptions." At the start of Phase 2, these assumptions are questioned and often overhauled:

At their calendar midpoints, groups experience transitions – paradigmatic shifts in their approaches to their work – enabling them to capitalize on the gradual learning they have done and make significant advances. The transition is a power-ful opportunity for a group to alter the course of its life midstream . . . Phase 2 . . . takes its direction from plans crystallized during the transition. (Gersick, 1988, p. 32)

Gersick describes several group work pathologies that spring from the application of her model: some of the teams she observed were not successful in making a viable and complete transition from Phase 1 to Phase 2, for example.

The usefulness of a coherent and widely adopted model for group processes is apparent, and the search for such a model is likely to con-tinue. Groups could be more easily controlled, and group members expec-tations managed, if a "normal" sequence for group progress were under-stood and agreed upon by group members. Such a model would aid in the process of establishing group-level control: group members could attempt to control each others' behaviors in reference to the model's standards. A powerful and generally accepted model would also have many implica-tions for development of CSCW applications, though it is possible that such a model would not readily translate from the face-to-face group configuration to computer-mediated settings.

Organizing group activity in terms of discrete stages is one of the ways in which we try to make our environments orderly and sensible. None of us could tolerate conditions that we perceive as being in complete disorder and lacking sense. Cooperative work efforts have aspects that can sometimes seem mysterious, chaotic, and apparently random. Constructions of "normal" group work patterns, forms, labels, sequences, and ideal types are attempts to make sense of group activity, although they can also be employed to place unduly strong constraints on the dimensions that activity can take. These constructs can be utilized by managers and administrators in their efforts both to control groups directly and to stimulate self-control on the part of group members.

Group work pathologies play complex roles in construction of groups. Weick (1979) describes various organizational enactment processes – ways that organizations and groups impose some degree of order on their environments. Organizations "enact" their environments, according to Weick; organization members "act" as if certain conditions exist, which has real ramifications for their environments. One common enactment process is that of the self-fulfilling prophecy:

A person who acts on the premise that "nobody likes me" will behave in a distrustful, stiff, defensive, or aggressive manner to which others are likely to react unsympathetically, thus bearing out the original premise. What is typical about this sequence and makes it a problem of punctuation is that the individual concerned conceives himself only as reacting to, but not as provoking, those attitudes. (Watzlawick, Beavin, and Jackson, 1967, pp. 98–99)

An example of a self-fulfilling prophecy is that of a person (X) who believes that another person (Y) is "angry" or has a "bad temper." X's belief may make him or her act in ways that would make anyone (including person Y) angry. (Person X may deliver snarling accusations about the temper of person Y, for instance.) Organizations and groups that act as if communicative ambiguity, isolation, or lack of group cohesion are dysfunctional will very possibly enact environments in which apparent displays of those qualities become problematic. On the other hand, groups for which the "unexpected is expected" may open up new, creative opportunities for future interaction.

Some conclusions and reflections

Just what is cooperative work? The models, norms, labels, and images discussed in this chapter have been utilized in recent years to structure and make sense of joint enterprise. The longevity and popularity of the "social technologies" described have to do with their understandability and ready application by relevant actor groups – as well as their interactions (or potential interactions) with other technologies for support of group work, including CSCW applications. Needs of social scientists for social technologies that fit into established research methodologies and agendas (that lend themselves to examination, measurement, and experimental treatments) are also factors in many of the technologies' success.

Should we attempt to "tame" our workgroups, to mold our groups into certain structures and interaction patterns? Should we devote our energies to steering our groups away from workgroup pathologies? Some amount of controlling and shaping our groups is inevitable. However, the genius of good group leaders involves knowing when to let groups evolve and develop on their own. Only a few of the current set of models and accounts of cooperative work include intangible and "slippery" factors such as "synergy" and "chemistry"; these factors deserve closer examination, along with the ones that are more readily quantifiable.

Today, the talents of a good workgroup facilitator or a strong team member are often in demand and are widely respected. What some managers, administrators, and group members do to make their groups work happily and function well is still considered to be little short of magic. Some of the trends in group work are apparently away from "magic" and toward "formalization," however. If workgroup procedures and structures are standardized (or "routinized," to use Bravermanic terminology), it is likely that the roles of many middle-level managers and administrators will be changed. The shaping of groups – the identification and treatment of workgroup pathologies – now is largely in the hands of middle management. Network-based system technologies may work to replace the human facilitator with a combination of computer- and peer-enforced mediation, reinforced with higher-level management oversight and control. Skills of facilitators may become less valued as a result.

The kinds of insights on group work that are drawn on in this chapter could be used as a cornucopia of possible workgroup routines and features; managers and group participants can utilize these strategies and perspectives in their efforts to experiment with and explore different styles of group activity, and to devise new ones. However, these notions (and the others that are currently being generated) can also be employed to limit the options of workgroups by placing research-supported restrictions on how groups should conduct themselves, and by compulsively identifying and eradicating all workgroup pathologies. The mental health model discussed in the preceding chapter provides some guidance as to which course of action will predominate: pathologies are likely to be avoided and "normal" group functioning strongly (and strictly) supported, by both managers and group members themselves. I hope that the more flexible and exploratory approach will be adopted, and the magic of group interaction allowed some room to flourish.

4

Shared resources and spaces: Lessons from the use of desks, tables, whiteboards, office settings, and video

> *In the end we design the tool for the material – in the end, but never in the beginning. In the beginning we have still to find out the first things about the ways in which the material is and is not workable; and we explore it by trying out implements with which we have already learned to work with other materials. There is no other way to start.*
>
> Gilbert Ryle, Dilemmas *(1962, p. 66)*

> *The general conception of the ideal plant newspaper is pretty well defined . . . it should carry lucid articles on efficiency, personal better-ment, shop news and personals, with the aim of securing cooperation.*
>
> Hi Sibley, Factory *(April 1918, p. 776)*

As Ryle laments, the initial stages of design with a new "material" often amount to solving yesterday's problems and meeting yesterday's require-ments. New possibilities and problems have indeed emerged in the era of CSCW applications. CSCW research and development communities have also taken on older, better-recognized, and still-important problems, prob-lems with their predecessors addressed in efforts to shape groups with the use of artifacts. Several salient cultural objects appear to have traveled with all of these kinds of efforts, most notably that of "efficiency."

A number of problems are associated with efforts to define or construct a group (in terms of its membership, sphere of action, and scope of accountability). Concern with these problems has surfaced in various forms since the early part of this century (as Sibley's advice in the epigraph suggests). Many managerial theorists, social scientists, design-ers, and users have suggested approaches to and perspectives on the problems:

1. The problem of shared access to resources – What access do group members have to various resources, and how are potential conflicts relating to access resolved? How are non–group members excluded from the use of these resources (if at all)? The problem of constructing resources so as to be amenable to shared access is linked with these issues, but has some distinct dimensions. How are organizational re-sources (physical, human, and informational) defined, and are group access considerations involved in this effort?

2. The problem of affording some sort of shared focus, involvement, or narration – As the number and variety of resources and possible perspectives on them increase, are mechanisms for the direction of attention of group members provided? Who can utilize these mechanisms?

3. The problem of maintaining a consensus on standard interpretations of group resources or vehicles for group expression, or of convincing individuals that there are such standard interpretations – How do group members interpret group resources or group expressions? Do managers or group leaders attempt to play a role in shaping these interpretations?

Users of various artifacts and their associated genres often become aware of these problems – as they are addressed in practice by designers, managers, and social scientists – either directly through discussion (for example, by asking or being asked the question, How will we devise strategies for sharing these resources?) or indirectly (for instance, through forms of managerial rhetoric or product advertisement). Users have also brought their own, related issues to the surface, bringing them to the attention of designers and managers or developing solutions of their own.

Unsafe at any speed? Efficiency in the context of the workgroup

The cultural object of efficiency has been tightly coupled with computing since the days of wiring boards and magnetic core memories. Efficiency and management have also been linked: the interest of many managers and team leaders in promoting specific social and task-related goals in the most efficient manner has been expressed in a variety of ways and has served to fuel the interest of social scientists in associated concerns. In his comments on American values, Williams (1960) writes, " 'Efficient' is a word of high praise in a society that has long emphasized adaptability, technological innovation, economic expansion, up-to-dateness, practicality, expediency, getting things done" (p. 428). Business historian Yates (1989) declares that "system, efficiency, and scientific became catchwords in the business world and beyond" after the influence of Taylorism (p. 15).

A variety of definitions of efficiency have been developed, most relating to some extent to economies in the pursuit of a certain goal or objective. Keen and Scott Morton (1978), in their discussions of decision support systems, define efficiency and effectiveness in terms of their relation to specific goals: "Efficiency is performing a given task as well as possible in relation to some predefined performance criterion. Effectiveness involves identifying what should be done and ensuring that the chosen criterion is the relevant one" (p. 7). Unlike Keen and Scott Morton, few of those who employ the notion of "efficiency" are careful about the specific usage of the word. Despite this imprecision, efficiency remains on the scene as a significant and frequently mentioned factor, often picking up a variety of managerial- and economics-related connotations and associations.

Managerial concern about the efficiency of group interaction has been stimulated by well-publicized research results: one example is Mosvick and Nelson's (1987) study, which shows that ineffectively managed meetings drained a Fortune 500 company of an estimated $71 million dollars yearly. Strassman (1985) states that managerial communications of all forms comprise the largest individual cost factor for American business (exceeding those of direct labor and capital, and greatly exceeding net profits). Despite the high cost of communication, the traditional meeting maintains a high level of utilization, and many managerial communication vehicles have not changed significantly since the early part of this century. Recognition of the high percentage of time many administrators, managers, and project leaders reportedly spend in meetings (estimates range from 60% to 70% for information systems managers to 30% to 80% for general managers) has reached the level of top management (Mintzberg, 1973). Hymowitz (1988) published a "Survival Guide to the Office Meeting" to dramatize the severity of the situation.

The quest for efficiency in communications has been a long-standing theme of business. In the early part of this century, T. C. Du Pont championed this quest, as evidenced in his 1913 statement describing "right attitudes" about communication: "Efficiency has come to stay, and in its application the first great essential is 'changing our minds' about the fundamentals of business" (see Yates, 1989, pp. 252–253). Du Pont characterized pejoratively the reluctance of many office and administrative workers to "change their minds" and part with some of the niceties of communication, including elements of etiquette and personal exchange.

Issues of efficiency also play an important role in some recent approaches to the academic study of human communication. Planalp and Hewes (1982) outline what they label as a "cognitive approach" to communication, one that focuses on the "cognitive capacities people have and use in communicating." They assert that optimum use of these capabilities involves efficiency as a "basic motivation":

Since people often have multiple goals that require the processing of large quantities of information with limited resources, the system must maximize efficiency . . . in both the representation and the processing of information. (Planalp and Hewes, 1982, p. 56)

This notion of efficiency in communication directs researchers to look for a system's overall goals and to devise measures of how quickly and with what level of resource usage those goals are met.

Efficiency is tightly coupled with CSCW applications in many published accounts and advertisements. A *Byte* article describes groupware in terms of its potential to make communications "easier and faster":

There's no question that a well-designed groupware package can enhance the productivity of your business. If you can get people to use the package, they will find that it makes their communications easier and faster. (Rash, 1990, p. 96)

"Economies of scale" concerning group interaction is a construct related to efficiency that is playing an important role in discussions of CSCW applications. The notion refers to the number of group members that can be accommodated in a meeting while maintaining the desired "quality of interaction" (that is, while providing adequate platforms for participation of group members). Group size can be expanded nearly indefinitely; one can simply build larger and larger meeting facilities. Development of adequate vehicles for group members' expression adds levels of complexity, however.

Consideration of economies of scale in group interaction has had a long history. Economist Mancur Olsen describes the detriments of having group size expand beyond the optimum number (however determined):

When a partnership has many members, the individual partner observes that his own effort or contribution will not greatly affect the performance of the enterprise, and expects that he will get his prearranged share of the earnings whether or not he contributes as much as he could have done. The earnings of a partnership . . . are a collective good to the partners, and when the number of partners increases, the incentive for each partner to work for the welfare of the enterprise lessens. (Olsen, 1971, p. 55)

An alternative explanation for these inadequate individual contributions to the group is that in groups beyond a certain size, group members can feel that their individual expressions will be "lost" or unrecognized, and thus can have little incentive to produce.

James (1951) posits that face-to-face groups have some upper limit on optimum group size, with "action taking" groups (groups with the objective of producing something) having a smaller optimum size than those not taking action. On a similar theme, the sociologist Georg Simmel (1950) asserts that "small, centripetally organized groups usually call on and use all their energies" (p. 92). The decades-long quest to widen the "span of control" of the group (to be able to include more individuals under the aegis of the group, while maintaining acceptable "quality" in terms of the contribution of each individual) has continued with current CSCW research.

The question of whether collaborative efforts are more efficient or productive than individual efforts (whether or not computer support is involved) has often been addressed through anecdotal evidence; it has also been a target of more systematic research. Gere and Abbott (1985) reviewed 17 pieces of research to support their contention that collaborative writing is more efficient than noncollaborative writing. Lunsford and Ede (1986) draw comparable conclusions, and report their survey that posed the question, In general, how productive do you find writing as part of a team or group as compared to writing alone? The response they received from 59% of the recipients was "very productive" or "productive."

Cultural objects or themes that apparently run counter to the cultural object of efficiency include that of "personality" (for example, as embodied in the personal touches in correspondence ridiculed by Du Pont decades ago). The personal and the efficient have had an uneasy relationship in business: calls to introduce efficiency into communications have often amounted to limiting the means individuals are afforded a "persona" in their communications – that is, expressive elements that relate to themselves as individuals. Correspondence is often considered efficient if it is apersonalized, standardized, and formalized, whether or not it serves the function of getting a point across. Segregation of the personal from the efficient is a common theme in design and implementation of a number of workplace artifacts and genres. A larger degree of leeway in terms of personality is afforded in many of today's computer applications, along with enhanced capabilities for filtering out unwanted and extraneous aspects of others' communications. Special "touches" such as elaborate fonts, color, and graphics features allow individuals to tailor their expressions while remaining within acceptable bounds of economy and efficiency.

Virtual individuals and groups can involve broad ranges and scopes of personal and group expression. "Information richness" (Daft, 1992), defined as the number of sensory modes incorporated in a particular communication medium, can have some influence on personal expressiveness, but is not a determining factor: a signature, a perfume, or a silhouette (all fairly limited vehicles) can be very expressive in certain contexts. Linkages to commonly understood and accepted "characters" can make for more highly expressive virtual individuals and groups. A signature that reflects an artist's flair can be most expressive, along with a perfume that has a characteristic trait or essence.

Another theme that has been linked with the design of efficient workplaces and workplace technologies is the "positioning" of the worker – that is, placement both physically and in terms of his or her relation to various organizational routines. This theme has long historical roots; Leffingwell (1925) in his book *Office Management* flatly asserts that much time could be saved by designing office routines so as to eliminate the need for individuals to rise from their desks (and thus have opportunities to communicate about nonbusiness matters). He states that desks should be organized so that correspondence and other shared material can be exchanged without "the necessity of the clerk even rising from his seat." We thus owe to Leffingwell some of the early notions of rooting or anchoring individuals to one place in the office or workplace. This approach is reflected in many of today's computer workstations, in which all the communications and support tools required for adequate job performance are reportedly incorporated.

In his efforts to build sets of organizational routines that can be incorporated into computer applications, CSCW designer Anatole Holt describes "an active organized work area" (that is, an office or other workplace) as akin to an "organization machine":

"Organization machines" are in some ways similar to and in other ways different from, other typical machines. Like all ordinary machines, organization machines really are physically organized utilitarian structures, with static as well as moving parts. Their parts are described in terms that the work participants understand, such as "the conference room," "the Xerox machine," "Building 20," "parking lot B," "the mechanical drawings," and "my memo." (Holt, 1988, p. 111)

Holt (1988) contrasts "organization machines" with machines in general by stating that in the former "their users are in them instead of outside of them" (p. 111). Holt developed the notion of a "diplan language," a formalized graphical language for describing organizational activities, as the underpinnings for his CSCW applications. Holt asserts that "diplans describe organization machines." Diplans are designed to make the "motions" and "connections" of the organization machine explicit; Holt argues that diplans do not create novel ways of conceptualizing coordination, but expose and support already-present notions. Diplans are intended to have effects on individual behavior by "lead[ing] their users to take the physical and responsibility aspects of human work into account" (p. 124). Diplans are parts of functional descriptions of "coordination environments" (CEs), which are " 'electronic territories' under unified administration in which work communities and their constituent organizations, teams, and work groups can set up to conduct business electronically" (p. 121). CEs are described in system software packages called "coordination bases": "Just as operating systems 'understand' programs and program relationships, so coordination bases 'understand' diplans and diplan relations" (p. 121). Holt says that diplans express more than computer operations, however; they are specifically developed for "expressing, organizing, and coordinating" the activity of individuals in terms of spatial relations (p. 120).

As with Leffingwell's organizational "routines," Holt's interdependent work plans, linked in a coordination base, are designed to create efficient organizational processes. Holt (1988, pp. 123–124) describes the following benefits for organizational participants:

- There is less to remember and less to think about in order to keep coordinated with one another.

- The routine aspects of working yield to mechanization, leaving the non-routine to personal management. Since what is routine and what is non-routine changes over time (sometimes rapidly), adaptability is an essential feature.

- There is greatly improved contextual information to guide what one chooses to do.

- A uniform operating style prevails, encompassing wide domains of work performed at computers – all of this in the context of physically distributed organizations using a physically distributed medium.

Holt's uniform operating style distinguishes organizational routines (which include many, fairly standardized aspects of communication and interaction among participants) from nonroutine elements of organizational functioning (aspects that require more specific attention from individuals). In Holt's system, the primary control for these routines – including many decisions about who can interact with whom and when – is placed in central authority. Leffingwell's routines required human supervision for their support; in contrast, Holt's routines are primarily rooted in automated control, and "shift coordination effort from the shoulders of participating people into computer-programmed mechanisms" (p. 123).

Such network-based system applications as workflow support environments are providing new sets of routines for positioning the worker. Using these applications, managers, peers, and staff can determine the worker's legitimate areas of functioning. Positioning the worker in physical terms has also been given new dimensions in an age of pagers, lap-top computers, and personal digital assistants (PDAs). Work that required extensive on-site office support can now be performed out of office settings, making work at home, on clients' turf, and in various field settings more feasible. The strategy of moving work out of the office predates the computer. "Lap desks" are old inventions. Thomas Jefferson employed a mahogany lap desk (one with various cubbyholes and a smooth writing surface) in the early 1800s. Lap desks were often a requirement for writing because of the paraphernalia associated with writing: "To create a legible document, one needed a pen holder, nib, a bottle of ink, and a blotter or sander to absorb the ink," as well as other tools such as knives and sealing wax (Kovel and Kovel, 1993, E3).

If a worker is adequately positioned, managers, project team leaders, peers, subordinates, visitors, and others can locate the worker in terms of his or her relation to specific organizational routines, or in relation to various physical settings (and sometimes both); narratives about the worker's activities are more easily constructed. There are also enhanced possibilities for control. When the worker was associated with a specific desk, efforts at positioning were relatively straightforward. When workers are more mobile, and move throughout a building or area (as required for many team activities), positioning is more difficult. *Active Badges* are devices employees wear that increase the level of positioning of employees in contexts of increased mobility by tracking their movements in a building or locale. Information about employee movements can be stored for future processing.

Positioning issues are increasingly focusing on the positions of virtual individuals and groups, rather than the physical locations of workers, although there are a number of analogies between the two issues. Distribution of virtual individuals and groups within organizational contexts is performed in a wide number of modes. Personality and positioning issues have many linkages: some virtual individuals are designed for mass distribution within an organization, and others are targeted for limited contexts and special purposes. Personality and positioning issues can be seen in terms of a matrix: in terms of personality, virtual entities can vary from high to low in terms of expressiveness (from being impersonal to being highly tailored and expressive of those with whom they are associated). In terms of positioning, virtual entities can vary from being specifically positioned (earmarked for certain contexts and locations) to having multiple purposes and being widely positioned (whether or not they are actually given wide distribution, they could well be). Trends in computer support are toward the creation of more highly personalized and widely positioned entities, entities that increasingly speak for those associated with them in a variety of organizational and societal contexts.

Shared work spaces and resources, and the construction of virtual individuals and groups

Affording shared access to various spaces and resources is a central aspect of the construction of a group: "members" are generally afforded more extensive access than "nonmembers." CSCW researchers Ellis,

Gibbs, and Rein (1991) discuss these issues in terms of "access control," emphasizing the need to decrease the likelihood of interference among group members in resource access:

Access control determines who can access what and in what manner. Effective access control is important for groupware systems, which tend to focus activity and to increase the likelihood of user-to-user interference. (Ellis, Gibbs, and Rein, 1990, p. 54)

Ellis et al. assert that access control can be linked with role definition: "If a group task is viewed in terms of its participants' roles, access constraints are usefully specified in terms of roles rather than individuals" (p. 55).

Greif and Sarin (1987, p. 201) declare that two of the most critical issues for CSCW application development are access control and the synchronization of concurrent actions. As with Ellis et al. (1990), Greif and Sarin's system MPCAL (1987, p. 201) defines "roles" in terms of access specifications:

- Each calendar has a collection of role definitions (whose structure is described below), a set of user definitions (listing the names of roles that each named user is allowed to assume), and a default role to be assumed by users who are not specifically named.
- Each role has a name and a description and a set of rules determining access to each type of operation on each type of MPCAL object (for example, SHOW DAY or CHANGE APPOINTMENT).
- Each rule, for a given role and a given operation, is a specification of whether or not a user in the given role can perform the operation in question, and if so, what variant of the operation.

Users may thus have different privileges depending on what roles they are currently playing. Similarly, in the Quilt system for cooperative writing, users with different roles are afforded different levels of access to the shared material (Fish et al., 1988).

Along with network-based CSCW applications, shared working spaces and resources often take the relatively mundane forms of tables and file cabinets, blackboards and whiteboards. In the 1980s, 3M's Post-It Notes (often recognized as one of the most influential and successful recent office innovations) turned ordinary sheets of paper or other printed material into shared working spaces. Individuals can write their suggestions, additions, or comments on the sticky little colored papers and append them to the document in question. Attaching Post-It Notes allows individuals' contributions to be distinguished, while retaining the overall identity and integrity of the group product. Potentials for interference among users (the access control issue) are addressed by having the original document remain unmodified, and suggested corrections and additions merely pasted over the document (or pasted over each other, in some cases).

Personal and shared resources both serve important roles in construction of virtual individuals and groups in organizational contexts. Various physical objects have been utilized to precipitate the formation of virtual individuals and groups and to shape group process. Consider the desk. The Wooton desk (the "King of Desks") was reportedly used by Queen Victoria, as well as many others who had (or believed they had) positions of authority in the last half of the nineteenth century. William S. Wooton of Indianapolis was one of the better-known desk designers in the 1800s, a "great age" for desks (Tenner, 1990). Advertisements for the Wooton desk emphasized the themes of control, order, and mastery:

One hundred and ten compartments, all under one lock and key. A place for everything and everything in its place. Order Reigns Supreme, Confusion Avoided . . . With this Desk one absolutely has no excuse for slovenly habits in the disposal of numerous Papers . . . Every portion of the desk is immediately before the eye. (quoted in Tenner, 1990, p. 12)

Along with the notion of external mastery and control, self-control is also underscored in this advertisement: the desk is designed to help the individual overcome "slovenly habits" concerning paperwork by creating a display that placed relevant paperwork in open view. The advertisement was aimed at the purchaser/user of the desk (who would be an individual of some means, since Wooton desks were top-of-the-line) and provides some evidence that paperwork was considered an overwhelming burden in the upper echelons of society even in the nineteenth century.

Wooton and similar styles of desks were designed for the person who had to serve as manager, personnel officer, and sometimes accountant. The layers of management and administration common in today's organizations were virtually unknown in the nineteenth century. Desks helped to define and distinguish managers and assist them in juggling their many roles. In the era of the Wooton desk, organizations themselves were much smaller in size; even the "large" organizations of the day had no more than a few thousand employees (Coleman, 1974). The bulk of employment opportunities were still related to agriculture and to very small, craft-oriented concerns.

As the average size of organizations increased, desks and other information-handling tools changed. The Wooton desk allowed one individual (possessor of the key) access to the compartments within. The key thus provided an early version of an "access control system." It is possible that this individual could remember what was in all the little drawers, but what of his or her assistant or staff? How could other people access the contents of the desk and understand its system of organization?

The Wooton desk was apparently not intended as group-oriented technology: as partial evidence of this, its associated advertisements were targeted to the tastes and needs of the individual user. The last Wooton desks were produced in the 1890s (Yates, 1989), about the same time that managerial levels began to expand in depth. Invention and dissemination of the tab card (a stiff card placed among papers with a protruding section that carries a label) and associated tabbing schemes helped to displace the multicompartment desk as a primary organizational document-handling and storage vehicle.

Tab cards afforded group-oriented access to various categories of papers for teams of office workers (teams that were growing in number and size in this period). Organizational participants (secretaries, accountants, assistants) could all be educated in the tabbing classification scheme, and the benefits in terms of order and organization would be comparable to having the documents placed in all those little Wooton desk drawers. James Newton Gunn (a management consultant with ties to librarianship who joined the nascent Harvard Graduate School of Business in 1908) is credited with invention and early dissemination of the tab card and other filing strategies (Tenner, 1990).

The tab card and, later, the vertical file shaped how information-oriented work was conducted and viewed. The large file cabinets with tab cards that can be observed in daily use in nearly any of today's offices demonstrate the remarkable versatility and power of this tool. In David W. Duffield's (1926) *Progressive Filing and Indexing for Schools,* there is a succinct definition of the vertical file and its role in stimulating efficient management: ". . . the bringing together, in one place, all correspondence to, from, or about an individual, firm, place, or subject, filed on edge, usually in folders and behind guides, making for speed, accuracy and accessibility" (p. 12). Vertical filing also provided an incentive for limiting each unit of correspondence to a small range of topics, since multiple subjects in a single document made its filing under tabbed topic headings problematic. An expert in records management recommended "as far as practicable each letter be confined to a single subject" (Williams, 1910, p. 19; see also Yates, 1989).

The strategies of limiting a piece of correspondence to one subject and of labeling it appropriately for group access and filing are often incorporated in advice on how to make electronic mail exchange more efficient. Lists of unread electronic messages (and of read but unfiled messages) can grow quickly: many individuals commonly receive several hundred messages a day. A number of informal electronic mail conventions have arisen that (like Williams's advice in 1910 about filing) attempt to place a definite structure on e-mail correspondence and computer conferencing entries, thus streamlining the handling and storage of messages (Belew and Rentzepis, 1990, p. 30):

1. Make good use of the subject line. As a start, I propose we use the Roman Numerals (I, II, etc.) that label the major topics of our syllabus to provide a first-pass indication of where the message fits into our larger conversation . . .
2. Make good use of the To: line. When you're starting a new topic send it to all of us . . . But if you are responding to the message of someone else, send your mail to the person(s) most directly associated with your reply, and simply carbon-copy the rest of us . . .
3. Keep each message pretty short and on one particular point. If you have several things to say, send several messages, each to the appropriate recipients.
4. When referring to others' messages, make the references as clear as possible.

The perceived problem of how to shape expressions so that shared access is feasible has not dissipated. Shared access is construed as requiring genres of correspondence that produce (1) succinct, (2) easily identifiable, and (3) subject-specified units – units that are (4) targeted to a particular audience.

The issue of how much personality should be brought into a piece of business correspondence has been transferred to the realm of e-mail. Yates (1989) describes how in 1923 the New York Board of Education sought to define how business correspondence should look. Memos exchanged within an organization were to be like "miniature reports," sharing their "explicitness, literalness, and cool impersonality of statement." Memos should have a "strictly business-like tone," and be brief and direct (p. 97). Concerns of a similar nature have arisen in relation to computer-mediated correspondence. Discussions of how much informality and personal style should be allowed in workplace exchanges are common. The notion that e-mail exchanges should be seen as closer to "conversations" than "minireports" (the latter being the form most memos have taken) has become fairly popular. Meticulously edited memoranda are often construed as products of an e-mail neophyte.

Problems relating to "flaming" in e-mail and computer conferencing – a demonstrated surfeit of personal and emotional content – have concerned social scientists, organizational researchers, and managers (Kiesler,

Siegel, & McGuire, 1984; Kiesler, Zubrow, Moses, & Geller, 1985; Dubrovsky, 1987). Flaming involves the expression of heightened emotion in a computer-mediated exchange – for example, passion (as in steamy love letters sent online) or anger (in a style of confrontation and bluntness). Explanations of flaming include the possibility that the rich variety of norms for face-to-face and paper-based interaction (norms pertaining to how individuals are to regard and treat each other) have apparently not yet successfully transferred to computer-mediated interaction (Oravec, 1989b). Heim (1987) attributes flaming to a mix of e-mail features: messages can be written with dispatch, they arrive instantaneously, and yet they can be read at leisure. The first two features may make individuals feel that it is unnecessary for them to buffer possibly disturbing, personally directed messages with small talk and other conversational niceties; the last feature gives the receiver the opportunity to examine, analyze, and steam over the messages at length. The phrase "transmit in haste, repent in leisure" is an appropriate characterization of the effect of flaming on individuals and their careers.

Preprocessing of personal expression – for example, buffering emotionally charged messages with small talk – is a common feature of interaction and an element in the management of impressions. I not only deliver my message to you, but I give you cues (both verbal and nonverbal) about how I'd like you to receive it. An example in face-to-face communication is the way we often accompany a request with a smile or a wink, with the strategy of influencing how the request is received by others.

A correlate of preprocessing in the world of e-mail interaction is the strategic use of small versus capital letters ("jO aNN"), double and triple punctuation ("!!!"), and various nonletter symbols ("%") as part of signaling a potential "flame." Preprocessing can send a notice that an emotionally charged message is about to be delivered, with the aim of somewhat softening its potential effect on the recipient. Various conventions have arisen along these lines in research organizations and institutions of higher education, places where many individuals have gained years of experience in e-mail interaction. The new varieties of computerized exchanges (e-mail, e-mail with graphics and voice, and so on) may be best characterized not as speech or formal writing, but as new forms of linguistic entities; each has its own variations of syntax and pragmatics. These emerging entities have some elements that users have consciously designed: widespread awareness of flaming (and recognition of the need for "flame retardants") have stimulated the creation and adoption of specific mechanisms for ameliorating its effects.

With the widespread availability of CSCW applications, the preprocessing, framing, and labeling of correspondence may play increasingly salient organizational and social roles. Information Lens is an early, influential CSCW e-mail system that employs "semistructured messages," which are "messages of identifiable types, with each type containing a known set of fields, but with some of the fields containing structured text or other information" (Malone, Yates, and Benjamin, 1987, p. 116). Malone et al. discuss the benefits (the "surprising usefulness") of semistructured messages in terms of their efficient processing and preprocessing of correspondence:

Semistructured messages enable computers to process a much wider range of information than would otherwise be possible [italics removed]. By letting people compose messages that already have much of their essential information structured in fields, we eliminate the need for any kind of automatic parsing or understanding of free text while still representing enough information to allow quite sophisticated processing of the messages. (Malone et al., 1987, p. 116)

With Information Lens, receivers can specify rules for automatically filtering and classifying incoming messages into "folders" (rules that apply the same set of dimensions and categories used by senders in constructing the messages).

Malone and his colleagues provide the following vignettes of user inspiration and insight (that is, how users have projected the future of semistructured message capabilities):

Two of the people in our informal interviews mentioned simple examples . . . One remarked about how helpful it would be if any memo requesting some kind of action included, in a prominent place, the deadline by which the action needed to be taken; a second commented about how wonderful it would be if all meeting invitations he received included a field about why he was supposed to be there. (Malone et al., 1987, p. 117)

Individuals select which kind of semistructured message to use in a particular situation (in other words, they preprocess their own correspondence). Information Lens message types can also be defined by their users. Lens developers assert that they are not sure whether the number of useful message types developed by users will be in the dozens or orders of magnitude larger; they state their intent to observe user-initiated activity in this area.

Even without the benefit of Information Lens–style semistructured message types, the task of reviewing a piece of correspondence for its possible relevance to its intended recipient can be largely taken on by the recipient's own "active agent" or "surrogate." The agent can be programmed with the expressed preferences of the individual and with the ability to recognize when those requirements are met by a unit of

correspondence. How a piece of correspondence is framed or prepro-
cessed will determine its inclusion or exclusion from the higher-priority
slots, and thus increase its likelihood of ultimately being noticed by its
intended (human) recipient.

With employment of active agents, message length considerations may
not be critical: the agent or surrogate may be able to do some simple
summarizing or key word extraction (or even make grammatical alterations for those offended by certain stylistic variations). These capabilities
could address dimensions of the cultural object of efficiency in the realm
of business correspondence without much direct effort on the part of the
individuals involved. For example, time that writers spend pruning and
editing lengthy, rambling messages (and the time readers spend plowing
through them) could be utilized elsewhere; however, some aspects of
personal style in interaction may be diminished in importance. (Other
issues involving the role of agents in personal expression are discussed in
a later chapter.)

Desk set: Constructing the individual and workgroup in office settings

The desk – commonly a flat surface near which an individual's chair is
placed – organizes and distinguishes more than the task activity itself. An
individual's range of working functions can be reflected in this space.
Many of today's organizational participants need not move from their
chairs and desks to do what is considered a "day's work."

Many current computer workstation designs have followed a similar
theme, attempting to combine most of the working tools an individual is
called on to access on one machine (if not on one screen, in a "windowed"
configuration). The very name "workstation," which has, with little objection, become a standard term for a variety of large-scale, graphics- or
numerical-processor-enhanced personal computers since the mid-1980s,
implies that individuals should be able to perform their tasks without
moving from this restricted setting, or even shifting their gazes more than
a few inches away from the computer screen. Airborne extensions of
these individual workspaces have been developed by Douglas Aircraft in
its double-deck MD-12.

The file cabinet provides much the same organizing and segregating role
for the group as the desk does for the individual worker. The centralized
file cabinet is often considered "group property." In many organizations,
however, the individual worker's desk and associated space have retained
a veneer of privacy and are often protected against invasion by both
custom and benign legal rulings. Controversies over how "personalized"
individuals' desks or working areas can become (for example, what indi-

vidually chosen decorations they can surround themselves with in the work setting) have often been heated. Aesthetic- and efficiency-related benefits of standardization among desks in a certain area are often explicitly weighed against employees' rights of choice and self-expression (see Sundstrom & Sundstrom, 1986). Granting employees rights to express themselves in workplace contexts has been construed as a way to compensate for other job perquisites, as in this account in a widely circulated business magazine:

The rewards of the past – more space, a windowed office, a larger staff – have become too costly in the face of high rents, collaborative work styles, and new technology . . .
Psychologists tell corporations to compensate for lost perks by giving employees more control – even if it remains intangible. Managers need to foster what Steele calls "tactical autonomy" among employees: the fine art of getting work done by choosing one's own work habits and shaping one's own workplace. (Flanagan, 1990, p. 115)

Workplace decoration rights are being increasingly linked to the autonomy granted to employees. Flanagan argues that employees should be allowed the amount of leeway they require in order to instill some element of personal expression into the environment:

Personalization – the act of decorating the workstation with private mementos or using eccentric filing habits – was anathema to the tidy office-scape of the 1980s. Now, the behavioral experts maintain, family photos establish personal turf; managed clutter is a form of self-expression. (Flanagan, 1990, p. 115)

These shifts in managerial strategies concerning workplace personalization are opening up markets for associated products, such as adjustable trays and racks for employee gear.

The ability to control one's own territory (for example, whether to allow others in, keep them out, or personalize the space somehow) is construed by Goffman (1971) as being "somehow central to the subjective sense that the individual has concerning his selfhood, his ego, the part of himself with which he identifies his positive feelings" (p. 60). Claims on one's physical surroundings – on the "territories of the self," in Goffman's phraseology – play critical roles in constructing self and group. From the choice of what pictures and colors to have on one's PC screen saver to the placement of political posters, the workplace provides an arena for delineation of self–group boundaries. Extensions of these territorial restrictions and affordances in the realm of "information" are the topics of the next section.

The information resource: Centralized databases and "informating" work

Some managerial theorists have recommended that the centralized office file cabinet become electronic, and its reach extended to the entire organization. Advanced information technologies have been called on to "informate" work (a word coined by Zuboff, 1988) – and thus serve as aids in dispersing information about various aspects of organizational processes to every level of the workforce. These technologies include multimedia computing (Johnston, 1990) and hypermedia. Zuboff (1988) pictures the organization of the future as being focused around a central database. "Members can be thought of as being arrayed in concentric circles around a central core, which is the electronic data base" (p. 396). "Intellective skills" play critical roles in Zuboff's formulation. They are skills required to construct linkages between various symbols in the database and an objective "reality" (with the linkages thereby constructed having a certain degree of general consensus, as well as managerial approval).

What would happen if different kinds of constructions emerge – if managerial constructions differ from those of lower-level employees, for instance? The constructions of "meaning" that Zuboff describes appear to be relatively unproblematic and without conflict or differences of opinion. In Zuboff's ideal organization, all organizational participants are involved to some extent in "learning" – that is, contributing to the central core of information and acquiring new intellective skills.

Zuboff contrasts the kinds of group organization that were associated with "action-centered skills" (noninformation work) with those that will emerge when a focus on intellective skills predominates:

The social psychology of group life in a world of action-centered skills is likely to differ from collective activity in an informated environment that places a premium on the exercise of intellective skill. In the first case, the context is more likely to be accepted as a given, and action know-how is displayed within that context. (Zuboff, 1988, p. 206)

In contrast, the informated organization is focused around the "dynamic, electronic text." Individuals are drawn into sharing their accumulated information and exchanging perspectives as to its interpretation:

In an informated environment, the electronic text displays the organization's work in a new way. Much of the information and know-how that was private becomes public. Personal sources of advantage depend less than developing mastery in the interpretation and utilization of the public, dynamic electronic text. This kind of mastery benefits from real collaboration. Communicative compe-

tence requires psychological individuation, which introduces a new sense of mu-
tuality and equality into group life. (Zuboff, 1988, p. 206)

Zuboff's vision is that cooperation and group cohesion will follow from
the construction and maintenance of a centralized databank. She assumes
that individuals' reluctance to share information will generally not subvert
these efforts, and that there will be enough consensus as to the interpretation of the information to afford "intellective skills" the status of "skills,"
that is, relatively unproblematic and teachable tools for linking sets of
abstractions with organizational reality.

Zuboff follows a long line of twentieth-century managerial theorists
who seek to centralize the "information resource" – and thus lessen the
control individuals and groups have over the information associated with
them. Treating information as a resource is generally held to imply that it
should be centrally managed and controlled (forms of control similar to
those given many other institutional resources). Even though they might
not be knowledgable of technical aspects of databases, Zuboff contends
that managers should become closely involved in the control of the organization's information resources.

The notion of information as a resource and related economic and social
concepts are linked with an ongoing societal discourse on the place of
information in society. Advocates of such notions have documented the
transformation of the U.S. economy from an agricultural, to an industrial,
and then to an informational base (following Machlup, 1962; Bell, 1973;
and Porat, 1977). Perceived needs for standardized accounting and handling of information resources have been given some academic underpinnings, as well as support in legislative efforts (including the Paperwork
Reduction Act, P.L. 96–511). They have also been upheld by various
members of the professional communities of data processors, record han-
dlers, managers, and public administrators (Horton, 1979). A large per-
centage of the techniques and methodologies considered under the rubric
of "information resources management" are directly borrowed from other
resource management strategies (such as those established for manufacturing and human resources).

Strategies of separating information from the groups and individuals
who are associated with it and of instituting forms of information control
are some of the means through which administrators and managers have
attempted to precipitate the formation of a focused group outlook, a
common work effort, and a unified reflection of the group's external
environment. Zuboff and others purport that care, maintenance, and utilization of a centralized database will unite the entire organization (or in the
case of CSCW applications, the group associated with the application).

Gathering around the table: Work tables, conference tables, and seating arrangements

Consider now the conference tables found in the meeting areas and board-rooms of many offices, schools, and universities. Whether or not a conference table is used in a meeting or for other occasions (for instance, the table may be used for a holiday party's refreshments) most organizational participants still can glean some information about its intended functions from certain of its physical facts and its relation to other objects in the room. There are generally from 10 to 18 seats at such tables, thus underscoring the "appropriate" number of individuals in a face-to-face working group; a "small group" generally has less than 20 or 30 members (Olson, 1971; Shaw, 1981). The tables are often rectangular or oblong shaped. Other objects in the room (for example, black- or whiteboards, overhead projectors, and other focal points) are usually placed in relation to the table so that a "head" of the table (a place that the discussion leader or other major figure may sit at) is designated, and a "natural" focus of group attention established. Efforts to establish a head of a conference table are comparable to the ways family structures are reinforced through placement of parental figures in a certain position around dining room tables.

Sociologist Dorothy Smith describes the role played by meeting room tables in the symbolic separation of "talking heads" from flesh-and-blood, functioning bodies:

The table surface organizes meetings of people around it; it differentiates the body parts above and below it, stashing away the lower part of the body and allowing the talking heads to function with a discreet suppression of legs and genitals under the table. (Smith, 1990, p. 201)

The talking heads arrangement described by Smith is another tool through which information (in this case, the group member's oral contribution) is distinguished from his or her other personal expressions and associations. Consider alternative arrangements, such as those used in the encounter and discussion groups popular in the 1960s and 1970s. Without tables or other physical boundaries or barriers, individuals would face each other (perhaps while seated in a circle) and view each other as physically whole individuals (as in the encounter groups described in Oden, 1972, and Lieberman, Yalom, & Miles, 1973).

Some recent research efforts have targeted the question of how to afford groups the opportunity to "personalize" (or, rather, "groupicize") their meeting room setting. Zimmer and Cornell (1990) assert their aim of supporting the rise of teamwork in corporate America through the development of such flexible arrangements. Zimmer and Cornell's group work spaces use easily repositioned tables, chairs, lounge furniture, rolling partitions, and storyboards; they assert that response to the spaces by users has been positive.

Joseph Kauffman of the University of Wisconsin at Madison relates a story about the early days of the Peace Corps in the 1960s and how its director, Sargent Shriver, utilized room size as a strategic tool for generating group momentum. Meetings of various sorts would be scheduled in rooms much smaller than needed, with the crowding reportedly affording the participants the feeling that something exciting was about to happen. After the room would be packed to overflowing, meeting participants would leave to find and then readjourn in a bigger room – gathering other interested meeting participants in their journey through the hallways.

Although they are considered to be critical social factors today, the potential impacts of physical and spatial entities on social situations were understated in sociology until the 1930s. One of the first sociologists to emphasize the importance of the interactions of the physical and spatial environment with the social realm was Emory S. Bogardus (1931), who asserted that "it is only as social and physical facts can be reduced to, or correlated with, spatial facts that they can be measured at all." Steinzor's (1950) research in discussion group seating arrangements around a conference table was among the first to document these interactions.

Identification of the "Steinzor effect" stimulated many studies on and much concern about the physical–social nexus. The "effect" was that people sitting directly opposite each other in a conference room setting – that is, individuals who can see each other without turning their heads – tend to interact more frequently. Hearn (1957) found that leadership can serve an intervening variable in the Steinzor effect. With minimal leadership, the Steinzor effect held (individuals directed more comments to those across the table). However, when leadership was strong (that is, when an active leader was involved in the discussion), individuals directed more of their comments to those sitting in adjacent seats. The Hearn study has triggered interest in the role that eye contact plays in discussion groups. Presence of a strong leader may encourage individuals to restrict their glances to those physically closest (Sommer, 1969) or to those who are between their line-of-sight and the leader.

A number of office and educational environment features have been intentionally designed to direct our attention and focus, and thus to shape the ways we interact with each other. CSCW applications are entering educational, office, and professional environments that already have been arranged in ways intended to encourage or discourage the conduct and formation of relationships. Library seating arrangements, for instance, are often configured in a manner that is intentionally "sociofugal":

> Knowledge of how groups arrange themselves can assist in fostering or discouraging relationships. A library that is intended to be sociofugal space, where interaction is discouraged, requires knowledge of how to arrange people to minimize unwanted contact. One possibility is to use the rank order of preferred arrangements of interacting groups as arrangements to be avoided in sociofugal space. (Sommer, 1969, pp. 72–73)

Sommer recommends that "corner" seating (the type of seating that would encourage communication in many seating arrangements) should be avoided in libraries and substituted by opposite or distant seating.

Messages from space: How to influence people with spatial arrangements

The notion that socialized individuals are able to decipher information conveyed symbolically through various architectural settings and space allocations is a common theme in many recent perspectives on design; this perspective thus leads designers to include in their set of design issues the question of what messages should be conveyed. CSCW application designer Holt (1989b) asserts that buildings and roads provide coordination signals that individuals can translate. Mehrabian (1976) contends that there is an implicit "dominance hierarchy" in many office buildings, one that reinforces social status structures of organizations:

> Few office buildings are designed for a particular company and its particular needs; rather, there is a more or less standard set of floor plans which assume that the company, whether it has forty employees or 4,000, will have a pyramidal organization, with most of the employees forming the base and a handful forming the apex. To properly reflect this dominance hierarchy, the floor plans usually embody a reverse pyramid in terms of space and design, allotting the most space and the most desirable locations to the fewest number of employees . . . In large, older buildings, individual floors often express the dominance aspects implicit in the hierarchy. (Mehrabian, 1976, pp. 140–141)

Mehrabian asserts that even within the floor plans of such buildings, there are "intricate formal and informal patterns of status" (p. 141), patterns that adequately socialized and aware individuals are able to interpret.

One of the philosophical movements that has provided underpinnings and inspiration for architectural efforts and that also has useful parallels in some current computer applications design initiatives is the German

Bauhaus movement. One of the major themes of the movement is that introduction of architecture into an environment imposes a set of cultural values on residents (Hooper, 1986). Leaders of the movement developed a set of design concepts rooted in the assumption that architecture has a predictable and controllable impact on human beings; they recommended that designers make choices among alternative design options on the basis of these projected impacts. Hooper and others have mapped strong similarities between the design perspectives of the Bauhaus movement and those of a number of software developers who assume that cultural values can be imparted to users in various computer applications.

The "open office" movement is an architectural initiative that also has strong linkages with trends in computer system design. Its prominence peaked in the 1970s, but it still has a number of strong proponents today. Rationales for the institution of open plan offices are often based on implicit behavioral assumptions about the positive impacts physical proximity has on office workers (Crouch and Nimran, 1989a). Simply put, many open office advocates purport that removing office walls and placing workers in closer contact (the essence of the open plan) will improve their ability to communicate with each other, and hence will increase productivity.

Some research results on the impacts of open plan office settings support these design rationales: for example, Allen and Gerstberger's (1973) results show an increase in communication and coordination after the office setting they observed was shifted to an open plan. Other results provide contrary evidence. Sundstrom, Herbert, and Brown (1982) observe no change in ease of communication among workers after a similar open plan shift. Crouch and Nimran's (1989a) research on open plan offices supports the notion that presence of other individuals in a worker's environment (rather than the physical features of a setting) is the primary influence on behavior. Focuses on "social presence" in the literature on computer-mediated interaction provide a parallel to Crouch and Nimran's perspective. In a pioneering effort, Williams (1977) asserts that social presence, or "a feeling of contact" among group members, decreases with the use of conferencing strategies that do not include face-to-face association; he claims that with lower "bandwidth" (fewer channels of communication), there is less social presence. Hence, telephone conversations (in which only sounds are exchanged) supposedly have less social presence than videophone conversations.

A number of CSCW designers have employed similar assumptions, contending that the use of high-bandwidth vehicles, or the increase of bandwidth by employing several vehicles for interaction (such as the combination of video and computer conferencing), can simulate social proximity. Abel describes the following results from a video link of two research facilities, 600 miles apart:

> Our experience showed that there was a sense of group cohesion in our distributed lab despite the 600-mile gap between the sites. Personal and working relationships were able to grow between distributed lab members. How were these things possible? We might speculate that they were possible primarily because we were able to simulate physical proximity to some extent via technology. (Abel, 1990, p. 506)

Some designers have believed that considerations of physical presence are critical enough to propose the creation of whole-body electronic representations as "stand-ins" for their owners at conferences (Heeter, 1992). Electronic meeting rooms are designed to take advantage of the reported power of social presence to stimulate intellectual productivity by incorporating workstations – as well as various projection devices and shared displays – in a "conference room" setting.

Electronic meeting rooms: Merging workstations, shared displays, and conference tables

Early electronic meeting room prototypes were developed by Douglas Engelbart in the 1960s and 1970s. One of the best-known pioneering initiatives in electronic meeting room development is the PlexCenter Planning and Decision Support Laboratory at the University of Arizona, which combines eight networked personal workstations on a U-shaped conference table. Workstations on the conference table are positioned so that participants can see over them (and thus maintain the kind of eye contact common in conference room settings). The PlexCenter setting includes four "break-out" rooms for caucusing, as well as a projection system and large screen so that a common display can be viewed; material from the individual participants' screens can be placed on the common display. The PlexCenter can also accommodate large group meetings.

The Nick meeting room environment combines a network of eight workstations, clustered in a rectangular table setting, and an electronic blackboard that all participants can view from their seats. Users can speak to each other directly, enter both private and shared information into their workstations, and contribute and manipulate shared resources on the electronic blackboard (Rein and Ellis, 1989). Many electronic meeting rooms are designed with the express purpose of combining one or more of the following: (1) the influences associated with social presence, (2) users' previous associations with seminar or conference rooms, and (3) the ability to communicate face-to-face as well as in computer-mediated vehicles.

"Clearboard" CSCW applications also utilize the power of social presence by allowing pairs of collaborators to see the faces of their co-workers superimposed on their working spaces. Clearboards (such as *TeamWorkStation*) are designed so that the directions of the gazes of the collaborators are ascertainable by co-workers (Ishii, 1990). Clearboards incorporate translucent overlays of individual workspace images, a technique that involves "superimposing two or more translucent live video images of computer screens or physical desktop surfaces. The overlay function created with this video synthesis technique allows users to combine individual workspaces, and to point to and draw on the overlaid images simulaneously" (Ishii and Miyake, 1991, p. 41).

Face-to-face meetings often employ a shared display of some sort. Most electronic room configurations also incorporate a single shared display area. Latour and Woolgar (1979) label such vehicles as "inscription devices," or artifacts for representation. One of the major inscription devices employed in education, business, and research for the past several centuries is the blackboard (or its recent counterpart, the whiteboard). In scientific research, blackboards serve a number of functions, as captured in this account of the blackboard-based interchanges in Crick and Brenner's laboratories:

On any given morning at the Laboratory of Molecular Biology in Cambridge, one observer writes, the blackboard of Francis Crick or Sydney Brenner will commonly be found covered with logical trees. On the top line will be the hot new result just up from the laboratory or just in by letter or rumor. On the next line will be two or three alternative explanations, or a little list of "what he did wrong." Underneath will be a series of suggested experiments or controls that can reduce the number of possibilities. And so on. The tree grows during the day (Schrage, 1990, pp. 93–94)

The gesturing and pointing to blackboard inscriptions that often accompanies their production provide a visual aspect to the presentation that an individual (or team) makes to other group members. This animation generally serves to be the focus of participants' active displays of attention, even when the individual who has the chalk is not the one who is currently speaking. It is indeed hard not to follow the person at the chalkboard with our eyes, even if our minds are on our taxes or where to get dinner that night. Controlling group members' involvement in a conference setting has been a long-standing concern for management; Goffman (1974) describes how lecturers also have the problem of maintaining at least the appearance of common involvement on the part of the group. Blackboards and other common displays have considerable roles in sustaining this involvement and in organizing the theatrics of group interaction. Willard C. Brinton (1914) in *Graphic Methods for Presenting Facts* reports that reflecting lanterns (or lanterns used with slides) were occasionally used to project charts or graphs on the wall so that meeting participants could share information and maintain a common focus in meetings (p. 304). Today, utilizing light pens and highly stylized colored graphics to perform these tasks has generated concern about the graphics' capacities to mesmerize their audiences and inhibit critical thinking.

Constructing a common focus or narration in a meeting room situation often involves the use of a pointer or similar device on a readily visible projected document or display. Except for face-to-face meetings, however, most facilities for group exchange have the capability of transmitting physical marks or inscriptions, but cannot convey to group members a sense of the activity that went into making those marks or inscriptions. This omission is apparently of critical importance in some contexts; for example, in their studies of group design sessions, Bly and Minneman (1990) assert that the activity of creating and using marks on a writing surface such as a whiteboard is "as important as the marks themselves" (p. 184). Suchman (1988b) hypothesizes that use of a whiteboard for communication among researchers is a "second interactional floor, co-extensive and sequentially interleaved with that of talk" (p. 320). She states that the whiteboard may be used to (1) document the talk and thereby display the writer's understanding; (2) continue the writer's previous turn; or (3) project the writer's next turn, thus providing objects to be used in subsequent talk. In some cases, two or more users may have control over whiteboard space.

The role of whiteboards and similar artifacts is one of constructing group expression from individual contributions – a critical transition that is usually closely managed by group members. The whiteboard is not individual property, or group property, but both. It and its associated inscriptions stimulate and play a role in creative production by providing a common group space. When individuals place an item on a whiteboard, they signal that it has become (to some extent) common group property and thus open to expansion and linkage to other items by members of the group. The private idea or comment becomes public. Inscriptions placed on the board may (or may not) retain association with the individuals who contributed them originally, with the likelihood of this depending on a number of factors (including demographic ones such as age, race, and gender and agreements of group members). Mere physical identification of the marks made on the board with the individual who produced them does not ensure continuing individual–mark–idea associations.

Use of the whiteboard for dramatic displays and emphasis is apparently common in design efforts; Bly and Minneman recorded and classified the activities of physically copresent designers who used a shared drawing surface, visible to all group members:

> In every session, the designers rapidly moved among drawing, writing, and gesturing, frequently performing all of these actions within the space of a few seconds. When possible, the designers used the drawing surface regularly for references . . . All sessions were characterized by frequent use of the drawing surface for emphasis. (Bly and Minneman, 1990, p. 186)

Telephone sessions among designers were observed by Bly and Minneman; even in those sessions (where the designers could not see each other) they actively created marks and employed gestures to punctuate their oral expression.

The Commune system (Xerox PARC) was modeled on a "shared pad of paper," a "sequence of sheets through which the user could page back and forth" (Bly and Minneman, 1990, p. 186). Commune is intended to support designers who work remotely but co-synchronously in teams. Design goals of system developers (p. 186) include the following:

1. Each designer's marks and gestures must be visible simultaneously to all other designers.
2. Designers must be able to switch quickly among drawing, writing, and gesturing.
3. All designers must be able to mark and gesture in the shared space simultaneously.
4. The tool should be as "natural" as possible (for example, a familiar writing/drawing instrument, marks appearing at the point of input).

Commune's workstations have a digitizer and penlike stylus, as well as a horizontally oriented monitor. In the attempt to meet Commune's design goals, its cursor can be employed either for writing or drawing, as well as be moved without making marks (so that the cursor can be used for gesturing and dramatic emphasis). Each of the cursors and associated marks have a distinctive color so that an individual's activities are linked with him or her. Cursor actions are transmitted to all of the stations in the network.

Direct linkage of an individual with a mark through color coding may affect some of the negotiations concerning who is responsible for the sequence of ideas that follow and are linked with the mark, but this in no way ensures that the individual will be considered the originator of, or even maintain association with, these ideas. Once part of "group space," however, direct and simple individual–mark–idea linkages are generally not the primary issue (unless group members choose to engage in a discussion that backtracks a narrative sequence for purposes of establishing credit).

Identification of a mark and associated idea with an individual can serve as another source of labeling and help to distinguish the ideas produced in a certain situation; as the kinds and number of ideas climb in a particular meeting, a variety of different identification devices are generally utilized. Even with an established procedural mechanism for idea identification, context-sensitive conventions can develop: an idea can be associated with labels such as "Sally's comment" or "the first point we discussed after lunch." The individual–mark–color linkages provided in CSCW applications such as Commune may play some role in negotiations concerning who is the "narrator" of a certain sequence, and thus who has some right to extend the narrative sequence further – but, again, the negotiations are many-factored and may produce varying results.

The transition from a set of individual contributions to a group product through means of a shared space can be problematic. In the "Capture Lab" electronic meeting room, Halonen et al. (1990) explored "hardware sharing" notions. Their system involves a "public machine" (connected to a projection device, with all members being able to view the common projection) that is networked with eight privately controlled workstations arranged in a conference table–style configuration. The "clipboard transfer" facility (provided by the Macintosh operating system) is the method employed for transferring data from the private workstations to the public machine (the "shared space"):

A user may copy a portion of a document to his or her clipboard, access the public machine, and paste from the clipboard into a document on the public machine. Alternatively, a user may transfer information from the public computer to his or her individual machine, for example, to further develop or reword material individually. (Halonen et al., 1990, p. 165)

Halonen et al. found that users preferred "social protocol" (informal discussion) as a means for regulating access to the public machine rather than the more elaborate, enforced systems designed by Capture Lab researchers. (Users of the Lab were all clustered around a single table, however, so the social protocol mechanisms were not tested over a distance.)

In relation to their "electronic chalkboard" efforts, Stefik, Bobrow,

Foster, Lanning, and Tatar outline the WYSIWIS notion ("What you see is what I see"):

WYSIWIS creates the impression that members of a group are interacting with shared and tangible objects. It extends to a group conversation the kind of shared access to information that is experienced by two people sitting together over a sketch. WYSIWIS is the critical idea that makes possible the sense of teamwork illustrated in the barn-raising metaphor. (Stefik et al., 1987, p. 33)

Maintaining WYSIWIS (or relaxed versions of it) becomes complex as a number of actively used, networked workstations are involved. For instance, individuals may want to work independently for a while and later display their efforts; strict WYSIWIS entails that everyone sees where everyone else is pointing to and has access to what they are doing. The systems Boardnoter and Cognoter described by Stefik et al. both relax WYSIWIS to some extent, yet attempt to afford construction of a shared group resource.

Every picture tells a story

Research and analysis of the use of video in group contexts may help to illuminate some of the problems and potentials of CSCW applications. Video is often a component of CSCW applications, as described in Mackay (1988); in this section, its use will be described in ways that may or may not depend on its integration into the applications. Whether or not an explicit CSCW component, video has aspects of use that are similar in important ways to the current set of CSCW initiatives.

Videos and films can provide a common focus for a group – much like the blackboard and other shared displays just discussed. We generally view videos and films in rooms where lights are somewhat dimmed and group attention is focused on a screen or tube. The reverence with which many Americans view the media of video and film can be linked with many hours of family television viewing, hours often spent in a relatively sedate atmosphere and a group setting. The tight coupling with the construction of "real" situations that video and film have established in Western society may have distracted many of the theorists who work with group-oriented video applications in business and education from producing critical analyses of video and its use as a vehicle of expression. The assumptions that "video (or film) reflects reality" and even that "video is reality" are often adopted without significant attempts at analysis. Whittock (1990) declares that despite their metaphorical status, film images "testify to the presence of objects in a direct way that words do not," providing an "existential link to a preexisting world" (p. 22) that is missing in writing. Bazin (1971) compares the process of taking a photograph to that of making a death mask, asserting that "one might consider photography in this sense as a moulding, the taking of an impression, by the manipulation of light."

Both Wollen (1969) and Metz (1974) capture the effect of photography and video in the word "trace":

Because still photography is in a way the trace of a past spectacle – as Andre Bazin has said – one would expect animated photography to be experienced similarly as the trace of a past motion. This, in fact, is not so; the spectator always sees movement as being present (even if it duplicates a past movement). (Metz, 1974).

It took a number of centuries for written words to be considered reflections of "reality," as described in the historical accounts of Eisenstein (1969, 1979) and others. Clanchy (1979), in his account of twelfth-century scholarship, recounts the following description by a medieval author of how "letters" relate to "things": "Fundamentally letters are shapes indicating voices. Hence they represent things which they bring to mind through the windows of the eyes. Frequently they speak voicelessly the utterances of the absent."

Photographic, film, and video technologies apparently took much less time to be accepted as providing reflections of reality. Solomon-Godeau (1986) gives an account of the evolution of documentary photography. She contends that the expression "documentary photograph" was seldom utilized until the late 1920s; before that time, the "preponderance of photographic uses previous to the term's introduction were what we would now automatically designate as documentary" (p. 193). For about a hundred years, the photograph was largely viewed as a "transcriptive" medium:

The late arrival of the category "documentary" into photographic parlance implies that until its formulation, photography was understood as innately and inescapably performing the documentary function. Self-consciously defined art photography aside, to nineteenth century minds the very notion of documentary photography would have seemed tautological. (Solomon-Godeau, 1986, p. 195).

The "designative authority" and documentary value of video, film, and photography described by Solomon-Godeau are apparently still high, even though the abilities of video and photographic technicians to alter and retouch the images are increasing, as is the potential for intentional distortion. These capabilities for distortion may have a substantial impact on construction and dissemination of news, as well as on public trust in news as an information vehicle:

> You look at two TVs – one's got a picture of Ronald Reagan shaking hands with Gorbachev, and the other set has a picture of Ronald Reagan punching Gorbachev in the nose, and you can't tell them apart. One's on videotape and one was synthesized on computer . . . What's going to happen to electronic newsgathering when the validating function of videotape no longer exists? Television will no longer be a verification medium. (Zeltzer quoted by Brand, 1987, p. 223)

Other commentators speculate that the authority now placed in the photographic, video, or film image itself – the authority to "verify" – may be transferred to photographers themselves as professionals or dedicated amateurs (Oravec, 1995). Despite their potential for alteration, the role of videos in the verification of certain social conditions has indeed been enormous. In 1991, a bystander's video of a police beating in Los Angeles verified to a national audience conditions that many inner city residents had been all too familiar with. Later in that year, a high school student's surreptitiously produced video of classroom behavior in Milwaukee city schools displayed for the nation conditions hardly conducive to education. Videos have been strongly associated with the power of the individual to expose injustice and fight back against poverty.

Even in the most simple or amateur video production (with no attempts at retouching), various choices and selections are made that often have dramatic effects on what the vehicle delivers. Through the video involved in teleconferencing and CSCW-related productions, a certain perspective on the individuals being taped is achieved (a perspective that varies depending on whether they are shown as clustered in a group, for example, or in close-up). Choices of perspective and focus provide a kind of narrative, coupling words (that is, who is speaking) and pictures (that is, who or what is pictured), as well as linking scenes across time. Even with these obvious and influential choices, the assumption that an unbiased "reflection of reality" is being produced is prevalent among designers as well as users. The apparent immediacy of video, film, and photography has a strong pull. We need to develop narratives that adequately capture the nuances of retrospection, editing, and shaping in video, film, and photography. Photographers, filmmakers, and video artists certainly have a rich vocabulary that would aid us in our efforts; making those notions more accessible to those of us whose daily interactions in the workplace are now or will soon be videotaped or otherwise captured will help us to develop and be sensitive to these genres.

The diagnostic image: Video self-portraits and group portraits

Video technology has been utilized in group settings for a variety of purposes, including therapeutic. An example of video to assist group psychotherapy efforts is found in Fryrear and Stephens (1988). They investigated the effectiveness of a psychotherapy program using both video and masks to facilitate inter- and intrapersonal communication. Cox and Lothstein (1989) describe the videotaping of group therapy sessions with young adults, and note the "extraordinary appeal" of such a method to a generation reared in front of the television screen. They claim that "it has a seductive power by drawing attention to the exhibitionistic and voyeuristic aspects of the self" (p. 250).

Cox and Lothstein characterize the "videoself" that is composed in a young person's confrontation with the medium as a "public self for all to see, enjoy, admire, and love"; videotaping processes may play a "symbolic mirroring role" for the self, providing a means for the self to unfold its contents. They assert that in group therapy, however (where a number of competing, individual "selves" are revealed), the confrontative power of videotaping comes into play. They claim that the "flaws" of the self become more obvious when "exposed" in such videotaping efforts, and a more vulnerable self may be experienced. The assumption that videos reveal pathologies – that they can serve as powerful diagnostic tools – is strongly demonstrated in Cox and Lothstein's work.

Many of Cox and Lothstein's patients composed "video self-portraits," as well as group portraits; the effect of the former is described in the following way:

> The actual taped product, the self-portrait, may also function for most patients as a kind of observing ego, providing them with the possibility of reinternalizing previously experienced negative emotional states in a new, positive light. The self is no longer experienced as diminished and isolated, but is enhanced and part of a larger totality. (Cox and Lothstein, 1989, p. 250)

In their roles as therapists, Cox and Lothstein advise that such video-based treatment is not self-sufficient (that is, it should be conducted along with other forms of therapy); however, they express a good deal of optimism about its future.

When video cameras first became available for home use, individuals were challenged to "get in touch with reality" by producing video portraits of their own family lives and day-to-day circumstances:

> One of the first things to do when you get a portable home video camera is take it home and live with it. Tape everyday ordinary events: eating, sleeping, talk-

ing, making love . . . You should feel absolutely no compulsion to show these tapes to others, or even save them. This is inherent in the economy of videotape because it's erasable. (Shamberg, 1971)

Shamberg states that in home movies and films, people's behavior is "abnormal" or "forced," partly because the expense of those media compels individuals to perform some activity ("do something") when being filmed. He argues that videotape has been able to capture more realistic imagery because people know it can be overwritten and as a consequence are less active in staging their behavior.

Other attempts to integrate video into psychological therapy and self-actualization efforts include those described in Petitti (1989). Petitti discusses a drama therapy group in which videotape was used as an externalizing object rather than as a reflection of self. "Externalizing objects" are inanimate objects intentionally linked with the roles of significant others in order to establish a fictional relationship to real-life conflicts, a relationship that can be explored in dramatic terms (generally with the help of a psychotherapist).

These and other uses of video can be seen in terms of Mead's (1934) social-psychological framework, in which construction of an "other" – whether the "generalized other" of a community or that of an authority figure – plays a prominent role. Mead's notion that "self arises only when one steps out of immediate subjective experiencing and becomes an object to oneself" is readily linked to the study of video-based group therapy. Videotaping has been used to assist in this temporary objectification:

Suddenly, the self is not swimming amorphously somewhere beneath the skin but is being represented upon a screen several feet away from the body. The initial shock effect of this situation has been noted by all observers. (Skafte, 1987, p. 398)

Skafte discusses the initial resistance to video feedback by individuals that is often observed in adults (see also Harrison et al., 1990); she contends that it is related to the fear of entering the reflecting, observing mode.

Video has been used by psychologists and psychotherapists to stimulate role exploration within a group context, as well as to serve as a catalyst for the self-explorations described by Skafte:

As individuals begin to realize the dazzling array of dimensions that each one of them embodies, a new freedom and excitement enters their relationships with each other. The group becomes more than a hall of mirrors. It becomes a hall of doorways that open into new vistas of the self. (Skafte, 1987, p. 400)

Skafte's description of the power of video technology in group proceedings is enthusiastic, but omits consideration of participants' varying perspectives on video as a medium, as well as the inevitable distortions in video imagery previously discussed in this chapter. Constructing "video as reality" can have dramatic effects on the quality of video-focused group psychotherapy. Skafte describes how a number of therapists utilize video technology to create "instant replay" situations (my phrase), confronting individuals with video-captured images of "what really happened" in the group:

Video technology also enables individuals to view themselves more accurately in the group setting. They can witness the immediate effects of their words and actions on others . . . Direct viewing tends to blast through defenses, particularly rationalization and denial . . . By the same token, group members can review certain interactions and discover that, indeed, their original perceptions were correct. (Skafte, 1987, p. 399)

Skafte asserts that video helps group members achieve "more accurate interpretations of the social phenomena around them" (p. 399). These instant replays of group proceedings may distort important aspects of their interaction, however. Seldom does a video slice provide the context needed to understand a situation. Selection of what slice for the group to examine (and reexamine) can give the therapist a large degree of control.

Rhetoric that supports the veracity of the group portrait (the "video as reality" perspective) can play considerable roles in its construction as a shared resource. If various group members consistently concentrate their energies on discussions of their own interpretations of what is on the video screen, attention can be directed away from other, equally vital, group activities; rhetoric can often serve to reduce if not stifle these debates. Just as in the case of the individual portrait (whether in marble, on canvas, or in words), in order for video to be usable as a vehicle for group portraits and diagnostic efforts group members must be able to interpret and identify with the video format to a certain extent. "Interactive plausibility" must be achieved (Oravec, in press): the video must reflect relevant aspects of group process, and of the texture of interaction among group members.

In practical terms, however, a group conference is generally not a video- or film-criticism session (although these can indeed be interesting). A delicate balance is sought: for the group to feel that the video portraits produced are coextensive with the group (and are noncontrovertible evidence of its activities) would invest in the video format far more than would be appropriate and useful. On the other end of the continuum, no identification at all would render the video portraits meaningless; the camera might as well be directed to an empty wall. A tape recording of a string quartet fails to deliver some of the interactive dimensions that can be constructed by eyewitnesses and thus be low in interactive plausibility; similarly, a video recording may catch aspects of visual interaction in two dimensions, but fail in regard to three-dimensional aspects. Mediated expression has limitations, many of which are astoundingly difficult to characterize.

Video and film are tools that are utilized to construct and structure situations. Carroll (1988) suggests that the structural analysis of film reinforces the metaphor that "film is language." In the same way that a linguistic grammar formally partitions the world into sequential and non-sequential objects, a structural theory of film partitions the world into those objects that are – and those that are not – narrative film scenes. Search for a video or film "logic" (a search often comparable with efforts through the ages to construct logics associated with the printed text) has spanned several disciplines, including communication arts, literary criticism, and various social sciences. Sociologist David Altheide (1987) uses the term "mediation" to refer to the influence of the logics of the media involved in the communication process. Media "formats" are "rules for the recognition, organization, and presentation of information and experience" (p. 130), and can consist of such factors as grammar, syntax, rhythm, and style (Altheide, 1985). Media logic refers to the application of rules and procedures that are supposedly "implied" by the various media's formats.

Altheide presents the following example of media logic from television:

TV news allocates air time on the basis of visuals, especially videotape showing drama, conflict, and action. Newsworkers, who take for granted the visual format of TV news, select and approach potential events with these criteria in mind. In short, it is through formats that things look like one kind of experience or another. In the case of television, a program looks like news and not a talk show or a situation comedy, but this understanding itself reflects at least a general familiarity with media logic. (Altheide, 1987, p. 130)

Media indeed provide constraints in expression, as in the example of the string quartet. How these constraints and affordances are constructed and characterized in relation to other media – and whether and to what extent users are familiar with these constraints and affordances – are critical to the way media are viewed and utilized as shared resources.

As described at several junctures in this chapter, users (along with designers and developers) have been involved in a number of ways in modifying resources for purposes of shared access and use, from the shaping of documents to fit the requirements of tabbing schemes to the tailoring of e-mail correspondence for electronic filing purposes. Media logics should not be viewed as sets of mysterious inner qualities and affordances that media manifest in their utilization, but as general approaches for the construction of genres suitable for group discussion, development, and record keeping.

The "sound bite" of network TV news and much of video production provides an example of constructing a shared resource. The public's awareness of the fact that TV airtime is a limited quantity has triggered general discussion of how news is packaged in small, readily deliverable units (as well as of some of the political and social ramifications of this practice). Politicians and other public figures now attempt to talk in sound bites for the camera; even random observers interviewed in real-life accident situations are to some extent aware of the network news' constraints and attempt to conform to them. I recently was involved in taping and editing "off-the-street" interviews for a large-scale video project; the individuals I interviewed for the most part were keenly aware of our time and taping limitations (except for one extraordinarily long-winded college professor). In this example, shared resources (network news clips and documentary footage) were being constructed – objects for subsequent analysis and discussion – and many individuals actively sought out information on how best to contribute to this overall effort.

Our national fascination with video distortion techniques and "morphing" (combination of a series of images so that one blends into another) is demonstrated by their utilization in many music videos and commercials. Correlates of the statistical notions of "averaging" or "norming" are moved into the realm of the image. We can see an "average citizen" through the morphing of facial images. Synergistic applications of computer, photographic, and video techniques have thus become part of the "logic" of film and video. Another form of synergy is found in some recent applications that associate specific objects on the video screen with textual explanations. Film and video logic must increasingly consider such synergies among media and consider the relevant social transitions – transitions of comparable influence to those sound had in transforming the silent movie into a "talkie."

Capturing group interaction: Videoconferencing and CSCW research in video

Before videoconferencing, there was the Picturephone, the concept of which was first explored by Bell Labs in the 1920s (Ives, 1930; Egido, 1988). In the late 1960s, Bell Telephone forecast that one million Picturephones would be in operation by 1985 (Dunlop, 1970). However, at the same time, some technical problems were also announced by Bell: if 10% of Bell subscribers desired these phones, Bell projected it would have to double the size of its exchanges.

Julius Molnar (executive vice-president of Bell Laboratories) declared in a 1969 *Bell Laboratories Record* that Picturephone service, like telephone service, would "enrich the lives of everybody":

Most people when first confronted with Picturephone seem to imagine that they will use it mainly to display objects or written matter, or they are very much concerned with how they will appear on the screen of the called party. (from Martin, 1977, p. 141)

Despite these immediate reactions, Molnar predicted the eventual popularity of the Picturephone:

Once the novelty wears off and one can use Picturephone without being self-conscious, he senses in his conversation an enhanced feeling of proximity and intimacy with the other party. The unconscious response that a party makes to a remark by breaking into a smile, or by dropping his jaw, or by not responding at all, adds a definite though indescribable "extra" to the communication process. (from Martin, 1977, p. 141)

Molnar displayed confidence that the Picturephone would succeed both technologically and in the marketplace: "Clearly, 'the next best thing to being there' is going to be a Picturephone call." Technical, economic, and social difficulties led to the early demise of the Picturephone, however. Egido (1988) cites the *Economist*'s 1969 description of the Picturephone as a "social embarrassment" that is akin in use to "talking to a mentally defective foreigner" (p. 15). However, the related technology of videoconferencing maintained experimenters' interest through the 1970s; research on videoconferencing was at a high level from 1972 through 1976 (Kraemer, 1982).

Video is utilized as a part of CSCW application development and research work at the Center for Machine Intelligence (CMI) (Horton, Eluart-Keys, & Kass, 1989). In CMI, video technology is a multipurpose tool: it is employed in efforts to analyze the collaborative work that occurs in CMI's electronic meeting room and to support the activities of the room's users and experimental subjects. CMI's electronic meeting room (mentioned previously) is called the Capture Lab, a name that has interesting connotations: a "captured" account of a certain situation apparently connotes a stronger, more lifelike image than a mere description. Archives of meetings in the Capture Lab include both the video recording of the meeting and all of the participants' computer activity.

Videotapes and computer logs are both time-stamped, which allows the captured computer activity to be used as an index into the video archives. Recording of interaction thus takes place on two, integrated levels.

The Design and Media Spaces Area at Xerox PARC also employs video as a part of its "Media Space" demonstration environments:

> What is a Media Space? It is a system composed of video, audio, and computer technologies that allow individuals and groups to create environments that span physically and temporally disjoint places, events, and realities. It is also a way of working – of being "media aware" – that brings the illusory power of media into everyday work. (Harrison et al. 1990, p. 97)

Media Space research is an "exploration of what the workplace will be like when video communications supplant text" (p. 96).

The Media Space team's experience with video as a tool for the support of design efforts are summarized (Harrison et al., 1990, p. 90) in the following statements:

1. The necessary facility both to use and act effectively in video can be acquired quickly by designers and integrated into work practice.
2. The use of real-time video connection can result in an intense task focus not evident in face-to-face interaction.
3. The medium retains many of the vital qualities of face-to-face interaction (ambiguity, negotiation, visual communication) that are lacking in other representations.
4. Some people resist being recorded on video and do not cooperate in its use; of these, some lose their resistance if they see that video is under their control and can serve them.
5. Backstage is brought onstage. Video tends to diminish the distinction between public and private. By making it more convenient to capture and replay casual elements of design activity to improve design process, more formerly private activity is given public display.

Harrison et al. stress the similarities of video with face-to-face interaction, with the major differences including an observed increase in task focus and the erosion of the backstage–frontstage dichotomy. These two exceptions could most certainly be linked: the notion that formerly private (previously unseen) activity is now being captured in video might serve to stimulate an increase in task focus.

There is already a large amount of documented experience in the use of video for various forms of communication. Educational and business uses of videoconferencing have increased dramatically in the past several years as its availability has increased and a number of technical advances have improved transmission quality. The primary function of such conferences has changed from the avoidance of travel costs to such varied purposes as (1) helping firms manage the process of merging with other firms, (2) educational outreach, (3) corporate training programs, (4) public relations efforts, and (5) releasing new products and services (see Powell, 1989). In 1989, Boeing Corporation already had 400 videoconferencing rooms located on customer sites; Apple Corporation has built a video network of "briefing centers" that are part of its strategy to help sell Apple systems to corporate managers.

Although the educational and business applications of videoconferencing are increasing, one of the reasons that many videoconferences are not a success is that participants are worried (if not obsessed) about their appearances as transmitted via video. Cowan comments that video changes our expectations of what is involved in a conference situation:

Certainly no one would mind if a participant in a face-to-face conference had his or her tie askew or that his or her hair was not perfect, but with full motion television we expect perfection – that is what we are used to seeing. (Cowan, 1984, p. 206)

Many hours of watching professionally produced films and television segments have contributed to our extraordinarily high expectations for the quality of the visual experience associated with the video format. As a practical approach to this situation, Cowan recommends that a mirror be made available in an unobtrusive position so that teleconference participants can check their appearances at strategic times before the teleconference and during breaks. A mere check at the mirror will not serve to offset the considerable advantage photogenic individuals have over the rest of us, however. Unfortunate arrangements and clumsy technical assistance could also serve to subvert even the best efforts of individuals to manage their own presentations, as in the case of bright footlighting in one videoconference that Cowan reports made one group of executives look like a "satanic worship society."

In a review of the research on the differences between face-to-face and mediated communication, Williams makes the following pessimistic assessment of the audio-video teleconference:

Audio-video media seem not to be as effective as was suspected at first. Early enthusiasm that such media were "just like face-to-face" has not been confirmed, and in most of the previously mentioned experiments, audio-video has turned out to be more similar to audio-only than face-to-face. (Williams, 1977, p. 973)

Sundstrom and Sundstrom (1986) comment that video is a "second-class" medium for conferencing, and that its use reflects poorly on the occasion.

Dissatisfaction of many individuals with the video impressions they

produce and receive in video conferencing has served to erode some of
the force of the "video reflects reality" assumption. Newscasters who are
not photogenic are soon out of a job; however, few individuals outside the
realm of broadcasting have been fired because the camera is not friendly
to them (although this may indeed change as utilization of video in organizational contexts expands). Images transmitted in video have more than
occasionally been perceived as a distraction rather than an aid to communication (the audio itself would be preferred) – although increased familiarity with the medium and advances in video technology are serving to
change this situation. In a review of research on videoconferencing, Egido
(1988) asserts that "results generally point to the dubious value of adding
a visual channel . . . performance does not improve significantly over
that achieved with narrower bandwidths" (p. 19). On the other hand,
"performance" in many of today's organizations is still largely measured
in terms of the production of linear-oriented, paper-based documents; as
these notions of performance shift, so may opinions on the value of
videoconferencing and related technologies.

Video introduces new forms of narrative into organizational contexts.
Ishii and Miyake (1991) state that they have chosen video as a basic
medium for collaborative design efforts because it fuses a set of "tradition-
ally incompatible visual media," such as papers, images, and computer
files (p. 39). In this fusion, video cannot help but pick up some of the
nuances associated with paper- and computer-related genres. Associations that video currently has with broadcasting and entertainment media
also influence the character of video-based narratives; the fact that video
is tightly linked with broadcast media places special emphasis on the
management of impressions and the construction of self. We are all well
aware of the great pains that television stars go through to present suitable
images to the camera. Use of video to capture group interaction will
engender a variety of defensive responses in the medium, as individuals
seek to construct images of themselves that wear well in subsequent
viewings of the tape. An "I told you so" delivered after an unfortunate
group-level decision or organizational incident may need to be confirmed
by subsequent viewings of video accounts. Demonstrations of unity and
consensus will take on broader levels of public, as well as group significance, possibly changing their timing and the kinds of gestures and language used.

Some conclusions and reflections

Groups have been defined, and their expressions consciously structured,
through a large number of vehicles; our virtual individuals and groups

have long been shaped and supported by artifacts such as desks, video-tapes, and whiteboards. How should we think about these vehicles, and how should we characterize the forms that individual and group expression in the workplace may take? This chapter reviews answers to these questions that have been delivered by managerial theorists, media specialists, and social scientists. Many of these answers were framed in terms of the cultural objects of efficiency and control. Examples in this chapter are provided from various artifacts and genres that have already had a presence in the workplace, as well as from CSCW applications that have not as yet made it out of the laboratory.

What impacts can designers, architects, and system implementers have on social interaction and personal expression? Some designers and theorists concerned with the physical–social environment nexus posit that both individuals and their environments are highly malleable. Sundstrom and Sundstrom (1986) assert that people and their physical environments "exert mutual influence and together form interdependent systems" (p. 1). Sommer (1969) holds that humanity itself is shaped through environmental influence and often changes in response to the constraints that designers establish: "Good design becomes a meaningless tautology if we consider that man will be reshaped to fit whatever environment he creates" (p. 172).

In the twentieth century, business correspondence became highly formalized and routinized. With the onrush of new vehicles for individual and group expression, expressions of individual and group personality can become a broader and more important dimension of organizational communications. A variety of interesting characters are emerging (Chapter 7 has a further discussion of the "character" notion and strategies for character development). Peters (1992) encourages managers and designers to "take seriously the flavor of everyday experience" when it comes to our interactions with individuals and institutions; certainly, the styles of the virtual individuals and groups associated with institutions provide a fair share of this flavor.

In this book, notions of genre-responsive design are developed, a strategy that places both designers and users in fairly active roles constructing artifacts and genres. Some examples of user awareness of genre considerations were provided in this chapter (including the case of sound bites), as were examples of the development of conventions by users (as in flame-buffering strategies). Group expression often involves combining individual contributions as elements or aspects of a group product: some vehicles (such as whiteboards and blackboards) supply a common space that is neither entirely group nor entirely individual territory and in which these transitions can be negotiated by group members.

Accounts of how twentieth-century social scientists and managerial researchers have worked to design and develop strategies for the use of various artifacts in group expression and information exchange support the idea that the problems today's system developers are tackling have seen treatment in previous eras. These accounts often incorporate distinctions that designers have constructed between the realms of the personal and the efficient. The notion that a set of common interpretations of resources is required for the resources to be sharable is often introduced. CSCW-related rhetoric (for example, identification of a certain product as being a cooperative work tool) can assist groups in their efforts to label certain resources as "shared resources" and to negotiate the transitions that individual contributions make in order to be considered group products. Analogies and linkages between the design of physical settings and the design of computer-based environments should be explored (following the lead of Hooper, 1986), if only to get a longer-range perspective on those basic problems of design: people have been designing buildings and furniture for millennia more than they have been designing computers.

5
Cultural objects and technological dreams: Dependence, autonomy, and intellectual augmentation

If our computer systems break down, we might find an enormous dependency of which we were not truly aware. We may, by then, have become functionally illiterate – unable to deal with each other except with the aid of mechanisms.

Laurie (1979, p. 141)

A tool is but the extension of a man's hand, and a machine is but a complex tool. And he that invents a machine augments the power of a man and the well-being of mankind.

Henry Ward Beecher (1813–1887),
Proverbs from
Plymouth Pulpit

Genres are associated with various cultural objects, objects that can attract us to the genres, make us suspicious of them, or even avoid their use. Sites for constructing, expressing, and modifying cultural objects include debate, writing, speeches, legal decisions, imagery, and design, as well as CSCW and other network-based system applications. Construction of cultural objects, like that of artifacts and other physical objects, should be considered in light of its reflexive dimensions. The objects serve to shape the cultures, individuals, and genres that are associated with them, and in turn are given shape.

Issues of dependence, autonomy, and intellectual augmentation are critical aspects of construction of the "first-person plural" – which involves the authority to attach the word "we" to a document, product, or decision. This authority is not automatically given by group members, and is often not recognized by parties outside the group. In some situations, establishment of this authority may depend on the ability of group participants and audiences to segregate the group from the "computer-mediated group." For example, to claim that a certain decision was really a product of the group as a unit, group participants may need to demonstrate by argument or imagery that the decision would have been forthcoming regardless of the kind or extent of computer support.

Images, fantasies, and dreams about technologies are often downplayed in favor of more straightforward descriptions of how technologies are viewed and utilized. In opposition to this trend, Romanyshyn (1989) attempts to map linkages among technologies, fantasies, and dreams. "The technological world is a work of reason but of a reason that reaches deeply into dream" (p. 10). In this chapter, dreams and fantasies about CSCW applications will be explored in the context of dependence (Are we "locked into" the use of some technologies?), autonomy (To what extent can we be seen as standing "on our own," without technological support?), and intellectual augmentation (Can technologies be employed in ways that will extend or amplify our intellectual capabilities?).

The third of these objects, augmentation, has developed particularly intense, dreamlike qualities. Augmentation (or amplification) is a long-standing vision of some computer pioneers and has profoundly influenced the way computing tools are talked about, advertised, and designed. The amplified intellect is constructed as one that has been specially equipped and prepared to take on the challenges of an increasingly complex civilization – an intellect coupled with computer-based tools and information sources, and networked with others whose intellects have been similarly amplified. The computer-augmented environment is framed as one that merges electronic systems into the physical world, enhancing our capacities for analysis, imagination, and interaction.

Intellectual augmentation is playing a growing role in making acceptable the utilization of computing tools in certain group interaction contexts, and thus in influencing the character of some of the dependence issues just described. For example, in a number of decision situations, the use of computer assistance of any sort is either explicitly forbidden by rule or excluded by custom: for example, juries must deliberate face-to-face without computer mediation, as must many arbitration panels and government committees. Face-to-face interaction of some kind is still generally considered a requirement for the true "will" of the group to be elicited.

Other examples of such strategic restrictions in the use of information technology abound. Individuals still take many important examinations without computer assistance, often without the aid of a calculator or word processor. Game show contestants battle each other or the scoreboard unaided. Societal construction of the cultural object of augmentation could be critical here: if the intellect is viewed as being augmented (that is, extended and enhanced) rather than altered (or even replaced) by computer assistance, the formal and informal strictures on computer utilization in many sensitive contexts might be lifted. (Whether such loosening of restrictions is indeed desirable is a different but related matter.)

Not just the technologies themselves, but the process of design can be seen as shaped by its relations with cultural objects. Discourse on genres and design methods often centers on these methods' relation to certain cultural objects or to various shared fantasies. For example, design methods associated with "appropriate technology" (or intermediate, human-scale technology) have a number of linkages with dependence and autonomy issues. Cultures are often considered as monolithic entities; I assume that cultural issues are best viewed in an active, developmental sense, with close consideration of artifacts and environments. I close this chapter with the recommendation that design efforts in advanced information technology begin with the sharing and examination of accounts of cultural objects and shared fantasies that appear to be relevant to the context, process, and products of design.

Technological dependence in societal context: Warnings and alarms

Warnings about how dependent our society is becoming on modern information technology and what these dependencies portend for individuals, groups, and communities are far from rare in both academic and popular literatures. Examples are provided by Laurie in the epigraph and in political scientist Langdon Winner's comments:

There is a tendency to think that in an increasingly interdependent technological society or world system, all of the parts need each other equally. Seen as a characteristic of modern social relationships, this is sometimes upheld as a wonderfully fortuitous by-product of the rise of advanced technics. The necessary web of mutual dependency binds individuals and groups closer together; lo, a new kind of community is forming before our very eyes. (Winner, 1977, p. 184)

Winner continues that this apparent "mutual dependency" can often disguise an unhealthy and dysfunctional dependency: there may be significant variation in the power each unit in the network has, variation that can serve to slight and even overwhelm some of the less powerful units in certain contexts.

Some of the images of dependence on technology have taken on tones even more sinister than those presented by Winner. Ralph E. Lapp describes technology as outside of anyone's control, and as leading us all into catastrophe:

We are aboard a train which is gathering speed, racing down a track on which there are an unknown number of switches leading to unknown destinations. No single scientist is in the engine cab, and there may be demons at the switch. (Lapp, 1973, p. 29)

The prospect of dependence on modern information technology has also been placed in a less severe light, however. Christopher Evans provides the following description of a technologically dependent society:

The fact is that the industrialized world has already reached the point where it can no longer survive without using computers . . . [Computers] have not arrived on the scene for aesthetic reasons, but because they are essential to the survival of a computer society . . . [just as are] food, clothing, housing, education, and health services. (Evans, 1981, pp. 67–68).

Evans's phrasing of the statement that computers are "essential to the survival of a computer society" is telling: he reflects the place that computers have taken in societal imagery as well as its functioning.

Mitroff and Pauchant frame our relationship with its technologies as "ironic": technologies widely adopted in the United States (those associated with the images of "mastery" and "independence") have served to lock it into conformity and various kinds of dependence. They proclaim that it is ironic that the

very technologies that the U.S. so quickly and thoroughly adopted because of the incredible emphasis that the U.S. placed on such values as continual innovation and individualism actually contributed to their erosion. The widespread adoption and infusion of the machine into every aspect and fiber of American society actually led to the decline and suppression of both individualism and innovation. (Mitroff and Pauchant, 1990, p. 160)

Mitroff and Pauchant contend that the United States is "one of the most conformist societies on the face of this planet" (p. 160), partly as a result of its imposition of mass media and certain information technologies on individuals.

Discussions concerning a very common and popular form of technology may shed light on these often confusing and contradictory issues: the telephone has often been construed as supporting personal autonomy and independence. Many examples are provided by Pool (1977) that bolster the case that telephones have served to "empower" individuals. In contrast, the telephone has also been constructed as increasing the dependence of individuals, and as forcing them to tend to others' intrusions on demand. An example of the latter construction is this account of physicist Robert Wilson's contemptuous attitude toward the telephone:

There was no telephone in Robert Wilson's office . . . The damned device, he said, kept intruding on his thought and his conversations. So in a moment of anger one day he tore the phone out of the wall and threw it into the hallway. Later, when he moved into his permanent quarters, a new phone lay in wait for him. Not long afterward, when his secretary Judy Ward wanted to put a call through to him, she went into his office, noticed that there seemed to be no phone, and began to look for it. She finally found the cord, which led to a large potted plant in the corner. Wilson had taken the phone and buried it in the moss and dirt. (Hilts, 1982, p. 31)

Annoyance with the intrusions that a ringing telephone presents is a common theme for social critics, essayists, and comedians, signaling a high level of cultural preoccupation. In contrast with these criticisms of the telephone, Illich (1973) in *Tools for Conviviality,* asserts that the telephone is a "structurally convivial tool" – that is, one that nearly anyone can use and that no one is required to use. Even Robert Wilson could effectively disable his telephone with the potted plant approach. Telephone technology is indeed becoming more complex (and less convivial), however, as reflected in the widespread concern about the privacy implications of Caller ID. These alternating societal themes of dependence and independence, freedom and enslavement, apparently often travel with critically important communications and information technologies.

Conviviality is an often-repeated theme in studies of technology and has emerged often in the computing literature (see the volume edited by Norman & Draper, 1986). The aim of constructing computing tools that everyone can use can lead designers to posit an "average user" – and may indeed result in products that appeal to a sizable market. However, the special needs of individual users are often overlooked in such an approach, as Jonathan Grudin relates:

Muffling individual users' voices meant that in the 1980's, as computer use spread and usability became an issue, product developers focused on the generic aspects of the human–computer dialogue that are shared by almost all users. Motor control, perception, and lower cognitive processes – the "look and feel" of software – were explored by researchers and developers in the field of human–computer interaction. (Grudin, 1991, p. 62)

Grudin argues that "projects for multiuser systems are more challenging than single-user applications" (p. 62), which is related to the fact that the approach of designing for a generic user does not work as well on the multiuser level.

The group as suspect: Second thoughts about teamwork

Just as societal-level dependence on computing has raised suspicions and triggered warnings in the United States, so has dependence on one's team, group, or association. Although in our society one is often called on to be a good team player, one must also be functionally autonomous – that is, able to stand on one's own feet both intellectually and socially.

The cultural object of "dependence" has an especially strong linkage to American culture, having direct ties to such concepts as "freedom" and "self-determination." Erikson and Hewitt both assert that cultural objects are closely linked with, and should be viewed in terms of, their apparent opposites or competitors. In recent years, dependence-related discussions have taken on increasingly negative connotations: for example, there are a number of books and television broadcasts about the social dimensions of various kinds of dependence, co-dependence, and addiction. Our society as a whole has been labeled as "addictive" in the numerous publications of Anne Schaef and her supporters: "Many of the behaviors considered 'normal' for individuals and organizations are actually a repertoire of behaviors of an active addict or nonrecovering codependent" (Schaef and Fassel, 1988, p. 4). Addiction and dependence are often related to powerlessness and weakness; autonomy, in turn, is generally associated with strength.

In the 1800s, Thoreau declared that we were becoming "the tools of our tools." Wilkinson (1988) underscores the continuing opposition to dependence, an opposition often manifested in a fear of "being owned" or "enslaved":

I use the term "owned" in a fairly wide range of senses. It includes the subjective condition of believing one is in some sense enslaved. It also includes the idea of psychological ownership by those who can manipulate one's identity. Indeed, as authority has become less brutal and more subtle, the idea of psychological invasion has grown. (Wilkinson, 1988, p. 73)

Wilkinson contends that strong antiownership threads may result in such logical sequences as the following: "I am supposed to be in total control of my life. I am not in control of it. Therefore illegitimate forces are controlling me" (p. 88). On the international scene, the fears described by Wilkinson are manifested in our deep national hatred toward groups that take individual American citizens as political hostages. In the case of organizational computing technology, these "illegitimate forces" are primarily construed as technological and managerial: managers are often construed as imposing inappropriate restrictions and standards, many of which are enforced through technological means.

Discourse on dependence in the United States is often framed in a fairly stark way. Hewitt (1989) provides examples of how American culture "seems to foster an extremist outlook on life," especially when matters concerning independence and liberty are involved. "Freedom," for example, is construed by many as an all-or-nothing entity. American culture is often associated with objects that are portrayed in striking terms, as Hewitt captures in his discussion of independence:

American declarations of independence thus seem to protest not only abuses and usurptations of the authority of employer, family, or state but also the possibility that the individual might actually need the aid or company of others. (Hewitt, 1989, p. 106)

However negatively the prospective lack of independence is portrayed, the cultural object of dependence is often expressed and discussed positively in comparably powerful imagery: witness the many portraits of the dependence of sports team members on each other or the dependence attributed to family members or co-workers. Although we paint bold images of our independence, we also characterize ourselves as needing others.

Seeming contradictions and variations are also found in the social science literature's consideration of individuals and groups. The attention that psychologists and sociologists have given groups as units has varied significantly in the past century (Steiner, 1983). In some periods, the group has been constructed as a critically important unit of analysis, and much attention has been paid to it. At other times, the reverse has been the case, and contributions to research on groups have sharply declined. From the time of LeBon's (1895/1960) *The Crowd,* social science's studies of group processes, pressures, and influences have often focused on issues in which the group is seen in less than a positive light. The question of why mobs and gangs of individuals form (Zimbardo, 1970) – how individuals as group members can engage in kinds of behavior they might not otherwise condone or be involved in, such as rape and murder – has been one of the major topics of concern.

Another issue that social scientists have targeted involves bystander intervention, the conditions under which a Good Samaritan will emerge from a group (Latane and Darley, 1970). Presence of bystanders (the perception that other people are also witnessing an event) was shown to decrease significantly the likelihood that a witness will make efforts to intervene in an emergency (p. 73). The "diffusion of responsibility" that may result from the presence of others either in organized groups or in unplanned associations was linked by Latane and Darley and other social theorists with some dramatic, shocking events, such as the murder of Kitty Genovese (which 38 people witnessed, but did not intervene in). The diffusion of responsibility notion has also been applied by social theorists to the less bizarre group decision settings of educational and business conferences.

The topic of group polarization has also garnered attention in social science literature. It too is often framed in ways that could make us suspicious of the group as an entity. Group polarization is "the tendency of group discussion or some related manipulation to extremitize the aver-age of group members' responses on some dimension from pre- to post-discussion in the direction of the prevailing tendency" (Turner and Oakes, 1989, p. 256). Social psychologists Moscovici and Mugny (1983) assert that groups generally have been conceived as "conformity producing machines," and the deviants within groups as "troublemakers, anomic, non-assertive individuals" in both social science and popular accounts (p. 45).

Concerning group decision making, the discussion of dependence on versus independence from the group has often focused on Janis's (1972, 1982) "groupthink" notions and Asch's (1956) work on conformity, both of which direct our attention to some experimental results that are not very favorable to the group as a decision-making unit. According to Janis (1972, p. 10), groupthink involves six critical defects in group process, defects that lead even highly intelligent decision makers to omit critical considerations and fall into dangerous traps:

1. The group's discussions are limited to only a few alternative courses of action.
2. The group fails to reexamine the course of action initially preferred by the majority of members.
3. The members neglect courses of action initially evaluated as unsatis-factory.
4. Members make little or no attempt to obtain information from experts.
5. Selective bias is shown in the way the group reacts to factual infor-mation.
6. The members spend little time deliberating about how the chosen policy may be hindered . . . ; consequently, they fail to work out contin-gency plans.

Janis (1982) added "incomplete survey of objectives" to this list, making a total of seven.

Janis (1982) links the groupthink phenomenon in part to the effects of membership in a cohesive group on individuals' assumptions about the kinds of critical review that a proposal or assumption may require: "When groupthink dominates, suppression of deviant thoughts takes the form of each person's deciding that his misgivings are not relevant, that the benefit of any doubt should be given to the group consensus" (p. 247).

Since the early 1970s, groupthink has received a large amount of aca-demic and popular discussion (Moorhead, 1982; Myers, 1987) and related empirical research (Leana, 1985). Some scholars have criticized Janis's presentation of the groupthink notion as being unclear – of linking groupthink with a number of different, and perhaps contradictory, explanatory variables. Individuals who dispute the criticality of the notion itself include Longely and Pruitt (1980), who assert that seeking concurrence can indeed be problematic – but it becomes dangerous only if it precedes conscientious evaluation of the important alternatives.

Groupthink-related accounts of national and corporate decision making snafus have had enormous influence on the way accounts of the group are constructed, both on the broad level on which many historians focus and on much smaller, more intimate scales. Failures in group process have been held to blame for many major military and political catastrophes and near-catastrophes in recent history, including the Bay of Pigs invasion, the response to the Cuban Missile crisis, and the escalation of the Vietnam War (Janis, 1972; McCauley, 1989). Narratives of these incidents developed with the groupthink theme were apparently enlightening and served to introduce the word "groupthink" into common parlance (as well as into the vocabulary used at the highest decision-making levels). The idea that the group could be an untrustworthy decision-making entity was thus reinforced.

Asch's (1956) work on conformity similarly warns us against the intellectual operations of the group. In the general model of Asch's conformity experiments, an individual is placed with a group of individuals. He or she is asked about the shape, size, or other dimensions of a projected object (or objects) and is given information about the opinions of others in the group. The information given the individual about the others' opinions is intentionally faulty: group members are portrayed as unanimously characterizing the object in a different way than it is displayed to the individual. The high frequency in which individuals accept the characterizations of the group, and apparently bypass their own capabilities of perception, have been of concern to social psychologists.

A variety of interpretations of the results of Asch-style experiments have been explored:

The naive subject expects to agree with the unanimous majority in the Asch paradigm because she or he has categorized the others as identical to self in relevant respects (e.g., having normal vision, being naive subjects under the same task instructions, operating from the same visual perspective) and assumes they are looking at the same invariant stimulus. If people are similar as perceivers (they look at things from the perspective of the same goals, values, sensory apparatus, etc.) and face the same stimulus situation, then they should and ought to agree – this is a natural and rational expectation. (Turner and Oakes, 1989, p. 250)

Turner and Oakes's explanation posits the individual as indeed being rational (in some senses of the word) in conforming to group opinion, although other interpretations of Asch's results place the individual in a less positive light.

The foregoing reasons for not having much confidence in the group are closely linked to the many constraints that are placed on group decision-making processes and group writing efforts (formal meeting protocols, for instance). To attach the word "we" to a report or decision – to assert that the product really stems from the group, and not from one or more dominant individuals – groups must often demonstrate that they have gone through a certain set of procedures and performed certain functions. Safeguards against what are perceived as common group foibles must often be taken. One of the most explicit of these safeguards is that of the "voice vote" or roll call taken for many important decisions. Members must declare with their own voices what their votes are. This activity also serves to signify that no direct coercion or subterfuge is involved in the voting process. Group-level constraints often serve functions akin to that of the QWERTY keyboard: they can serve to slow down the group, and make its processes more methodical (just as the QWERTY keyboard was originally designed to slow down typists so that typewriter keys would not jam).

Accompanying social science's mistrust of groups and its warnings against dependence on them is its legacy of suspicion about the seductive-ness of media:

So much of the post–World War Two political and sociological literature on in-formation and communication was laden with moral imputations about the risks and dangers of succumbing to the blandishments of bureaucratic or mass society that the explosion of possibilities opened up by radio, television, and satellite communication became strangely converted into threats and predicaments for in-tellectuals. (Horowitz, 1986, p. 16)

The danger of being habituated to media – from overdependence on television as a news and information source to video game addiction – has been a recurring motif in education, social science, public policy, and communications studies, from Newton Minow's "vast Wasteland" senti-ments of the early 1960s to recent discussions of the possible dangers of immersion in virtual reality (see Perry, 1994). The notion that individuals are losing a "clear sense of truth from untruth" and of "self in relation to others" because of flights into technology-mediated fantasy has been expressed in many cultural commentaries:

Without truly binding the individual, mass organization had taken over and dis-torted his or her sense of reality through its array of media instruments, from ad-vertising and managed news to television shows and videos. Information was increasingly secondhand and prerecorded. Society had become a "hall of mirrors" in which fictions mocked other fictions ("soaps" spoofing other "soaps"), leaving to individual dignity only a sense of ironic detachment. (Wilkinson, 1988, p. 32)

Distinctions between "real" performances and those that have been technologically modified have stimulated debate as to what constitutes a human performance as opposed to a simulated or virtual performance. William Safire (1994) calls for closer demarcation between human and "electronically enhanced" portions of performances and various entertainment vehicles. He contrasts "organic entertainment" (such as a 1960s recording or a live performance by a cabaret singer) with the "plasticity" and "virtual venality" of retouched or electronically doctored pieces. All performances involve creation of virtual individuals and groups; however, some are indeed considered less contrived than others, reflecting more fully and more naturally the expression of the individual. Similarly, some photographic retouching is considered within acceptable bounds in terms of its presentations of individuals, and other reworkings are viewed as distortions or manipulations of the image for purposes of self-aggrandizement or mockery. (This issue is taken up again in the conclusion of this chapter.) Several incidents in which performers have received major awards for presentations in which they were not fully involved (for example, songs that they lip-synched) triggered national attention on these issues, as have "new releases" by recording stars who have passed away.

Work on CSCW applications and related technological innovations is continuing at full speed, despite the concerns outlined so far in this chapter. Mistrust of the group (as manifested in the social science perspectives described in this chapter) is still considerable. However, the group is increasingly being seen as meriting the attention of managers, technologists, and researchers (as the earlier chapter on the emerging varieties of collaborative groups supports). CSCW applications can be constructed as ways of taming the group – of making it a known and safe entity (in contrast with the unpredictable and dangerous gang or mob); developers and implementers of these applications are designing technologies to shape and constrain the group, as well as to harness its power for various organizational purposes.

Concerns about the negative influences of mass media and communications technology are also being overridden, as these media are incorporated into many organizational strategies. A number of changes are occurring: skills once framed as individual properties are rapidly being transferred to the group level for purposes of analysis and control (Greenbaum, 1988). A number of managerial researchers have championed the group or team as a critically important organizational unit (see

Peters, 1987; Malone, 1988; Scott Morton, 1991). Many kinds of tools are being developed and employed in efforts to link group members and facilitate group interaction – including CSCW applications.

Intellectual autonomy, the personal computer, and CSCW applications

The unit of focus of much of philosophy and education is the self-contained individual. When considered as self-contained or autonomous intellectual units, individuals are construed as facing the task of performing and controlling each stage in the sequence of intellectual activity they engage in. Relatively few scholars have deviated from this path (see Hardwig, 1985, and Blais, 1987, for notable examples); few have attempted to describe in more precise terms what is involved when individuals accept the premises, logic, and results (or partial results) of other individuals – and thus become directly dependent on intellectual activities of others. When one accepts and incorporates into one's own intellectual activities important insights or intellectual products of others, one is faced with a number of issues: How competent are the individuals or groups whose results one accepts? Did one understand the results and their original contexts, and receive them without distortions or critical errors in transmission? These questions are often not considered as "philosophical" matters – but the perspective they lend can modify the construction of the individual as an autonomous intellectual unit to one who is more socially aware and intellectually dependent on others and on various information-processing media.

Intellectual autonomy (the capacity to stand on one's own as a complete and self-contained intellectual unit) incorporates an amalgam of political and social aspects, as well as themes related to the sociology of knowledge and philosophy of technology. As stated by A. Whitney Griswold, former president of Yale, the presumption that only the individual is creative has roots in the divine:

Creative ideas do not spring from groups. They spring from individuals. The divine spark leaps from the finger of God to the finger of Adam, whether it takes ultimate shape in a law of physics or a law of the land, a poem or a policy, a sonata or a mechanical computer. (Griswold, 1959)

In order to ensure that individuals are indeed autonomous intellectually (at least in image), American educators have provided a variety of signals that competence in certain knowledge-related activities is important. Many educators fought the introduction of calculators into education, particularly in the examination room (Abelson and Hammond, 1980; Ralston, 1987); others have denied their students access to word processors in examinations. Very few formal examination settings afford students opportunities to interact in other than covert ways, even though many of the activities they will engage in later in life require such interaction. These educational decisions serve to convey the notion that the desired product of the educational system is an individual whose intellect is effectively "self-contained" – who indeed requires nothing more than a No. 2 pencil to be a competent thinker and problem solver.

The PC has had close and continuing ties with the cultural object of autonomy. One facet of this autonomy is self-sufficiency. Some pioneering designers of PCs went so far in the direction of supporting individual self-sufficiency that they attempted to produce computers that (1) could be repaired easily by their owners, and (2) for which replacement parts could be made out of scrap items, in case a major national emergency would occur.

Another aspect of autonomy in the computing context is ability to tailor a system to one's own perceived needs. Nicholas Negroponte wrote of a "personalized computer," one that has direct ties to a specific human being:

I coined the term "idiosyncratic system" to distinguish a personal computer from a personalized computer, one that knows its user intimately and can accordingly invoke all the necessary inferences to handle vagaries, inconsistencies, and ambiguities. I offered the following hypothetical scenario as an example:
"Okay, where did you hide it?"
"Hide what?"
"You know."
"Where do you think?"
"Oh."
(quoted in Brand, 1987, p. 153)

The ideal PC that Negroponte describes has been so closely tailored for and is so intimate with the individual user's needs, tendencies, and foibles that little direct conversation between user and machine is required for the machine to perform its functions.

The popularity of the notion that computers can indeed be tailorable to an individual's needs is tightly coupled with the reduction in the scales, sizes, and prices of computing-related artifacts that occurred when the PC became mass-marketed. The early 1980s heralded the era of the widely accessible computer, an age signaled by *Time* magazine's appointment of the computer as the 1983 "Machine of the Year":

Computers were once regarded as distant, ominous abstractions, like Big Brother. In 1982 they truly became personalized, brought down to scale, so that people could hold, prod and play with them. (Meyers, 1983, p. 3)

Yet another dimension of autonomy involves control. The high degree of individual control often associated with the PC has been seen by a number of users and user advocates as being subverted by CSCW applications and associated network technologies, systems that supposedly make the PC less immediately reflective of the individual user's needs and directions. Threats that networking and CSCW applications have directed toward individual autonomy have been taken quite seriously; as discussed in previous chapters, many CSCW applications have indeed been promoted by managers who wish to regain control over organizational computing functions. Williams (1989) describes as "absurd" the idea that computer users would need to be dependent on each other in the advent of computer networking, since, even without connecting to a larger system, "everyone is now able to have the computing power of a mainframe on his desk." Whittaker (1991) makes this case in similar terms, contrasting the power of computer mainframes and networks with the freedom many users associated with the PC. He claims that in the 1980s many users consciously chose such "freedom" over the computing "power" they might otherwise have gotten from maintaining their allegiance to the mainframe configuration.

Many early developers and users of PCs delivered strong statements about how computing could increase their autonomy, and declared that they would just as soon be left alone with their machines to develop self-sufficient applications – applications that a single user working alone could benefit from. In contrast, others wanted to be able to switch readily from a "personal tool" mode to a "communication" mode, as reflected in this account by the developers of Xerox PARC's *Alto* in the 1970s:

People often need to do things in groups. There are times when we want to use the *Alto* as a personal tool, and times when we want to use it as a communication medium, and times when we want both. Our purpose in bringing all that computer power to individuals was not to allow them to isolate themselves. We wanted to provide the gateway to a new information space, and ways to fly around in it, and a medium for community creativity, all at the same time. (Robert Taylor, quoted in Rheingold, 1985, p. 224)

Construction of the PC as having a "dual nature" – as a personal tool and a communications device – is evidenced by the spread of a number of buzzwords, including "compunications" and the "interpersonal computer" (the former linked with Anthony Oettinger and the latter often attributed to Steve Jobs of Next, Inc.).

Some dimensions of dependence and autonomy issues

Dependence of individuals on advanced information technologies and on the group as a unit is often presented as involving a variety of possible dysfunctionalities, including the atrophy of intellectual versatility (Oravec, 1988a). VR applications have attracted similar controversies: some social critics have expressed strong concern that participants in VR activities will become locked into various virtual worlds, and thus lose their connections with more traditional, and socially acceptable, manifestations of "reality." This section analyzes facets of technological and group dependence issues, and discusses means that have been proposed or implemented for mitigating undesirable consequences that may be associated with them. The dimensions of technological dependence discussed are not completely distinguishable in their effects: all have the potential of working in conjunction with and reinforcing the others.

Individual and group dependence rooted in "externalization"

Is the externalization of various intellectual processes dysfunctional? Externalization involves a kind of dependence: if we must utilize tools (or be able to get in contact with certain people) to perform certain mental activities, we become less self-contained and self-reliant. With the advent of the calculator, Hardin (1982) declares, the calculation skills that his father and predecessors had "internalized" (that is, had available without any mechanical assistance or prompting by others) are becoming increasingly rare. "Externalization" in the realm of the intellect is generally constructed as including the recording, scripting, or (in the case of the calculator) mechanizing of some intellectual processes that were previously manifest only in internalized form. Hardin points out dangers of such externalization, in part by discussing the likelihood that intellectual skills will undergo atrophy if they are not utilized (just as teeth may experience a certain level of atrophy if not challenged sufficiently with suitably textured food).

Notions concerning the dangers of externalization can be readily extended to various group-level functions. In groups, many social functions and rules are externalized to some extent: rituals can be scripted and recorded in various formats (religious ceremonies are one example), roles can be described, and procedures codified. CSCW applications can be seen as extending this externalization, providing mechanisms for interpretation and enforcement of many social functions and rules that were previously the province of memory and habit. As an example of this externalization, social roles are defined in the Quilt collaborative writing system in terms of the kind of access allowed to documents (Fish et al., 1988). The levels of negotiation and interpretation that are usually involved in largely internalized processes concerning social roles may to some extent be overridden when the system-provided accounts are accepted and incorporated by the group.

Some forms of externalization may serve to impair the flexibility of human associations. Groups that have utilized certain CSCW applications for some time, yet have not developed resilient, robust interpersonal relationships outside of their CSCW-based contact, may find themselves locked in certain behavior patterns stipulated or encouraged by the applications, and frozen into certain aspects of their virtual groups. These groups may subsequently not be able to shift their modes of interaction as required for intelligent adaptations to changes in circumstances (such as the shifts in human needs of group participants).

An example of these concerns in a related context is expressed by some group psychotherapists: they observe that groups fall into rigid patterns as a result of certain kinds of therapeutic intervention. Such a dependence raises group effectiveness problems (the therapeutic power of the sessions may wane as groups become stuck in these routines). It also brings to light various professional concerns for therapists. Therapists may be called to question their own abilities to extricate themselves from their group therapy efforts sufficiently to gain perspective on the group.

Dangers associated with "exposing" group process and giving it an "objective" examination are critical ones for group therapy, as well as for CSCW application development and implementation. CSCW researchers and group psychotherapists both introduce new vocabularies and new perspectives to users and clients. Both CSCW research and psychotherapy are generally afforded the imprimatur of scientific objectivity, and their accounts are often given greater weight than folk wisdom or "common sense" about group interaction. Parallels between CSCW research and group psychotherapy may indeed be a promising avenue for future research (an avenue not yet heavily traveled by researchers in either the CSCW or group psychotherapy camps).

Individual and group dependence based on economic and social investment

Investments that groups make in network-based computer system technologies are themselves often associated with dependence, on both personal and group levels. Training one individual to use a technology is a large investment; training a group of individuals to utilize appropriately a group-based technology includes added, complex factors. The substantial resource investment involved in introducing new technologies can stifle their growth: Saffo (1991) declares that "office real estate is too scarce for companies to dedicate rooms to groupware systems" (p. 50). The possibility that simple space considerations may indeed turn out to be an important factor in the success of a form of CSCW application certainly underscores the difficulties involved in developing forecasts about technological futures.

Warnings about the level of intellectual and social investment required for CSCW applications are often appended to even the most optimistic assessments of the technology, as in this discussion of hypermedia:

Adult readers of printed documents have come to take their ability to read for granted. Reading hypermedia graphs will require the acquisition of at least some new skills. False expectations to the contrary may be an impediment to widespread acceptance. (Begoray, 1990, p. 128)

Not all discussions of technological investment are downbeat: some CSCW proponents enthusiastically claim that such applications as Lotus *Notes* offer an economic return on investment of over 100% (Hamilton, 1992), as well as substantial social and personal payback.

Formation of groups as units involves an "investment," whether or not the groups are computer-mediated. There is fairly little available in terms of economic thinking on whether forming a group to solve a problem is a better investment than having a single individual attempt to solve it (or over just flipping a coin). The choice to employ a group or team rather than an individual in solving a problem or writing a document ties up organizational and personal resources that could otherwise be utilized. Kraut et al. (1988) contend that it is not uncommon for teams to take more than a year to go from introductions and their first cups of coffee together to a congealed project plan or grant proposal. That is indeed a large investment of time and emotional energy for everyone involved, which often creates a huge psychological and social investment in the team's continued existence. Even when team members are better off apart, they might not consider separating unless circumstances sever their ties.

McGrath provides a sampling of the issues that collaborative workgroup members must resolve:

What will I get out of it [the workgroup]; what will it cost me; whose ox is to be gored and whose ax is to be ground; how much stroking will I have to do in order to get appropriate responsiveness from my partners; and the like. (McGrath, 1990, p. 58)

He recommends that time should be invested in such issues early in the relationship. Following through on McGrath's recommendation commits substantial resources to the team, since the discussion of these issues in itself is time consuming (as well as risky in terms of the future interactions of the individuals involved).

Dependence based on image and association

CSCW and other kinds of network-based system applications may become tightly associated in image with the group as an entity, and those associations may be construed as a kind of dependence. For instance, there are strong images associated with networks (both their technical and social components) and with certain sets of group procedures (especially democratic procedures such as majority rule). Just as it is difficult to think of Congress without thinking of the building in which it meets, its associated rules of order, and the video or film images of its members meeting in session, various network-based applications may be tightly coupled with the group. Many CSCW applications have video components, as described in an earlier chapter; reflections of group performance and functioning that these systems provide may capture our imaginations as much as the images we see of Congress from newscasts or C-Span often do.

Ceremonial functions of decision making, group writing, and conflict resolution are important to consider in relation to network-based applications (although little attention has yet been directly targeted to their consideration). Organizational ceremonies can serve to reinforce specific values and create or remind people of organizational heroes and heroines (Deal and Kennedy, 1982). Up to this point, CSCW applications have been heavily associated with efficiency-related images (as previously discussed), but other images and themes, possibly in consonance with organizational and group ceremonies, may well be reflected by designers in the future.

Dependence based on job or task redesign

The tasks that groups perform may be redesigned so that certain network-based systems may be desirable (or even necessary), thus creating a kind of dependence on the technology. Many jobs have already been configured so that an individual is required to use a computer to perform them. Our modern systems of welfare, transportation, and other vital services cannot easily be decoupled from the computer technology that supports and enhances them. Administrators, managers, and project leaders may soon be making demands on groups that apparently can only be met with the assistance of CSCW applications and related technologies.

Weizenbaum (1979) comments on the tight couplings between today's welfare systems and the computer, couplings that often have unfortunate ramifications for innovation:

If the computer had not facilitated the perpetuation and "improvement" of existing welfare distribution systems – hence of their philosophical rationales – perhaps someone might have thought of eliminating much of the need for welfare by, for example, introducing negative income tax. The very erection of an enormously large and complex computer based welfare administration apparatus, however, created an interest in the maintenance and administration of the welfare system itself. (Weizenbaum, 1979, pp. 30–31)

Weizenbaum argues that many of the social problems that have been "solved" by the computer (problems that are widely considered as offshoots of the growth and complexity of society) would have been met with innovation and ingenuity if the overwhelming interest in perpetuating computer systems had not provided "substantial barriers" to such innovation.

The ways in which we structure task activities can mandate (or at least strongly suggest) the use of certain forms of technology. Some of the ways that CSCW applications can and have played roles in shaping our notions of what can be done within the scope of a task activity include the following:

Complexity. The CSCW application may enable job designers to increase the complexity of the task, so that the task would not be performable by the group without the aid of the application. Linkage of a decision-making task with a set of statistically complex rules and procedures would fall into this category.

Time frame. CSCW applications may be used to alter our constructions of a time frame for a task. For example, they may speed up our standards of what is an "acceptable" length of time for task completion. The fact that committee meetings can be slow is a part of American legend and lore, and is often accepted with a shrug and a grin. The introduction of a new technology designed to make these meetings more efficient could change our constructions of what is a tolerable time frame for a gathering. Time considerations are emphasized in CSCW applications in an assortment of ways: for instance, Timeslips Corporation's *Timesheet Professional* is targeted to corporate workgroups that need to track hours spent on projects (Simon, 1991), and group calendaring programs such as Russell Information Sciences, Inc.'s *Calendar Manager* are aimed toward organizational environments where there is a complex intermeshing of project teams (Busse, 1993).

Numbers and varieties of participants. CSCW applications may afford opportunities for more participation, as well as more broadly based participation. Some electronic meeting systems have been designed to accommodate hundreds of active participants, with even larger assemblages in the works. As for varieties of participation, Engelbart and Lehtman (1988) assert that CSCW applications support and encourage the development of diverse kinds of groups – for example, groups that are geographically distributed and engaging in asynchronous interaction – along with traditional, co-located groups.

Dependence based on convenience

Another facet of the dependence issue is our society's apparent fixation on "shortcuts" and other time-saving methods. Once implemented, network-based computer systems may save the group some time with certain aspects of its decision-making, message-handling, and other group-related processes. The group may thus utilize these systems even when it is not otherwise considered appropriate to do so (that is, even when there may be important reasons not to use such systems, such as the sensitivity of the decisions made or of the messages exchanged). A good deal of current research in group decision support and related CSCW applications does not yet show appreciable time savings as a result of system use. However, as experience with the systems grows, time savings may become more apparent. Kirkpatrick (1992) provides some accounts of project time cuts linked with the use of CSCW applications; some Boeing managers claim that *TeamFocus* (by IBM) helped them cut project time by 90%, for example.

Implications of dependence for power and control

Dependencies on vital resources of any kind have considerable implications for issues of power and control; the dependencies described in this chapter may thus have far-reaching effects on relations in the school or workplace, relations among socioeconomic groups, professional–client relations, and any other relations where power and control are critical factors. Concern for these issues at the group level can be traced at least to the 1950s. Thelen describes the dependencies that groups can have on those who train group members in skills related to group participation:

The problem of functions served by the trainer is also the problem of desired versus undesired qualities of dependency. The trainer must learn to distinguish among the various aspects and conditions of dependency. Acceptance of certain forms of dependency on him is part and parcel of the dynamics of training, be-

cause the group's trust in the trainer is actually the source of his ability to train
. . . There are other aspects that are acceptable initially but will disappear as the
group develops its own resources. (Thelen, 1954, p. 171)

Thelen advises group trainers to be conscious of the level and timing of
states of dependency, and to work to increase group members' consciousness of them.

Some of the other professions that deal with matters of group interaction have also taken strong stances toward group dependence and control
issues. For example, J. Scott Rutan, former president of the American
Group Psychotherapy Association, delivered the following, passionate
remarks in his 1988 Presidential Address concerning the conditions and
the ethics of group psychotherapy:

Groups are complex and powerful, with impressive capacities to heal and
wound, to enhance and detract from the individuals in them. In your hands alone
is the momentous task of determining how to make society's groups more therapeutic . . . a new language [should] be invented, a language that by its form and
content will protect the individual from the group and the group from the individual. (Rutan and Groves, 1989, p. 14)

Similar discussions have taken place in single-client psychotherapy.
Maranhao (1986) describes the problems of dependence that may develop
between a psychotherapist and his or her client. The client is in a vulnerable position, faced with deep-seated images and powerful impressions that
have surfaced in the session. Boundaries between client and therapist can
thus be seen as muddied; the therapist has introduced new ways of
thinking and talking, and has coaxed out various feelings and impressions
that might otherwise not have been psychologically available to the client.
A certain level of dependence between client and therapist can thus be
constructed – often consciously and willfully by both parties.

Dependence issues also loom large in the workplace. It is in the best
long-range interests of any administration or management to have work-
forces that are not dependent on any one technology, but are flexible and
easily retrainable (as outlined by Peters, 1987, and others). Constant
change is a fact of life in organizations, and a flexible workforce is often an
important factor in facing such change. Cross-training employees in various technologies, and instituting other strategies for empowerment, require expenditures of time and effort – but the level of resource utilization
is not as important as the will of management needed to allow for and encourage this empowerment (and the consequent shifts in power relations).

Issues associated with "learned helplessness," which is linked with
individuals' constructions of situations, should also be considered in light

of the discussions in this chapter. For instance, construing that a certain set of group processes or intellectual operations needs computer assistance may lead individuals to feel that the situation requires such assistance. Research in learned helplessness is thus potentially fruitful in this area; some psychologists have attempted to understand the behavior and thinking patterns related to learned helplessness. Individuals who lose contact with their basic social and intellectual capabilities and intuitions may lose touch with other important aspects of their work lives as well (aspects that involve their political and social well-being). Sociologists once linked this unfortunate situation largely with assembly-line workers and others who deal with routine tasks. As Perrolle (1987), Garson (1988), and others have noted, many workers with higher-level positions are also serving in "electronic sweatshops." "Routinization" of group processes may take its place along other forms of routinization in some organizational contexts, with the nuances of group interaction ignored in favor of a more standardized and mechanized (and possibly more rigid and less adaptive) approach.

Individuals who are (either in their own perceptions or in others') "locked into" one form of technology are obviously in a less advantageous power position than those who are skilled in and comfortable with several forms of technology, or who have flexible skills that allow for easily learning various alternatives. Individuals who have a healthy "detachment" from the technologies that they work with on a day-to-day basis, who understand the limitations and strengths of those technologies, and who have some control over their use, simply have more power in their workplace or educational environments. Such detachment from our vehicles of expression and interaction is not readily come by. Marshall McLuhan contends that detachment is required for understanding media and information technologies of all kinds: "Media, after all, are only extensions of ourselves. The road to understanding media begins with arrogant superiority. If one lacked this sense of superiority – this detachment – it would be quite impossible to write about them" (in Stern, 1967, p. 284).

Appropriate technology, organizational simplicity, and open technology

The question of whether and how designers, implementers, and users of network-based computer systems should work in direct ways to avoid group dependence on the systems (or mitigate the dependence that does result) is a difficult one. Appropriate technology approaches provide some handles on dependence issues. The work of Schumacher (1973) and others in human-scale ("intermediate" or "appropriate") technology has inspired similar approaches in computing, as well as in educational technology.

Schumacher outlines the appropriate technology approach as an alternative to design approaches that present "more" technology as being "better" technology. Rather than being "antitechnological," appropriate technology concentrates on the relation of the technology to the specific tasks and situations in which it is utilized and to the people who use it. (Schumacher often stated his preference for the word "intermediate" over "appropriate," although he conceded that the latter term rapidly took on the most recognizability.)

Until recently, most appropriate technology design efforts were largely outside the high-tech arena, involving either agricultural or basic industrial innovations. Jequier and Blanc's definitional criteria for appropriate technology broaden the notion in a way that serves as a good starting place for the consideration of computer application design:

low investment cost per workplace, low capital investment per unit of output, organizational simplicity, small scale operations, high adaptability to particular social or cultural environments, sparing use of natural resources, and very low cost of the final product. (Jequier & Blanc; 1979, p. 8)

Clegg (1988) provides a pioneering exploration of the theme of appropriate technology in the management of information technology, arguing that many otherwise-successful companies make inappropriate choices concerning the scope and extent of computer applications.

Using Jequier and Blanc's characterization of appropriate technology, Machanick (1988, p. 7) generated the following criteria for investigating whether a computer design approach reflects an appropriate use of technology:

- Hardware should be low in cost.
- Multiuser or networked configurations should be avoided.
- The software should be easy to use.
- Minimal training should be required.
- The user interface should readily adapt to new languages.
- The functionality should easily adapt to new contexts.
- The approach should apply to a wide range of people and localities.
- The cost per user should be low.

Machanick emphasizes the difficult role of the designer in defining and resolving issues such as "ease of use" in contexts where users and developers need first to establish basic communication (as in intercultural design projects where spoken language may be a barrier), and where there is little prior experience in the development of computer applications of any sort. Human-scale information system approaches to network-based system design have been instituted by Eriksson and Kalmi (1986) and Nurminen (1982). In these approaches, cooperative work applications are construed as collections of toollike, individual applications that communicate with each other by simple message exchanges. These approaches do not involve manipulation of shared material by users, an element that the designers assume would introduce complexity and (perhaps) confusion for users (Sorgaard, 1987). Other designers have underscored the importance of individuals who use CSCW applications to be able to work in environments that they are familiar with and that have close connection to the work they perform outside the group context (see Halonen et al., 1990; Ohkubo and Ishii, 1990). The CSCW efforts that this group of designers describe all involve some manipulation of shared material, however, unlike those of the preceding set.

People work with shared material in a variety of noncomputerized contexts (although such work can be fraught with difficulty); working with shared material can certainly be considered a human-scale endeavor (and thus fit within the constraints of the appropriate technology approach). As technical and conceptual problems with the manipulation of shared material in a computer system context are overcome, the question of how to handle shared material may play a less controversial role in appropriate technology design efforts than it does today.

A CSCW application effort that apparently fits Jequier and Blanc's criterion of organizational simplicity is the Answer Garden (Ackerman & Malone, 1990) developed by MIT's Center for Coordination Science. The system provides a database of answers to commonly asked questions. The "organic" analogy involves the fact that the system grows as new varieties of questions arise and are answered by "experts." In the case of the first iteration of Answer Garden, the questions are technical questions concerning an operating system. The "key ideas" of the system include: (1) a branching network of diagnostic questions to help users find the answers they want, (2) automatic routing of new questions to appropriate experts and insertion of questions (along with their answers) into the network, and (3) system capabilities that allow experts to modify the diagnostic branching network in response to users' problems (for example, if the network is misleading or inefficient). A key idea that apparently emerged from the user community is to allow users themselves to annotate the entries; in the first version of the Garden, only staff members and local experts could make changes in the information database. Users have also requested to build their own "access trees" out of database segments (branching networks designed to suit their own needs).

One of the most interesting facets of the Answer Garden is the apparent humility of its designers (as reflected in their descriptions of the system). The account of the system published in an Association for Computing Machinery conference proceedings ended with the following proviso: "The Answer Garden is not a radically new kind of system. We believe it shows, however, how a relatively simple combination of well-known concepts can provide a surprisingly powerful platform for a new kind of cooperative work application" (Ackerman and Malone, 1990, p. 36). Combining familiar tools may provide one of the more fruitful approaches to network-based system design work – and is certainly compatible with the genre-responsive approach of this book.

A design approach closely related to appropriate technology is the "open technology" perspective. Hutchins (1990) argues that the design of a tool can affect its "suitability" for use in a group context. For example, he declares that "watching someone work with a chart is much more revealing than watching someone work with a calculator or a computer" (p. 217). The tool's "openness" (in this case, the chart's graphic depiction of position and motion) helps the interaction of those working with the tool to be more easily deciphered and understood by others working alongside them. The notion of "open tools" in the realm of information systems has been expanded by Ted Nelson:

A globe is my model of a proper information system. A globe does not say "good morning"; it does not bother you with menus, icons, or prompts. You turn it and move your head to the most useful position for overview or detail, that's all. (Nelson, 1990, p. 248)

Appropriate technology has indeed stimulated a good deal of thinking about design approaches in general, and presents a well-worked alternative to design concepts and methodologies that place a premium on complexity. Although appropriate technology approaches have detractors (for example, Florman, 1981), the themes of technological simplicity, "small is beautiful," and human-scale technology have filtered into discourse on politics, economics, and organizational design, as well as computing.

The augmented virtual individual and virtual group

Cultural objects and group fantasies are not readily separable from the technologies associated with them. One of the objects most closely linked with the development of CSCW applications to this date is that of intellectual "augmentation." Ellul (1964) talks of the "self-augmentation" of technology, the notion that technological growth seems to have taken a life of its own and is effectively out of human control. The augmentation I discuss in the following section is different from Ellul's (although many claim that the human–computer symbiosis associated with intellectual augmentation may similarly be out of our control).

Intellectual augmentation is generally presented alongside such apparently benign notions as the support and amplification of human intelligence – and the dreams of technologists who declare their aims to see farther and think more deeply. Birnbaum (1985) declares that augmentation is part of the "great promise" of computing: "The great promise of computing technology is that it will expand human memory, augment human reasoning, and facilitate human communication" (p. 1234). Advocates of augmentation often wax poetic about what will happen when humans will be able to take full advantage of computer assistance. For example, Timothy Leary (1990) predicts that "the information technologies of the next ten years are going to link amplified individual minds into a global supermind" (p. 230), a notion reminicent of the "group mind" projected by Fleck (1935) and others earlier in this century.

Linked with intellectual augmentation is the notion that individuals will someday come to "inhabit" computers – that they will cast off their physical forms and reside more comfortably in a computer framework. *The Wall Street Journal* carried a front-page story on these ideas (Carroll, 1990); the work of Hans Moravec as described in his book *Mind Children* (1988) also explores them. When augmentation is associated with group interaction, such drastic means of obtaining human–computer symbiosis are generally eschewed in favor of such comparatively mundane interfaces as computer screens, keyboards, and mice.

Vannevar Bush's description of the memex, apparently one of the only successful early projections of the notion of the PC, links its use to a form of scholarly augmentation. Many accounts dealing with intellectual augmentation issues begin with a discussion of the memex:

The owner of the memex, let us say, is interested in the origin and properties of the bow and arrow. Specifically, he is studying why the short turkish bow was apparently superior to the English long bow in the skirmishes of the Crusades. He has dozens of possibly pertinent books and articles in his memex. First he runs through an encyclopedia, finds an interesting but sketchy article, leaves it projected. Next, in a history, he finds another pertinent item, and ties the two together. Thus he goes, building a trail of many items. Occasionally, he inserts a comment of his own, either linking it into the main trail or joining it by a side trail to a particular item . . . Thus he builds a trail of his interest through the maze of materials available to him. (Bush, 1945, p. 107)

The memex went far beyond the notepad and library in expanding human intellect: it built a "trail of [the owner's] interest."

The name of Douglas Engelbart is the one most firmly associated with the cultural object of intellectual augmentation (although Engelbart credits Bush with his early inspiration). Engelbart (1989, p. 189) relates the initial insights that led to his notion of intellectual augmentation in terms of the following "flashes":

FLASH-1: The difficulty of mankind's problems was increasing at a greater rate than our ability to cope.

FLASH-2: Boosting mankind's ability to deal with complex, urgent problems would be an attractive candidate as an arena in which a young person might try to "make the most difference." (Yes, but there's that question of what does the young electrical engineer do about it? Retread for a role as educator, research psychologist, legislator . . . ?)

FLASH-3: Ahah–graphic vision surges forth of me sitting at a large CRT [cathode ray tube] console, working in ways that are rapidly evolving in front of my eyes (beginning from memories of the radar-screen consoles I used to service).

Engelbart relates that within weeks of these flashes, he had committed his career to "augmenting the human intellect." Engelbart developed an intellectual structure for his augmentation notions in the Stanford Research Institute (SRI) report "Augmenting Human Intellect: A Conceptual Framework," which was condensed into a chapter of a book published the next year (Engelbart, 1963).

Engelbart (1963, pp. 4–5) describes the following basic classes as extensions of human capabilities (or "augmentation means"):

1. Artifacts – physical objects designed to provide for human comfort, and the manipulation of things or materials, and the manipulation of symbols.
2. Language – the way in which the individual classifies the picture of his world into the concepts that his mind uses to model that world, and the symbols that he attaches to those concepts and uses in consciously manipulating the concepts ("thinking.")
3. Methodology – the methods, procedures, and strategies with which an individual organizes his goal-centered (problem-solving) activity.
4. Training – the conditioning needed by the individual to bring his skills in using augmentation means 1, 2, and 3 to the point where they are operationally effective.

In capabilities (1) through (4), Engelbart did not explicitly include interaction with a group as an augmentation means, but in his experimental efforts groups played substantial roles.

Many of the aspects of Engelbart's efforts – for example, his "Computer Based Knowledge Workshop" plans – incorporate attempts to equip not just the group but the individual group member as well, thus providing for some individual autonomy:

> Any Workshop user at the gathering can call on part of his online notes, or use his familiarity with certain material, to bring special information before the assembly. Or, the whole assembly can see the display being controlled by another individual (or assembly) at a remote site, in shared-display dialogue. (Engelbart, 1988, p. 6)

In Engelbart's ideal, agendas can be altered dynamically – as the meeting progresses – so that the group is not unnecessarily locked into a prearranged sequence that may not fit its emerging needs.

In his history of the early pioneers in computing, Rheingold provides an account of a schism between Engelbart's vision and those of colleagues and associates who were oriented more toward the PC and less toward the use of mainframes. Engelbart's early augmentation strategies were indeed rooted in a centralized mainframe (the networks of workstations we are familiar with today were not available):

> There were those who felt that even Doug's technological ideas, although they might have once been radical and futuristic, were becoming outmoded. The idea of augmentation teams and high-level time shared systems began to seem a bit old-hat to the younger folks who were exploring the possibility of personal computers. (Rheingold, 1985, pp. 202–203)

PCs offered a different horizon in the eyes of many who were working with augmentation notions. Those who developed the "PC vision" often posited the machine itself as both a physical and intellectual extension of the user; the "computer as tool" notion became more tightly defined in terms of the machine on the user's desk and his or her own, specially tailored programs. In the PC vision, the user and machine became a unit. The PC was constructed as a personal memory, a home base, and a buffer between the individual and the organization (both socially and technically); individuals and their PCs became teams.

Some criticisms of the augmentation notion relate to its lack of clarity and specificity (Mahmood, 1989). Augmentation of the human intellect (as described by Engelbart) did not begin with the computer, but rather with language itself. What would *not* serve to augment human intellectual capabilities? Historian Carl Becker (1965) describes writing as an augmentation means, increasing "the power of . . . mind as formerly the flint hatchet increased the power of [the human] hand" (p. 46). Becker goes on to describe writing as presenting an "artificially extended and verifiable memory of objects and events not present to sight or recollection," echoing the externalization theme outlined by Hardin (but casting it in a more positive framework).

Many other questions arise about augmentation. It can be seen in relation to the "bounded rationality" notions that became popular in the 1960s (notions associated with the work of Herbert Simon, 1963/1981). Bounded rationality is defined by Daft in the following terms:

Managers have only so much time and mental capacity, and hence cannot evaluate every goal, problem, and alternative. The attempt to be rational is bounded (limited) by the enormous complexity of many problems. There is a limit to how rational managers can be. For example, an executive in a hurry may have a choice of fifty ties on a rack, but will take the first or second tie that matches his suit . . . [he or she] simply selects the first tie that solves the problem and moves on to the next task. (Daft, 1992, p. 367)

In the context of a managerial and administrative literature that has strong ties to the notion of bounded rationality, concerns arise about augmentation: Can human capabilities (either as individuals or in teams) reach a limit at which augmentation can go no further, and possibly at which subsequent augmentation efforts would be detrimental? One is reminded here of human physical capabilities, such as those exercised in track or swimming. Records continue to be broken, but the margins by which they are being broken are becoming smaller, stimulating speculation about the point at which runners and swimmers will not be able to top their predecessors' speeds.

The "stage" or "level" model of intellect is often associated with augmentation, and can be employed in attempts to answer such questions. Heim (1987) describes augmentation as attempts to increase human intellectual capabilities at each stage or level, with synergetic relationships among stages leading to an overall augmentation effect. Although there may be only slight gains at any one level as a result of utilizing augmentative means, synergy may amplify their impact. Thus, the constraints associated with bounded rationality are given some opposition (although specific accounts of the kind and degree of synergism involved have yet to be formulated).

Some designers are not content with amplifying one or a limited number of levels, and then counting on synergy to perform its magic. For example, Rao and Turoff (1990) state that augmentation efforts must support all stages of intellect in order to be effective as group communication devices and intellectual support tools. Hypertext systems, they assert, "must be rich enough to accommodate the full range of human reasoning or intellectual abilities to serve the group communication process."

Intellectual augmentation also involves aspects of imagery and rhetoric.

Appearing "intellectual" not too long ago meant associating ourselves with books, chess, and classical music; today, these associations include the capable utilization of various computer applications. However powerful the rhetoric, though, there is a tendency to search for the individuals (or groups) who are "behind the curtain" of their augmented capabilities (just as Dorothy found a very human-appearing Oz behind the curtain in the *Wizard of Oz*). Many of us wonder about the sources of statistical information we use, or the graphics we view; the traces of the author or artist that we are apparently able to distill provide some underpinnings to these products and support or diminish our confidence in them.

Augmentation or replacement?

Intellectual augmentation has been contrasted with the replacement or externalization of human intellectual power. For instance, along with their use of the term "augmentation" to describe their EUCLID hypertext-oriented computer environment, Bernstein, Smolensky, and Bell directly label their application a "support" system and contrast it with efforts designed to replace human intellect:

We created an environment which augments human reasoning ability by providing a canvas on which the user may construct arguments and a palette of tools from which to choose . . . In EUCLID, the computer plays a role analogous to acoustic or print media in verbal or written argumentation: it provides a medium – an extremely powerful one – for supporting logical discourse among human users. We are not proposing to use computer reasoning to replace human reasoning. Our goal is to give users the expressive and analytic power necessary to elevate the effectiveness of their own reasoned argumentation. (Bernstein, Smolensky, and Bell, 1989, pp. 1–2)

One of the reasons that hypertext has been associated with augmentation (besides historical ties with Bush and Engelbart) is said to be its "wonderful, universally applicable, powerful, natural, human-oriented model for organizing and accessing knowledge" (a slightly tongue-in-cheek description by Raskin, 1987, p. 325). Hypertext and related technologies are often associated with augmentation because of the assumption that they somehow model or reflect a more "natural" way of accessing data – one that extends and enhances human intellect rather than forcing humans into a Procrustean relationship with their information storage and access technologies.

Carlson (1990) describes hypertext as "reducing the tedium" in a variety of complex intellectual tasks, which she claims has the nontrivial implications of encouraging the learner to deal with competing explanations of events, and of fostering an appreciation for multiple points of view. In another defense of hypertext, Landow (1987) argues that the use of hypertext will stimulate forms of critical thinking on the part of users: "The emphasis upon linking materials in hypertext simulates and encourages habits of relational thinking in the user . . . particularly that which builds upon multi-causal analyses and the relation of different kinds of data" (p. 333). Others criticize hypertext for supporting only one dimension or stage of thinking – generally the early, exploratory stage (Beeman et al., 1987).

In efforts to augment the intellect, human intellectual capabilities are often constructed as "processes," processes that once discovered and recognized by designers can be given support. Many of the initiatives labeled as "augmentation efforts" have strong ties to artificial intelligence (AI), as in Bernstein et al. (1989); however, they take a slightly different approach than traditional AI efforts (efforts that generally involve attempts to construct an autonomous machine intellect). In these AI-inspired, but nontraditional approaches, designers often assume that to "augment" human reasoning, applications must to some extent reflect or have significant similarities with human intellectual capabilities.

Sometimes this strategy becomes a kind of "AI in reverse," in which a system is designed to reinforce in individuals that use it certain habits of thinking. For others (including Bernstein et al., 1989), the system provides a "clear, precise, and relatively standardized" language that users are called on to adopt along with other tools for performing intellectual activities (for example, conducting certain forms of argumentation). The stated assumption of some of the designers engaging in AI-inspired approaches is that human intellectual functions can be shaped in ways that are consonant with their "natural" directions. Intellect is supposedly enhanced and amplified by the systems – not replaced or subverted.

These discussions about augmentation and hypertext reflect the fact that discourse on augmentation vehicles is generally focused on a rather small set of information and communication technologies (even though Engelbart included a lengthy list of "augmentation means" in his early attempts to characterize augmentation). Much of the discourse seems bent on attempting to place hypertext or various AI-related applications in some sort of context with other intellectual tools. As these discussions extend beyond hypertext to a large and increasingly expanding range of augmentation means, new dimensions of the cultural object of augmentation are likely to emerge.

Video systems are another means of augmentation and have been characterized as "technology of the self, instrument[s] of personal transformation" by Gene Youngblood (1987, p. 324); in this formulation, they have inspired discussions similar to those concerning hypertext about matters of technology and augmentation. The Chicago school of video art promoted the use of personalized video machines for self-exploration and discovery:

I think culture has to learn to use high-tek *[sic]* machines for personal aesthetic, religious, intuitive, comprehensive, exploratory growth. The development of machines like the Image Processor is part of this evolution. (Dan Sandin, quoted in Tamblyn, 1991, p. 305)

Youngblood describes the use of video for individual amplification in the following terms:

The personal instrument becomes an instrument of the persona and electronic visualization finds its most complete expression as a technology of the self. "If we make it convincing enough, it'll work, we'll become it," [Jane] Veeder asserts. "We convince ourselves. In a way it electronifies everything. The medium becomes the environment in which you evolve. We do that intentionally. It's a kind of consciousness-raising. We really are looking to evolve into these beings we are trying to simulate." (Youngblood, 1987, p. 341)

Extension and development of the individual and group through the use of video technology have a number of parallels to the augmentation means just discussed (including Vannevar Bush's memex, Douglas Engelbart's initiatives, and hypertext). Utilization of an artifact as a device for expression, reflection, storage, and communication is involved in each case. The malleability of the artifact itself is also a salient issue: for example, in the Chicago school, individuals and groups are portrayed as having a large degree of control over the shape and form of the video production process, affording them substantial means for self-expression.

Some conclusions and reflections

In this chapter, I have attempted to unravel the notions of dependence, autonomy, and augmentation in the context of group interaction and the various genres associated with it (including CSCW application genres). Each of these cultural objects has deep roots in American culture; none of these objects is without considerable implications for control. Dependence on vital resources of any kind can have significant political and social consequences. The dependencies described in this chapter may thus have far-reaching influences on how relations in organizations are constructed, as well as on relations among various socioeconomic groups, professionals, and clients. Shaiken (1986) writes that when work is "electronically demeaned . . . the repercussions carry far beyond the work-place" (p. 278).

Augmentation as a cultural object has ties with American technological wonders and inventions. It is linked with the notion that technology can indeed "save" us, that the problems presented by technology (such as that of the nuclear bomb) can only be met by the application of even more powerful technologies. Clement (1994) writes: "Computers in the 1980s had to be user-friendly. Now, it seems they have to positively *empower* their users." Dimensions of augmentation that once seemed esoteric have become an expected part of many computing genres, creating an escalation of application features (and associated rhetoric).

Augmentation indeed is a more socially acceptable concept than dependence, although it may be seen as incorporating many of the aspects of dependence; a tight coupling between human and computer is still involved. There are also strong linkages between augmentation and autonomy, although the unit that has autonomy is the human–machine pair. Vannevar Bush's memex incorporated efforts to make the individual–machine symbiosis intellectually self-sufficient – not dependent on others' memories and intellects, or even on libraries and other information storage repositories controlled by other individuals or organizations. Those of us who have engaged in lengthy intellectual projects begin to develop a gut sense of how extraordinarily dependent one can become on somebody else's decisions about what is and what is not appropriate material to add to a university library's holdings. Control of access to knowledge is control over the individual, and over the range of his or her intellectual interactions. The augmented, empowered individual or group would be less vulnerable to this form of control.

Some application designers are avoiding use of the word "virtual" in preference to augmentation-related terms. Wellner et al. contrast their efforts to construct computer-augmented environments with those of VR designers in strong terms:

Instead of using computers to enclose people in an artificial world, we can use computers to augment objects in the real world. We can make the environment sensitive with infra-red, optical sound, video, heat, motion and light detectors, and we can make the environment react to people's needs by updating displays, activating motors, storing data. (Wellner et al., 1993, p. 26)

Augmenting the overall environment so it is more responsive to human needs is yet another approach for designers.

Augmentation issues in the realm of virtual individuals and groups are just emerging. Capabilities for doctoring photographs, hiring editors to shape our written expressions, and modifying our personae were once solely in the province of the wealthy; now the "rest of us" have ready access to these tools. How far will our groups and our organizations allow us to go in augmenting ourselves in workplace contexts, and in setting agents to do our work? Conversely, will organizational leaders bent on augmenting individuals and groups force us to employ these tools (or use them themselves in routine fashion on our virtual individuals), whether or not we ourselves are comfortable in doing so? Many of these issues have close correlates to issues of portraiture, fashion, and style. I am certainly allowed to have a photographer touch up my portrait a bit; such minor changes are expected. I will be considered rather odd, though, if I have my portrait retouched so that it looks like a person half my age (or twice my age), or to the point that it cannot be readily distinguished as a recent photograph of myself. It is not perceived as "fair" to associate myself so closely with a photograph that is heavily retouched, just as it is not fair in most circumstances to wear an ornate headpiece and powdered wig (however becoming they may be).

My virtual individuals must apparently retain some association with myself, within limits that are closely maintained by various experts or by convention in photography, human relations, and etiquette. How these limits will be set (and be overridden by creative efforts) will occupy an ever-increasing proportion of the attention of social scientists, managers, advice columnists, and CSCW application users of the near future.

6
Privacy, anonymity, and agency: Applications of computer networking and the development of social analogues

> *Overconcern for privacy may indicate retreat from responsibility and sagging motivation.*
>
> *Propst (1968, p. 2)*

> *Half the world today is engaged in keeping the other half "under surveillance."*
>
> *McLuhan and Nevitt (1972)*

What can "privacy," "anonymity," or "agency" mean for members of a collaborative workgroup? The presumption that groups are supposed to work together in harmony and close contact may seem to exclude the need for private spaces, the opportunity to make an anonymous contribution, or the capacity to have one's work done by an agent or surrogate. However, these cultural objects have served to shape CSCW and other network-based system applications.

Privacy, anonymity, and agency in the realm of the societal construction of computing applications have a number of common denominators. Each has special associations within the group level: individuals' expectations for privacy, or the meanings they attach to a statement delivered under the cloak of anonymity, are affected by whether or not they are working in a group or team context. Roles that agents play in computing applications are also sensitive to group context; for instance, groups may set standards for the kinds of activities in which they can be utilized.

These three cultural objects have also been topics of frequent discussion within computer application design communities. "Social analogues," system features that are intentionally linked by developers to specific cultural objects, have been formulated for each of the three. The question of whether a social analogue will be successful in maintaining a strong linkage with a certain cultural object (beyond the association that designers have attempted to make) has a number of complex dimensions. For example, labeling a system feature as "privacy-related" may indeed forestall some privacy concerns on the part of system users. However, whether the feature will continue to be linked to privacy in significant ways – that is, continue to address individuals' concerns about privacy – is another matter. Users may become more aware of privacy and demand

223

more extensive privacy safeguards than they perceive are associated with the feature.

Cultural objects are many-faceted and constantly changing, as demonstrated in the social history of privacy concerns in the United States provided in upcoming sections. For a social analogue to be accepted as a response to or a reflection of a cultural object, the analogue may need some adjustment (and subsequent readjustment), often in light of users' own formal and informal experiments with it. Attempts to "market" the analogue or stress its relations to the cultural object in question might also be required. Cultural objects are themselves reexamined and reshaped in light of the social analogues associated with them.

Concerns about information access and about privacy have been closely coupled; in the past few decades there have been major changes in discourse on information, changes that are also reflected to some extent in privacy-related discourse. Machlup's 1962 study, *The Production and Distribution of Knowledge in the United States,* was one of the first efforts to characterize from an economist's perspective reported changes in the United States concerning "information production" (roughly characterized as an amalgam of various educational, research, office-related, and economics-related functions). Consciousness of the "information age" – the age of the knowledge worker – has permeated literature and discussion about education, business, government, and other sectors of American life. Threats associated with "Big Brother" have become construed in information- and computer-related terms, although Orwell's own efforts in *1984* extended beyond the information realm and did not directly encompass computing technologies.

In the 1960s and 1970s, information per se became broadly recognized as an entity or resource in its own right, a powerful economic, social, and political factor. Bell's (1973) account of the postindustrial society delineated dimensions of various societal changes:

1. the change from a goods-producing to a service society,
2. the centrality of the codification of theoretical knowledge for innovation in technology, and
3. the creation of a new "intellectual technology" as a key tool of systems analysis and decision theory.

Many current American constructs of information privacy are intimately linked to the notion that information is a "resource," often one over which people or organizations have certain kinds of proprietary rights. Many if not most of the rights concerning the disposition of information about individuals in the United States are not automatically assigned to those individuals, however, but reside rather in collectors, processors, refiners, and subsequent purchasers of the information. A number of legal rulings have given increasingly extensive rights to these "owners" of personally identifiable information (Samuelson, 1991).

Various attempts have been made to explain the fact that individuals are generally afforded little control over the information collected about them. Rule, McAdam, Sterns, and Uglow (1980) find the following assumption prevalent among administrators and policy makers: both individuals and organizations share an interest in the enhanced efficiency through which organizational decisions are made. This premise is often used to justify the collection, storage, and processing of any and all information about individuals perceived as relevant to the making of those decisions. In similar terms, Westin (1982) describes the following set of attitudes toward the collection of personally identifiable information in the 1960s and 1970s:

If there was one lesson that was learned during the first part of the computers-and-privacy debate, it was that personal information is the vital lubricant of the data-based social system we have been building since the 1950s. Knowledge of consumer preferences and behavior is central to marketing of goods and services, extension of credit, decisions about employment and insurance, and many other activities. Computerized personal information is equally sought by government for a host of rational and administration purposes such as tax compliance, law enforcement, licensing, program eligibility, etc. (Westin, 1982, p. 102)

With perceived needs of American society so heavily linked to the "data-based social system" (Westin's phrase), the rights of individuals in terms of information collection and dissemination have generally been construed in the courts and in the sphere of public policy as largely limited to matters concerning accuracy of information collected and some aspects of its use.

Privacy as a cultural object

Along with efficiency and dependence, privacy is a cultural object with close and long-standing linkages to computer-mediated interaction. Hewitt (1989) asserts that individuals not only learn about, but also come to own, cultural objects associated with their societies: "Once accepted, the object became theirs to pursue, to worry about, to interpret, to devise ways of detecting or even evading" (p. 71).

Such ownership is especially applicable to the cultural object of privacy. An enormous number of strong, if not passionate, public declarations of support of privacy rights – as well as the considerable number of attempts by those less concerned about these matters to deflate others' opinions of the importance of privacy – are at least some index of the extent to which individuals feel "ownership" in relation to privacy. In the 1980s, influential statements of support for privacy rights came from the Association for Computing Machinery (ACM), whose Code of Professional Conduct has the following two ethical considerations related to information privacy:

An ACM member should consider the health, privacy, and general welfare of the public in the performance of the member's work. (E.C. 5.1)

An ACM member, whenever dealing with data concerning individuals, shall always consider the principle of the individual's privacy and seek the following: to minimize the data collected; to limit authorized access to the data; and to provide proper security for the data; to determine the required retention period of the data; and to ensure proper disposal of the data. (E.C. 5.2)

In March 1991, the Association took an even more proactive stance on these issues, with publication of the following:

Whereas the ACM greatly values the right of individual privacy;

Whereas members of the computing profession have a special responsibility to ensure that computing systems do not diminish individual privacy;

Whereas the Code of Fair Information Practices places a similar responsibility on data holders to ensure that personal information is accurate, complete, and reliable;

Therefore be it resolved that

(1) The ACM urges members to observe the privacy guidelines contained in the ACM Code of Professional Conduct;
(2) The ACM affirms its support for the Code of Fair Information Practices and urges its observance by all organizations that collect personal information; and
(3) The ACM supports the establishment of a proactive governmental privacy protection mechanism in those countries that do not currently have such mechanisms, including the United States, that would ensure individual privacy safeguards. (White, 1991, pp. 15–16)

Increased attention that the ACM and other organizations of computing professionals (including the Computer Professionals for Social Responsibility and Data Processing Management Association) are paying to privacy issues in the 1990s provides a signal that privacy concerns are rising in the priorities of many associated with the computer industry.

Knowledge of the extent of privacy legislation, related constitutional protections, and administrative safeguards in the United States is restricted to very few people, unfortunately; these concerns receive minimal coverage in our schools, universities, and in the news (although press coverage has occasionally increased when specific cases or incidents come to light). Many Americans pull out their plastic credit cards on numerous occasions in a single day, but know very little about where information associated with the transaction they are about to make is going. A good deal of publicity has indeed been given to the exploits of computer system intruders (often known as "hackers"). However, far less press coverage has been given to the activities of individuals and groups who collect, process, and sell the personal information that hackers are often able to obtain illegal access to.

General interest in privacy issues in the United States has not diminished significantly over the past 12 years, as expressed in public opinion polls and in activities of some professional associations (such as the ACM) and government bodies. A sharp increase in privacy concerns was shown in the 4-year period between two Harris polls (taken in 1979 and 1983); the 1,200 Americans interviewed considered privacy more important in the 1980s than in the preceding decade. A similar, 1990 Harris poll found that 71% of individuals surveyed felt that they had lost all control over how personal information concerning themselves is circulated and utilized by business; 79% agreed with the statement that privacy is the same kind of fundamental right as "life, liberty, and the pursuit of happiness" (Betts, 1990).

Percentages just outlined for 1990 are higher than or comparable with those taken in 1979 and 1983. Alan F. Westin, one of the advisors for the poll and a major figure in the history of privacy concerns in the United States, states that results of the 1990 poll reflect the public's continuing distrust of large institutions, and of technology itself. However, despite strong privacy concerns expressed in the study, the majority of the individuals surveyed did not want to give up the benefits of having a credit system in order to diminish possible privacy losses – one sign that privacy-related issues are often overshadowed by other personal concerns.

Taylor and Davis (1989) found that personal information most directly related to jobs (for example, pay rate, fringe benefits, and educational history) was deemed "most sensitive" by a sample of white-collar and administrative employees. Respondents in the study noted that they were more concerned with the prospect of certain types of individuals and groups accessing this information than about the kinds of information processing and storage tools utilized. Taylor and Davis label as "computer desensitization" the decreased concern respondents had about the fact that information was being collected and stored about them in a computer-based format versus their fears about what individuals or groups had access to this information. The job world is not the only realm in which privacy issues arise: the field of education (from preschool years to postdoctoral work) is information intensive and has a special stake in matters relating to privacy. Proposals to streamline the handling and analysis of educational records have included some that are problematic in light of privacy issues. For example, Rushby (1990) outlines the notion of a "learning credit card" that employs "smart card" technology for support and management of learning. Rushby's plan is to utilize a credit card–sized piece of plastic with a microchip to store an individual's detailed educational history.

The issue of privacy has received support from a number of sources in American life in a variety of contexts and for a number of different reasons. The late President Nixon, in a statement in the *Congressional Record,* January 30, 1974, asserted that "one of the basic rights we cherish most in the United States is the right of privacy," and noted that technological advancements had threatened that right (H372). Meg Greenfield, in a *Newsweek* commentary, outlined what she describes as the current American attitude toward privacy issues:

Privacy in our shameless society these days has little to do with demureness, discretion, solitude, or, for that matter, good taste. It is a generic term for personal freedom from the poking and pawing, the intrusions and prohibitions of government – federal, state, local, or, equally, merely institutional, meaning all the various bureaucracies that are always asking you questions and telling you what to do. (Greenfield, 1987, p. 100)

The special ramifications of information technology for the privacy of individuals and groups include the fact that it is no longer necessary to have a large amount of direct human intervention in monitoring and survelliance (see Marx, 1985). Many activities generally considered invasions of privacy by Americans have been depersonalized and even routinized with the utilization of various communication and information-processing applications.

The right to be let alone: Some background on privacy concerns in the United States

One of the first explicit legal constructions of the right of privacy in the United States was set forth by Judge T. Cooley in 1888:

The right of privacy, or the right of the individual to be let alone, is a personal right, which is not without judicial recognition. It is the complement of the right to the immunity of one's person. The individual has always been entitled to be protected in the exclusive use and enjoyment of that which is his own. The common law regarded his person and property as inviolate, and he has the absolute right to be let alone. (Cooley, 1888, as cited in *Pavesich v. New England Life Ins. Co.*, 122 Ga. 190, 50 S. E. 68, 78, 1905)

Warren and Brandeis further developed the "right to be let alone" in an 1890 article (referencing Cooley's 1888 notion). Warren and Brandeis's privacy formulations were triggered by outrage toward newspaper accounts of matters relating to the Warren family: "To satisfy a prurient taste the details of sexual relations are spread broadcast in the columns of the daily papers. To occupy the indolent, column upon column is filled with idle gossip, which can only be procured by intrusion upon the domestic circle" (p. 196). Warren and Brandeis argued that a privacy invasion should be considered a tort "because it impaired the individual's sense of his own uniqueness, trammeled his independence, impaired his integrity, and assaulted his dignity" (cited in Dionisopoulos and Ducat, 1976, p. 20).

Lack of a clear constitutional basis in the United States for many aspects of personal privacy rights has profoundly affected the character of the debate concerning privacy – and has served as a foundation for the cases of critics of privacy-related policies. Simply put, the word "privacy" is not mentioned in the Constitution, although many privacy rights have been derived from the Bill of Rights. The First Amendment to the Constitution declares that Congress shall make no law abridging freedom of speech, freedom of the press, or the right of people to assemble peaceably and petition the government for redress of their grievances. Thus, with very few and very limited qualifications, an individual has the right "to speak one's mind, to argue unpopular cases, to publish anything" (Burnham, 1983).

Specifically, with regard to the rights of individuals concerning information directly related to them, the First Amendment places limits on government inquiries into political and religious beliefs and affiliations (*NAACP v. Alabama*, 357 U.S. 449, 1958); the courts have also determined that the First Amendment limits the government's use of those kinds of information (*Shelton v. Tucker*, 364 U.S. 479, 1960; *Torcaso v. Watkins*, 367 U.S. 488, 1961). The Fourth Amendment has been a mainstay of many defenses of privacy rights; it states:

The right of the people to be secure in their persons, houses, papers, and effects, against unreasonable searches and seizures, shall not be violated, and no Warrants shall issue, but upon probable cause, supported by Oath or affirmation, and particularly describing the place to be searched, and the persons or things to be seized.

The amendment has been held by the courts as restricting the means used by the government to collect information from places in which an individual has "a reasonable expectation of freedom from governmental intrusion" (see, for example, *Mancusi v. DeForte,* 392 U.S. 364, 368, 1968). Supplemented by wiretapping and postal statutes, the Fourth Amendment also places strict limits on wiretapping, electronic eavesdropping, and the opening of mail by governmental agencies (see, for example, *Berger v. New York,* 388 U.S. 41, 1967).

The Fifth Amendment also places some limitations on information collection practices of the federal government and has been applied in information privacy–related cases. The amendment reads in part: "No person . . . shall be compelled in any criminal case to be a witness against himself." This section of the amendment has been used to limit the means applied by the government to collect incriminating information from an individual in a variety of contexts, as well as limiting the scope of questioning during criminal proceedings themselves (see, for example, *Miranda v. Arizona,* 384 U.S. 436, 1966).

There is thus no mention of privacy per se in the Constitution, and protections of the privacy rights of individuals are often said to form a permeable "patchwork" rather than a single, solid shield. The stability and effectiveness of this patchwork is linked to the level of awareness and concern about privacy issues by the public, the courts, and various levels of government. In some eras, this concern has been strong. On August 12, 1974, President Gerald Ford declared, "There will be hot pursuit of tough laws to prevent illegal invasion of privacy in both governmental and private activities" (Adams and Haden, 1978). During 1974, there were 102 privacy bills (and a total of 207 sponsors) in the House; the Senate's privacy initiatives had 62 sponsors. The post-Watergate privacy movement in Congress maintained substantial momentum even after enactment of the Privacy Act of 1974. In 1975, there were still more than 100 privacy bills of various sorts in process in Congress.

The Privacy Act of 1974 remains the bedrock piece of privacy legislation in the United States. In its final form, the act benefited from a number of contributions, including (1) legislation proposed by Representative Edward Koch and Senator Sam Ervin; (2) *Records, Computers, and the Rights of Citizens,* a government-sponsored report that Alan Westin spearheaded; and (3) International Business Machines' (IBM's) "Four Principles of Privacy" (which were given wide advertisement in periodicals and newspapers in the early 1970s). In the Privacy Act of 1974, Congress finds:

1. the privacy of an individual is directly affected by the collection, maintenance, use, and dissemination of personal information by federal agencies;

2. the increasing use of computers and sophisticated information technology, while essential to the efficient operations of government, has greatly magnified the harm to individual privacy that can occur from any collection, maintenance, use, or dissemination of personal information;
3. the opportunities for an individual to secure employment, insurance, and credit, and his right to due process, and other legal protections, are endangered by the misuse of certain information systems;
4. the right to privacy is a personal and fundamental right protected by the Constitution of the United States; and
5. in order to protect the privacy of individuals identified in information systems maintained by federal agencies, it is necessary and proper for the Congress to regulate the collection, maintenance, use, and dissemination of information by such agencies.

(5 U.S.C. 552a, section 2.(a))

Despite the declaration in point 4, and despite the enthusiastic support given to privacy protections in point 5, there has been a substantial decline in congressional oversight of the Privacy Act and most certainly in administrating its provisions on the agency level. One major area of oversight is in the administration of computer matching programs, described shortly.

One of the longest legacies of the privacy initiatives of the 1970s belongs to the "Fair Information Practices," a set of principles developed by a U.S. government study committee in 1973 (chaired by Willis Ware of Rand Corporation):

1. There must be a way for a person to prevent information about the person that was obtained for one purpose from being used or made available for other purposes without the person's consent.
2. There must be no personal data record-keeping systems whose very existence is secret.
3. There must be a way for a person to find out what information about the person is in a record and how it is used.
4. There must be a way for a person to correct or amend a record of identifiable information about the person.
5. Any organization creating, maintaining, using, or disseminating records of identifiable personal data must assure the reliability of the data for their intended use and must take precaution to prevent misuses of the data.

The practices have often been cited in efforts of both private and public organizations to get a handle on privacy issues. As chair of the Privacy

Council of the State of Wisconsin, I led the Council in composing a set of fair information practices applicable to state and local governments.

Toward a national depository of virtual individuals: National Data Center strategies

The cultural object of privacy in the United States still has close linkages to proposals for a National Data Center. Proponents of nearly any technology or administrative measure that relates to information collection and management in the United States are still (in some way, by some party) reminded of the aborted efforts of those who sought to establish the Center. The basic concept behind the Center was a relatively straightforward one: the government might be able to save a lot of money – as well as provide better physical security safeguards – by centralizing their disparate collections of personally identifiable information.

As Smith (1979) relates, "With a centralized computer system in which information could be retrieved by an individual's name or number, each Federal agency would not have to collect and store duplicate information, nor would the agency have to ask the individual to fill out a lengthy form each time he or she applied for benefits" (p. 87). In 1965, a study commissioned by the U.S. Bureau of the Budget proposed that such a Center be created so that personal data collection on citizens could be streamlined. Two other government studies concurred with the Bureau's findings.

The National Data Center proposal stirred a great national uproar, however. House and Senate hearings soon were held concerning the Center and its possible implications for privacy, hearings described in the following way by Baran:

The dissection of the Data Bank proposal in Congressional hearings, particularly the analysis of the depth of thought that went into anticipating its long-term consequences, was both painful and amusing. It was a case where some otherwise erudite witnesses believed that they were dealing with unsophisticated Congressmen – always a bad mistake, but doubly bad if one hasn't done his homework. When questions were asked about privacy controls and the ease of misuse of the files, it was clear that the proponents of the system had not only neglected their homework, but they tried to design the system details "at the blackboard." (Baran, 1969, p. 221)

During Congressman Cornelius Gallagher's (D-New Jersey) 1965 hearings on the Center, he declared that the idea would lead to "the computerized man," an individual stripped of identity and privacy: "His life, his talent, and his earnings would be reduced to a tape with very few alternatives available." Vance Packard (a highly vocal and effective social critic) testified that the Center would lead to a "depersonalization of the American way of life." The House and Senate hearings were sufficient to squelch the idea, at least temporarily. As stated by Smith (1979): "Americans have an immediate distaste for centralization, computerization, and demands for personal information. When the three are combined in a proposal for a National Data Center, the public reaction is immediately negative" (pp. 87).

The National Data Center concept had been endorsed by many economists, planners, and top managers of the executive and administrative branches of government; however, the concept had not been formally endorsed by the Johnson administration. In 1967, Carl Kaysen, chair of the commission that originally recommended the Center and president of the Institute of Advanced Study, stated that the Center proposal was primarily a response to the "inadequacies of our over-decentralized statistical system." Kaysen (1967) declared that the Center would not contain "dossier" information (in which the specific identity of the individual would be "central to its purpose") but be a "statistical data file" in which identification of the individual's identity would be "merely a technical convenience for assembling in the same file the connected set of characteristics which are the object of information" (p. 57). Kaysen stated that proper management of the Center as a repository for statistical data files (and not dossiers) would indeed have to be "checked and overseen by politicians" so that administrators and bureaucrats involved would not slip into a dossier-like mode of operation. However, despite the effort that would obviously be involved in this oversight, Kaysen lamented that nuances of the dossier–statistical file distinction were simply lost on the politicians who rejected the proposal.

A widespread awareness of privacy issues – issues related to the construction of virtual individuals by the government – was apparently triggered, quite suddenly, by the National Data Center proposition. In the realm of political rhetoric, implications of the Center were indeed catastrophic. No longer could Americans be described as facing an open frontier and endless possibilities: their destinies were shaped forever by credit, employment, medical, criminal, and educational records – records often compiled and disseminated by their own government. Moving to the next town, next state, or even the other coast would not help: the records were ever-present, readily accessible on the other end of a satellite transmission.

Although the Center concept was defeated politically, many of the objectives of the Center's designers were instituted with the technological assistance of widespread computer matching. "Computer matching," as defined by the Computer Matching and Privacy Protection Act of 1988, involves computerized comparison of two or more automated systems of personally identifiable records (or the comparison of a federal system of such records with nonfederal records) for the purpose of (1) establishing or verifying eligibility for a federal benefit program or (2) recouping payments or delinquent debts under such programs. Since the 1970s, matching has often been conducted without notification of individuals whose records are involved.

Matching can serve to create a de facto National Data Center by comparing various record series for certain purposes. Although the Privacy Act of 1974 stipulates that information collected from individuals be used only for purposes for which it was originally collected, matching programs are often conducted by federal, state, and local agencies in ways that violate the Privacy Act. The Computer Matching and Privacy Protection Act was an effort to control proliferation of such matching by agencies – for example, by requiring that "matching agreements" that clearly outline the purpose and legal authority of the matching program be filed with the Senate Committee on Governmental Affairs and the House Committee on Government Operations.

Effectiveness of the Computer Matching Act in putting reins on Privacy Act violations has yet to be determined. What is most interesting about matching is the fact that it has been applied largely to individuals – and not corporations. Richard L. Fogel, of the Government Accounting Office, told a subcommittee of the House that computer matching could indeed be effective in constraining corporate tax violations:

> Growing budget deficits, increasing corporate noncompliance, and declining audit coverage all point to the need for a corporate document-matching program similar to the one that has so effectively promoted voluntary compliance and full income reporting for the vast majority of wage earners. (*Chicago Sun Times*, 1991, p. 51)

Use of computer matching as a tool to construct virtual individuals (and thus, in effect, to control individual behavior), along with the neglect of its use for corporations, send loud signals about the aims and perspectives of the U.S. government today.

Computer "profiling" is another tool utilized to help governmental agencies control the behavior of individuals. Profiling involves construction of a variety of statistical patterns and other information about target individuals, as well as information about recent social conditions, into various composites or caricatures. These caricatures of the target individuals (or "profiles") are then applied to statistical information about a certain section of the population in order to obtain lists of individuals who match the profiles – lists that can be used for further investigation. For example, various governmental agencies have constructed profiles of likely smugglers or tax evaders, based on information about previously identified smugglers' and tax evaders' characteristics; profiles have also been constructed of students who have a high probability of dropping out of high school based on statistical information about existing high school dropouts. Similar techniques are used in workplaces to target individuals likely to be high performers or poor performers, pilferers or drug users.

Critics of profiling techniques decry the way the techniques effectively declare individuals "guilty" before they have actually committed a crime; individuals may be given certain treatment on the basis of certain aspects of statistical information about them without adequate investigations of their situation. The kinds of problems projected by opponents of a National Data Center – problems involving temptations of having a great amount of readily accessible information about Americans – are indeed manifested in the combination of computer matching and profiling techniques and applications that the government and many private-sector organizations now have in place.

Controversies concerning the prospects for a standard identification number provide another theme in the history of American privacy issues. As stated in the Department of Health, Education, and Welfare (HEW) report on privacy matters (*Records, Computers and the Rights of Citizens,* 1973), a standard universal identifier (SUI) is a "systematically designed label that, theoretically at least, distinguishes a person from all others." To fulfill this function as a "unique identifier," an SUI must meet most, if not all, of the following criteria (pp. 109–110):

1. Uniqueness: It must be unique for each person. No more than one person can be assigned the same SUI, and each person must have no more than one SUI.
2. Permanence: It must not change during the life of the individual and should not be reused after his death until all records concerning him have been retired.
3. Ubiquity: Labels must be issued to the entire population for which unique identification is required.
4. Availability: It must be readily obtainable or verifiable by anyone who needs it, and quickly and conveniently regainable in case it is lost or forgotten.
5. Indispensibility: It must be supported by incentives or penalties so that each person will remember his SUI and report it correctly; otherwise systems will become clogged with errors.
6. Arbitrariness: It must not contain any information. If it does, for example, state of issuance, it will be longer than necessary, thus violating

the "brevity" criterion. It may also violate the "permanence" criterion if changeable items, such as name or address, are incorporated. Most important, if items of personal information are part of a SUI, they will be automatically disseminated whenever the SUI is used; in our view, this would be undesirable.

7. Brevity: It must be as short as possible for efficiency in the recognition, retrieval, and processing by man or machine.
8. Reliability: It must be constructed with a feature that detects errors of transcription or communication.

In its report, HEW argued that the SUI would have a number of practical advantages, including the following: (1) it would allow for easier updating, merging, and linking of records about individuals for administrative, statistical, and research purposes; (2) duplication and error in record keeping would be reduced; and (3) individuals would be spared the burden of recalling and transmitting a variety of different identification numbers (for example, for credit card transactions and bank transactions).

However, the very notion of an SUI has stimulated (and continues to stimulate) broadly based concern in the United States. The 1973 HEW report states that "many people both feel a sense of alienation from their social institutions and resent the dehumanizing effects of a highly mechanized civilization." The report concludes with a stern warning about use of an SUI:

The Committee believes that fear of a standard universal identifier is justified. Although we are not opposed to the concept of a SUI in the abstract, we believe that, in practice, the dangers inherent in establishing a SUI . . . far outweigh any of its practical benefits. Therefore, we take the position that a standard universal identifier should not be established in the United States now or in the foreseeable future. (HEW, 1973, p. 112)

In a separate report (independently compiled), the National Academy of Sciences Computer Databanks Project reached a similar conclusion (Westin, 1972). There were some dissenting voices from information-processing and public policy communities, however. In a 1969 address, J. C. R. Licklider of MIT placed as an element of his proposed "information bill of rights" the right to an SUI, a "unique and redundant identifier – unique in that it identifies him as distinct from all other individuals in a population and redundant in that a randomly constructed identifier is unlikely to be the identifier of an actual individual" (Licklider, 1970, p. 23). Licklider argued that this identifier would play an important role in providing privacy and security safeguards.

The social security number is the closest approximation to an SUI in the United States. It was established to number accounts for the 26 million people who were first covered under the Social Security Act of 1935. First mention of the social security number in a law or agency regulation is in a Bureau of Internal Revenue regulation of November 5, 1936, which specified that an identifying number (then called an "account number") would be applied for by each employee and assigned by the postmaster general or Social Security Board. There was an added, interesting safeguard: the regulation provided that "any employee may have his account number changed at any time by applying to the Social Security Board and showing good reasons for a change" (T.D. 4704, 1 Fed. Reg. 1741, Nov. 7, 1936).

Through a variety of administrative regulations, the social security number's use as an identifier has been heavily emphasized since 1943 and the issuance of Executive Order 9397. This order (still in effect) provides for the following:

WHEREAS certain Federal agencies from time to time require the administration of their activities a system of numerical identification of accounts of individual persons; and . . .

WHEREAS it is desirable in the interest of economy and orderly administration that the Federal Government move towards the use of a single, unduplicated numerical system of accounts and avoid the unnecessary establishment of additional systems;

NOW THEREFORE . . . it is hereby ordered as follows:

1. Hereafter any Federal department, establishment, or agency shall, whenever the head thereof finds it advisable to establish a new system of permanent account numbers pertaining to additional persons, utilize exclusively the Social Security account number.

The Privacy Act of 1974 explicitly prohibits federal, state, and local agencies from denying a benefit to an individual because he or she refuses to disclose his or her social security number (5 U.S.C. 522, Sec. 7) – that is, unless the agency involved has authority to do so in a law or regulation on the books prior to 1975. In 1976, this provision was amended to exempt state motor vehicle, tax, and welfare departments. In 1974 Congress also amended the Social Security Act to require all members of a household receiving public assistance to supply social security numbers. In 1977, the same requirement was added to the Food Stamp program. Controversies concerning the use of the social security number as an SUI continued into the 1990s: in early 1991, congressional hearings were held by Representative Andy Jacobs (D-Indiana) concerning the use of social security numbers to link files belonging to an individual. However, use of the number to identify individuals has become far less important as sophisticated

computer database tools have made retrieval on any one (or a combination) of available indices easier.

The cases for a National Data Center and an SUI demonstrate the
complexity of attitudes and approaches toward privacy considerations in
the United States. Strong opposition was expressed to specific proposals
related to the Center and to an SUI – opposition often linked with themes
of our basic freedoms, individuality, and the American frontier. Supporters countered that the benefits of the Center and an SUI in terms of
efficiency could be substantial: centralized, secure, and well-managed
record keeping, to name a few.

In the years since the height of the Center and SUI controversies, most
of the objectives of the Center and the SUI have been obtained by
governmental agencies in other ways, through computer matching initiatives (many of which are widely considered as running counter to the
Privacy Act of 1974) and profiling. Public protest against computer matching and profiling, however, has been much more muted than the wild
outrage previously expressed about the Center and SUI. It is indeed far
more difficult to imagine and project the implications of composite records
pieced together when required or desired by government agencies than
the impacts of the same material held in composite form in a centralized
storage system. Similarly, dangers to privacy of the use of a single numerical identifier seem more austere than the use of an individual's name and
other markers to perform similar kinds of identification.

Where everybody knows your name: The self, the group, and privacy

Privacy as a cultural object has often been associated with seclusion, a
life apart from community or group interaction. However, in privacy-
related literature and discussions in recent years, the meaning of "privacy" has been increasingly intertwined with social and political aspects
of human life. Post (1989) goes so far as to claim that "privacy is for us a
living reality only because we enjoy a certain kind of communal existence" (p. 1010). Similarly, Merton (1957) argues that intensely social
environments (such as those associated with modern industrial societies)
would not be feasible or even tolerable without privacy protections for
the individual and his or her associations.

Many of the social and political issues concerning privacy can be
framed in terms of the virtual individuals and groups constructed by
various governmental agencies and other public and private organizations.
For instance, computer matching and profiling create composite portraits
of individuals, portraits that play a role in determining whether or not
individuals are placed in the categories of "benefit recipient" or "potential

defrauder." Much of the information collected about individuals by the government is not gleaned directly from the individuals themselves, but is compiled and disseminated in ways the individuals have little direct awareness of.

Scholars writing on privacy issues have taken a number of different approaches, some in politically motivated support of privacy proposals, others in more theoretical efforts to place privacy among other kinds of values. The following is a sampling of these approaches, with an emphasis on those that more directly deal with social dimensions of privacy:

Privacy as instinctual

Some of the reasoning in legal cases involving privacy portray it as being derived from natural law: "The right of privacy has its foundation in the instincts of nature. It is recognized intuitively . . . A right of privacy in matters purely private is therefore derived from natural law" (*Pavesich v. New England Life Ins. Co.*, 122 Ga. 190, 194, 50 S. E. 68, 69–70, 1905). When privacy is construed as a basic instinct, the social roots or underpinnings of privacy are often not developed. Individuals (that is, "normal" individuals) are projected as having basic privacy instincts. This approach has the shortcoming that it cannot account for significant cultural variations in construction of privacy. Although most societies seem to afford at least some measure of personal or group privacy, there are indeed major variations (as Altman, 1977, describes). Clarifying the notion of a privacy "instinct" and identifying its dimensions would thus be problematic.

Functional definitions of privacy

Merton (1957) argues that privacy (which he defines as "insulation from observability") is "an important functional requirement for the effective operation of social structure." He constructs a functionalist definition of privacy, asserting that pressure to conform to the vast array of (often conflicting) social norms would be "literally unbearable" if not for relief afforded to the individual by buffers provided by the range of privacy norms.

Social pressures and tensions that accumulation of records and traces on individuals can foster are captured in this section of Solzhenitsyn's *Cancer Ward:*

As every man goes through life he fills in a number of forms for the record, each containing a number of questions . . . There are thus hundreds of little threads radiating from every man, millions of threads in all . . . They are not visible, they are not material, but every man is constantly aware of their existence . . . Each man, permanently aware of his own invisible threads, naturally develops a respect for the people who manipulate the threads. (Solzhenitsyn, 1969)

Solzhenitsyn's portrait is of individuals who are constantly and permanently aware of the existence of the virtual individuals associated with them. In contrast, in recent years, many of these "threads" have been spun with only the slightest awareness by the individuals with which they are associated. Collection of personally identifiable information is conducted as a by-product of such everyday transactions as a call to a consumer help line or purchase of groceries at a store with a credit card.

Privacy constructed in terms of privacy infractions

Given the difficulties in framing a definition of privacy, Ware (1982) proposes that we need rather to devise ways of recognizing privacy infractions. By getting a handle on the "invasion of privacy" notion (that is, possible intrusions on privacy), our constructs of privacy can be framed in more pragmatic terms. A striking metaphor for these invasions of privacy is provided by Simmel (1950), who identifies an "ideal sphere [that] lies around every human being" – a sphere that "cannot be penetrated, unless the personality value of the individual is thereby destroyed" (p. 321).

Ware (1982) outlines the following steps in determining what is involved in privacy: (1) identify a space of concern, (2) identify possible intrusions, (3) identify the consequences of each intrusion, (4) determine what "injuries" are involved in each intrusion, and (5) address legal actionability (including potential courses for redress). The steps just outlined (especially 3 and 4) involve current societal standards for what is "acceptable" and "inacceptable" in terms of an intrusion upon an individual, standards that may vary given changes in his or her living conditions and other contexual factors – as well as the positions and perceptions of others. Katz and Graveman (1991) develop a strategy for categorizing privacy intrusions that is similar to Ware's; important cultural institutions (family, home, church) are examined individually as to their possible intrusions on privacy.

"Neutral" definitions of privacy

In contrast to the preceding definitions of privacy based on functionality and infractions (both of which underscore the importance of social norms), Ruth Gavison (1980) has sought a "neutral" concept of privacy, rooted in information-related considerations. Gavison posits that privacy losses can be measured objectively in terms of the extent that others (1) pay attention or gain access to the individual, and (2) obtain information about the individual.

Post (1989) and others argue that Gavison's account of privacy is not compatible with consideration of social norms – norms that can serve to frame privacy concerns in ways that cannot be captured in the "objective" style of accounting Gavison outlines. Although a relatively simple method of determining the extent of a privacy invasion would indeed be useful, Gavison's attempt to construct such a method is seen by many privacy experts and legal scholars as not hitting the mark.

Privacy as a possession of self

The notion that individuals "own" their privacy – that it belongs to individuals in the same way other possessions do – has been expanded by some sociologists and legal scholars:

The "social space" around an individual . . . belongs to him. He does not acquire [it] through purchase or inheritance. He possesses [it] and is entitled to possess [it] by virtue of the charisma which is inherent in his existence as an individual soul – as we say nowadays, in his individuality – and which is inherent in his membership in the civil community. [It] belong[s] to him by virtue of his humanity and civility. A society that claims to be both humane and civil is committed to [its] respect. (Shils, 1966, pp. 281, 306)

Ownership of information about oneself is also construed in terms of its economic dimensions. Property rights related to privacy in mediated communications (including telephone, telegraph, and fax) have been recognized in various legal and social contexts in the United States for some time:

The function of a telephone system is . . . to enable any two persons at a distance to converse privately with each other as they might do if both were personally present in the privacy of the home or office of either one . . . A third person who taps the lines violates the property rights of both persons then using the telephone, and of the telephone company as well. (*Olmstead v. U.S.* 438, 1928)

However celebrated these rights are, it has been difficult to associate monetary damages with them. Defining and securing a property interest in information privacy could make privacy invaders open to assessments of real monetary damages, and thus might have a kind of deterrence effect that other social and moral sanctions lack.

Privacy infractions as involving the commodification of individuals

A commodification of individuals approach to privacy concerns has a number of similarities to the one just described, but has different historical and analytical roots. Commodification of "information" in general (traced in Bellin, 1990) has a correlate in the commodification of information relating to personal characteristics of individuals and their associations. Secondary and tertiary products incorporating personally identifiable information – ones that violate the "fair information practices" principle that information about individuals be used only for purposes for which it was collected – often become commodities and are marketed in ways unknown to the individuals with whom the personal information is associated.

Bloustein commented on a legal case involving use of a photograph of a person without his consent in advertising copy:

No man wants to be "used" by another against his will, and it is for this reason that commercial use of a personal photograph is obnoxious. Use of a photograph for trade purposes turns a man into a commodity and makes him serve the economic needs and interests of others. In a community at all sensitive to the commercialization of human values, it is degrading to thus make a man part of commerce against his will. (Bloustein, 1964, p. 988)

Abhorrence that many Americans express toward the use of individuals' photographs without their consent has unfortunately not been directed toward development and use of other kinds of "portraits." Statistical portraits of individuals have often been utilized for purposes related to commerce without the associated individuals' consent or knowledge.

Privacy initiatives in Europe that relate to commodification issues have apparently progressed more quickly than those in the United States. The European Community (EC) has proposed that member nations not move computer files containing personally identifiable information into nations that do not have adequate privacy protections (Fakes, 1991; Miller, 1991). Rights for data subjects supported by EC directives include rights at the time information is collected from the subject, rights to know about the existence of personal data files and their purposes, and rights to correct data and have certain data erased. The EC initiatives are framed by their designers as attempts to prevent the packaging of information about individuals by both private and public sectors in ways that disable individuals' efforts to see and correct the information – as well as to control its use and dissemination.

One of the proposed ways to circumvent commodification of individuals through sale of portraits and profiles constructed by others is the recognition in precise economic terms of proprietary rights individuals have in information about themselves. Copyrighting some of an individual's personally identifiable information could be one step in establishing and supporting these rights, although only a handful of individuals have as yet explored this option and few legal precedents have been set.

Commodification issues will be of special importance as mechanisms for the construction of characters in organizational contexts expand in number and variety. Some of the images, labels, and other means to distinguish personae that are associated with individuals in their organizational exchanges (for example, those that emerge through CSCW application–supported interaction) could be especially successful, and various organizational participants may want to profit from them. Protecting virtual individuals and groups from commodification and other forms of exploitation will provide a number of practical difficulties, but may be a cornerstone of the establishment of personal and social rights.

Privacy as support for intellectual independence

Privacy is construed in many accounts as providing opportunities to plan, reflect, self-observe, become absorbed in intellectual activities, and produce evaluations independently of others' opinions (Chapin, 1951; Schwartz, 1968; Altman, 1975; Moore, 1984). These opportunities can play a role in processes of self-definition and individuation.

Whyte's popular *Organization Man* posits the need for a certain level of privacy from social pressures for individuals to do creative work. Creativity, Whyte claims, is not a group-level phenomenon:

The most misguided attempt at false collectivization is the current attempt to see the group as a creative vehicle. Can it be? People very rarely think in groups; they talk together, they exchange information, they adjudicate, they make compromises. But they do not think; they do not create. (Whyte, 1956, p. 51)

Whyte opposes what he identifies as trends toward "false collectivization" (building groups for the sake of being in groups), which he claims will stifle creativity and intellectual initiative.

Issues of privacy in the sphere of intellectual work are especially relevant for CSCW and other network-based system applications, which are used in a variety of intellectual contexts. Brand is cited by Katz and Graveman as describing some uses of the information that can be collected easily through network statistics – information about specific aspects of intellectual activities of scientists and researchers:

Brand has argued that there is a legitimate value in knowing what materials have been read by what scientists. He points out that such information could resolve questions concerning scientific discovery and plagiarism or imitation from coincident work. It would also be helpful in rating articles so that others could seek key knowledge more efficiently. (Katz and Graveman, 1991, p. 81)

Collection, dissemination, and utilization of this information could well be influential in intellectual property disputes, tenure or promotion battles, and other matters of concern for scientists. The perception that privacy is being eroded in a system may provide a "chilling effect," convincing many users to avail themselves of other means of expression and communication (if possible) or of changing the content or style of their modes of interaction on the suspect medium.

CSCW application designers have developed some specific means for individuals to be able to work in privacy, then submit their contributions to the group. For example, HyperBase (a hypertext database supporting collaborative work of programming teams) maintains global (as well as local) versions of programs that teams are working on. "Local versions make it possible to further develop different parts of the program in privacy and commit the changes to the running version whenever the parts are tested and ready" (Wiil, 1993, p. 24). HyperBase's communication and support message facilities clarify the status of group and individual contributions for team members, chronicling relevant changes.

Privacy versus the "ideology of intimacy"

Linkages of American notions of individuality with privacy have been strong, often leading to relative neglect of privacy issues in disciplines that have substantial counterindividualistic currents. Bloustein presents a case for a strong coupling of individualism and privacy:

The fundamental fact is that our Western culture defines individuality as including the right to be free from certain types of intrusions. This measure of personal isolation and personal control over the conditions of its abandonment is of the very essence of personal freedom and dignity, is part of what the culture means by these concepts. A man whose home can be entered at the will of another, whose conversation may be overheard at the will of another, whose marital and familial intimacies may be overseen at the will of another, is less of a man, has less human dignity, on that account. He who may intrude upon another at will is the master of the other and, in fact, intrusion is a primary weapon of the tyrant. (Bloustein, 1964, pp. 973–974)

Bloustein thus contends that a certain level of privacy expectation and protection are critical for the construction of individuality.

One of the forces counterbalancing privacy is the cultural object of intimacy. Sennett and Parks both claim to have tracked an "ideology of intimacy" in recent American literature and social thought on administration, organizations, and communication (Sennett, 1977; Parks, 1982). Sennett outlines this ideology in striking terms:

The reigning belief today is that closeness between persons is a moral good. The reigning aspiration today is to develop individual personality through experiences of closeness and warmth with others. The reigning myth today is that the evils of society can all be understood as evils of impersonality, alienation, and coldness. The sum of these three is the "ideology of intimacy": social relationships of all kinds are real, believable, and authentic the closer they approach the inner psychological concerns of each person. (Sennett, 1977, p. 259)

The cultural object of intimacy has close linkages with individuation: one of the tools of individuation (as discussed in Chapter 2) is the individual's disclosure of "private" information, whether on a voluntary or involuntary basis. The fact that many members of the social science community have vested interests in continuing disclosure of information by individuals is seldom underscored by those who promote intimacy as a value. Unless individuals are willing to confide in experts, produce information for surveys, or submit to experimentation, a variety of kinds of social analysis would cease to be feasible.

Parks attempts to outline roles that the cultural object of intimacy and its related ideologies play in developing constructs and identifying measures of effectiveness in various forms of interpersonal communication: "Effectiveness is frequently equated with openness, authenticity, honesty, and empathy or awareness. Since we are constantly changing, we must constantly disclose" (Parks, 1982, p. 79).

Discourse on the meaning and value of "self-disclosure" has often emerged in the social science literature. Failure to disclose information about the self, as well as the withdrawal from or limitation of interaction with others, have been painted in a very harsh light by many social psychologists, psychiatrists, and communication and organization theorists. Rosenfeld (1979), McCroskey (1977), and Zimbardo (1977) construe attempts to avoid the disclosure of personal information or to otherwise curtail interaction as signs of emotional illness. In the psychological literature, Bennett (1967) has labeled privacy as merely a "graceful amenity" that should yield to other moral or social concerns.

A good share of theory and research in self-disclosure relates to the work of Kurt Lewin (whose efforts in group dynamics were discussed earlier). Lewin developed a theory of personality in which the self is modeled as a series of concentric circles (called "boundaries"), which are also sectioned into wedges (or "ridges"). The model presents the self as a sort of circular library that shelves information about the self according to both its centrality (how deep in layers) and its type (which set of ridges). The more central, close-to-the-core aspects of personality are thus more difficult to access, since outer layers must be permeated first (Lewin, 1935).

Lewin contended that patterns of an individual's disclosure of information about him- or herself provide clues about his or her personality, what is central and critically important and what is not. Altman and Taylor (1973) expand Lewin's model and describe the growth of a relationship among individuals as a mutual process of sharing of the self – a process that proceeds inward from outer levels and broadens across ridges. Rather than use the term "self-disclosure," Altman and Taylor coined the phrase "social penetration" to refer to this phenomenon; their shift in terminology is an attempt to signify that a broad range of exchanges (both verbal and nonverbal) are employed in mutual discovery. One apparent contrast between Lewin (1935) and Altman and Taylor (1973) is that the possibility that social penetration models overemphasize "openness" at the expense of privacy considerations is explicitly lamented in the latter work.

The self, the group, and intellectual activities

Privacy issues on the level of the group have intellectual as well as interpersonal dimensions. The issue of whether or to what extent the privacy of the individual group member is a major factor in his or her intellectual functioning has been a topic of research and debate at least since the days of Goethe, as sociologist Barrington Moore relates:

Modern societies have developed a social interest in privacy for another reason. The professions have begun to play an indispensible role in modern life. Without the sciences and scholarship that support the professions, contemporary society would soon grind to a halt . . . As Goethe remarked when this demand had just begun to grow, the development of talent requires peace and quiet . . . In a word, one needs privacy, both to acquire professional skills and to exercise them. (Moore, 1984, p. 76)

Moore underscores the importance of functional needs for intellectual privacy, needs he claims that Western society generally recognizes even though the privacy required can be costly to provide. In an artistic format, Virginia Woolf (1929) declares that "a room of one's own" – a separate, protectable space – is a requirement for adequate intellectual work for women.

Group work is often constructed as requiring a certain "letting down of barriers" among group members, however. Various intrusions on one's time, on one's office space, and even on one's personal life are permitted (if not encouraged) in a workgroup or team context, intrusions that would be nearly unthinkable in other situations. Partial results – such as barely started manuscripts – are often shared among team members, along with speculations, dreams, and half-baked notions that would normally not be deemed suitable for public distribution. The intimate atmosphere of a small meeting room (in contrast with a large work room) is linked in imagery with this type of sharing; team members meet in such rooms to "swap ideas."

Many individuals will swear that some of the most important encounters they ever had in group or organizational settings have been chance occurrences – a random meeting in a hallway or courtyard, or the occasion of running into someone in the parking lot. A number of CSCW researchers have targeted the facilitation of such informal contacts among individuals (Goodman and Abel, 1987; Johansen, 1988; Root, 1988). In Allen's (1984) *Managing the Flow of Technology,* the importance of such informal social interactions for organizational "effectiveness" is underscored. Many computer conferencing systems have incorporated some means for informal, less structured contact among participants.

Visions of the "electronic hallway" (or "virtual hallway") and "social browsing" were presented in an article by Thompson (1975), although the origin of the phrase "electronic hallway" is often associated with Orr (1986). Johansen describes a hypothetical electronic meeting involving an informal encounter:

> It is almost midnight when Betsy is ready to log off the system. Just then, the system notifies her that Karen has logged on. They type messages to each other briefly before shifting to an audio link. (Neither of them is interested in a video link at midnight.) A long conversation ensues, the kind that rarely occurs in the office while everyone is rushing about. (Johansen, 1988, p. 36)

Social browsing devices are social analogues designed to afford opportunities for informal contact among organizational participants. When does "informal" contact become intrusive, though, and possibly involve unwanted "snooping" or monitoring? Contacts in hallways and through open office doors in a face-to-face situation generally involve some measure of mutual consent for the parties involved. A leisurely trip to the coffee machine provides generally recognizable signs that one has a few moments to spare for off-the-cuff conversation. The question of how social analogues for such consent and the various conventions associated with it can be provided in network-based systems has occupied the concern of a number of designers and researchers.

Issues involving privacy aspects of social browsing are surprisingly difficult to handle. "Symmetry" is often construed as an important dimension in social analogues of informal contact situations: "The use of information/communication levels is symmetrical for both occupant and visitor: an occupant cannot make a channel unavailable to a visitor but have the channel open to monitor the outside world" (Root, 1988, p. 33).

In the version of the electronic hallway described by Root, individuals are allowed to engage in social browsing only if they are themselves open to be browsed upon. In another social analogue of informal interaction, the University of Toronto's Cavecat system utilizes cameras on each workstation, allowing Cavecat participants to see each other while they interact (Gruman, 1991). This system employs "locked-door" and "please-knock" signals to serve as privacy-related social analogues. Which of these analogues (if any) will successfully capture the imaginations of users may depend on the attractiveness of their imageries and compatibilities with other system features.

The relationships that group members form often have certain expectations for internal, group-level privacy, which some network designers are taking into account. Katz and Graveman (1991) assert that, in large networks, small-group communication "should have the expectation attached to it that files not be forwarded or distributed further without explicit permission of the originator" (p. 75). Constructing underpinnings for privacy protections remains problematic, however, whether or not such expectations can be created and narratives about group privacy exchanged. Once information is released in a workgroup context, doors are opened to further release. Once privacy protections have been eroded in the group context, however necessary the erosion may seem to getting the work of the group done, they may continue to be eroded on other organizational fronts (and possibly on the Internet as well), creating a problem with both technical and social dimensions.

Many of the intellectual privacy issues related to CSCW applications involve the establishment of boundaries between self and group. The question of whether or when an intellectual product associated with an individual becomes the group's product – when the individual no longer is afforded control over its dissemination and modification by others – is central to many privacy concerns. For example, partially completed contributions (which the individual might feel are not yet ready for public circulation) may be readily accessible by other group members in some CSCW and other network-based system applications. Similar issues indeed also arise for groups that have no computer assistance – but it is hard to deny that technological considerations can play critical roles in shaping the kinds and extent of access that individuals can have to each other's work.

One of these technological considerations is computer monitoring. The following is a description of some monitoring capabilities currently available on local area networks (LANs):

> Remote-control LAN products allow PC managers to remotely connect to other PCs on the network. Most are designed as LAN management tools, but some have an extra capability that lets managers monitor more than just the network load.
>
> Some packages give users the power to share screens, which translates into the ability to take control of a remote user's screen and, less often, the keyboard. This means that a supervisor of a LAN can call up an employee's screen on his own screen. The authority to set the notification/no-notification option varies; some allow only the supervisor to configure the package. Triticom doesn't have a notification option in its Argus/n program because customers wanted it that way. (Fickel, 1991, p. 50)

The network administrator package *Close-Up LAN* from Norton-Lambert is advertised as allowing team leaders or supervisors to "toggle from PC to PC, helping some, monitoring others [and] remotely supervis[ing] employees' work" (Fickel, 1991, p. 51).

The following are some of the possible modes of access to an individual's contributions in current network-based system environments:

1. Ready accessibility by the team leader or supervisor: In network-based systems where monitoring is involved, the supervisor or team leader could have access to whatever individuals are working on, including partially completed contributions. Other group members may not have this kind of access, however. Whether or not the individual receives notification of when he or she is being monitored is another variable here. Notification can be general (individuals may be told that their work may be monitored), or specific (when monitoring occurs, individuals receive notification).

2. Ready accessibility by all group members: In some network-based computer system configurations, no workspaces are constructed as "private." Once an individual enters data into the system they become accessible to other members of the group; an "intermediate" space, where an individual can sketch out ideas before releasing them to the group, is not available within the system.

    Not having a system-supported private space does not prohibit individuals from sketching out ideas on a piece of paper or other medium. However, it does often prevent individuals from working on some kinds of common tasks (for example, those involving some kinds of computer-based tools or resources) without their intermediate results being readily accessible to other group members.

3. Private hardware and public hardware: In the "shared hardware" ap-
    proach there are both "private" and "public" spaces; workstations con-
    trolled by individuals are coupled together for certain purposes but
    remain autonomous for others. Individuals can formulate their contri-
    butions, then make them accessible to the group if and when they feel
    the contributions are ready.
4. Private hardware, swapped disks: If CSCW or comparable applications
    are not in use, individuals may either swap disks that have their contri-
    butions on them (also known as "sneakerware") or send comparable
    packets of material to each other via the network.

Release of an individual's partial work results and work-related profiles
in the context of group sharing via network-based systems, as in options
(1) and (2), may effectively make those results and profiles available to
higher levels of management and to much of the rest of the organization
as well. Constructing an individual as a member of a workgroup may
thus erode that individual's abilities to conduct intellectual activity that is
not in direct view or control of others. New levels of privacy protection
may be required for the individual to be able to contribute as a full and
active group member as well as to maintain a certain level of individual
privacy – to have buffers both from the group and from the organization
as a whole.

Anonymity in computer-mediated group interaction

Privacy and anonymity are closely associated cultural objects. In terms
that Merton employs to describe privacy, anonymity can also be considered as affording certain types of relief from the massive pressures that
society places on individuals to conform to various norms. In many
contexts in our lives we are effectively "anonymous" (whether or not we
want someone to know our name or to construct other aspects of our
identity, no one does). When we try to find help in a crowded library or
shop, when we attend a lecture in a large auditorium, we are indeed
considered a member of the category "human being" – but not a person
whose face and name are considered significant.

The cultural object of anonymity has special linkages in the group
context. Anonymous, faceless group members and the acts they can
engage in have been a source of fear and terror for millennia. (Some of the
fear of people banding together in groups that was previously described in
this book is often linked with this kind of anonymity.) The mask or
identity shield that protects group members from retaliation can also

serve to diminish their perceived levels of responsibility, even their sense of decency.

In other contexts, censure and other forms of personal attack faced by a group member who speaks out with unpopular opinions or political views also trigger fear. Anonymity in the political sphere has often been used as a means to protect free expression, both on the newspaper page and at the ballot box. Anonymity has long-standing associations with creative expression, as well; carnival masks allow for personal expression that might otherwise be stifled, and many authors have submitted manuscripts under the universal author's shield "by Anonymous."

"Anonymous characters" are playing important roles in some CSCW applications – virtual individuals that can be adopted by group members who wish to make certain kinds of points and deliver some varieties of messages. These characters are able to relate messages that would otherwise be stifled because of fear of possible retribution by higher-ups. However, contributions of anonymous characters are still often shaped or even censored by human facilitators. The success of these anonymous characters in making possible some forms of expression, and the level of acceptance of these characters by organizational participants, will be critical in the overall success of the CSCW application genres that support them.

Portraits of the general dimensions of anonymity issues are often rooted in the context of the group. One of these issues is whether, when, and to what extent individuals reveal markers of personal identification to other group members. A second, related issue is whether these markers are revealed to outsiders (that is how group membership and contributions are portrayed to nongroup members). For purposes of this discussion, the "group" will generally be a group of limited membership, in which group members know for the most part who else is in the group – as is the case in most cooperative workgroups.

Both dimensions have in common the notion of a significant identifying "marker." In many situations, names serve as such a marker. To use our names in a certain context points to us as individuals. In this society, the name (first name and surname) generally affords a useful marker, although in the case of a fairly common name (for example, Harry Smith) such a personal marker as a pointer to an individual might not be effective in some contexts. One's handwritten signature serves as a marker in a number of important social contexts. Digital analogues for the handwritten signature are being developed that will allow for electronic transmission of various legally valid forms and documents (such as wills and leases), complete with authenticated signatures. Numbers can similarly be employed as markers, as outlined earlier in the case of the standard universal identifier. Physical objects associated with an individual can also serve as markers – as in territorial claims. Individuals on crowded beaches employ beach towels or picnic baskets to hold their places in the sand while they swim.

In many community, organizational, and group contexts, individuals make a conscious choice of whether or not to place significant personal markers on a statement, decision, or other product – something that connects that entity to themselves as unique individuals. Some forms of linkage are afforded more significance than others; names (surname and first names) have long-standing associations with individuals in custom, popular connotation, and the legal system. Individuals are often afforded means to manage the extent to which some significant form of personal identification is associated with an idea or other intellectual product, but sometimes these means are significantly limited.

There are a number of obstacles that prevent an individual from maintaining a continuing association with an idea – either within the group or in extragroup contexts – even if the individual is the first one to introduce the idea to the group or community. Plagiarism is one example. Wicklund (1989) asserts that even though protection of the original source of an idea has enjoyed some cultural support since early Roman law, other group members are often quick to "appropriate" ideas once they have surfaced in a group setting. (Wicklund occasionally uses the phrase "idea lifting" to refer to this activity.) The notion that appropriation of ideas by other group members may play a vital role in the eventual acceptance of the ideas and in the probability of their being acted upon is supported by standard lore and some social science results. Failure to associate a personal marker of some sort with an idea can itself be a form of expression, as in the act of "throwing an idea out to the group" in brainstorming sessions.

Our own decisions about associating a significant marker with an idea or event are not the end of the story. Others often make decisions concerning whether (or how) this should be done for us. For example, recent decisions by major news organizations to associate the names (significant markers) of rape victims with the publicized crime have taken away from victims the option to reveal or not to reveal their identities to the public at large. The news organizations in question have asserted that the public's need to know effectively overrides the victim's wishes for anonymity.

Anonymity is increasingly being considered as a multifaceted commodity by CSCW application developers. The range of anonymity affordances includes the following:

1. Enforced anonymity: a situation in which no association of significant markers with individuals is allowed for within the context of the situation (for example, an individual can discuss his or her voting behavior later, but no one else but the individual is witness to the act of voting). (Voting is used here as an example of individual participation and contribution.)
2. Universal identification: a situation of the face-to-face group with voice voting: members have many markers (factors associated with their identity); these markers are tightly coupled with their preferences and contributions. In communities where such a configuration is employed regularly for voting, a high level of "trust" among citizens is often said to exist.
3. Permissive anonymity: a situation in which there are few or no physical or technological anonymity protections, yet there are strong social norms protecting anonymity (for example, people can keep their eyes closed when voting occurs in a group context).
4. Monitored anonymity: a situation in which individuals can remain anonymous (for example, their contributions are not identified to fellow team members); however, certain persons (for example, system supervisors) can override any existing identity protections.

Only an enforced anonymity provides a nearly complete severance between an individual's significant markers and his or her contributions, although a permissive anonymity (where there is very strong social support for the cultural object of anonymity) can also provide some anonymity protections.

Some social situations provide contexts for explicit individual and group choices concerning anonymity. Myers (1987), along with an anonymous bulletin board user, asserts that "anonymity is part of the magic" of computer-mediated communications, allowing for creation of aliases and associated characters in conditions of "monitored anonymity." Myers interviewed a number of participants in a public electronic bulletin board as to why they created online characters rather than revealing the names and other biographical information associated with them in their day-to-day lives:

The character [alias] is an escape from the professional world I live in. The time spent as him is fun and allows the creative joy to develop again, that I've lost from time to time . . . he is a part of me, but a part locked away from work. ("Pete Moss," an engineer)

You can make the character behind the alias exactly like you, nothing like you, a combination of both, or even make it vary depending on the situation . . . if you use an alias, you can say pretty much what you want without others pinning what you say to your real name. In "real life," you have to wear a mask, trying not to say the wrong thing . . . under an alias, it doesn't matter. ("The Professor," age 14, a student)

Myers states that even though identities in the system "were changed as easily as hats," the power to create unique and personally meaningful identity was a highly valued and often-rare commodity. From his ethnographic analysis, Myers concludes that two types of leadership emerged in the bulletin board context: "social experts" assisted in others' quests to build interesting characters and engage in social interaction, while "system experts" demonstrated leadership in technical matters.

Graffiti provide yet another avenue for anonymous personal expression in public contexts. There are few studies by social scientists of social and personal functions of graffiti; the ones that have been conducted reflect close linkages between anonymous interaction and creative expression:

Graffiti are interesting because they are spontaneous and anonymous, giving expression to ideas and feelings which are normally taboo in other contexts. It may be proposed that the more anonymous the arena the more expressive the behavior. The writer can safely give vent to ideas and feelings without fear of discovery. (Kaplan, 1981, p. 405)

Kaplan describes how desk tops in schools often serve as "slates," vehicles for anonymous message sending to the next student to use the desk. In the 1990s, graffiti have served as communication vehicles for city gang members.

Morris describes how anonymity provides a shield for antisocial behavior of computer system users, and calls for its restriction:

The intrinsic anonymity of computer systems must be redressed by better ways of authenticating the creators and users of information. There are obviously situations in which anonymity is desirable – an AIDS conference, for example – but they are the exception. The use of authenticated communications must be made much more convenient; then a higher standard of identification could be demanded. (Morris, 1989, p. 449)

Morris states that this "intrinsic" anonymity has resulted in a number of problems, including the apparent difficulties in making individuals accountable for their supposed online misdeeds.

Anonymity issues have also been a recurring theme in matters related to telephone usage. Lester (1977) discusses roles of the anonymous counselor and anonymous client in a telephone counseling session, asserting that "anonymity minimizes the feeling of possible ridicule, abuse, censure, or hurt because of the counselor's evaluations" (p. 460). Lester claims that strangers are more easily confided in than friends or acquaintances, and that telephone counseling and crisis "hot lines" can thus serve many vital purposes. Shepard (1987) updates the account of phone-based therapy: although the counselors and clients described are not anonymous (they established previous relationships before moving to a telephone format), the fact that direct face-to-face interaction is not involved in the sessions is construed as playing a critical role in the way the sessions are constructed by the participants.

The advent of Caller ID and other technologies based on Automatic Number Identification (ANI) raises other issues concerning anonymity and communications. With Caller ID, purchasers of certain equipment and a special service are afforded access to the telephone number and sometimes the name of a calling party before the telephone is actually "answered." Some civil libertarians have defended the calling party's right to anonymity. AT&T, among others, has disagreed with this position, and produced and publicized a "Position on Customer Privacy":

Because a "right to anonymity" is not a reasonable expectation in any other form of human communication (personal interaction, mail service, electronic communication), AT&T does not believe it to be a reasonable basis for denying the benefits of technologically advanced products and services in voice communications. (AT&T, 1990, p. 3)

Conflicts between one party's privacy (the party whose phone is ringing) and another's freedom to remain anonymous (the calling party) have emerged in full force in Caller ID and related technological issues. The "social browsing" capabilities previously described present a similar set of concerns.

Association of the notion of "safety" with anonymity is common. For example, when a group of users and designers employed a participatory design approach in creation of CSCW applications for project management, they placed special importance on the ability to send and receive anonymous messages – in part to ensure that certain kinds of information could be exchanged without damage to individuals' careers (Muller, Smith, Shoher, & Goldberg, 1991, p. 85). The need for anonymity in communications was explained in terms of the following requirements:

1.   transmitting important information without personality issues;
2.   sending needed but "dangerous" information (for example, "you should never talk to the boss the way you did yesterday because . . .") without having to ensure that the recipient will keep the sender's role in confidence; and
3.   exploring a powerful person's response to a potentially risky idea before taking on the personal risk of being associated with that idea.

Muller et al. describe anonymous message exchange as "identity filtered" communications. Examples of "virtual personal addresses" created in their system in order to ensure such anonymity (while still identifying messages) include "humanUsers-ownersOf-projectComponent" and "anonymousSenderOf-MailReceivedEarlier-Regarding-topicKeyword."

Users of network-based computer system applications can seldom be completely anonymous in their message sending efforts: the source of their contributions can generally be traced by a system administrator (the "monitored anonymity" condition previously described). Their responses are also given some level of identification, if only to the extent that they are indeed members of the group – members with access to the mechanisms through which such a message can be delivered. The kinds of anonymity afforded thus depend on how system administrators choose to run the system, as well as other social assurances and agreements.

Anonymous characters in the context of the group

Organizational benefits of having anonymous modes of interaction, in which individuals can say certain things of importance to each other and to higher-ups, have been underscored in a number of recent publications. The following account of the benefits of anonymity in electronic-meeting-room-supported exchanges was published in the high-circulation magazine *Business Week:*

There's a bloody meeting going on. "This company has no leader – and no vision," says one frustrated participant. "Why are you being so defensive?" asks another. Someone snaps: "I've had enough – I'm looking for another job."
Rough stuff – if these people were talking face-to-face. But they're not. They're sitting side-by-side in silence in front of computer terminals, typing anonymous messages that flash on a projection screen at the head of the room . . . People become brutally honest. The anonymity of talking through computers "turns even shy people powerful," says Alethea O. Caldwell, president of Ancilla Systems, Inc. (Bartimo, 1990, p. 78)

Fox bolsters his statement that "assured anonymity will produce more and better quality input" in a meeting context with the following analysis of human nature:

It is human nature to try to please those in our work situation who control the things we need and want. Even when they are not right, we hesitate to disagree with them, to criticize their actions, or to "offend" them in any other way. And we don't act any differently when we enter a problem-solving meeting. (Fox, 1990, p. 146)

The *GroupSystems* electronic meeting system incorporates an "electronic brainstorming tool that supports group members in generating ideas, allowing them to simultaneously and anonymously contribute ideas and comments on a specific question" (McGoff, Hunt, Vogel, & Nunamaker, 1990, p. 41). (*GroupSystems* is a University of Arizona–rooted project that emerged from Plexysis.) Benefits of *GroupSystems'* social analogues for anonymity are described in glowing terms by some of its developers:

Anonymity is particularly beneficial in the meeting process. Historically, group meetings have been plagued by problems caused by incongruities in members' status, fear of reprisals, "groupthink," and so forth. The anonymity offered by *GroupSystems* solves some of these problems. (McGoff et al., 1990, p. 49)

Although some of these organizational problems were described as being addressed by the features, new problems have emerged. For example, some IBM managers decided to hold employee feedback meetings in *GroupSystems,* meetings in which questions concerning both local issues of immediate working conditions and global issues of corporate strategies would be discussed. Reportedly, participants found this experience "very rewarding." Managers, however, were faced with the following dilemma:

An analysis indicates that groups sometimes stray from the communication focus and offer opinions on peripheral issues. Facilitators take great care to ensure that groups do not gang up on the line manager in a non-productive way. (McGoff et al., 1990, p. 46)

Apparently, employees were taking advantage of their anonymity to discuss what they felt were real job-related grievances, thus deviating from the IBM-approved, socially accepted "communication focus." The utilization of human facilitators to circumvent such employee appropriation of meetings in *GroupSystems* was IBM's response.

A previously popular management-sponsored attempt to unleash the power of uncensored expression in the organization is the encounter group or T-group ("training group"). Encounter groups were a common tool of organizational developers in the 1960s and 1970s. The groups were rooted in goals that included: (1) facilitating emotional expressiveness, (2) generating feelings of belongingness, (3) fostering a norm of self-disclosure as a condition of group membership, (4) sampling personal behaviors, (5) making sanctioned interpersonal comparison, and (6) sharing responsibility for leadership and direction with the appointed leader (Lakin, 1972).

Encounter group leaders often found themselves in a position similar to that of the *GroupSystems* facilitators just described. They were often called on to steer supposedly spontaneous and free group proceedings in a way that would be beneficial to the goals of management, just as the *GroupSystems* facilitators are apparently charged with steering anonymous group exchanges away from issues that are potentially troubling for the organization.

Computer-mediated "masks": The effectiveness of anonymous characters

Varieties of anonymous characters are apparently emerging in some computer-mediated contexts. Discourse on anonymity links these characters with certain expectations for creativity, for quality and quantity of idea production, as well as for honesty and straightforwardness. Will these anonymous characters be considered useful developments – that is, worth the investment in systems (to provide adequate vehicles and protections for anonymity) and social structure (to support and interpret the protections)?

Consider the mask, that low-tech mechanism for modifying facial expression popular at parties, in theatrical productions, and on Halloween. The fashion of wearing masks in various Western societal functions developed at about the same time as conventions for anonymity and pseudonymity in writing (between 1650 and 1700). In many cases, the individuals behind the anonymous works were well known to some segments of their audiences; anonymity apparently served a number of expressive functions, being linked with modesty and lack of pretensions. Diderot's *Encyclopédie* has the following praise associated with "anonyme": "Any writer who, out of shyness, modesty, or scorn for glory, refuses to attract notice at the beginning of his work deserves to be commended" (Diderot, 1778/1978).

Associations of anonymity with masks are many-sided: today, writers normally choose not to submit a work anonymously (although it was, in some periods, a custom to do so), though pseudonyms still provide a partial mask for many authors. In many circumstances, the identity of the author in anonymous works is ascertainable without much difficulty, by either deduction or some simple sleuthing by those who wish to obtain that information. Similarly, masks are generally a voluntary accessory. They are donned on occasions where their values in hiding the identity of the individual are only partial and often temporary.

Most workgroups have limited membership. It is safe to say that in most groups, members are generally able to recognize each others' contributions; unlike most graffiti, one can often guess who said what. However, many electronic meeting system sessions that incorporate means for anonymous communication appear to "work" in that social restrictions are apparently lifted to the extent required for some things to be said that would not otherwise have been said. Individuals appear to be allowed at least some of the protections that a fairly high level of anonymity (few, if any, linkages from a communication to a specific individual) would afford.

In some organizations, hot lines and other means for presumably anonymous communications between whistle-blowers and organization-sanctioned watchdogs have been established and have had long histories of use. In other organizations, individuals can deliver complaints and make observations anonymously through suggestion boxes placed strategically in cafeterias or near time clocks. The often-recognized need for a way to break down social barriers at least for a short time in order to get some difficult and perhaps unpleasant points across may be one of the incentives that support anonymous communication in network-based computer systems – and that allow for the construction of some communications as "anonymous" that could indeed be readily identified with specific individuals.

The cultural object of anonymity could well be greatly affected by the success of systems that support "permissively anonymous" expression – expression that could most probably be traced to individuals (either through technological means or simple deduction) but is not. At masquerade parties, individuals "know" yet are "unsure" of who is behind the mask – the mask serves the social function of maintaining surprise and mystery. The social analogue of the electronic "mask" may serve the function of signaling to the parties involved that a communication is intended to be seen as decoupled from any specific individual, and thus not delivered with the force of that individual's presence behind it.

Benefits of anonymous characters to organizations have not yet been firmly established. If anonymity protections are less than "enforced" (and identities of individuals delivering remarks can be determined), those who attempt to deliver the proverbial "bad news" should beware. Careers were ruined when the warm glow of corporate-sponsored encounter groups faded and individuals (generally subordinates) were later held accountable for what they said. If similar scenarios transpire in the era of the electronic meeting room, the effectiveness of normative and technological anonymity shields will be eroded, and the development of anonymous characters will be stunted.

Agents (or surrogates) and CSCW applications

Surrogates for individuals or groups are a common part of our lives, with their use supported by custom and law. Surrogates can include other individuals (someone may commission you to buy tickets for a concert), as well as various physical objects (we may use a coat to hold our seat for us in a crowded library when we are looking for a book). Surrogates need not be of human form or of considerable size, however. The notion that a document or record can stand in for an individual and be used to interpret his or her wishes may seem bizarre – until we consider the "last will and testament," a common feature in many Western legal systems. After an individual's death, a properly witnessed will holds legal authority comparable to that of a living individual in some restricted financial and social arenas. Other documents, tokens, and stamps are given similar social standing.

Socially sanctioned surrogates extend the sphere and effective range of an individual's or group's clout. The ability to delegate certain responsibilities and to employ an "agent" to serve in one's place are long-standing features of organizational and social life; the CSCW applications environment is no exception. In the United States, as well as other nations, many statutes and extensive case law relate to the mutual responsibilities that agents and their principals have. In a group context, subgroups, subcommittees, and individuals can also be placed in the role of surrogates for the group as a whole, officially performing some aspects of the group's function.

The delegation process is not as simple as it may appear on its face, however. There are legal and social strictures against delegating certain tasks and functions in nearly any context. There are also a number of constraints associated with the personal qualities of the surrogate or delegate: surrogates must be apparently "competent" to carry out certain duties and functions. In many cases, a certain level of monitoring and supervision is required of a principal as an aspect of his or her relationship with an agent.

The possibility of incorporating intelligent agents (or surrogates – the two terms are used interchangeably) into CSCW and other network-based computer applications is attracting increasing attention from design communities, and many of the issues just mentioned about human surrogacy have taken on new dimensions. Origins of the agent notion are often traced to Alan Kay (currently a fellow at Apple Computer Corporation). Kay himself traces the roots in the following way:

The idea of an agent originated with John McCarthy in the mid-1950's, and the term was coined by Oliver G. Selfridge a few years later, when they were both at the Massachusetts Institute of Technology. They had in view a system that, when given a goal, could carry out the details of the appropriate computer operations and could ask for and receive advice, offered in human terms, when it was stuck. An agent would be a "soft robot" living and doing its business within the computer's world. (Kay, 1984)

Marvin Minsky (1987) uses the notion of agent extensively in his *Society of Mind*. Minsky's agents (which possess a number of humanlike qualities) are employed to model the functions and interactions of human intellectual capabilities and emotional characteristics, however, not as surrogates for individuals or groups.

Johansen gives examples of agents used in general computing applications:

programs that can search through databases for desired information, changing the definition of what is being sought "on the fly," based on the data found; programs autonomously and intelligently able to control telecommunications equipment; and programs that learn the preferences and habits of human users to make system interfaces more responsive. (Johansen, 1988, pp. 101–102)

As for CSCW applications, Johansen contends that agents will be used in the following ways:

Applications of agents in groupware might include bandwidth agents capable of dynamically reassigning bandwidth on demand according to group needs, agents capable of identifying and "signing up" participants in conferences on particular topics, reminder agents that help human participants to remember commitments, and topic agents that monitor a broad range of on-line conferences and alert their sponsor when items of interest arise. (Johansen, 1988, p. 102)

Not all of the potential applications of surrogates are considered as benign by Johansen: he also describes such "intrusive" applications as identifying group members who express unpopular opinions in conferences.

Agents are construed as effectively extending what individuals can attend to in a certain time frame. Herbert Simon (1977) has placed humans' limited capacities for attention as one of the most critical problems of our information-rich world: "A wealth of information creates a poverty of attention and a need to allocate that attention effectively among the overabundance of information sources that might consume it" (pp. 40–41). Miyata and Norman (1986) explore problems of attending to a number of tasks cotemporaneously when using a computer system. The designer of computer-mediated systems faces the dilemma of potentially disturbing one human–task involvement in order to alert individuals of other pending requirements for their attention.

Kay's ideas for a agent-controlled news service, NewsPeek, provide a glimpse of the "personalized" services an agent may be able to provide:

NewsPeek stays up all night looking for the newspaper you would most like to read at breakfast. It logs into a half dozen information systems including NEXUS, AP, The New York Times, etc., looking primarily for topics of interest to you, but also those that are especially interesting to humans in general. It reads the articles to the best of its ability – when it comes across a famous name, like "Mitterand," it finds his picture on a video disk. (A. Kay, 1990, p. 205)

As well as presenting news (the public sphere of news that the mass media deliver today) Kay's system redefines "news" to include personal items:

> The major headline might be "Your 3:00 Meeting is Cancelled Today" because one of its sources is your own electronic mail and it wants to bring important things it finds there to your attention. A sidebar might read "Your Children Slept Well Last Night." (A. Kay, 1990, p. 205)

Kay asserts that two areas where agents will become popular in computer systems are (1) performing tasks that require considerable strategy and expertise and (2) doing tasks that can be done while you are involved with something else (p. 205). In an academic context, a NewsPeek-style agent can be programmed to glean electronic indexing services periodically for relevant articles on particular topics related to one's projects.

Computer programs with the agent or surrogacy theme have also been incorporated into filtering systems for electronic mail. Sproull and Kiesler describe some social implications of using such filtering programs:

> In a filtering system, people can write a rule to filter out messages sent by a person who is known to send inappropriate mail . . . Then those using filters no longer have to see the offending messages. The person whose behavior is offensive, however, gets no feedback on that behavior; he or she does not know that his or her messages are being filtered out and continues to behave inappropriately. (Sproull and Kiesler, 1991, p. 139)

Sproull and Kiesler develop a scenario in which all the individuals in a group use filters: no one receives peer-level guidance as to what appropriate social participation might constitute. Thus, Sproull and Kiesler underscore the value of direct peer-to-peer interchange concerning the character and quantity of communications, advice about what works and what falls short in communicating online.

There have been many attempts to build "intelligent" functions in computing systems. Why are some of these functions construed as agents (with the many connotations such a label provides) and others simply constructed as programs? One of the aspects often used to distinguish agents from many other kinds of intelligent operations is that agents must perform for their principals in specific environmental conditions, in real time, and generally without complete information. In a group context, the agent–principal relationship appears to be an especially useful construction: agents and their relations with their principals must also be understood to some extent, and perhaps even accepted as legitimate, by other group participants, just as the relationships between principals and their human agents are.

An example of incorporating an intelligent agent in a CSCW application is Liza (Gibbs, 1989), part of a groupware toolkit:

> When Liza joins a session, a picture of an intelligent-looking android is also displayed, indicating to the group that Liza is participating. Liza's participation means that a set of rules owned by Liza become active; these rules monitor session activity and result in Liza suggesting changes in content or form. (Ellis, Gibbs, and Rein, 1991, p. 43)

The picture displayed of Liza (a small portrait of a female) alerts group members that Liza is "active." However, group members need to have some acquaintance with Liza over time in order to have a good notion of what Liza's "activity" entails; a picture alone does not suffice.

Bond (1990) employs the notion of "commitment" derived from the sociological works of Becker (1960) and Gerson (1976) to produce a model of an agent that could provide support in human organizations (for example, solve organization-related problems and maintain various objectives and goals). Bond explicitly designed his "agent" notions so that they also have implications for distributed AI (Bond and Gasser, 1988) and for the modeling of organizations. Bond constructs his agents in terms of specific commitments they are designed to make and fulfill. In this stage of Bond's work, the relationship of these agents to their principals (as perceived by the principals themselves or other principals or their agents) is not presented as a major factor in their design or use. The agents that emerge from this design strategy may thus be of limited value in relation to role taking in a group context.

Individuals in a group situation are often primarily interested in what a principal (the human being who is a member of the group) is doing or thinking, and are looking to agents for clues. Unless we can see some kind of a relation between an agent and its principal – whether or how the principal is altering (or can alter) the agent's actions because of certain events – we may not be able to learn about the principal (and to role-take) by watching the agent and its responses to various circumstances. In some cases, the agents of others are the first "audience" for what a group member produces; unless the group member can get an item past the agents of its intended recipients – and directly into human hands – creation of the item may be for naught.

Agents and role taking

How can social analogues for agents be constructed? In face-to-face interaction, individuals often stand in for others. If we need to step out of a meeting for a short while, we can ask an associate to take our places.

The associate can be construed as serving a number of functions: (1) he or she can represent the fact that the meeting is considered important enough by us for us to arrange for a representative in our absence; (2) he or she might also represent the fact that we had pressing business we considered more important than the current meeting; and (3) he or she can receive and relate information to us, perhaps deliver a message or two from us, and to some limited extent act on our behalf in the group. Other group participants learn about us from our relationships with our agents – what we have commissioned our agents to do for us in the group proceedings.

The virtual individuals and groups described in previous chapters can all serve as surrogates for the individuals and groups involved, just as the human surrogate does in the meeting just described. For example, our projected images can in many ways "stand in" for us in a group context. (Consider the presence created by ornately framed pictures of company luminaries in many board rooms.) To have an effective presence, agents need not always be under direct control (although some level of supervision is often involved), and need not be active or exhibit intelligence to any great extent. What is important is that the agent is recognized by group members and other interested parties as having a "character" in the group context. The agent plays a role in relation to the narratives or stories that the group constructs.

In conjunction with the design of agents, some network-based computer system designers are experimenting with "group spaces" that stand in for a normal physical group meeting environment. One example of such a group space (a visual setting that serves as a social analogue for an office or meeting room) is the "televirtual" three-dimensional world currently being developed at the Human Interface Technology Lab (of the University of Washington in Seattle). Bob Jacobsen of the lab defines televirtuality as the "sharing of virtual worlds by two or more people in remote places or even at different times." Jacobsen contends that the people involved in televirtuality "partake of that [computer-mediated] model to experience the place as if they were really there" (quoted in Keizer, 1991, p. 84).

A description of how televirtual worlds could be used in business situations is provided by Keizer:

Rather than use telephones or video cameras and screens to pull together scattered executives, for instance, a company could transmit a complex, three-dimensional world over fiber optic telephone lines. Participants would see the same computer-created room, perhaps filled with a computer rendering of a prototype. Participants could see the prototype in three dimensions, move around it, even enter it . . . A meeting could adjourn for an instant field trip to gather information, without anyone getting out of his [or her] chair. (Keizer, 1991, p. 84)

In some organizations, employees already relate to network-transmitted attempts at motivating individual and group effort:

It doesn't matter much that Mia Daniel, a sales manager for American Express Co. who lives in West Palm Beach, Fla. rarely sees her supervisor . . . She [receives] a daily cheerleading missive from her boss via AmEx's private network to her laptop, wherever she is working. "Let's end this year with a massive finish," reads one. "THINK BIG. THINK GIGANTIC. THINK HUMONGOUS. THINK ABSOLUTELY ASTRONOMICAL. DON'T STOP AT NOTHIN'." (Baig, 1995, p. 105)

One of the ways we learn about ourselves and each other is through how we interact with and respond to the virtual individuals and groups with which we and others are associated. Our own programming of the agents associated with us can often serve as a form of self-individuation, a self-profiling of some aspects of our preferences within the constraints provided by the system.

For example, to program a system such as Kay's proposed NewsPeek, we consider and analyze our own reading and scanning preferences. (We may trust the system to analyze our previous reading selections and project our future needs from these, but this analysis may leave out consideration of our goals and ideals, as well as future projects and plans.) Similarly, the observations we are afforded of other individuals' agents can provide information that signals how those individuals relate to certain rules, objects, and events – and what their own reading and scanning preferences are – and can thus play a part in role-taking activities. Rather than simply being a by-product of the creation of agents, the use of agents in personal exploration and in role taking may thus be one of their most critically important functions. If the agents are obtuse, and difficult for ourselves and others to understand and interpret, some of their benefits as a medium for expression and interpersonal communication may be eroded.

The social dimensions of agents are many and varied. Employing agents as our personal ambassadors, interpreters, or social facilitators may provide some difficulties, however. Kay (1990) warns that the use of agents in sensitive interpersonal realms could backfire: "It would not do for an agent to randomly insult clients with whom it is trying to make appointments. It is indeed hard to undo an insult!" (p. 206).

The agents that Brennan (1984) proposes – agents designed to make complex interfaces easier to use – have explicitly represented, humanlike personae. Laurel (1986) notes that designers are tempted to design agents of this kind as a "model of human personality, with human-like knowledge and thought processes" (p. 84). However, Laurel contends, less powerful AI approaches than those projected by many AI researchers may be required to perform the requisite functions adequately. She provides the example of Weizenbaum's "Eliza" program in her argument, a program relatively simple in structure (largely a set of branching statements) yet effective in some contexts in representing a human being.

Among Laurel's (1990) criteria for a good agent are the following: "[It] will do what I want, tell me all I want to know about what it's doing, and give me back the reins when I desire" (p. 357). Kay (1990) asserts that an agent's "safety and ability to explain itself in critical situations" will be the primary criteria for an "acceptable" agent, with common sense also being a vital component. (Designing systems with common sense has been a long-standing objective of some AI theorists, including John Mc-Carthy, 1984.) Negroponte (1990) sees "trustworthiness" as a necessary attribute of an agent. Negroponte also claims that agents must have a certain amount of discretion and autonomy, however, because if every aspect of a task had to be explained to the agent, the "relentless explicitness" required for agent–human communication would erode its practical value (p. 351).

The question of how far designers should go in terms of anthropomorphism – designing artifacts so they will appear or function as humanlike entities – has been raised in a number of contexts and takes on increased salience in the realm of agents. Bright Star Technology, Inc., has developed a Macintosh desk accessory *(At Your Service)* that features a picture of a bow-tied male "actor" named "Phil." Phil provides a number of services for users, including the following:

Phil offers greetings, with a time-of-day-specific salutation whenever you boot up; reminders can be delivered hourly, weekly, annually, and more; Mail Call alerts you to incoming Microsoft *Mail* and CE *QuickMail* messages; and in Health Watch, Phil monitors keyboard and mouse activity and tells you when to take a break. (*Infoworld*, 1991, p. 18)

Phil is intentionally designed as humanlike, "speaking" (along with facial movements and expressions) when he communicates with human users. Would Phil be just as effective without these human resemblances? Probably not. Phil's image helps to attract and focus our attention to the activity at hand, just as a human helper at our side would. Robotics designers have approached similar conceptual issues for the past several decades, considering whether humanlike qualities and functional resemblances should be constructed as essential parts of industrial robot design and operation (Miller, 1983). Placing humanlike images on robots, or designing robot parts that have correlates with human ones, has often aided integration of these machines into manufacturing contexts.

Not all of the computer community supports the promotion of computer anthropomorphism: some computer system designers and researchers have stated opposition to the conscious injection of anthropomorphism in various aspects of computing, including the design of agents. For instance, Nelson (1990) contends that "crypto-social" entities – "perky or sassy personalities full of greetings and apologies" – have no place in computer interfaces: "We do not need gratuitous social interaction, but rather clear, sensible models of the working domain" (p. 238). Microsoft's *Bob* software was both lambasted and warmly received in 1995 for the talking animals it uses to communicate with users.

Designers are beginning to explore the social dimensions of interface agents employed in a group context – agents particularly designed to be used in environments where more than one individual will control them and have access to them. Problems involved in designing agents that relate to one individual and his or her individual tastes and needs can differ substantially from those employed as group-oriented entities. In constructing a group-oriented agent, the images, sounds, words, and/or icons associated with the agent must have significance to a good share of the group members – not just to a specific individual. Development and utilization of a group-oriented agent could be seen as part of the process of group narrative construction. The character of the group is reflected in the agents it selects, along with how the agents are represented, programmed, and utilized in practice. Group agents signal areas of concern deemed important enough for the group to keep an eye on; they also identify activities that the group constructs as being programmable and specifiable – and thus capable of being handled by an agent rather than consuming group members' time and attention.

How do we experience the agents associated with us, and over whom we have some control? Hill (1989) distinguishes among three ways of "experiencing AI" – that is, of responding to and dealing with AI programs. Hill's distinctions are useful in analyzing how we approach and use agents (both our own and those of others). First-person experiences of AI programs are those in which the user feels as if he or she is doing the bulk of the intellectual activity involved in the human–computer relationship; the computer serves as an intellectual "prosthesis." Examples that Hill provides here include graphic extensions to Prolog debuggers (such as Coda).

Second-person AI experiences (which Hill claims are most common and will probably remain so) are those in which the user interacts with the intelligent program as an "other," as "a you to converse with" (p. 36). The question-answering system pioneered by Weizenbaum (named "Eliza") is considered by Hill as belonging in this category (Weizenbaum, 1979), along with a number of expert systems.

Third-person experiences of AI can be characterized by the inclusion of an authorship dimension: "The program's system image must mediate authorship" (p. 36) and be viewed by others as an artifact created by someone. Hill provides the example of Malone's message system Lens (Malone et al., 1987) as an AI program that is usually experienced in this way.

Agents utilized in a social situation such as a group or team context can be seen as falling into all three categories, and others as well. The person with whom the agent is most closely identified may relate to the agent in the first-person mode, as an intellectual extension or tool. Other group members are also in relationship with this agent, however, and may evaluate the competence of both the agent and the individual with whom the agent is associated by how well the principal–agent team operates in certain circumstances. The agent is thus viewed as a team member – as part of a partnership with its principal. Other group members may construe the agent as a vehicle for influencing the principal (either directly or indirectly) – for example, by employing the agent to communicate messages to the principal (just as children of divorced parents are often employed as vehicles to convey messages between their mothers and their fathers).

Aspects of authorship (Hill's third-person AI experience) are thus involved in agent–principal relationships, but these relationships are often better characterized as continuing and iterative authorship and monitoring. Our reaction to what is happening to the agents associated with us (agents who serve as virtual individuals) is a signal to others of our interest and attention levels. Our agents can be seen as having a "character" – one created in part through these interactions – and as playing a role in narrative creation. Reactions of others to our agents (what others allow our agents to do, or how others constrain our use of our agents) are an aspect of others' reactions to us. In the case of the group agent (the agent that has a number of team members as principals), the group as a whole may desire a common understanding of what the agent is doing – and thus the agent's actions may serve as another sort of group expression and communication device. The agent serves as an extension of the group, a vehicle through which the group can explore its common (as well its divergent) purposes.

For example, if some group members compose an agent to glean various electronic news services and newsletters for information relevant to our project, and we perceive that a good deal of the information being gleaned is not relevant to the project, we will most probably surmise that there is either a problem in the agent's programming or some significant difference in the way we construe the project's goals and objectives in comparison to the way other group members do. To get a handle on what differences exist between ourselves and other group members, we may review how the agent was programmed and possibly experiment with other configurations. However, the prospect of personally programming and reprogramming all of the agents that a busy group will be utilizing in future systems is unlikely. If we find other agents to be similarly puzzling, we will most probably at some point quiz our fellow group members about their perspectives on the project, and/or watch for other clues that we are somehow out of touch with what other members are doing. In many cases, we may consider our differences with fellow group participants concerning these agents as providing useful signals about the group's overall direction.

Development of group agents may serve to extend and modify the available notions of agent anthropomorphism. If negotiation and shared understandings are emphasized when agents are constructed, the common product may seem more like a child with several, possibly domineering and conflicting parents than a butlerlike servant (the latter being the image most often associated with agents today). Multiple agents representing different, competing group factions may also be created, and thus also serve to distinguish subgroups; these sets of agents could forestall the groupthink (the restriction or stifling of some group intellectual processes) that might result if a single set of agents is employed by the group.

As an example of close human–agent association, Myron Krueger (1991) observes that individuals often identify intensely with visual images associated with them in an "artificial reality" configuration. He describes what often transpires when a projected image of a hand controlled by and associated with an individual is "touched" by the hand image associated with a "stranger" (in this case, a hand controlled by Krueger, behind the scenes): the individual quickly moves his or her hand image away from the stranger's. Krueger concludes that strong personal identification with the images is involved, and that societal prohibitions against allowing strangers to touch one's hands have apparently been transferred to the electronic realm.

Understanding and explaining such identifications, along with creating agents that are effective in social contexts, are formidable undertakings for which there is little direct precedent. Computer science and AI have long-standing connections with a cognitive science rooted in the model of replicating human intellect (as described by Turkle, 1984; Gardner, 1985; and others). Designing a carefully monitorable, personal or group "surrogate" in a social situation is at variance with the many AI initiatives that seek primarily to create a kind of autonomous intelligence, one that is not modeled on or otherwise linked with any individual or group. However, there is more involved with designing effective agents than replicating a humanlike intellectual unit (which is not to underestimate the difficulty of the latter task). Some notion of how intellectual units function in the context of a system (in this case, a group) is required for this design effort. Constructions of how individuals identify with and relate personally to these agents may also be needed. Some efforts are moving closer to constructing AI as involving (if not emphasizing) human–computer partnerships and symbioses, as related in these projections by AI researcher Hans Moravec:

Today, and for some decades into the future, the most effective computing machines work as tools in human hands. As the machinery grows in flexibility and initiative, this association between humans and machines will more properly be described as a partnership. In time, the relationship will become more intimate, a symbiosis where the boundary between the "natural" and the "artificial" partner is no longer evident. (Moravec, 1988, p. 75)

Integrating various social and personal perspectives into AI may serve to enrich its supply of narrative themes and characters, thus triggering new kinds of research initiatives (such as the tangents that research in cooperation and intelligent agents are currently taking).

Agents as puppets, protagonists, and progeny

Agents can be constructed as puppets, as protagonists, and as progeny, ways that often overlap in individual cases. An agent can be constructed in more than one of these roles, although one way seems to predominate in a specific setting. Agents serving primarily in the capacity of puppets are seen as reflecting as directly as possible the wishes of their individual users and are generally closely monitored or controlled by them.

In contrast, when agents are constructed as protagonists, they serve as one of the main characters in the group's or individual's narratives, "around whom the action centers" *(Webster's New World Dictionary)*. The actions of protagonist agents are often constructed as largely independent of specific human users or of the group as a whole, although they may have a strong linkage with the CSCW or other network-based system application with which they are associated. Protagonist agents may include those that are designed to help with difficult decision making and information searches (for instance, agents that have expert system and advanced database capabilities).

Agents in the role of progeny exhibit obvious signs of being a product of more than one individual (or of the group as a whole), taking on associations with various group members. Progeny agents are like children, at times being constructed as (1) associated with the group as a whole, (2) independent and having a will of their own but still relating to the group, and (3) closely linked with one or more specific individuals. An example of an agent that is best considered in the progeny mold is the "activity assistant" of ESPRIT's EuroCoOp project. It serves as an assistant for the group as a whole:

The activity assistant enables users to define, enhance, or modify cooperative activities, supervise work progress, make joint use of documents and services in the activity context and exchange information. The activity assistant distributes activity descriptions, appended documents and information to the participating users in a consistent manner. (Kreifelts, 1993, p. 5)

The way that agents are constructed – as puppets, protagonists, or progeny – has tight linkages to notions of delegation. Although we may closely monitor or associate ourselves with our agents, some level of task delegation from human to agent occurs. If one must monitor agents too closely and not trust them, at least to some extent, their usefulness will be minimized (as Negroponte related in an earlier section).

Tondl (1989) defines "delegation" as the process of transfer of some specific human actions to machines, a transfer "based on some conceptual schemes or models of human actions (usually rational actions based on some capabilities, skills, knowledge prerequisites, and so forth) to information technologies" (p. 321). A long-standing topic of discussion in the computer application design and philosophical communities concerns the kinds and quantity of functions normally performed by humans that can (or should) be delegated to computers. Moor (1985) asks whether there are "decisions computers should never make," realms in which delegation of the type that Tondl specifies should not be allowed. Moor argues that two questions should be asked before we delegate decision-making functions to computers:

First, what is the nature of the computer's competency and how has it been demonstrated? Secondly, given our basic goals and values, why is it better to use a computer decision maker in a particular situation than a human decision maker? (Moor, 1985, p. 129)

Weizenbaum (1979) takes the strong position that computer intelligence is "absolutely alien to any and all authentically human concerns" and as such should not be utilized to assist in decision making in sensitive areas of human life (p. 227).

Various kinds of failures involving delegation have been distinguished: for example, agents may be programmed incorrectly or applied in contexts for which their programming is not relevant. Rosenbrock characterizes such failures in the following terms:

When a computer fails, either through a hardware fault or a software error, its behaviour no longer expresses the human purpose which was induced in it, but a different purpose arising from its faulty condition. Failures in the human organism can equally result in aberrant behaviour expressing the purpose of a faulty organism. (Rosenbrock, 1991)

Rosenbrock continues that a "sane actor can represent a madman; a mad actor represents only himself, and is spontaneously mad in his own way." Machines that fail are thus severed to some extent from the purposes and plans of their human designers.

In the principal–agent relationship, failures involving delegation may result from failures of the principal to monitor the agent sufficiently and/or from the agent's own opacity (for example, its failure to communicate appropriately with the principal or to be available to the principal for monitoring purposes). For agents constructed as puppets, this monitoring may be extensive and constant. For protagonist agents, longer periods of operation without monitoring may be required for the protagonist to perform its functions.

Since protagonist agents are constructed as performing difficult, sometimes poorly defined or unstructured tasks, their failures may be construed quite differently than those of a puppet agent (whose tasks are more delimited). These may be considered as task-definition failures, rather than those of the agent itself, although this distinction may indeed become blurred; one may expect many principals to concentrate their efforts on reprogramming agents after such failures, rather than in reconstructing the task situation (the former generally being far easier than the latter). In the group context, delegation and possible failures associated with it have a number of additional, complex dimensions. If an individual is allowed with little or no protest to utilize an agent in the group context (for example, in certain interaction- or decision-related functions), the group to some extent has sanctioned that relationship and may be seen as at least partly responsible for the resulting failures. Group members may indeed decide not to continue condoning the use of agents in areas in which such failures have occurred. Similar situations may develop with agents that are constructed as progeny (agents associated with the group as a whole).

Some of the failures related to agent delegation may involve the inability of principals and observers to shift from one mode of agent construction to another when appropriate. They may not be able to focus on the progeny-related aspects of agents in a group context, for instance, or recognize that an agent is being constructed by others as a protagonist rather than a puppet in certain situations. Consensus (or dissensus) concerning the status of agents will indeed have a critical role in how and where the agents are utilized and whether or not their activities are "successful."

Some conclusions and reflections

A good deal of our lives and livelihoods are wrapped up in what happens in organizations of various shapes and forms – educational and nonprofit, governmental and corporate. We thus have a great deal at stake in how we as individuals – as well as the groups we belong to – are constructed in those settings, regardless of the extent of computer mediation of our activities. Cousins warns us that we have to protect our personal identities in our roles as organizational participants:

Human beings in a world of computerized intelligence are taking on a quality of spindled artifacts; they are losing their faces. They are also losing their secrets. Their mistakes and indiscretions are metabolized by a data base, never to be forgotten. Nothing is more universal than human fallibility; nothing is more essential than forgiveness or absolution. Yet statistical maintenance is as remorseless as it is free of redeeming judgments nourished by intangibles or the passing of time. (Cousins, 1981, p. 104)

Our notions of what is acceptable in terms of constraints on our freedom to express our individual identities have deep roots in our economic and political systems. In most cases, the burden rests on individuals to explain why certain actions by authorities constitute distortion of their images, "invasions of privacy," or other forms of encroachment on their well-being. Many civil libertarians take wholly different approaches in these matters, however. For example, Rapoport (1961) asserts that "the individualist maintains that every restraint imposed on the individual be justified by specific circumstances, must be enforced impersonally in terms of objectively identifiable, publicly stated criteria, and must be confined to overt acts" (p. 348).

Why is there such tolerance in the United States for activities that are indeed considered by many to be invasions of privacy, including the creation and manipulation of virtual individuals and groups? The American craving for demographic, behavioral, and attitudinal information noted by Wilkinson (1988) and others provides one rationale:

Taking the national pulse is a recurring pastime for newspapers and magazines. What is "the nation's mood"? What changes are underway in Americans' attitudes to themselves, their work, other people, the future? "New findings show that seven out of ten Americans . . ." (Wilkinson, 1988, p. 5)

Although Americans find these portraits of society and community of interest, fewer are willing to contribute directly to them by filling out forms or answering a survey taker's questions. An increasing number of surveys are being conducted with passive data subjects, through information gleaned as by-products from various transactions (such as credit card purchases).

As portrayed in this chapter, the cultural objects of privacy, anonymity, and surrogacy have a number of aspects in common in the context of computer applications, especially those for support of group expression and interaction. All three involve issues of the individual's management of aspects of his or her personal identity. All three involve critical dimensions of the construction of individuals and groups. Many aspects of information privacy involve creation and manipulation by others of virtual individuals and groups that are linked to us in our workplace or educational associations. For instance, recent discussions about information privacy often include concerns about utilization of computer profiling and other social science and statistical techniques to characterize and provide interpretations of individual behavior.

Social analogues associated with anonymity also involve dimensions of virtual individuals and groups; these analogues can provide system-enforced means for the control of personal expression (there may be no way for an individual to express certain aspects of his or her identity in the group context, for example). Social analogues associated with agency afford individuals and groups means to construct entities that are tailored for specific purposes and with which they often have high levels of personal identification.

Virtual entities that are decoupled from the individuals and groups associated with them in time and context are dangerous entities. These entities often have only a tentative linkage to individuals, but can affect these individuals and their livelihoods profoundly. Statistics collected about our economic activities can show up years later in job interviews;

educational, political, or medical records may constrain our future activities no matter what the records' relevance is to them. The voices of individuals and groups, the expressions of their needs and personalities, are muffled and distorted. Designers can work to construct systems that support the production of virtual entities that are meaningful and relevant.

7
Toward a genre-responsive design approach for computing applications

The requirements for design conflict cannot be reconciled. All designs for devices are in some degree failures, either because they flout one or another of the requirements or because they are compromises, and compromise implies a degree of failure.
David Pye, The Nature and Aesthetics of Design *(1978)*

Each electronic medium has come into its own only when we recognized its newness and stopped trying to use it as a container of the old.
Tony Schwartz, Media: The Second God *(1981)*

In building a design approach for computing applications that is responsive to their social and ethical dimensions, Pye's remarks are certainly instructive. He counsels us that all designs are in some senses compromises, and are therefore "failures." Schwartz's comment prods us to look for new dimensions and possibilities in design, as well as to develop new ways of seeing media – not just new ways of applying new media to old problems. We tend to view new technologies with standards and expectations formed in previous eras: it is indeed difficult to do otherwise. The upshot of Pye's and Schwartz's counseling, simply put, is that computing applications and network-based system approaches in particular are likely candidates for revision, rethinking, and revision again.

I develop the notion of "genre-responsive design" in this chapter, along with some specific considerations for designers, managers, and users. Genres reflect complex political, social, and economic interactions among the individuals and groups with which they are associated. Couplings that genres have with various cultural objects serve to shape users' expectations of those genres, as well as affect the scope of the genres' utilization for constructing virtual individuals and groups. Designers should be sensitive to genres, but not be overwhelmed by them; the influence of genres is powerful, but designers indeed have some means through which genres can be modified and extended for particular purposes and contexts.

Both speaker and audience are constructed in CSCW application genres. For example, agents or surrogates can be constructed as both audience and speaker by the various parties that relate to them. The notion of narrative emphasizes the instability and volatility of efforts to construct speaker and audience; narratives often emerge without a firm connection to any one speaker, and the audience for a narrative has a similar lack of clarity. Who is "speaking" when an oft-repeated tale is told? When the audience fills in the gaps in a set of narrative fragments, who is the speaker and who the audience? With hypertext applications, where speaker and audience, reader and writer often merge, construction of the various parties can take especially creative and interesting twists.

The narrative paradigm: *Homo narrans* and the construction of group character

Attention to narrative as a model or "master metaphor" has cut across disciplinary boundaries. Administrative theorists have described "organizational narratives" and "stories" as playing important roles in organizational culture (Martin, Feldman, Hatch, & Sitkin, 1980). Social psychologists have explored narrative as a mode of self-construction (Gergen and Gergen, 1986). Communication theorists and rhetoricians have gotten into the act as well. Walter Fisher (1985, 1987), from the rhetorical camp, outlines the "narrative paradigm" in the following terms:

humans are . . . storytellers; the paradigmatic mode of human decision-making and communication is "good reasons" which vary in form among communication situations, genres, and media; the production and practice of good reasons is ruled by matters of history, biography, culture, and character. (Fisher, 1987, p. 7)

CSCW application genres introduce new dimensions of issues concerning both individual and group narration, including questions about control of group narrative production, development and maintenance of participant roles, construction of an "audience" for the narratives, and placement of narrative accounts in time frames.

Application of the term "paradigm" is often considered honorific: only ideas and theoretical frameworks of momentous impact are generally construed as being worthy of the term (see Kuhn, 1970, and hundreds of subsequent discussions). Fisher employs the phrase *"Homo narrans"* as well as "paradigm," adding an extra emphasis. Fisher presents a lengthy defense of his high regard for narrative – arguing that to assert that humans are storytellers is not to deny rationality but to extend its boundaries beyond those of logic and argumentation. Fisher contends that as storytellers and as rhetorical beings, humans are as much "valuing" as they are "reasoning" animals. He asserts that value judgments humans make are inevitable; the judgments are not irrational just because they are not well described in the terms of traditional logics. They do not admit of a fully realized and explicit consensus: "No analytically ground[ed] hierarchy of values will ever claim universal audience" (p. 105).

Gergen and Gergen (1984), along with Fisher, assert that potential benefits of the narrative paradigm for a number of fields and pursuits are many and varied. These benefits may include (1) providing a focus on sequences of symbolic actions and their meaning; (2) helping to make apparent that texts have historical, situational, and biographical contexts; and (3) underscoring that the meaning and value of accounts (or stories) are influenced by how any account stands in relation to other accounts that the audience has. Considering that a credit record, a computer-generated profile, a retrospective account of a decision, or a task force report tells a "story" in much the same way as a novel or a play does opens the door to new forms of analysis.

One of narrative's benefits for research in CSCW applications is that it has relevance not only for written and printed communication, but for oral, pictorial, and electronic as well (Chesebro, 1984; Haynes, 1989). The experience that has been gained in the exploration of narrative's political and social dimensions is also of value for our investigations. Many CSCW applications in active development or operation are multimedia, employing both video and computer conferencing (as in Xerox PARC's Media Space), or both face-to-face and computer-mediated components (as is the case with many electronic meeting systems).

Social science investigations of groups and their interactions often focus on group members' own satisfaction and perceptions of group proceedings, and downplay or ignore ways in which group members attempt to shape the image of the group, the group's products, and the group's proceedings for others (including other group members). Groups have "audiences," both external and internal, for their interactions. Groups are constructed, in part, in relation to external audiences, those construed as "outsiders." Many members of this external audience have some stake in what transpires in the group, however. CSCW applications may serve to alter the ways in which these audiences have access to the group and its products, and thus play a role in constructing the audiences themselves. Agents that group participants utilize for various purposes in network-based systems themselves comprise a kind of audience, and are a part of the computer-facilitated creation of narratives.

Narrative, audience, and the first-person plural

Group efforts in narrative construction have many dissimilarities with those that are considered to be "individual" efforts – but there are also a number of commonalities and couplings between the two. In collaborative writing activities, in group decision making, in discussion, and in conflict resolution, groups compose narratives that relate events and sequences relevant to the group (events and sequences that can have a number of common threads or be quite disparate in form or features). For instance, in group decision making, events and sequences can include group members' statements of their assumptions, issue presentations, alternatives generated by the group, discussion topics, decision recommendations, and future plans to continue debate or carry out the group's decisions.

In some group narrative efforts, identities of group participants are submerged and the individual has a certain level of anonymity. For example, collaborative writing can involve the construction of a single, unified voice (the "we"), as well as a cacophony or mosaic of individual voices. In the social psychology literature, the state of reduced focus on the individual is often labeled as "deindividuation":

> Deindividuation seems to be an important element in the savagery of a lynch mob, just as it seems to be an important element in the path toward enlightenment. Reducing self-focused attention seems to be a necessary, but not sufficient, condition for the very worst and the very best of human potentials. (Mullen and Hu, 1986, p. 10)

Deindividuation is only one of the ways to characterize a decreased emphasis on the individual as a unit. An individual (or individuals) can be "written out" of an account of a certain set of proceedings, whether or not his or her own self-focus and awareness are diminished (or whether the individual is indeed aware of how his or her contributions are being presented).

Apostles of anonymity in group interactions have been increasingly vocal in its support. Fox (1990) writes in glowing terms of the value of submerging individual identities in group decision-making efforts, downplaying possible negative consequences of deindividuation or reduced consideration of the individual decision maker: "The fact is, assured anonymity will produce more and better-quality input . . . getting participants to speak frankly, and to tell more" (p. 146). The deindividuated self as part of a group writing effort or decision-making team can be seen in contrast with the highly individuated writer or decision maker of some group efforts – for example, the individual who is distinguished in the group by composing a dissenting opinion or who is openly credited with an idea or motion. Composition or demographics of a group can be construed as a critically important factor in group process considerations, particularly when the members involved serve as representatives for absent constituents (such as in assemblages required in representative democracies, in contract negotiations, or in policy making). The manner and extent to which identities or representative standings of group members are revealed or are otherwise involved in group proceedings are aspects of construction of the group's character. "Character" construction is an essential aspect of narratives. Toolan declares that reader and writer, listener, and teller participate in the creation of characters:

Character is an illusion in which the reader is a creative accomplice: a variety of descriptions of some posited individual, together with descriptions – implicit or explicit – of that individual's actions and reactions, suffice to lead most readers to conceive of a person of whom these references and insights are just glimpses. (Toolan, 1988, p. 91)

Toolan uses an "iceberg principle" to describe how readers may "read" a character: they generally assume that much more lies behind the surface than can be captured in a description of the character. How do readers or listeners project what is beneath the iceberg? Fowler outlines some core character traits of individuals, traits that often appear in narrative construction:

The novelist and his readers make reference to a stock of physical, behavioral, psychological, and verbal attributes out of which fictional characters may be put together in somewhat the same way as the police assemble an "identikit" picture out of a set of pictures of segments of different kinds of faces. In modern "realistic" fiction, the semes tend to reflect the cliches and stereotypes in terms of which the society which supports the literature sees itself: aggression, materialism, possessiveness, piety, innocence, naivete, ambition, sensitivity, physical power. (Fowler, 1977, p. 35)

Various audiences also attempt to construct how group members interact, to understand how matters of control are apparently resolved in the group, and to ascertain who group members are in their roles both inside and outside the group context. Some of the stock concepts of collaborative workgroups that can be used to flesh out a character for a group come from the descriptions and models of workgroups described in Chapter 3. This is an evolving set of notions, with different ones developed as interest in and attention to workgroups increases and the genres associated with groups flourish. Number and variety of popular and formal accounts of "what work teams are like" are growing at a rapid pace, and reflect an interest in obtaining ready characterizations of workgroups. For instance, in the August 1991 edition of *Computer Language,* an article entitled "Pull Together!" provides a characterization of study groups (small groups of people who meet regularly to discuss new ideas). The article also presents some vocabulary for talking about study groups and outlines various issues, applications, examples, problems, and possibilities for them in the context of computing and information-related work (Cohen and Keuffel, 1991).

Narrative requires not only a description of a state of affairs; it also involves descriptions of change, of action, or of difference, which all assume some kind of temporality. Todorov (1990) distinguishes "succession" and "transformation" as two kinds of temporality in narration, the former a mere chain of events, placed in chronological sequence. Transformation, in contrast, involves a kind of substantive change from one time period to another. Transformations are often involved in group narrations – narrations that include decisions, task force reports, and theater productions. Narrations provide accounts of how certain changes have occurred – how observations, assumptions, and statements of value are incorporated in and transformed into decisions and plans, for example. The perspective that individual and group decision making can be best characterized as a "web" of reasons, arguments, and ideas is at variance with traditions that present decision making either normatively or descriptively in terms of a linear sequence.

An aspect of the narrative approach that is often neglected in literature (but is of special relevance to our discussion of CSCW applications) is that of the "group" or "team" as narrator. Groups can produce narrative accounts primarily for their own consumption, to record the details or make sense of a certain situation, and/or as a part of a decision event. Narrative accounts can also be developed for consumption of non–group members or non–group entities – for example, as task force reports that an appointed team delivers to the head of an administrative unit.

An example of a group narrative is the "oral memory" of villages, tribes, and kinship groups, as described by Vansina (1985): "They [oral memories] are all institutionalized to some extent. They are told officially on formal occasions. They are often the property of a group" (p. 19). Vansina characterizes the process through which the reminiscences or news of an individual are added to the village's or tribe's oral memory as follows: "Their content has to be adapted. [The reminiscences] become part of an existing corpus of history" (p. 19).

The audience is viewed as critical in a number of formulations of the narrative paradigm. In group narratives (such as the group saga, told around campfires or at ceremonial gatherings), possible distinctions between the story's authors and listeners become blurred. Bennett (1983) describes the group saga as being told and retold more for purposes related to group cohesion and reminiscence than for the dissemination of information (although the latter certainly is a factor in the use of group sagas to convey information across generations). Thus, as Polanyi (1989) describes, fictionality is not only tolerated but also appreciated in some group contexts.

In several other forms of group narrative, careful attention is paid to constructing an account that most group members accept, even if the account is fairly sketchy. For example, minutes that are kept of a meeting and approved in ceremonial fashion at the beginning of the next meeting of the group are usually a sparse and selective record of what transpired, and are generally not considered controversial. One person is assigned the role of taking minutes, but full participation of group members is obtained at least symbolically when the minutes are approved. The minutes serve as a kind of "group memory" – analogous to an individual's own memory.

Many kinds of group narrative are characterized by overlapping or "multiphasic" accounts. The group memory comprising such accounts is thus often not a consistent or integrated one:

It may be that a collective style of telling is more frequently adopted where there is individual and collective uncertainty about just what happened and how things ended up; each in the group helps to piece the story together. (Toolan, 1988, p. 174).

Even when there is a single record of a meeting or transcript of an event, the notion that a group memory is or can be a seamless, integrated entity is problematic (as will be discussed in a later section).

Narratives may not be structured in a linear sequence, but they can be given some useful classifications as to their form. In his review of narrative types in literature, Todorov (1990) identifies three major narrative types:

1. Mythological: relating to simpler narrative forms in which succession and transformation (previously discussed) link narrative segments.
2. Gnoseological (or epistemical): relating to the logic of succession among segments or units of the narrative as governed by our changing perceptions or knowledge. (New information is provided or new perspectives introduced that link one unit of the narrative to the next.)
3. Ideological: relating to abstract rules or ideas that connect the various propositions or scenes. Actions or incidents are linked through the intermediary of an abstract formula.

Mythological narratives can apparently include scientific lab notebooks in which only the day's activities are recorded. (The genre of the scientific notebook serves as a diary of daily lab work.) Gnoseological accounts can include many scientific journal articles, either refereed or nonrefereed (accounts in which scientists tell the story of an experiment or research project from the vantage point of knowledge and insight gained from later analyses and subsequent experiments). Examples of ideological accounts are those academic books, textbooks, or review articles in which a theme or set of themes links the various subaccounts, propositions, or units. (The theme of "genre" ties together much of the material in this book, for example.) One of the criticisms often made of books is that authors fail to follow the same theme throughout the document – which can indeed be fairly difficult to do.

In the bulk of his work, Todorov apparently downplays group author-ship factors, factors that construct and convey the presence of an autho-rial "we." In my consideration of CSCW-application-supported and other group-oriented narratives, I add to Todorov's list the following forms of narrative linkage:

4. Procedural: relating to various application-oriented or procedural con-siderations (such as those involving sequences of deliberation or stages of decision making). This could be seen as a variety of "ideological" association, except that procedural considerations are generally associ-ated with the production tools utilized in constructing the account (such as CSCW applications). They are known before the account is created (or clarified as a feature of the account). In contrast, ideological link-ages are often considered as part of the "content" of the account and often emerge as the account proceeds.

5. Transactional: relating to some index of the composition or member-ship of the group (that is, aspects of virtual individuals associated with group participants or of virtual groups associated with the group as a whole). Disciplinary affiliations of group members are often di-rectly and explicitly utilized in these narrative linkages. These linkages are thus especially relevant for interdisciplinary groups in academic and research spheres, where part of the authority for the accounts produced rests in the variety and scope of group affiliations of their cre-ators.

6. Consensual: relating to construction of areas of perceived consensus, common understanding, and/or general agreement achieved among group members. For example, this kind of narrative linkage presents issues or topics in terms of whether they were addressed by the group and whether consensus was or was not obtained on certain aspects.

7. Conflictual: relating to areas of perceived conflict among subgroups (or among two or more of the groups producing a joint narrative). These conflict-related narratives include those structured by area of disagree-ment (with points of contention discussed in a point–counterpoint fash-

ion) and those focused on the conflicting parties themselves with their perspectives and particular positions outlined in depth.

When groups engage in and present accounts of decision making and collaborative writing efforts, one or more of these types can be employed in developing transitions among propositions, units, or elements in order to develop a "complete" or satisfactory narrative. Choices among these transitions or linkages depend on whether they are primarily used for "making sense" of narratives (for shaping partially or wholly developed narratives for particular audiences) or for "eliciting" their development (inspiring or stimulating narrative production). The use of transitions that make sense of narratives helps the group explore its emerging character; for example, a group may use such transitions in an effort to "sort out" images and stories about itself. In comparison, elicitation transitions serve to shape the group by stimulating narrative production of a certain kind.

Many CSCW and network-based system applications, including both collaborative writing and group decision support systems, provide vehicles for constructing narratives that are heavily focused on the "procedural" (the fourth kind of linkage). A set of system features and protocols relate the various stages of writing or decision making with each other, and lead group members through a particular sequence. Such systems help participants "tell a story" about what happened in group interaction – how a particular account or decision was produced in the context of a particular system genre. "Transactional" narratives include accounts that are apparently constructed in a round-robin format (every group member gets a turn, and biographical information is available). Such accounts are segmented by academic disciplines or similar allocations of narrative space. The group's "collective consciousness" or "group mind" has been associated with "consensual" accounts (the sixth kind of linkage). The narrative the group produces can be a mosaic of the topics it has covered in its interactions, along with some indication of how the topics were received by group members (how deeply and thoroughly they were discussed and whether or not some common understandings were reached).

Divided groups – or groups in conflict – have often "agreed to disagree" on various points and may structure the conflict-related narratives they produce jointly (the seventh kind of linkage) to underscore these areas of disagreement. The group character constructed in these narratives may reflect these schisms by emphasizing the few areas of agreement that do exist and/or by outlining clearly the issues where there is obvious or open discord.

Several variations of CSCW applications have been developed or proposed for support of conflict resolution (Klein, 1990, provides a review of this work); the "first-person plural" is clearly divided into parts in these efforts. Generally, two or more identifiable parties are involved in an intergroup or intragroup relation that is labeled a "conflict" situation. These parties are defined in terms of this conflict: in other words, part of their identity as a group rests in the conflict or disagreement in which they are engaged. In a "collaborative negotiation tool" implemented in Object Lens, conflicting parties are prompted through a set of ideal problem-solving and consensus-building stages. As they proceed iteratively through the stages, the parties are redefined as consensus-oriented groups; they move closer to a collaborative solution through the process of shaping rough cuts of a solution with each other.

Notions of narrative construction and group character are highly applicable to the discussion of conflict resolution systems. The very fact that the system chosen for use is labeled as a "conflict resolution system" sends strong signals about the situation. For example, individuals or subgroups involved may perceive themselves as sufficiently divergent in certain matters to engage in conflict resolution (rather than decision making or problem solving per se); they may also see themselves as divided into segments, so that various sides or opposing viewpoints can be distinguished. CSCW applications that deal with conflict resolution can help groups negotiate the transitions between a group character that distinguishes them as being in conflict and separate, and one that recognizes new areas of consensus (and perhaps harmony).

The well-tempered workgroup: Issues of time and control

Despite the strong rhetoric about efficiency that is associated with CSCW applications and other group work vehicles, considerations other than efficiency often play major roles in forming narrative linkages and in other aspects of narrative production. Some relatively common group writing conventions and decision-making procedures apparently relate to traditions in which groups are seen as needing to be slowed down – encouraged to be more methodical – rather than made more efficient. Such conventions as forming a problem statement or outlining assumptions (both in collaborative writing efforts and in decision making) call for group members to pause and contemplate before jumping headlong into writing or deciding. For example, roll call voting procedures take time but ensure that an individual's voice will be heard (if only for a moment). Many of our group writing and decision-making conventions may indeed have served over the years to make group narrative construction more deliberate and systematic.

When an individual constructs a narrative, he or she speaks, writes, draws, or otherwise performs an activity. Images of the group as a whole constructing a document or decision are powerful: we say, "Congress came to a decision" or "The jury decided in favor of the plaintiff." Nevertheless, groups take action through the individuals that comprise them, and someone (or something, in the case of an agent or surrogate) must perform some activity. Network-based computer systems, campfire circles, and corporate meeting rooms all have mechanisms through which individuals can take turns at constructing the group narrative, or through which they can work simultaneously or in conjunction.

The fact that an increasing number of group-based decision and writing procedures are composed of fragments of activities that are scattered in space and time – and not largely constructed in a face-to-face meeting of the group as a whole – makes the notion of narrative even more useful. What makes an account that is pieced together over long distances and through asynchronous interaction a "satisfying" account? Issues of who has control over how an account is constructed loom large in the answer to this question.

Dickson et al. (1989) describe three different approaches to control of group decision support systems: user-driven, chauffeur-driven, and facilitated. In the first, each user in the group has equal control of the system; each has a workstation and can access shared resources, as well as his or her own individual resources. Chauffeur-driven systems have a human facilitator who generally takes directions from the group concerning how to proceed in the meeting. These systems are designed for situations in which the technical problems of running the computer may be considerable, but in which group members themselves want control over the meeting. Facilitated systems have a human facilitator who exercises considerable control over the meeting. When meeting participants themselves run the meeting (no human facilitator is involved), one of the participants is usually afforded a larger amount of control over the proceedings than others. Some CSCW applications currently have capabilities that support the activities of moderators – individuals who resolve conflicts among group participants in their efforts to contribute to the group. In a group environment where individuals can see each other, such conflicts may be resolved through informal means (as in motor vehicle driving, where a hand wave and a glance can allow for some ad hoc changes in rules of the road); in a long-distance connection, more formal means for sequencing may be warranted.

Aspects (by Group Technologies) places a heavy emphasis on the role of the conference moderator. It allows from 2 to 16 individuals to work on specific documents, as well as view changes that others make to documents while those changes are in progress. In this CSCW application, the conference moderator has considerable control over the character of group proceedings and group products. He or she determines who is to participate and when: "The person who starts a meeting becomes, by default, the conference moderator, with responsibility for keeping the proceedings running smoothly" (von Biel, 1991, p. 210).

The moderator of an *Aspects* session chooses from three different "mediation levels":

> Free-for-all mediation lets all participants edit a document at the same time; this mode is essentially for brainstorming or informal conferences with few partici- pants. Medium mediation allows only one editor at a time per document, al- though participants can edit other documents while someone else is editing the main document. Full mediation allows only one editor at a time to make changes to any document. (von Biel, 1991, p. 210)

Support provided by some sort of conference moderation may be neces- sary for constructing a linear, coherent document or other product that speaks in a single voice (the kind that most of the individuals using *Aspects* are probably preparing). However, a document with identifiable segments (for example, a conflict-related or transactional document) may allow for different construction strategies, strategies that need not lead to the eventual congealing of the document into a uniform, integrated whole.

Many aspects of control over who participates and when, how partici- pants' accounts are exhibited to others, and other aspects of narrative production in CSCW applications are not directly and immediately en- forced by human facilitators (who can often be quite flexible), but are, rather, shaped by various application parameters or features. These pa- rameters can provide reflections of how group participants perceive and conduct themselves as a group.

The apparently voluntary and improvisational image associated with a good deal of face-to-face group interaction (the image of individuals voluntarily acceding to the group's constraints) is thus altered to a consid- erable extent. Narratives produced by members concerning how their group is functioning are constrained by the kinds of accounts provided by application parameters, features, and vehicles for recording. An individ- ual's or group's compliance (or lack of compliance) with many kinds of application-based system meeting procedures is therefore less readily constructed as a matter of choice, volition, and personal expression than it is in the face-to-face meeting. Even in applications where expression is tightly constrained, there is the possibility of some manifestation of dis- sent, however. Poole and DeSanctis (1990) explore the idea of "ironic" compliance with the constraints provided in computer-mediated interaction, a kind of compliance in which individuals either (a) violate the spirit of the application's structure, but retain its operations (often using them in ways not intended by designers), or (b) alter both the spirit and the operations of the application.

When a narrative account (for example, a book, article, record about an individual, or decision sequence) is produced and then recalled or otherwise utilized, it enters "textual time," losing many of the connections and references to the context in which it originally appeared or was generated: "In textual time, the processes of working up the formulation become invisible. The account comes to stand for the actuality it claims to represent" (Smith, 1990, p. 74). In characterizations of textual time, Smith and others are largely referring to records that are printed on paper (which is considered the primary vehicle of development and dissemination). Paper-rendered text has a relatively long-range orientation (for example, in comparison with accounts delivered face-to-face or immediately broadcast to a wide audience). Documents that will be printed many times and require typesetting may enjoy a particularly long organizational or societal lifespan.

Extending Smith's notion of textual time, individuals' perceptions of retention periods (their notions, however gleaned, of how long an account will be readily available or will be retrievable from storage) are important to consider, as well as the ability of others to amend, distort, or modify the account. An additional, related factor relevant to considerations of textual time is the "granularity" of the narrative sequences produced. Large-grained narrative sequences (for example, textbooks and lengthy volumes) generally provide a good deal of background in their coverage of issues and often have a high level of internal consistency in style of presentation. In contrast, in narrative sequences produced from transcripts of a face-to-face meeting (with smaller-grained monologues and dialogues), issues are often introduced without much background, and widely divergent perspectives can emerge without much warning.

Accordingly, accounts constructed in network-based systems have a time frame I label "application sequencing." Application sequencing is linked both to individuals' perceptions of the retention periods associated with the narratives and to the degree of granularity (the amount of information and background) of these narratives. As in textual time, accounts in application sequences become disconnected from the original contexts with which they were associated. They retain or later develop a number of interrelations and sequences, which are often given some structure or unity by various features of the application involved. Application sequencing considerations are especially important in the early stages of genre development – before a form of "genre habituation" sets in. Engelbart provides the following account of development of the Journal in the early 1970s, a way of linking documents in a workgroup context:

A document could go in and be catalogued into a system called the "Journal" which was similar to the idea of pasting it down on a table. We had linkages and internal addressability, so an embedded link in one document could directly cite an arbitrary passage in any other. Successive documents could be entered in the system and easily be cross-referenced back to each other. This supported what we called our "recorded dialog." (Engelbart, 1988, pp. 212–213)

Engelbart recounts his group's hypothesis that "recorded dialog" of the kind supported by the Journal would be a critically important tool for collaborators. He notes that, at first, some individuals had second thoughts about contributing to the pool of Journal entries:

I think that one person actually never could bring himself to enter a memo into the Journal – the idea that it was "forever" stopped him cold. Another person, a very valuable contributor, felt violently opposed to the basic concept, and it possibly hastened his departure. (Engelbart, 1988, p. 213)

Opposition to the notion of the Journal reportedly diminished, and Engelbart's group accumulated more than 100,000 Journal entries in 5 years. The prospect that one's work will be catalogued and linked to others "forever" does not greatly surprise and bother many people today – we have become familiar as a society with some of the basic notions behind such applications.

For an example of application sequencing, consider a meeting of a departmental faculty committee in which a quasi-formal, nonrigorous application of a set of procedural rules is applied (a common configuration in faculty meetings). Committee members are considering the general issue of whether a certain course should be offered by the department. There are a number of specific motions raised: some are discussed further, others are dropped, but none are voted on. Finally, a motion is raised, discussed, and carried.

Questions of relevance to narrative production include: How is the meeting process constructed by those in attendance – what narratives about it are related for their own consumption and that of outsiders? How are those narratives linked to each other, or what sequences do they usually follow? What aspects of interaction during the meeting are retained for immediate reconsideration and/or for future reference? Are specific discussion points recorded, along with some identification of the individual who made them? Does the account identify those who voted for the successful motion, those against, and those who abstained? How is the successful motion itself described? How long is the account of the meeting retained or remained in storage? Answers to these questions help to capture what kind of narrative is being produced in the meeting, and thus what kind of "group" is being constructed in the perspectives of both group participants and relevant audiences.

Issues of who is speaking in an account often loom large in narrative construction. The question of who is speaking can have a number of interpretations, including the following: (1) Who is in control of the process of narrative construction? (2) Who is constructed as the apparent or immediate "speaker" (that is, whose "voice" is being heard in an account, or who currently has the floor in a group setting)? (3) Who is constructed as speaking "behind a character" (that is, whose voice is being heard when an agent or other character speaks)? (4) Who is constructed as speaking "for the group" (that is, which voice, if any, is considered the voice of the group as a whole)? Various CSCW applications add new dimensions to these issues, including the capacity to employ active agents or surrogates and to have a number of individuals effectively "on the floor" at one time (that is, to allow more than one individual to produce narratives simultaneously). The question of whose voice is constructed as the "group's" is an especially critical one, since production of a single, coherent group product is often considered an objective by those who use these applications.

Collaborative writing support: Constructing a group character

Gide (1931) wrote that "no *chef-d'oeuvre* was ever produced by several people together." Few of the works that are labeled "great literature" and studied by literary critics and scholars are considered to be produced in a group context, even though there are many accounts of the tremendous influence of collaborators, editors, and commentators in molding many of the works of renowned writers.

Samuel Clemens (Mark Twain) delivered a severe comic blow to collaborative writing efforts in his description of the team writing of a newspaper serial:

Mrs. F. was an able romanticist of the ineffible school – I know no other name to apply to a school whose heroes are all dainty and perfect. She wrote the opening chapter, and introduced a lovely blonde simpleton who talked nothing but pearls and poetry and who was virtuous to the verge of eccentricity. She also introduced a young French duke of aggravated refinement, in love with the blond. Mr. F. followed the next week, with a brilliant lawyer who set about getting the duke's estates into trouble. (Twain, 1869/1984, pp. 798–799)

Clemens did not choose to expand on why group writing is a difficult activity and why the medium of the newspaper serial was not conducive to group writing. However, he did underscore quite effectively the difficulties that differences in personality, attitude, and writing style can provide in team writing efforts. The group of writers that Clemens portrays apparently aims to create a single, unified serial, not an amalgam of highly disparate styles and characters – hence the humor in their efforts. If they portrayed themselves as a group of writers taking successive stabs at the task of the column's production, Clemens might have had a harder time making us laugh.

Despite Clemens's trenchent comedic attacks, ready availability of computer networking facilities has served to inspire a number of efforts at collaborative writing. *Invisible Seattle* is a 1983 collective effort – a 15-chapter mystery story written by a group of Seattle citizens chosen through an unscientific cross-sampling. The equipment used to link the authors included six small PCs, two larger ones, and various video arcade game parts (Rheingold, 1985). The Electronic Information Exchange System (EIES) system pioneered by Hiltz and Turoff at the New Jersey Institute of Technology also was the site of some pioneering collaborative writing efforts.

The CSCW application genre of collaborative writing support has strongly influenced the general notions of groupware and CSCW. Most academicians, public administrators, and business people have undertaken at least one major group writing project of some sort – whether a grant or project proposal, a business plan, or a task force report. Many of us have found the experience to be a highly frustrating one and have contemplated (at least in passing) why this is the case. CSCW applications have generated substantial interest, in part because of their potentials for making group writing projects proceed more smoothly.

The impact of introducing computing into the work of writing has dramatic psychological and social dimensions. Barrett (1988) asserts that there is a "natural affinity between writing and computers, almost a genetic relationship" (p. xvii), with both being mechanisms for knowledge representation. Slater (1989) states that the problem of developing systems that support the coauthorship of documents is "as much a psychological research area as a technical one" (p. 109), and involves the restructuring of human relationships. Similarly, Bolter (1989) asserts that the use of computers in writing promises to redefine relationships among authors, readers, and "writing spaces." Heim (1987) contends that the use of a word processor itself transforms the process of writing from an individual-based to a collaborative one. Daiute (1985) observes that writing with a

word processor feels more like talking than writing with pen and paper –
in other words, it has more of the character of a casual, iterative conversation with another human than does the activity of moving a pen over a
piece of paper.

Reither and Vipond (1989) declare that perspectives that construe writing (any and all kinds of writing) as "collaboration" are more fruitful than
those that view writing as an individual activity:

> We find it more helpful to think of writing (and knowing) not as social, but, more
> specifically, as collaborative. Instead of asking "in what ways is writing a social
> process?" we ask "In what ways are writers collaborating with others as they
> write?" Phrasing the question this way brings into focus writers' relationships
> with other writing and other writers. (Reither and Vipond, 1989, p. 856)

Accounts produced in a collaborative setting can be framed in ways
that serve to establish or reinforce the positions of individuals within the
group, as well as establish participants' and the group's position in relation to non–group members. These two concerns can have a large degree
of overlap, but may diverge in various circumstances (as the number and
kinds of audiences for the group and its products expand). In their attempts to identify certain stances or objectives as belonging to the group,
some group members may include in a document items that are largely for
internal consumption. Though possibly serving important roles within the
group, these inclusions may not be significant to the non–group members
who read them.

The construction of self and group through writing can indeed be problematic. A reviewer of Clifford Geertz's popular anthropological work
Local Knowledge notes with a critical bite that reflection of an author in a
text can sometimes be taken too far:

> But surely the most striking thing about the . . . passage is that it so insistently
> calls attention to itself as a piece of writing, reminding us in virtually every
> phrase of the literary presence behind the text. Indeed, it tells us much more
> about Mr. Geertz than about its putative subject. It informs us, quite gratu-
> itously, that he is familiar with both Immanuel Kant and Wallace Stevens. At the
> same time, it is also eager to assure us that he is no ivory tower intellectual but a
> regular guy who knows the colloquial meaning of "square" and would sooner die
> than be thought smug. (Robinson, 1983, p. 11)

Robinson continues his vitriolic criticism of Geertz's style by stating that
the author's essays "exist less as a forum of ideas than as occasions for
the author to display himself." Geertz's "knowing self-consciousness," in
Robinson's viewpoint, works to distance readers from the issues at hand,
rather than enhance the text.

Writing involves the construction of the author, as well as the presentation of content. Sometimes authors labor to present a portrait of themselves as authorial (as Geertz apparently did); at other times authorial portraits emerge without (or despite) the author's efforts. There has been a good deal of debate among literary theorists on the functions of the "implied author," a notion associated with the work of Wayne Booth:

> As [an author] writes, he creates not simply an ideal, impersonal "man in general" but an implied version of "himself" that is different from the implied authors we meet in other men's works . . . the picture the reader gets of this presence is one of the author's most important effects. However impersonal he may try to be, his reader will inevitably construct a picture of the official scribe who writes in this matter. (Booth, 1961, pp. 70–71)

In Booth's formulation, the implied author can differ in each production an author has. However, there may certainly be strong linkages among the implied authors in an author's various works. Toolan (1988) declares that "the pictures we have of authors are always constructions, so that all authors are, if you like, 'inferred authors' " (p. 78).

Considerations of actual and implied authorship have extended beyond print material to the full range of media production. The idea of "individual authorship" for a film or video emerged as a popular force in the 1950s; Bordwell (1989) asserts that in this period the director became celebrated as the creative source of meaning, producing a repetition and enrichment of creative themes and stylistic choices similar to that of the author of print material. Other analyses of film and video production have stressed its collaborative aspects, with an emphasis on team interaction, and countered the idea that a sole "author" (the director in some cases, a producer in others) can or should be distinguished. Many participants in the Chicago school of computer-mediated video production have taken the notion of video authorship to an extreme, designing personalized video tools and claiming that they have themselves "become" their video products, echoing themes also expressed by VR developers: " 'I am the project that is under development,' says Jane Veeder . . . 'The actual works are just periodic research reports; the titles could be the date' " (Youngblood, 1987, p. 335).

With the heavy societal emphasis on the notion of an individual author, there has been far less commentary and discussion of group-authored narratives and the role they play in constructing an "implied group author." Many groups become very aware of their constructions of a virtual group (for example, in the form of the team descriptions and group biographical material attached to a document). One of the ways that an implied group author is formed is by constructing narratives about group interaction – stories about how groups produced their writing or other collaborative products.

Which kinds of accounts of collaborative writing activity and other forms of joint production are "satisfying" – that is, accounts that convince their various audiences (including group members themselves) that indeed a group product has emerged – and which impart information about the group? Attention is increasingly being directed toward this question. Some efforts have been made in an educational context to explore and experiment with the linkages among various constructions of group process and collaborative writing. Raymond (a psychologist) and Yee (a professor of English) have collaborated to conduct a university class that relates group process considerations to team-based writing (Raymond and Yee, 1990).

Raymond and Yee first present a model to their class of "three phases of group development": (1) a stage involving orientation, hesitant participation, overdependence on the leader, as well as the definition of goals, structure, and boundaries; (2) a stage that manifests conflict, dominance, and rebellion; and (3) a stage in which cohesiveness is developed, a bonding that "submerges" individual differences. The three stages were derived from the work of Yalom (1975) in group psychotherapy. After the stages are discussed with the students, class meetings are spent in simulations and discussions of group problem situations linked with the stages (for example, they developed a "scenario of a team of technical communicators experiencing the second, conflict-ridden stage in their group"; p. 79). Raymond and Yee assert that through role playing various group work dilemmas (pathologies that correspond to problems in progressing through the three stages), students become better collaborators in team writing efforts.

Use of certain collaborative writing activities in stimulating group exchange and cohesion has been extended to the production of online help aids. In *Text, ConText, and HyperText,* Price discusses the "sociability" of these aids:

Can an entire workgroup pitch in to revise your help aid, making it more useful for them? To what extent do you set it up to encourage people to talk to each other, asking questions, responding with their own helpful comments, so that gradually the help contains a collection of shared solutions, a little library of that group's solutions. (Price, 1988, p. 340)

Online help aids are thus construed as part of the environment in which teamwork is fostered and the group is unified.

Problems involved in creating and maintaining effective teams of computer programmers have also undergone scrutiny; contributions of individuals must be integrated seamlessly into a working program, despite variations in working styles and levels of talent. In 1971, Gerald Weinberg wrote *The Psychology of Computer Programming,* in which "egoless" programming strategies were developed. Henry Ledgard rephrased and championed Weinberg's ideas 15 years later in the following terms:

Individual egos must be sacrificed for something higher: a collective ego. Resistance to criticism is detrimental to achieving the objective; the cooperative attitude is necessary. As one realizes that one's own special talent – even one's own ego – is necessary for the project at hand to succeed, the gut response will not be "I can do it," but "We can do it." (Ledgard, 1986, p. 13)

Constantine (1990) describes the quest for "genuine consensus" on technical design issues as being important because it means full group resources have been used and creative integration of diverse contributions has been achieved.

Links that bind groups together: Construction of group character in hypertext

Hypertext applications offer a model of collaborative writing in which the "author" and "reader" roles are intertwined. Many applications for support of collaboration are designed to enhance production of documents and other materials that are now or could readily be put into a paper-based vehicle. A number of hypertext initiatives, however, are ends in themselves and will not be eventually recast in paper-oriented formats for consumption by an audience.

Hypertext (or nonlinear text) has been widely portrayed as a means for supporting collaborative authoring. Ted Nelson (who is credited, with Vannevar Bush and Douglas Engelbart, with some of hypertext's conceptual underpinnings) defines it simply as "non-sequential writing with free user movement among links" (Nelson, 1987, p. v) and in more elaborate terms as "a combination of natural language text with the computer's capacity for interactive branching, or dynamic display . . . of a nonlinear text . . . which cannot be printed conveniently on a conventional page" (Nelson, 1981). Conklin (1987), in a document that soon became widely regarded as a definitive source on hypertext, associates the growing interest in the applications of hypertext to the availability of cheaper and more powerful workstations. As these workstations became equipped with advanced graphics, optical media, and video production facilities, the notion of "hypermedia" came into wide circulation – referring to the broad range of hypertext-oriented vehicles for access of music, words, pictures, simulated voices, video segments, and nearly anything else that can be placed in digitized form. Some notions associated with hypertext were further popularized in the advent of the World Wide Web, in which countless numbers of documents, graphics files, and the like are connected.

One of the ways that hypertext system developers have gone about their activities is to incorporate "print analogues" (features that have roots in print-oriented terminology) into their designs. Oren (1987) describes several print analogues: (1) hypertext "bookmarks," which are "simply links to a document which are generated at the user's request and stored with some associated comment or picture"; (2) hypertext Post-It Notes, which are "constructed by putting a link in the increment file, targeted to a new notepad document stored on magnetic disc"; and (3) hypertext "writing," which involves some form of document versioning (p. 294). Designing print analogues is one way designers have sought to decrease the amount of time users need to become familiar with hypertext features and functions; learners bootstrap their learning efforts with their previously gained knowledge of the associated print analogue.

Hypertext has been widely described as "a state of mind" and as a "tool to enhance the user's mental abilities." Hypertext has strong linkages with the cultural object of intellectual augmentation discussed earlier. Some educators have undertaken experiments with hypertext in the classroom, and have extended these experiments into examinations of what "education" itself constitutes. Brown University's Intermedia is one of these pioneering experiments: it is a "networked hypermedia" system. The networking comes about because individual workstations are connected via a network, and the "hypermedia" label is appended because the system enables linkage of images, sound, and text. Yankelovich, Landow, and Cody (1985) describe Intermedia as permitting groups of authors "to link information together, create paths through a corpus of related material, annotate existing texts, and create notes that point readers either to bibliographic data or the body of the referenced text" (p. 18).

Group characters associated with hypertext production efforts are often linked with antiauthoritarianism. For example, Landow makes a case for the "democratic" or "leveling" nature of the Intermedia system. He claims, for example, that he has "observed graduate students reading documents by freshmen and freshmen reading works by advanced graduate students," and states that the system "allows collaboration not only among those of equivalent academic rank or status, but also among those of widely different rank or status" (pp. 422–423). Nelson (1987) posits as a basic concept of hypertext a democracy of access as well as production: "Everything should be available to everyone. Any user should be able to follow origins and links of material across boundaries of documents, servers, and networks, and across boundaries of individual implementa-tions" (Nelson, 1987, p. v). These group characters are also associated with experimentation and exploration (Beeman et al., 1987; Smith, Weiss, & Ferguson, 1987), as well as an emphasis on idea expansion and connec-tion (even to the point of losing track of the initial point of an investigation).

Hypertext and associated hypermedia productions enlarge opportuni-ties for expression of the individual and the group. The individual "ego" has various modes for expression (individuals are given substantial leeway to employ personal style in their contributions to hypertext, as well as in their usage of it), and distinctive group characters often emerge as well. Links among units of sounds, texts, and images create meaning, along with the units themselves. Designers of World Wide Web pages are dis-covering that the choice of what linkages to form among their home pages and others are at least as important as their "content-related" choices.

It is in the cards: Index cards and the organization of information

The structure and sequencing of a group product are vehicles for expres-sion of group character. Indexing systems employed by a group are one kind of vehicle. An early proponent of the index card was the abbe Rozier, who in 1775 used playing cards with alphabetical headings in some of his large-scale scholarly projects (Tenner, 1990). Before the advent of the index card and related office innovations, the bound book (pages held together with a permanent binding) was a primary information storage and dissemination vehicle. In the early part of this century, before a piece of outgoing business correspondence was sent out, it was hand copied into a bound book (Yates, 1989). This was obviously a labor-intensive activity, but served to promote a certain continuity and standardization of se-quence.

Bound books still have a vital role in information handling protocols. For example, the artifact of the bound book is still popular in scientific laboratories. They are used as lab notebooks, permanent records of a laboratory's daily activities that are often involved in resolution of dis-putes about patents, procedures, and priorities. Bound books are linked with modes of information presentation that are linear and sequential. Index cards, in contrast, afford a different sort of presentation; the "card" itself serves as a basic unit, and the card ordering system places an external structuring on the cards (although some aspects of what is printed or written on the card can influence this ordering). Since each index card is an individual unit, these cards can be produced by collaborators work-ing separately, and can be assembled (and reassembled) into a desired sequence at a later date.

Some index card concepts and terminology have been employed in hypermedia applications. NoteCards is "first and foremost an authoring system designed to provide its users with facilities for creating and modifying hypermedia structures" (Halasz, 1988). Not unlike the index cards associated with abbe Rozier, this system uses stacks of 3×5 cards as its information storage and retrieval metaphor. The term "arbitrary" is heavily underscored in Trigg and Irish's (1987) specifications of the system: the network is formed by (1) "an arbitrary amount of editable substance," (2) "each in an arbitrarily sized window," which is then (3) "connected to other cards by arbitrarily typed, directed links" (p. 90).

Difficulties that many users had with the NoteCards system in its early iterations prompted Halasz to declare that the simple node and link model (the "arbitrary" model just described) "is just not rich and complete enough to support the information representation, management, and presentation tasks that these users will want to accomplish using their hypermedia system" (pp. 364–365). Similarly, a critique that has been levied against Intermedia and related approaches relates to the cultural object of efficiency: the form of the system is held by many as not providing explicit "checks and balances" for the production process. The documents linked "can add material not included previously, qualify existing approaches, and even simply contradict existing presentations of individual topics" (p. 421).

In paper-oriented vehicles, these checks and balances can be obtained in an assortment of ways. The physical size and shape of the document in itself can provide some constraints on expression; many authors seek to maintain a relatively standard paragraph and chapter size, for instance. One of the ways that efficiency considerations have been proposed for hypertext design is to "match additional power with additional control and structure" (Smith et al., 1987, p. 212). Smith et al. argue that hypertext (in its basic concept and form) is most consistent with the "exploratory" stage of thinking. When thinking proceeds beyond this stage (which is often an early stage in the development of ideas), they declare that more structured and constrained tools are needed. They suggest that "in the long term, constraints may turn out to be more important than raw power" (p. 212). Barrett (1988) states that hypertext may not afford writers the capability of presenting a "unique structuring of ideas for a particular purpose" of the kind that technical communication may require (p. xx).

One of the major tasks of designers is to attempt to structure how their applications are used. The search for new ways to impose structure on hypermedia production – to construct various narratives of how hypermedia is created by individuals and by groups – has been the focus of a number of recent development efforts. No one story has yet emerged as a powerful, unifying account of hypermedia production and utilization, although a number of candidates are currently being explored. For example, VR–based "navigational aids" have been developed for hypertext systems, and offer the potential of stimulating new thinking on the problem of how to balance user freedom with application usability and organization. Some VR applications employ three-dimensional spatial representations as vehicles for presenting user options in hypertext database search and browsing.

Electronic meeting systems: Group decision support environments and electronic meeting rooms

Decision making is one form of group narrative construction, a form in which the suggestions and choices of individuals are transformed and constructed as a group product (for example, a decision or recommendation for further study). Various forms of group procedure play vital roles in decision-making events. It is often the case that the more a group decision is constructed as "critical," the more the method through which the decision is reached is proceduralized (Davis et al., 1989). In group decision support environments, a number of proceduralized aspects are introduced and their implementation controlled not by the immediate facilitation of a human leader or by convention, but through aspects or features of the application being utilized. Individuals who select the application, and who can set its various parameters and control its functioning, thus can wield a good deal of control over group proceedings.

As in collaborative writing efforts, group decision-making procedures provide vehicles for the construction of a "first-person plural" – a group voice or character. A single voice – the group's – emerges from many decision-making efforts, although dissenters are occasionally afforded a carefully delimited platform. Violating the constraints of group decision-making procedures is often seen as other than an artistic statement (as it may be construed in collaborative writing efforts) – rather, it is viewed as a moral abuse, an affront to the group and perhaps to "democracy" or other cultural objects as well. For example, if majority rule is agreed upon, its constraints are generally held to, at least until the end of the group's current session.

Various devices have been developed in the past several decades to facilitate formation and maintenance of a group voice. Consider the Harwald Group-Thinkometer:

The Harwald Group-Thinkometer . . . Most group-relations people would probably disown it as too stringent a tool, yet it seems a perfectly logical development.

The Group-Thinkometer is an electric meter the dial of which is graduated in degrees of interest. Feeding into it are ten remote-control switches which can be distributed around, or under, the table, and by pressing the switch members of the group indicate approval or disapproval. Since the needle on the meter shows only the accumulated group reaction, one can veto a colleague's idea without his being the wiser, and, as the Harwald Company suggests, thus the personality factor is eliminated almost entirely. Extreme? (Whyte, 1956, p. 63)

Whyte (a vocal supporter of individual rights) asserts that the Group-Thinkometer "has only concretized . . . the underlying principles of the group philosophy" (p. 63), a philosophy that he claims is bent on dismantling bases for individual initiative.

Despite Whyte's stinging criticisms, many current systems for group decision support have aspects reminiscent of the Thinkometer. The CONSENSOR, a system developed in the 1970s to help administrative groups solve problems, has striking similarities to the Group-Thinkometer. The CONSENSOR was designed to meet "the need for a means of anonymous expression of individual judgment that could be transformed into a graphic display of group judgment, quickly and within the context of continuing discussion" (Burns, 1988, p. 27).

CONSENSOR is an electronic system for polling individuals anonymously on a set of issues. It consists of individual input terminals (up to 99) with two register dials, a microprocessor-based "reader" console, and a video monitor:

The terminals are designed to maintain the anonymity of individual participants, while allowing them to express a range of opinion. The video display presents a bar graph distribution of opinions read from the set of terminals, the mean of the set of judgments expressed, and the number of terminals counted. (Burns, 1988, p. 27)

Burns states that CONSENSOR provides instant polling at any point during a meeting, which he asserts can help to determine the range of opinion in a group. Burns asserts that the polls CONSENSOR produces are not "decisions"; rather, they serve to "reveal judgments and provide useful information at any point in the discussion" (p. 28). Burns is not clear on what would keep a group from construing a CONSENSOR judgment or informational poll as a "decision," however.

The Group-Thinkometer and CONSENSOR are attempts to obtain mechanically a sense of group direction and definition in relation to certain issues. They appear rather simple. Obtaining the mean of a set of judgments is primitive in comparison with the complex group decision protocols currently in development. However, these two devices are similar in spirit to many current decision support initiatives in their association of the group as an entity with results of anonymous, mechanically compiled polling procedures. Individual "voices" in the group are congealed by statistical means into a single voice, which is constructed as an indication of the group's direction. The systems are utilized as part of the group's storytelling as to how it progressed from the initial statement of a problem, to the polling of group members, to the final decision (if indeed one was reached).

Electronic meeting systems have become an increasingly popular tool of management and administration. Dennis et al. define these applications in the following terms:

> an information technology–based environment that supports group meetings, which may be distributed geographically and temporally. The IT environment includes, but is not limited to, distributed facilities, computer hardware and software, audio and video technology, procedures, methodologies, facilitation, and applicable group data. Group tasks include, but are not limited to, communication, planning, idea generation, problem solving, issue discussion, negotiation, conflict resolution, systems analysis and design, and collaborative group activities such as document preparation and sharing. (Dennis et al., 1988, p. 593)

Plexysis (which evolved into *GroupSystems,* a commercial application) goes beyond the simple strategies of the Group-Thinkometer and CONSENSOR to produce an early and influential meeting room environment, one considered relatively "complete" by its developers. The Plexysis environment is designed to enable groups to move from decision statement to discussion to a final decision, plan, or strategy – not just provide a polling facility. Vogel and Nunamaker (1990) include teams of high-level university administrators developing long-term strategies for their institutions, community groups specifying plans for local development, and senior executives defining objectives for their divisions as possible users for these decision support environments.

As characterized by its developers, Plexysis has the following stages and features:

1. Session director: helps the facilitator or group leader select the tools to be used in a session and suggests an appropriate sequencing of steps within a session.

2. Electronic brainstorming: supports the generation of ideas, allowing group members both to enter comments simultaneously and anonymously and to share information on a specific question. Participants begin by entering a comment in response to the question on their individual computer screens. These initial comments are then randomly distributed to other members of the group; group members can then enter "comments on comments" as they receive files containing the ideas and observations

of other participants. The typical length of an electronic brainstorming session in a Plexysis meeting is 30 to 45 minutes.

3. Issue analyzer: helps group members identify key items produced during the idea generation process (the process described in stage 2) and consolidate them into a smaller set. In the identification phase, individuals select topics they feel merit further consideration by the group, and can also append supporting comments from the idea generation session to those topics.

The result of the process described in stage 3 is, according to Vogel and Nunamaker, a "manageable set" of ideas and comments. This set can be either utilized for further discussion or employed as alternatives in a voting procedure.

4. Voting: provides a variety of standard measures for prioritizing, including agree/disagree, Likert scales, rank ordering, and multiple choice. The program is designed so that group members cast their ballots privately and the results are tabulated in an anonymous fashion.

5. Topic commenter: uses an identified list of topics in a multiwindow format to guide group discussion. Individual group members can respond to any or all of the topics in whatever order they choose. Participants can also examine the comments made by other group members. Topics can be further decomposed into subtopics.

6. Policy formation: supports the group in developing a policy statement or mission through iteration and group consensus.

7. Session dictionary: helps the group establish a glossary of words or phrases containing the group's agreed-upon definitions.

Commenting on the value of the session dictionary, Vogel and Nunamaker state that the program can help to provide a "valuable record of the group's activity that can be useful in future sessions or in its day-to-day activities" (p. 517). Vogel and Nunamaker assert that output from the use of any of the tools acts as an "organization memory" as groups return for additional sessions or as new group members are added.

Nunamaker et al. (1991) further develop the notion that an accounting produced with CSCW applications such as Plexysis can be construed as a group memory:

The EMS [electronic meeting system] can provide a group memory by recording all electronic comments, which is typically done by many, but not all, EMSs. Participants can de-couple themselves from the group to pause, think, type comments, and then rejoin the discussion without missing anything. This should reduce failure to remember, attention blocking, and incomplete use of information, and may promote synergy and more information. A group memory that enables members to queue and filter information may reduce information overload. (Nunamaker et al., 1991, p. 47)

The notion of a group memory – a common storehouse of group narratives – entails a considerable level of consensus on the part of group participants. Existence of this consensus may indeed become a common narrative theme in the accounts that participants construct of CSCW application-based activities. Prospects that a permanent account of the minute details of the interactions in a group session is being constructed automatically (through the means provided in a CSCW application) lend a significantly different character to an application-based group than to face-to-face groups. Conventional meetings generally have minutes – recorded by a secretary or transcribed from a tape – and relevant information can be copied from blackboards; meetings can also be tape-recorded or videotaped.

However, groups that actively work with the assumption that the results of their keystroked decisions and comments are being preserved in great detail and are accessible in a number of formats are creating a richer, more complex record than is rendered either by minute taking or conventional electronic recording devices. Records of these meetings (the narratives created through the various means afforded by the system) apparently increase in importance and scope of use in relation to the "actual" meeting event (if one indeed can be constructed) as the records' depth and ease of access increase. If there is a high level of acceptance by the group of the application-based account, the accessing of the account can be constructed in some senses as a substitute for meeting participation. It may indeed be difficult to construct significant distinctions between this accessing and "actual" meeting attendance and participation.

The various analyses and alterations that can be performed on network-based system meeting accounts add considerable complexity to the notion of a group memory. Group reconstructions of all sorts are, by their very nature, a patchwork of inconsistent and overlapping accounts. With various CSCW and network-based system applications, physical traces of the group's memory can also undergo extensive manipulation and distortion.

There is some precedent to having a group's records "tinkered" with in various ways after a meeting is held. For example, congresspeople can add to the *Congressional Record* material never heard on the floor of Congress, and thus "reconstruct" congressional proceedings. Similarly, an increased number and variety of reconstructions of the "meeting" as an event are likely to result as individuals use the meeting's records for intensive analysis, commentary, and perhaps revision. The capacity for altering a group's records may indeed affect perceptions of their reliability and quality. Shapiro (1991) posits that the construction of social reality is linked with the perceived reliability and quality of information sources.

The social reality of group interaction (that is, what is considered as happening or not happening within the group) may accordingly be linked with the reliability and quality associated with records and other traces that the application produces.

Electronic meeting system sessions generally involve a considerable time, resource, and preparation commitment on the part of groups (in contrast with the simpler polling devices previously described). One of the case studies provided by Vogel and Nunamaker involves the use of the University of Arizona facilities by the CEO and 12 key members of a health care organization. There were two sessions, each lasting for $3\frac{1}{2}$ hours. The cost of renting *GroupSystems* facilities to conduct a day's session can run into the thousands of dollars, and the time of the participants can cost thousands more. These factors should themselves have some impact on the intensity of meeting preparation and on participant attention levels.

Hypertext applications have been utilized both as separate decision-making tools and as components in electronic meeting systems. Minch (1989) asserts that hypertext can resolve some of the issues associated with variations in individual cognitive styles in decision support systems: predefined hypertext paths can be established for users who require a systematic, analytical, or sequential approach to an issue, whereas generalized browsing capabilities can be provided for users who do not want to avail themselves of a restricted approach. Strategies similar to the one described by Minch can be applied to the design of systems for group decision support. These systems may serve to extend the notion of a "group" decision event somewhat. Rather than attempting to ensure that all group members present at a gathering attend to the same information and analyses, hypertext-oriented group decision events afford participants the opportunity to explore various paths and conduct analyses independently as the meeting progresses (with all the potential for inefficiency such efforts may provide).

The question remains to be answered whether utilization of a hypertext system by a group whose participants will obtain independently tailored views of a topic will be constructed as a meeting. Whether the notion of a "meeting" will be largely restricted to events at which individuals share a common set of interactions (as in the conventional group meeting, where heads are generally turned toward a common focal point) will be better determined as experience with hypertext-enhanced events increases. If a "meeting of the minds" is not considered as occurring through hypertext-based activities, other, supplemental events may be needed so that group participants feel they have indeed "met" and achieved some commonality as a group (and so relevant external audiences also consider the group to have met).

Enhancing the expression of groups: Questions and issues for application designers

In genre-responsive design, intellects and imaginations of both users and designers are seen as being engaged to a large extent. Users select or reject various themes, and adopt, ignore, or refit social analogues. Design is not a spectator sport; all participants play a role and have a good deal at stake in it.

We as individuals make many efforts to construct and express our characters within our office, school, or other organizational environments. Look at the desks in the next office setting you visit. Decorating desks with pictures, mementos, plants, mugs, and calendars demonstrate the individuals' efforts to express aspects of themselves to others; such decorations are becoming increasingly popular as many administrators and managers recognize their importance (Sundstrom and Sundstrom, 1986). Obvious manifestations of the size of impending workloads (the inboxes placed prominently on their desks) are also commonplace. In computer-based interaction, opportunities for such expression are still relatively limited. Designers can work to broaden and enhance these opportunities.

Development of characters is a critical dimension of narrative construction. Designers can indeed provide a number of tools for both individual and group character development, characters that can be involved in constructing virtual individuals and groups. They can provide various themes and images for users to associate with their group or with themselves as individuals. Some of the themes and images that are particularly appropriate for a workplace context include the following:

1. Availability/lack of availability: the level of involvement in a group, and availability for further interaction, can be signaled by a particular image or set of images.
2. Uncritical acceptance/"devil's advocacy": many individuals preface their contributions to groups either with obvious signals of receptivity to others' ideas or with a devil's advocacy stance toward them. (These are not polar opposites, but relate to different stances toward others' contributions and positions.)
3. High/low levels of association with one's group contributions: in certain contexts, individuals generally desire to be closely associated with

their contributions to a group. However, in other contexts (such as brainstorming sessions and some kinds of information collection) such association is not sought after or desired.

Getting a sense of others' workplace characters (as constructed by them and by others) can help us to formulate expectations for further involvement with them, as well as aid in our current attempts toward expression and exchange. For individuals with whom we intend to have working relationships over time, we may choose to construct our own sets of character indices – character themes we view these individuals as expressing in a certain group or project context. Individuals may have an ensemble of characters associated with them, which may provide definite problems for the audiences with whom they interact. We can expect that many character construction efforts will result in strong, if not outlandish, characters in the attempt to clarify "who we are" in a particular situation (as opposed to another situation) and to distinguish our own character from those of others.

Genres have intimate connections with the societies in which they flourish. Todorov (1990) claims that "genres communicate indirectly with the society where they are operative through their institutionalization" and "bring to light the constitutive features of the society to which they belong" (p. 19). The fact that a certain social analogue associated with a genre is successful (becomes popularly utilized) reflects significant aspects of the society as a whole, as well as of the institutions or groups in which the analogue is utilized. Popularity of the heroic epic in a particular age can be seen as reflecting the age's perspectives and needs, for instance. A genre-responsive focus affords means for exploring the virtual entities that genres support.

Application-based capabilities for "anonymous" interaction appear to be increasing in variety and popularity in our own age. Many individuals are also constructing "readers" and "writers" as being merged or inter-changeable in various applications. Dimensions for constructing virtual individuals and groups in our society reflect aspects of our social conditions. We may find ourselves as designers (and consumers of design efforts) "reading" the currently popular and not-so-popular genres to find out about society. We may also, in turn, study aspects of society in order to construct more effective and accessible social analogues and other genre components.

Genre-responsive developers can play an especially significant role in construction of "generic" characters – such as the "anonymous character." This character relates to expectations for what will transpire in interactions for which there are some anonymity shields. Agents can also be associated with various character traits and images that designers can make available to users (although users will also be active in developing and choosing their own sets of agent character traits).

Few of us are members of just one group or team in the organizations we work, study, or play in. Users in the future will most probably be participants in many different groups, teams, and task forces (as group-level constructions in the workforce become increasingly popular). Keeping these various affiliations straight will be an increasingly difficult task. Development of distinct group characters – rooted in various models, images, and notions of group activity – can help in this task. Consider the following account of a CSCW application-based group:

Coordination Technology bills *Together* as an "operating system for people" . . . physical hierarchy is intact; each user is represented by an office, complete with a door ajar, and all the offices are displayed along a "hallway" . . . It also keeps track of the hierarchical relationship between co-workers, recognizing managers, subordinates, and users. (Reddy, 1991, p. 78)

A definite portrait of the group and its character is reflected in applications such as the one just described, a portrait that may have disturbing dimensions for some of us, but nevertheless permits a view into group process and structure. Users can also be afforded means to construct their own accounts and produce their own images of group activities, including retrospective accounts of what happened in group interactions, as well as accounts of their perceptions of group structure.

The activity of constructing characters of individuals creates certain expectations by them and for them; reader and writer, listener and speaker are all involved in character construction. In our daily activities, we as individuals assume more than one character. We build characters rooted in our roles as students, teachers, artists, professionals, and family members. Although consistency and stability of character are often considered a virtue (if not a necessity) in the bulk of our personal relations, active development of more than one character by individuals in a system environment could serve to heighten individuals' abilities to convey a variety of messages and to participate in activities that have conflicting demands.

Construction of "audiences" is another aspect of system development where designers have some creative leeway. We are very familiar with a number of "broadcast" vehicles, in which the audience is widely scattered geographically and often is heterogeneous in other dimensions. The perception of audience participation – for example, the notion that others are watching a television program at the same time we are – has an impact on our own experience of it. We similarly have had a good deal of experience with "one-to-one" communications, in which only a very limited number are party to the communication. "Groupcast" vehicles (such as many CSCW and network-based system applications) are less familiar, however. Groupcasting involves expression and exchange within a group: to apply an apparently circular definition, group membership makes one a party to the interaction, and being a party to the interaction makes one a member of the group (at least in some senses). "Classcasting involves expression and exchange in classroom contexts. System developers have various means of shaping impressions of who is in the group – in other words, of shaping perceptions of the audience for groupcast or classcast communications. For example, audiences can include the computer-based agents of participants as well as the (human) participants themselves.

Group narrative construction has much in common with the construction of narratives by individuals: both are forms of storytelling in which the audiences for the narratives play critical roles (and become co-authors in a number of senses). There are a variety of relevant differences, however: aspects involving group procedures, as well as comparisons and contrasts in a group's composition (including the disciplines or demographics that group members are affiliated with), often loom large in group narrative construction. The character of the group is to a large extent shaped by decisions concerning which individuals are afforded the means to participate in narrative construction, how and when opportunities to participate emerge, how individuals' contributions are framed and presented to others (both inside and outside the group), how matters of time frame and pacing are handled ("application sequencing" considerations), and other, related factors.

How consensus and dissensus are portrayed in the narratives – whether differences among group members are construed as large and/or significant enough to trigger the construction of "subgroups" or even conflicting groups or teams, or whether dissensus is handled in other ways – is another aspect of the creation of group character. Group characters draw from a growing set of commonly known images and models associated with groups in a certain context or culture, and are utilized in the construction of specific virtual groups.

Some of the answers to questions about how various CSCW and other network-based system genres can and will be utilized for narrative construction will not be ascertainable until the genres are used in a wider set of contexts and for more and broader purposes. As Crane (1987) and other designers lament, unless hypertext publications are given a status comparable to that of linear publications most academics are not going to expend the time and energies needed to explore the dimensions of hypertext and various forms of hypermedia.

Similarly subdued predictions have accompanied the advent of other CSCW and network-related genres. To attract a market and to be immediately useful, many CSCW applications have been developed and utilized largely as production vehicles for such "traditional" genres as paper-bound corporate reports and multiyear plans. Genres in the world of print publication often have peaks and valleys in their use and development as well (certain forms of poetry may wane as more individuals try their hands at the novel, for example) – but the need for a large-scale infusion of effort in the exploration of CSCW genres is indeed more critical than for these, more conventional modes of expression.

Genre-responsive design and the construction of characters

One of the purposes of this book is to provide underpinnings for a design approach to CSCW applications. Some practical issues that emerge from my characterization of genre and other considerations discussed in the book include the following.

1. The appearance of the individual's contributions: How do the individual's contributions or expressions appear to other group members? How do the individual's contributions appear in relation to what is constructed as the "group product"?

To what extent might these contributions be distorted (not appear the way the individual intended or believed they would appear) as a result of application-related modifications and influences? Even simple summary statistics (for example, an individual's average sentence length or mean time to submit a response) could have the effect of substantially altering individuals' contributions, and thus potentially of disabling individuals' attempts to save "face" (or otherwise manage their personal identity). Issues involving distortion generally have strong ethical and emotional dimensions and overtones.

2. "Positioning" of the individual and group: How are virtual individuals and groups distributed in the organization? Individuals and groups will have an assortment of virtual entities associated with them in organizational contexts; a means for keeping track of such entities' locations will give people needed senses of where they stand as organizational participants.

3. Restrictions or special privileges in the use of channels for social interaction: How are the forms and channels of interaction for group members structured? What restrictions for the use of these channels exist (for example, do some members have limited access to certain channels)? Are any of the group members (the group leader or supervisor, for instance) afforded "special" perspectives on group activity? If so, what

opportunities do these individuals have to exploit these privileged positions?

4. Required levels of involvement: How is "involvement" constructed within the context of the application (for instance, how do group participants demonstrate involvement)? What are the expected, required, or strongly suggested levels of involvement for individuals in system-mediated interaction? Are these levels explicit (communicated openly)? Do these levels of involvement change at any point in the interaction (for example, are they event driven, or can group leaders modify them)? Application designers and implementers should provide users with accounts dealing with these questions so that users will not be surprised (or embarrassed) by unexpected requirements for involvement – or so that they will be able to negotiate more reasonable expectations for involvement. VR environments can incorporate complex, multidimensional levels of involvement, and may thus be particularly problematic in this regard.

5. Construction of social roles: What attempts are made by designers to construct individuals' roles within the context of the application? To what extent do individuals' social roles (as supported by the application) affect the scope of their activities? For a designer to declare that individuals have certain roles within the application does not entail that those individuals and relevant audiences will accept or understand those roles. Social analogues for various roles thus may or may not be successful in communicating certain expectations to participants. Concerns that fall under this heading include the following:

a. Compatibility with spheres of accountability: Are application-supported social roles compatible with the individual's spheres of accountability within the group or organization? (In other words, is the CSCW application affording the individual adequate resources and scope of action to perform his or her organizational responsibilities?)

b. Opportunities for role taking: Are individuals afforded means for role-taking within the context of the application? Importance of role taking for ethics is discussed in Schwalbe (1988). "It should be apparent that the development and application of role-taking abilities can negate the tendency to objectify others" (p. 428). Opportunities to role-take in the context of CSCW application utilization may thus preserve a possibly essential element of ethical functioning. To take the role of another, an individual must be able to gain some perspective on the scope and dimensions of the other individual's role. System designers should consider whether individuals are afforded such opportunities within the scope of application-supported interactions. Role-taking activities (where individuals are encouraged to swap roles) could also be arranged by application designers and implementers.

c. Emergent roles: Do any of the system-supported social roles "emerge" as a function of system-mediated activity? (For example, might an individual be able to assume some special leadership role or obtain special information access during a system-mediated activity)? If so, what information do other individuals receive about the scope of these emergent roles, or on how to obtain such roles themselves?

6. Perspectives on system-level activity: How does group-level activity appear to the individual? If subgroup formation is supported in a CSCW application environment (as described in Stefik et al., 1987), what perspectives are individuals afforded on the composition of the various subgroups and their activities? Making accounts available about the amount and kind of application-based activity (including subgroup activity) could serve to mitigate feelings of isolation or disorientation that could result from application-based interaction, much of which may be conducted when participants are geographically dispersed.

7. In-group/out-group identification and segregation: What kinds of accounts are participants afforded of who is included in a group, and how "outsiders" are excluded, segregated, or otherwise distinguished? What accounts are given of relations of the group to the external organization (or to the broader community context)?

8. Group memory issues – time frames for retaining accounts relevant to group process: Is there an explicit "expiration date" on application-related records? If not, what kinds of understandings do group members generally have concerning these records, and how do they come about these understandings? What kinds of access to these records are group members afforded in various stages of the records' existences? Notions of application sequencing and account granularity (previously described) will take on increasing importance as the number and kind of accounts that individuals are called on to relate to increase, and as the amount of time and attention individuals can pay to any one account decreases.

A possible criticism of these points is that the availability of a large variety of accounts concerning modes of application-based interaction and expression could create a kind of "information overload" (or, rather, "account overload") for group participants. Most of the considerations introduced in this section relate to perspectives on situations and environments in which individuals spend their educational and working lives – and in which they have great personal investments. Levels of interest in these accounts are thus likely to be quite high, as will the tolerance for an abundance of information. Designers should work to present these accounts in a fashion that is economical of users' time and attention resources, however.

In an earlier chapter, the notion of the social analogue was developed. In many accounts of CSCW application design, designers assert that certain aspects of a system relate to privacy issues, or are intended to provide users with a vehicle for anonymous contribution. Despite the prayers and wishes of designers, there is no way to ensure that a certain association between a set of application features and a cultural object will take hold of the imaginations of users, and that they will utilize this association in the narratives they construct about the application.

One way that designers can be more effective in developing social analogues is to listen to how users talk about various applications, as well as to encourage them to adopt an experimental attitude toward application use. The often-rigid boundaries between designer and user should be eroded in these efforts: users should be encouraged to maintain a critical attitude toward social analogues, and to offer their own suggestions as to what would, for instance, affect their perceptions of their own privacy or anonymity. Results of informal, user-initiated experiments should also be considered in application design efforts. Much of the discourse on and the spirit of group interaction have an improvisational flavor: we "float trial balloons" in the groups we belong to or "raise a flag and see who salutes." Designers should tap this creative energy to propel their own design efforts.

Accounts of other genres (both active and extinct) and historical accounts of genre development should also be of assistance in design activity. Todorov (1990) goes so far as to claim that all genres spring from other genres. "A new genre is always the transformation of an earlier one, or of several: by inversion, by displacement, by combination" (p. 15). Todorov's assertion may indeed be rather broad, but does remind us of the value of historical insights. In Chapter 1 I discussed the development and evolution of the scientific journal in an effort to provide such perspective.

Some conclusions and reflections: Toward the sciences of the constructed

In this book, I portray the development of a genre and the artifacts linked with it as involving a complex amalgam of social, ethical, and technical issues. Recognition of how complex genre development and related design efforts are may leave designers and users of computer applications at a loss: How can they make meaningful and socially responsible contributions to the process of genre development? In the perspective presented in these chapters, many aspects of genre development are indeed out of the range of any organization's, group's, or individual's control.

Herbert Simon (1963/1981) declares that the "proper study of mankind is the science of design" (p. 159). Computer scientist Peter Wegner (1991, p. 1) follows Simon's portrayal of design as one of the "sciences of the artificial":

1.   A design should satisfy explicit or implicit goals specified by its requirements.
2.   Design structure should mirror abstract structure (phylogeny should reflect ontogeny).
3.   A design should determine behavior that realizes the required goals.
4.   A design should satisfy constraints of the design medium and application domain.

Pretenses and goals of genre-responsive design are much more delimited than these portrayals, particularly in regard to the third point (concerning the control of behavior of individuals). Genre-responsive designers relate closely to frameworks provided by past and existing genres, and to the associated expectations and forms of expression of individuals, groups, and communities.

Simon describes "artificial" in "as neutral a sense as possible, as meaning man-made as opposed to natural" (p. 6). Artifacts are interfaces between inner and outer environments:

An artifact can be thought of as a meeting point – an "interface" in today's terms – between an "inner" environment, the substance and organization of the artifact itself, and an "outer" environment, the surroundings in which it operates. If the inner environment is appropriate to the outer environment, or vice versa, the artifact will serve its intended purpose. (Simon, 1963/1981, p. 9)

For Simon, the goals of the designer are to create artifacts that serve their intended purposes, purposes established by designers. In contrast, in genre-responsive design, the designers' goals include positioning themselves and their genres in ways that make them more effective players in terms of the total picture of societal genre construction. The designers' roles evolve as the genres themselves evolve, from active development and labeling to defining newer, emerging genres in relation to older ones. The character of the designer is itself a focus of construction; it involves working in synergy with various existing genres, cultural objects, and other aspects of context (all of which will be affected by the changes they and other designers make). For example, designing a social analogue may influence one or more cultural objects; it may also have impacts on the way related genres are perceived and utilized. In ecological terms, genres find a "niche" in which they can flourish; designers can create or support these niches. The niches are apparently not isolated; a number of common themes emerge in comparative genre analysis.

Communication among designers, implementers, and users is an essential part of these processes. Genres do not naturally fit, or fail to fit, their environments. "Management of genre identity" is required; just as individuals manage their identities by being concerned with certain aspects of their "presentation" (in Goffman's terminology), the presentation of genres affects how (and whether) they will be used. Management of genre identity is a continuing, iterative process: cultural objects change rapidly, as well as do other genres. Artifacts are not created, then left to be "molded by the environment" (as in Simon's sciences of the artificial). Narratives about genres that designers, implementers, and users construct are critical aspects of genre development, and even the act of distancing oneself from a particular genre (as some developers have done with unsuccessful AI-related applications) has significance for genre development. The work of the designer is thus never entirely complete.

Application designers can have a number of areas of influence on the emerging CSCW genre and in any other design effort. For instance, they can effectively incorporate considerations into applications that will help users manage their own identities within the application's context. The major focus of genre design of any sort is provision of vehicles for the expression of individuals and groups. By obtaining a clearer picture of how they themselves appear in application-based interaction, and being given more clues as to the scope of activity in relation to the application, users can be more effective and expressive narrative builders. Designers and users can work together to expand the opportunities for expression that the genres afford. Genre developers can also explore, clarify, and in some cases redirect the linkages between their applications and various cultural objects (such as privacy, anonymity, intellectual augmentation, democracy, and dependence). Construction and refinement of social analogues are iterative processes, involving participation of designers, implementers, users, and their respective audiences.

Todorov characterizes Baudelaire as not being the "inventor" of the genre of poetry, but as having the following, laudatory role:

It was he who assured its status, who introduced it onto the horizon of his contemporaries and his followers, who made it a model of writing: a genre, in the historical sense of the word. (Todorov, 1990, p. 62)

Designers can play similar kinds of roles in relation to CSCW application genres: they can ensure the statuses of these genres; introduce them to various communities of users, developers, and researchers; and explore their possibilities as vehicles for expression. They can also be conscious of their own, emerging roles as designers.

We have searched for a "satisfactory" (aesthetically pleasing and useful) way to characterize the various genres associated with CSCW and other network-based system applications. In looking to narrative, to group characters, and to the dramatic for an approach, we are in good company. Psychologist Theodore Sarbin directs our attention toward the imagery of the theater and the skills of the novelist in posing and answering questions about social and personal aspects of expression:

It is my belief that no aesthetically satisfying account of the human condition can be constructed without taking into account the continually changing texture of events. Our job now is to find a way of satisfying our need to describe how people live their lives. Since neither fate nor mechanical causality are convincing descriptions, we are directed to seeking other ways of describing contexts. As a start I suggest we seek enlightenment from the efforts of dramatists, novelists, and other observers who view life as theater. (Sarbin, 1982, p. 33)

The success of dramatists and novelists rests in their abilities to construct ever-renewing plots and narratives – vehicles that reflect the "texture" of events. Development of genres for cooperative work requires comparable skills on the part of both designers and users.

Bibliography

Abel, M. (1990). Experiences in an Exploratory Distributed Organization. In Galegher, J., Kraut, R. E., and Egido, C. (Eds.), *Intellectual Teamwork*. Hillsdale, NJ: Erlbaum, pp. 489–510.

Abelson, P. H., and Hammond, A. L. (1980). The Electronics Revolution. In Forester, T. (Ed.), *The Microelectronics Revolution*. Cambridge, MA: MIT Press, pp. 16–28.

Ackerman, L. S., and Whitney, D. K. (1984). The Fusion Team: A Model of Organic and Shared Leadership. In Adams, J. D. (Ed.), *Transforming Work*. Alexandria, VA: Miles River Press, pp. 254–264.

Ackerman, M. S., and Malone, T. W. (1990). Answer Garden: A Tool for Growing Organizational Memory. *SIGOIS Bulletin*, 11(2–3), pp. 31–37.

ACM Member Net (1990). *The SIG World*, 1(1), p. 4.

Adams, A. S., and Thieben, K. A. (1991). Automatic Teller Machines and the Older Population. *Applied Ergonomics*, 22(2), pp. 85–90.

Adams, J. M., and Haden, D. H. (1976). *Social Effects of Computer Use and Misuse*. New York: Wiley.

Ahlberg, C. D., and Honey, J. C. (1951). *Some Administrative Problems in Governmental Research*. Washington, DC: Syracuse University, Washington Government Office.

Ahuja, S. R., Ensor, J. R., and Horn, D. N. (1988). The Rapport Multimedia Conferencing System. *Conference on Office Automation Systems*, ACM SIGOIS, pp. 1–8.

Albrecht, G. (1985). Videotape Safaris. *Qualitative Sociology*, 8(4), pp. 325–344.

Alexander, M. (1988). Adapting Tools to Work Groups. *Computerworld*, December 19, p. 31.

Alexander, M. (1990a). Meetings That Aren't Hard to Take. *Computerworld*, June 25, p. 20.

Alexander, M. (1990b). Lotus Litigation Draws Protest. *Computerworld*, August 6, p. 6.

Alford, C. F. (1991). *The Self in Social Theory*. New Haven, CT: Yale University Press.

Allen, T. J. (1984). *Managing the Flow of Technology*. Cambridge, MA: MIT Press.

Allen, T. J., and Gerstberger, P. G. (1973). A Field Experiment to Improve Communication in a Product Engineering Department: The Nonterritorial Office. *Human Factors*, 15, pp. 487–498.

Allport, F. H. (1924). *Social Psychology*. Boston: Houghton Mifflin.

Allport, G. (1932/1971). Social and Political Problems. In Achilles, P. S. (Ed.) *Psychology at Work*. Freeport, PA: Books for Library Press, pp. 199–252.

Allport, G. (1954). The Historical Backround of Modern Social Psychology. In Lindzey, G. (Ed.), *Handbook of Social Psychology* (Vol. 1). Reading, MA: Addison-Wesley, pp. 3–56.

Allwood, C. M., and Wang, Z.-M. (1990). Conceptions of Computers Among Students in China and Sweden. *Computers in Human Behavior*, 6, pp. 185–199.

Aloia, A. (1973). *Relationships Between Perceived Privacy Options, Self-Esteem, and Internal Control Among Aged People*. Unpublished Ph.D. dissertation, California School of Professional Psychology.

Alpher, R., Bethe, H., and Gamow, G. (1948). The Origin of Physical Elements. *Physical Review*, 63, p. 803.

Altheide, D. L. (1985). *Media Power*. Beverly Hills, CA: Sage.

Altheide, D. L. (1987). Media Logic and Social Interaction. *Symbolic Interaction*, 10(1), pp. 129–138.

Altman, I. (1975). *The Environment and Social Behavior*. Monterey, CA: Brooks/Cole.

Altman, I. (1977). Privacy Regulation: Culturally Universal or Culturally Specific? *Journal of Social Issues*, 33(3), pp. 66–84.

Altman, I., and Taylor, D. A. (1973). *Social Penetration: The Development of Interpersonal Relationships*. New York: Holt, Rinehart, & Winston.

Alvesson, M. (1990). On the Popularity of Organizational Culture. *Acta Sociologica*, 33(1), pp. 31–49.

Amabile, T. M. (1989). How Work Environments Affect Creativity. *1989 IEEE International Conference on Systems, Man, and Cybernetics*. New York: IEEE Press, pp. 50–55.

Ambrosio, J. (1990a). Groupware Gropes for Recognition. *Software Magazine*, June, 1990, p. 21.

Ambrosio, J. (1990b). Groupware Start-up Plans to Get It Together. *Computerworld*, July 2, p. 35.

American Psychological Association (1983). *Publication Manual*, 3rd Edition. Washington, DC: APA.

Ancona, D. G. (1990). Information Technology and Work Groups: The Case of New Product Teams. In Galegher, J., Kraut, R. E., and Egido, C. (Eds.), *Intellectual Teamwork*. Hillsdale, NJ: Erlbaum, pp. 173–190.

Anderson, J. R. (1981). *Cognitive Skills and Their Acquisition*. New York: Erlbaum.

Andriole, S. J., Ehrhart, L. S., and Aiken, P. H. (1989). Storyboard Prototypes for Group Planning and Decision-Making. *IEEE International Conference on Systems, Man, and Cybernetics*. New York: IEEE Publications, pp. 253–256.

Antonoff, M. (1990). Spreadsheets with Style. *Personal Computing*, 14(3), pp. 72–78.

Applegate, L. M., Konsynski, B., and Nunamaker, J. (1986). A Group Decision Support System for Idea Generation and Organizational Planning. *Proceedings of the First Conference on Computer-Supported Group Work*, pp. 16–34.

Archea, J. (1977). The Place of Architectual Factors in Behavioral Theories of Privacy. *Journal of Social Issues*, 33(3), pp. 116–137.

Archer, N. P. (1990). A Comparison of Computer Conferences with Face-to-Face Meetings for Small Group Business Decisions. *Behaviour & Information Technology*, 9(4), pp. 307–317.

Arms, V. M. (1984). Collaborative Writing with a Computer. *Technical Writing Teacher*, 11, pp. 181–185.

Arnst, C. (1995). The Networked Corporation: Linking Up Is Hard to Do – But It Is a Necessity. *Business Week*, June 26, pp. 86–89.

Asch, S. E. (1956). Studies of Independence and Conformity: A Minority of One Against a Unanimous Majority. *Psychological Monographs: General and Applied*, 70, pp. 1–70.

Ash, S., and Quelch, J. (1982). *The New Videotex Technology and Its Impact on Retailers in Canada*. Ottawa: Industry Trade and Commerce.

AT&T (1990). *AT&T Position on Customer Privacy, June 1*. (Provided by Wisconsin AT&T State Manager of Government Relations, James L. Leonhart.)

Auramaki, E., Lehtinen, E., and Lyytinen, K. (1988). A Speech-Act Based Office Modeling Approach. *ACM Transactions on Office Information Systems*, 6(2), pp. 126–152.

Austin, J. (1962). *How to Do Things with Words*. Cambridge, MA: Harvard University Press.

Back, K. W. (1979). The Small Group: Tightrope Between Sociology and Personality. *Journal of Applied Behavioral Science*, 15, pp. 283–293.

Bacon, F. (1879a). Novum Organum, in *Works*, ed. Spedding, J., Ellis, R. L., and Heath, D. D. London: Longmans.

Bacon, F. (1879b). The New Atlantis, in *Works*, ed. Spedding, J., Ellis, R. L., and Heath, D. D. London: Longmans.

Bacon, F. (1902). *Advancement of Learning*. New York: Collier.

Baier, K. (1965). Action and Agent. *Monist*, 49(April).

Baig, E. (1995). Welcome to the Officeless Office. *Business Week*, June 26, pp. 104–106.

Bailey, H. S. (1983). Reading, Writing, and Publishing in Academia. In Graubard, S. (Ed.), *Reading in the 1980's*. New York: Bowker, pp. 255–264.

Bales, R. F., and Strodtbeck, F. L. (1951). Phases in Group Problem Solving. *Journal of Abnormal and Social Psychology*, 46, pp. 485–495.

Bandura, A. (1989). Human Agency in Social Cognitive Theory. *American Psychologist*, 44(9), pp. 1175–1184.

Bannon, L. J. (1986). Computer-Mediated Communication. In Norman, D. A., and Draper, S. (Eds.), *User-Centered System Design*. Hillsdale, NJ: Erlbaum, pp. 433–452.

Banta, M. (1978). *Failure and Success in America: A Literary Debate*. Princeton, NJ: Princeton University Press.

Bantz, C. R. (1989). Organizing and the Social Psychology of Organizing. *Communication Studies*, 40(4), pp. 231–240.

Baran, P. (1969). Legislation, Privacy, and EDUCOM. *EDUCOM Bulletin*, December.

Barber, B. (1983). *The Logic and Limits of Trust*. New Brunswick, NJ: Rutgers University Press.

Barnard, C. (1938/1968). *The Functions of the Executive*. Cambridge, MA: Harvard University Press.

Barnard, C. (1948). *Organization and Management*. Cambridge, MA: Harvard University Press.

Barnett, A. H., Ault, R. W., and Kaserman, D. L. (1988). The Rising Incidence of Co-Authorship in Economics: Further Evidence. *Review of Economics and Statistics*, 70, pp. 539–543.

Barquin, R. (1989). Toward a New Ethics for the Computer Age. In Robinett, J., and Barquin, R. (Eds.), *Computers and Ethics: A Sourcebook for Discussions*. New York: Polytechnic Press, pp. 7–18.

Barrett, E. (1988). Introduction: A New Paradigm for Writing with and for the Computer. In Barrett, E. (Ed.), *Text, ConText, and HyperText*. Cambridge, MA: MIT Press, pp. xiii–xxv.

Barrett, E. (Ed.) (1989). *The Society of Text: Hypertext, Hypermedia, and the Social Construction of Information*. Cambridge, MA: MIT Press.

Barrett, E., and Paradis, J. (1988). The On-Line Environment and In-House Training. In Barrett, E. (Ed.), *Text, ConText, and Hypertext*. Cambridge, MA: MIT Press, pp. 227–250.

Barrett, W. (1987). *Death of the Soul: From Descartes to the Computer*. Garden City, NY: Anchor Books.

Barrie, J. (1890). Review. *British Weekly*, 9, November 20, p. 54.

Barry, J. (1986). Pleasure/Leisure and the Ideology of Corporate Convention Space. In Flak, L., and Fischer, B. (Eds.), *The Event Horizon*. Toronto: Coach House Press, pp. 253–266.

Barthes, R. (1977). *Introduction to the Structural Analysis of Narratives: Image-Music-Text*. London: Fontana.

Bartholomae, S. (1990). Micro, IS and Purchasing Managers Most Often Select Software Channels. *PC Week,* 7(26), p. 114.

Bartimo, J. (1990). At These Shouting Matches, No One Says a Word. *Business Week,* June 11, p. 78.

Baudrillard, J. (1988). *America.* London: Verso.

Baum, A. J. (1977). Introduction. In Baum, A. J. (Ed.), *Interdependence: An Interdisciplinary Study.* Albuquerque, NM: World Books, pp. 1–15.

Bazerman, C. (1987a). Literate Acts and the Emergent Social Structure of Science: A Critical Synthesis. *Social Epistemology,* 1(4), pp. 295–310.

Bazerman, C. (1987b). Codifying the Social Scientific Style: The APA Publication Manual as a Behaviorist Rhetoric. In Nelson, J. S., Megill, A., and McCloskey, D. N. (Eds.), *The Rhetoric of the Human Sciences.* Madison: University of Wisconsin Press, pp. 125–144.

Bazin, A. (1971). *What Is Cinema?* (Vol. 2). Berkeley, CA: University of California Press.

Beade, P. (1987). Comment. *College English,* 49, p. 708.

Beaver, D. B., and Rosen, R. (1979). Studies in Scientific Collaboration: Part 3, Professionalization and the Natural History of Modern Scientific Co-Authorship. *Scientometrics,* 1, pp. 231–245.

Becker, C. L. (1965). *Progress and Power.* New York: Random House.

Becker, H. S. (1960). Notes on the Concept of Commitment. *American Journal of Sociology,* 66, pp. 32–40.

Bedau, H. (1984). Ethical Aspects of Group Decision-Making. In Swap, W. S. (Ed.), *Group Decision Making.* Beverly Hills, CA: Sage, pp. 115–150.

Beeman, W. O., Anderson, K. T., Bader, G., Larkin, J., McClard, A. P., McQuillan, P., and Shields, M. (1987). Hypertext and Pluralism: From Lineal to Non-Lineal Thinking. In Smith, J. (Ed)., *Hypertext 87.* Chapel Hill: University of North Carolina Dept. of Computer Science, pp. 67–88.

Begeley, S. (1991). Gridlock in the Labs. *Newsweek.* January 14, p. 44.

Begoray, J. A. (1990). Hypermedia Issues, Systems, and Application Areas. *International Journal of Man–Machine Studies,* 33(2), pp. 121–147.

Belew, R. K., and Rentzepis, J. (1990). Hypermail: Treating Electronic Mail as Literature. *SIGOIS Bulletin,* 11(2–3), pp. 48–54.

Bell, D. (1973). *The Coming of Post-Industrial Society.* New York: Basic.

Bellah, R. N., Madsen, R., Sullivan, W. M., Swindler, A., and Tipton, S. M. (1985). *Habits of the Heart: Individualism and Commitment in American Life.* Berkeley: University of California Press.

Bellin, D. (1990). The Commoditization of Information: Societal Implications and Analogies to the Commoditization of Labor. *Computers & Society,* 20(3), p. 124.

Bendix, R. (1956). *Work and Authority in Industry.* New York: Wiley.

Benedikt, M. (1986). *Architecture and the Experience of Reality: Knowledge and Society* (Vol. 6), Greenwich, CN: JAI, pp. 233–250.

Beniger, J. R. (1986). *The Control Revolution.* Cambridge, MA: Harvard University Press.

Bennett, C. C. (1967). What Price Privacy? *American Psychologist,* 22, pp. 371–376.

Bennett, G. (1983). "Rocky the Police Dog" and Other Tales. *Lore and Language,* 3(8), pp. 1–19.

Bennis, W. (1956). Some Barriers to Teamwork in Social Research. *Social Problems,* 3, pp. 223–235.

Bentham, J. (1791). Panopticism. In Bowring, J. (Ed.), *Works of Jeremy Bentham* (Vol. 4). Edinburgh, 1843.

Berne, E. (1963). *The Structure and Dynamics of Organizations and Groups.* New York: Grove.

Bernstein, B. (1975). *Class, Code, and Control: Vol. 3, Towards a Theory of Educational Transmissions.* London: Routledge & Kegan Paul.

Bernstein, B., Smolensky, P., and Bell, B. (1989). *Design of a Constraint-Based Hypertext System to Augment Human Reasoning.* Department of Computer Science, University of Colorado at Boulder, January. Working Paper CU-CS-423-89.

Berscheid, E. (1977). Privacy: A Hidden Variable in Experimental Social Psychology. *Journal of Social Issues,* 33(3), pp. 85–101.

Betts, M. (1990). Consumers Fear Threat to Privacy. *Computerworld,* June 18, p. 4.

Bijker, W. E. (1987). The Social Construction of Bakelite: Toward a Theory of Invention. In Bijker, W. E., Hughes, T. P., and Pinch, T. J. (Eds.), *The Social Construction of Technological Systems.* Cambridge, MA: MIT Press, pp. 159–190.

Bijker, W. E., Hughes, T. P., and Pinch, T. J. (Eds.) (1987). *The Social Construction of Technological Systems.* Cambridge, MA: MIT Press.

Bikson, T., and Eveland, J. D. (1990). The Interplay of Work Group Structures and Computer Support. In Galegher, J., Kraut, R. E., and Egido, C. (Eds.), *Intellectual Teamwork.* Hillsdale, NJ: Erlbaum, pp. 245–290.

Bion, W. R. (1961). *Experiences in Groups.* London: Tavistock.

Birnbaum, J. (1985). Toward the Domestication of Microelectronics. *Communications of the ACM,* 28(11), pp. 1225–1235.

Bittner, E. (1983). Technique and the Conduct of Life. *Social Problems,* 30(3), pp. 249–261.

Bjerknes, G., Ehn, P., and Kyng, M. (Eds.). (1987). *Computers and Democracy: A Scandinavian Challenge.* Brookfield, VT: Gower.

Bjorn-Andersen, N. (1988). Are "Human Factors" Human? *Computer Journal,* 31(5), pp. 386–390.

Bjorn-Andersen, N., Eason, K., and Robey, D. (1986). *Managing Computer Impact: An International Study of Management and Organizations.* Norwood, NJ: Ablex.

Bjorn-Andersen, N., and Kjaergaard, D. (1987). Choices Enroute to the Office of Tomorrow. In R. Kraut (Ed.), *Technology and the Transformation of White Collar Work.* Hillsdale, NJ: Erlbaum, pp. 195–210.

Blais, M. (1987). Epistemic Tit for Tat. *Journal of Philosophy,* 7, pp. 335–349.

Blakeslee, S. (1990). Ethicists See Omens of an Era of Genetic Bias. *New York Times,* December 27, p. B–6.

Blanchard, C., Burgess, S., Harvill, Y., Lanier, J., Lasko, A., Oberman, M., and Teitel, M. (1990). Reality Built for Two: A Virtual Reality Tool. *Proceedings of the 1990 Symposium on Interactive 3D Graphics,* in *Computer Graphics (ACM),* 24(2), pp. 35–36.

Blanchot, M. (1969). *L'entretien infini.* Paris: Gallimard.

Blanchot, M. (1982). *The Space of Literature.* Lincoln: University of Nebraska Press.

Blau, J. (1982). Expert Collaboration and the Ethics of Practice. *Knowledge: Creation, Diffusion, Utilization,* 4(1), pp. 111–126.

Blau, P. (1967). *The American Occupational Structure.* New York: Wiley.

Bloustein, T. (1964). Privacy as an Aspect of Human Dignity: An Answer to Dean Prosser. *New York University Law Review,* 39, pp. 962–1007.

Bly, S. A. (1988). A Use of Drawing Surfaces in Different Collaborative Settings. *Second Conference on Computer-Supported Cooperative Work,* September 26–28, pp. 250–256.

Bly, S. A., and Minneman, S. L. (1990). Commune: A Shared Drawing Surface. *SIGOIS Bulletin,* 11(2–3), pp. 184–192.

Bobrow, D. G. (1991). AAAI-90 Presidential Address: Dimensions of Interaction. *AI Magazine,* Fall, pp. 64–80.

Bochenski, B. (1990). Workgroup Goals Push Groupware Boundaries. *Software Magazine,* November, pp. 69–79.

Bodker, S. (1987). *Through the Interface: A Human Activity Approach to User Interface Design.* Aahrus University, Computer Science Department, Working Paper DAIMI PB-224.

Bogardus, E. S. (1931). *Contemporary Sociology.* Los Angeles, CA: University of Southern California Press.

Boguslaw, R. (1965). *The New Utopians: A Study of System Design and Social Change.* Englewood Cliffs, NJ: Prentice-Hall.

Bolter, J. D. (1984). *Turing's Man.* Chapel Hill: University of North Carolina Press.

Bolter, J. D. (1989). Beyond Word Processing: The Computer as a New Writing Space. *Language and Communication,* 9(2–3), pp. 129–142.

Bolter, J. D. (1991). *Writing Space: The Computer, Hypertext, and the History of Writing.* Hillsdale, NJ: Erlbaum.

Bolton, C. (1967). Is Sociology a Behavioral Science? In Manis, J. G., and Meltzer, B. N. (Eds.), *Symbolic Interaction: A Reader in Social Psychology.* Boston: Allyn & Bacon, pp. 95–108.

Bond, A. H., and Gasser, L. (1988). *Readings in Distributed Artificial Intelligence.* San Mateo, CA: Morgan Kauffman.

Bond, A. H. (1990). A Computational Model for Organizations of Cooperating Intelligent Agents. *SIGOIS Bulletin,* 11(2–3), pp. 21–30.

Boone, J. (1983). Privacy and Community. *Social Theory and Practice,* 1(1–3), pp. 14–21.

Booth, T., and Miller, R. E. (1987). Computer Science Accreditation: The First-Year Activities of the Computing Sciences Accreditation Board. *Communications of the ACM,* 30(5), pp. 376–383.

Booth, W. (1961). *The Rhetoric of Fiction.* Chicago: University of Chicago Press.

Bordwell, D. (1989). *Making Meaning: Inference and Rhetoric in the Interpretation of Cinema.* Cambridge, MA: Harvard University Press.

Borenstein, N., and Thyberg, C. A. (1988). Cooperative Work in the Andrew Message System. *Proceedings of the Second Conference on Computer-Supported Cooperative Work,* Portland, OR, September 26–28, pp. 306–323.

Borgmann, A. (1984). *Technology and the Character of Contemporary Life: A Philosophical Inquiry.* Chicago: University of Chicago Press.

Bormann, E. G. (1985). Symbolic Convergence Theory: A Communication Formulation. *Journal of Communication,* 35(4), pp. 128–138.

Boulding, K. E. (1984). Crime Doesn't Pay: A Review of The Evolution of Cooperation. *Commonweal,* May 18, pp. 310–314.

Bourdieu, P. (1990). Social Space and Symbolic Power. *Sociological Theory,* pp. 14–25.

Bowen, M. (1978). *Family Therapy in Clinical Practice.* New York: J. Aronson.

Bramel, D., and Friend, R. (1987). The Work Group and Its Vicissitudes in Social and Industrial Psychology. *Journal of Applied Behavioral Psychology,* 23(2), pp. 233–253.

Brand, R. (1990). Personal communication, cited in Katz, J. E., and Graveman, R. F. (1991), Privacy Issues of a National Research and Education Network, *Telematics and Informatics,* 8(1–2), pp. 71–120.

Brand, S. (1987). *The Media Lab: Inventing the Future at MIT.* New York: Viking.

Braverman, H. (1974). *Labor and Monopoly Capital: The Degradation of Work in the Twentieth Century.* New York: Monthly Review Press.

Breer, P. E., and Locke, E. C. (1965). *Task Experience as a Source of Attitudes.* New York: Dorsey.

Brennan, E. (1989). Using the Computer to Right the Canon: The Brown Women Writers Project. *Brown Online,* 2, pp. 7–13.

Brennan, S. (1984). *Interface Agents.* Unpublished paper, cited in Laurel, B. (1986).

Brennan, S. (1990). Conversation as Direct Manipulation: An Iconoclastic View. In Laurel, B. (Ed.) *The Art of Human–Computer Interface Design.* Menlo Park, CA: Addison-Wesley, pp. 393–404.

Brenton, M. (1964). *The Privacy Invaders.* New York: Coward-McCann.

Brewster, Sir David. (1855). *Memoirs of the Life, Writings, and Discoveries of Sir Isaac Newton.* Edinburgh: Edmonston & Douglas.

Brill, N. I. (1976). *Teamwork: Working Together in the Human Services.* Philadelphia: Lippincott.

Brinton, W. C. (1914). *Graphic Methods for Presenting Facts.* New York: Engineering Magazine.

Broadhead, R. S. (1980). Individuation in Facework: Theoretical Implications from a Study of Facework in Medical School Admissions. *Symbolic Interaction,* 3(2), pp. 51–68.

Brod, C. (1984). *Technostress.* Reading, MA: Addison-Wesley.

Brooke-Rose, C. (1991). *Stories, Theories, and Things.* Cambridge University Press.

Brooks, F. B. (1967/1982). *The Mythical Man–Month: Essays on Software Engineering.* Reading, MA: Addison-Wesley.

Brooks, F. B. (1971). Why Is the Software Late? *Data Management,* August, pp. 18–21.

Brooks, F. B. (1988). Grasping Reality Through Illusion – Interactive Graphics Serving Science. Keynote Address, 5th Conference on Computers and Human Interaction, Washington, DC, May.

Brown, W. R. (1978). Ideology as Communication Process. *Quarterly Journal of Speech,* 64(2), pp. 123–140.

Brown, W. R. (1981). *Toward a Complementary Version of the Rhetorical-Vision Theory.* Unpublished manuscript, Ohio State University.

Browning, J. (1990). The Ubiquitous Machine. *Economist,* June 16, pp. 5–20.

Bruce, R. V. (1987). *The Launching of Modern American Science.* New York: Knopf.

Bruffee, K. A. (1986). Social Construction, Language, and Knowledge. *College English,* 48, pp. 773–788.

Bruffee, K. A. (1987). Response. *College English,* 49, pp. 711–716.

Brunsson, N. (1989). *The Organization of Hypocrisy: Talk, Decisions, and Actions in Organizations.* New York: Wiley.

Buber, M. (1958). *I and Thou* (Second Edition). New York: Scribner.

Budd, T. (1991). *An Introduction to Object-Oriented Programming.* Reading, MA: Addison-Wesley.

Buerger, D. (1993). "Workgroup Software" Lacks a Clear Definition. *Communications Week,* May 24, p. 50.

Buley-Meissner, M. L. (1990). Rhetorics of the Self. *Journal of Education,* 172(1), pp. 47–64.

Bulkeley, W. (1988). New Software Helps PC Users Work as Groups. *Wall Street Journal,* February 24, p. 26.

Bump, J. (1990). Radical Changes in Class Discussion Using Networked Computers. *Computers and the Humanities,* 24, pp. 49–65.

Bundy, A., and Clutterbuck, R. (1985). *Raising the Standards of AI Products,* (Vol. 2). Ninth International Joint Conference on AI, pp. 1289–1294.

Burgoon, J. K. (1982). Privacy and Communication, In M. Burgoon (Ed.), *Communication Yearbook 6.* Beverly Hills, CA: Sage, pp. 206–249.

Burke, K. (1937). *Permanence and Change: An Anatomy of Purpose.* Indianapolis, IN: Bobbs-Merrill.

Burke, K. (1945). *A Grammar of Motives.* Englewood Cliffs, NJ: Prentice-Hall.

Burke, K. (1955). *A Rhetoric of Motives.* Englewood Cliffs, NJ: Prentice-Hall.

Burke, K. (1966). *Language as Symbolic Action.* Berkeley, CA: University of California Press.

Burnham, D. (1983). *The Rise of the Computer State.* New York: Random House.

Burns, M. L. (1988). Participative Leadership Made Easier with Consensor: An Electronic Tool. *Educational Technology,* 28(4), pp. 26–30.

Burrill, V. (1993). The MOVIE Project: Mapping Objects on Video by Interactive Editing. *ERCIM News,* 15 (December), p. 15.

Burris, B. H. (1989). Technocracy and the Transformation of Organizational Control. *Social Science Journal,* 26(3), pp. 313–333.

Bush, V. (1945). As We May Think. *Atlantic Monthly,* August, pp. 101–108.

Businessland, Inc. (1990). Bottom Line Computing: The Challenge for the '90s. Advertising supplement to the *Wall Street Journal.*

Busse, T. (1993). Russell Enhancing Its Calendar Manager App. *Communications Week,* December 20, p. 13.

Caldwell, B. (1990). Big Brother Is Watching. *Information Week,* 275, pp. 34–36.

Callon, M. (1986). The Sociology of an Actor-Network: The Case of the Electric Vehicle. In Callon, M., Law, J., and Rip, A. (Eds.), *Mapping the Dynamics of Science and Technology.* London: Macmillian, pp. 19–34.

Campbell, D. E., and Campbell, T. (1988). A New Look at Informal Communication: The Role of the Physical Environment. *Environment and Behavior,* 20(2), pp. 211–226.

Carey, J. (1991). An "Information Superhighway"? *Business Week,* 3199, February 11, pp. 28–29.

Carlson, P. A. (1990). Hypertext: A Way of Incorporating User Feedback into Online Documentation. In Barrett, E. (Ed.), *Text, ConText, and Hypertext.* Cambridge, MA: MIT Press, pp. 93–110.

Carmody, D. (1991). Question of Quotes: Are They What the Speaker Really Said? *New York Times,* June 21, p. A8.

Carr, C. (1992). Planning Priorities for Empowered Teams. *Journal of Business Strategy,* 13(5), pp. 43–48.

Carringer, R. L. (1982). Orson Wells and Gregg Toland: Their Collaboration on *Citizen Kane. Critical Inquiry,* 8, pp. 651–662.

Carroll, N. (1988). *Philosophical Problems of Classical Film Theory.* Princeton, NJ: Princeton University Press.

Carroll, P. (1990). Good News: You Can Live Forever. *Wall Street Journal,* December 7, p. A–1.

Ceci, S. and Peters, D. (1984). How Blind Is Blind Review? *American Psychologist,* 39(12), pp. 1491–1494.

Ceteras, S. (1990). Through the Virtual Looking Glass. *ETC,* 47(1), pp. 67–71.

Chandler, A. (1977). *The Visible Hand: The Managerial Revolution in American Business.* Cambridge, MA: Harvard University Press.

Chapin, F. S. (1951). Some Housing Factors Related to Mental Hygene. *Journal of Social Issues,* 7, pp. 164–171.

Chesebro, J. W. (1984). The Media Reality. *Critical Studies in Mass Communication,* 1(June), pp. 111–130.

Chesebro, J. W. (1989). Text, Narration, and Media. *Text and Performance Quarterly,* 9(January), pp. 1–23.

Chesebro, J. W., and Bonsall, D. G. (1989). *Computer-Mediated Communication: Human Relationships in a Computerized World.* Tuscaloosa: University of Alabama Press.

Chicago Sun Times (1991). Use IRS Document Program on Businesses: GAO. June 11, p. 51.

Chisolm, D. (1989). *Coordination Without Hierarchy.* Berkeley: University of California Press.

Christiansen, P., King, S., and Munger, M. (1989). Groupware: E-Mail Meets Scheduling. *PC World,* 7(7), pp. 146–156.

Churbuck, D. (1990). Network Nettles. *Forbes,* 146(3), pp. 94–95.

Ciborra, C. C., and Olsen, M. H. (1988). Encountering Electronic Work Groups: A Transaction Costs Perspective. *Proceedings of the Second Conference on Computer-Supported Cooperative Work* (Vol. 2), Portland, OR: September 26–28, pp. 94–101.

Cicourel, A. V. (1990). The Integration of Distributed Knowledge in Collaborative Medical Diagnosis. In Galegher, J., Kraut, R. E., and Egido, C. (Eds.), *Intellectual Teamwork.* Hillsdale, NJ: Erlbaum, pp. 221–242.

Clanchy, M. T. (1979). *From Memory to Written Record: England, 1066–1307.* Cambridge, MA: Harvard University Press.

Clegg, C. (1988). Appropriate Technology for Humans and Organizations. *Journal of Information Technology,* 3(3), pp. 133–146.

Clement, A. (Ed.) (1993). Special Issue, *SIGOIS Bulletin,* 14(1).

Clement, A. (1994). Computing at Work: Empowering Action by "Low-Level" Users. *Communications of the ACM,* 37(1), pp. 52–63.

Cline, R. J. (1983). The Acquaintance Process as Relational Communication. In M. Burgoon (Ed.), *Communication Yearbook 7.* Beverly Hills, CA: Sage, pp. 396–413.

Coate, J. (1992). Innkeeping in Cyberspace. *Proceedings of Directions and Implications of Advanced Computing.* Palo Alto, CA: Computer Professionals for Social Responsibility.

Coates, J. F. (1991). Leaving the Computer Stone Age. *Computerworld,* April 1, pp. 23.

Coffee, P. (1990). PM Spreadsheets Take Different Tacks. *PC Week,* 7(29), pp. 75–76.

Cohen, R., and Keuffel, W. (1991). Pull Together! *Computer Language,* 8(8), pp. 36–44.

Cole, M., and Griffin, P. (1980). Cultural Amplification Reconsidered. In Olson, D. R. (Ed.), *The Social Foundations of Language and Thought: Essays in Honor of Jerome S. Bruner.* New York: Norton, pp. 343–364.

Coleman, J. (1974). *Power and the Structure of Society.* New York: Norton.

Collins, H. M. (1987). Expert Systems and the Science of Knowledge. In Bijker, W. E., Hughes, T. P., and Pinch, T. P. (Eds.), *The Social Construction of Technological Systems.* Cambridge, MA: MIT Press, pp. 329–348.

Collins, R. (1989). Toward a Neo-Meadian Sociology of Mind. *Symbolic Interaction,* 12(1), pp. 1–32.

Colonna, J. D. (1987). Computer Professionals Take A Stand on Social Issues. *Information Week,* September 14, p. 22.

Comer, D. (1983). The Computer Science Research Network, CSNET: A History and Status Report. *Communications of the ACM,* 26(10), pp. 747–753.

Comer, D., and Peterson, L. (1985). Conversations: An Alternative to Memos and Conferences. *Byte,* 10, pp. 263–272.

Computer (IEEE) (1989). Computer Mouse Inventor Gets Funding. May, p. 82.

Computerworld (1990). International Data Group, Inc. June 25, p. 116.

Conklin, J. (1987). *A Survey of Hypertext.* Technical Report No. STP-356–86. Austin, TX: MCC.

Conklin, J., and Begeman, M. (1988). *gBIS: A Hypertext Tool for Exploratory Policy Discussion.* Second Conference on Computer-Supported Cooperative Work, September 26–28, 1988.

Constant, E. W. (1987). The Social Locus of Technological Practice: Community, System, or Organization? In Bijker, W. E., Hughes, T. P., and Pinch, T. J. (Eds.), *The Social Construction of Technological Systems.* Cambridge, MA: MIT Press, pp. 223–242.

Constantine, L. (1990). Teamwork Paradigms and the Structured Open Team. In *Proceedings of Software Development '90.* San Francisco: Miller Freeman.

Cook, P., Ellis, C., Graf, M., Rein, G., and Smith, T. (1987). Project Nick: Meetings Augmentation and Analysis. *ACM Transactions on Office Information Systems,* 5(2), pp. 132–146.

Cooley, C. H. (1902). *Human Nature and the Social Order.* New York: Scribner's.

Cooley, C. H. (1909/1962). *Social Organization.* New York: Schocken.

Copple, R. F. (1989). Privacy and the Frontier Thesis: An American Intersection of Self and Society. *American Journal of Jurisprudence,* 34, pp. 87–132.

Corcoran, E. (1988). Groupware. *Scientific American,* 259, July.

Cortese, A. (1990). Coordination Offers Groupware. *Computer Systems News,* 473, p. 31.

Cortese, A. (1995). Cyber-Networks Need a Lot of Spackle. *Business Week,* June 26, pp. 92–96.

Coursey, D. (1988). Groupware: Not Just for Groups. *MIS Week,* 9(43), p. 26.

Coursey, D. (1991). Prodigy Denies Latest Charge, Starts Education Program. *Infoworld,* May 8, p. 6.

Cousins, N. (1981). *Human Options.* New York: Norton.

Cowan, R. A. (1984). *Teleconferencing: Maximizing Human Potential.* Reston, VA: Reston Publishing.

Cowan, R. S. (1987). The Consumption Junction: A Proposal for Research Strategies in the Sociology of Technology. In Bijker, W. E., Hughes, T. P., and Pinch, T. J. (Eds.), *The Social Construction of Technological Systems.* Cambridge, MA: MIT Press, pp. 261–280.

Cox, J. (1990). Olsen: Use Networks to Foster Employee Teamwork. *Digital News,* 5(4), p. 48.

Cox, J., and Lothstein, L. (1989). Video Self-Portraits. *International Journal of Group Psychotherapy,* 39(2), pp. 241–253.

Coyle, Grace (1926). *Some Personal and Social Values in Adult Education.* Grace Coyle Papers, box 6, file "Speeches, 1930's." Cited in Graebner (1987).

Coyle, Grace (1935). *Program Study Prospectus,* September 4, 1935, Grace Coyle Papers, Case Western Reserve University Archives, Cleveland, Ohio, box 1, folder "Biographies – Group Work, 1934–56." Cited in Graebner (1987).

Crane, D. (1972). *Invisible Colleges: Diffusion of Knowledge in Scientific Communities.* Chicago: University of Chicago Press.

Crane, G. (1987). From the Old to the New: Integrating Hypertext into Traditional Scholarship. In Smith, J. (Ed.), *Hypertext 87.* Chapel Hill: University of North Carolina Dept. of Computer Science, pp. 51–56.

Crick, F. (1989). *What Mad Pursuit.* New York: Basic.

Croft, B. (1990). Evaluating Computer-Based Tools in Organizations. *SIGOIS Bulletin,* 11(2–3), pp. 193.

Crouch, A., and Nimran, U. (1989a). Perceived Facilitators and Inhibitors of Work Performance in an Office Environment. *Environment and Behavior,* 21(2), pp. 206–226.

Crouch, A., and Nimran, U. (1989b). Office Design and the Behavior of Senior Managers. *Human Relations,* 42(2), pp. 139–155.

Crowston, K., and Malone, T. W. (1988). Intelligent Software Agents. *Byte,* 13(13), pp. 267–271.

Culliton, B. J. (1990). Harvard Tackles the Rush to Publication. *Science,* 241, p. 525.

Cushman, P. (1990). Why the Self Is Empty: Toward a Historically Situated Psychology. *American Psychologist,* 45(5), pp. 599–611.

Cuzzort, R. P. (1969). Humanity as the Big Con: The Views of Erving Goffman. In Cuzzort, R. P. (Ed.), *Humanity and Modern Sociological Thought.* New York: Holt, Rinehart, & Winston, pp. 173–192.

Daft, R. (1992). *Organizational Theory and Design.* St. Paul, MN: West.

Daiute, C. (1985). *Writing and Computers.* Reading, MA: Addison-Wesley.

Dalton, R. (1987). Group-Writing Tools: Four That Connect. *Information Week,* March 9, pp. 62–65.

Daly, J. (1991). Constitutional Scholar Calls for "High Tech" Amendment. *Computerworld,* April 1, p. 99.

D'Amico, P. (1990). Committee Coma. *Wall Street Journal,* August 6, p. A–13.

Danziger, J. N., and Kraemer, K. L. (1986). *People and Computers.* New York: Columbia University Press.

Danziger, K. (1987). New Paradigm or Metaphysics of Consensus? A Response to Harre. *New Ideas in Psychology,* 5(1), pp. 13–17.

Danziger, K. (1990). *Constructing the Subject.* Cambridge University Press.

Davidow, W., and Malone, T. (1992). *The Virtual Corporation.* New York: HarperBusiness.

Davies, D. (1988). Computer-Supported Co-operative Learning Systems: Interactive Group Technologies and Open Learning. *Programmed Learning and Educational Technology,* 25(3), pp. 205–215.

Davis, J. H., Kameda, T., Parks, C., Stasson, M., and Zimmerman, S. (1989). Some Social Mechanics of Group Decision Making: The Distribution of Opinion, Polling Sequence, and Implications for Consensus. *Journal of Personality and Social Psychology,* 57(6), pp. 1000–1012.

Davis, N. P. (1968). *Lawrence and Oppenheimer.* New York: Simon & Schuster.

Daviss, B. (1990). Grand Illusions. *Discover,* 11(6), pp. 36–41.

Daviss, B. (1991). Knowbots. *Discover,* 12(4), pp. 21–22.

Deal, T., and Kennedy, A. A. (1982). *Corporate Cultures.* Reading, MA: Addison-Wesley.

Dehnert, E. (1986). The Dialectic of Technology and Culture. In Amsler, M. (Ed.), *The Languages of Creativity.* Cranbury, NJ: Associated University Presses.

Delbecq, A. L., Van de Ven, A. H., and Gustafson, D. H. (1975). *Group Techniques for Program Planning: A Guide to Nominal Group and Delphi Processes.* Glenview, IL: Scott, Foresman.

Delisle, N., and Schwartz, M. (1987). Contexts – A Partitioning System for Hypertext. *ACM Transactions on Office Information Systems,* 5(2), pp. 168–186.

Denning, P. (1987). The Science of Computing: A New Paradigm for Science. *American Scientist,* 75, pp. 572–573.

Dennis, A. R., George, J. F., Jessup, L. M., Nunamaker, J. F., and Vogel, D. R. (1988). Information Technology to Support Electronic Meetings. *MIS Quarterly,* pp. 591–624.

Derfler, F. (1989). Imposing Efficiency: Workgroup Productivity Software. *PC Magazine,* 8(16), pp. 247–269.

Derlega, V. J., and Chaikin, A. L. (1977). Privacy and Self-Disclosure in Social Relationships. *Journal of Social Issues*, 33(3), pp. 102–115.

DeSanctis, G. (1983). Expectancy Theory as an Explanation of the Voluntary Use of a Decision Support System. *Psychological Reports*, 52(1), pp. 247–260.

DeSanctis, G., and Gallupe, R. (1987). A Foundation for the Study of Group Decision Support Systems. *Management Science*, 33(5), pp. 589–609.

Descartes, R. (1965). *A Discourse on Method and Other Works*. New York: Washington Square Press.

de Solla Price, D. J. (1963). *Little Science, Big Science*. New York: Columbia University Press.

Deutsch, C. H. (1990). Business Meetings by Keyboard. *New York Times*, October 21, p. F-25.

Deutsch, M. (1949). An Experimental Study of the Effects of Cooperation and Competition upon Group Processes. *Human Relations*, 2, pp. 199–232.

Deutsch, M. (1973). *The Resolution of Conflict: Constructive and Destructive Processes*. New Haven, CT: Yale University Press.

Devons, E. (1970). *Papers on Planning and Economic Management*. Manchester: Manchester University Press.

Dewey, J. (1922). *Democracy and Education*. New York: Macmillan.

Dewey, J. (1931). *Philosophy and Civilization*. New York: Minton, Balch.

Dewey, J. (1939). *Freedom and Culture*. New York: Putnam.

Dewey, J. (1948). *Reconstruction in Philosophy*. Boston, MA: Beacon.

Dewey, J., and Tufts, J. H. (1939). Intelligence in Social Action. In Ratner, J. (Ed.), *Intelligence in the Modern World*. New York: Random House, pp. 435–466.

Diaper, D. (1989). Task Analysis for Knowledge Descriptions (TAKD): The Method and an Example. In Diaper, D. (Ed.), *Task Analysis for Human–Computer Interaction*. Chichester: Horwood, pp. 108–158.

Dickson, G. W., Lee, J. E., Robinson, L., and Heath, R. (1989). Observations on GDSS Interaction: Chaffeured, Facilitated, and User-Driven Systems. *Proceedings of the 22nd Annual Hawaii International Conference on System Sciences* (Vol. 22), pp. 337–343.

Diderot, D. (1778/1978). *Diderot Encyclopedia*. New York: Abrams.

Didion, J. (1976). Why I Write. *New York Times*.

Diehl, M., and Stroebe, W. (1987). Productivity Loss in Brainstorming Groups: Toward the Solution of a Riddle. *Journal of Personality and Social Psychology*, 53(3), pp. 497–509.

Diener, E. (1979). Deindividuation, Self-Awareness, and Disinhibition. *Journal of Personality and Social Psychology*, 37, pp. 1160–1171.

Diener, E. (1980). Deindividuation: The Absence of Self-Awareness and Self-Regulation in Group Members. In Paulus, P. (Ed.), *The Psychology of Group Influence*. Hillsdale, NJ: Erlbaum, pp. 209–242.

Dilatush, L. (1977). Interdependence in Sociology. In Baum, A. J. (Ed.), *Interdependence: An Interdisciplinary Study*. Albuquerque, NM: World Books, pp. 122–131.

Dionisopoulous, P., and Ducat, C. (1976). *The Right to Privacy*. St. Paul, MN: West Publishing.

Doran, J. (1985). The Computational Approach to Knowledge, Communication, and Structure in Multi-Actor Systems. In Gilbert, G. N., and Heath, C. (Eds.), *Social Action and Artificial Intelligence*. Brookfield, VT: Gower, pp. 160–171.

Dowie, M. (1990). Friend or Big Brother? *Infoworld*, July 23, pp. 32–36.

Dreitzel, H. P. (1981). The Socialization of Nature: Western Attitudes Towards Body and Emotions. In Heelas, P., and Lock, A. (Eds.), *Indigenous Psychologies: The Anthropology of the Self.* London: Academic Press, pp. 205–223.

Dreyfus, H. L., and Dreyfus, S. E. (1986). *Mind over Machine.* New York: Free Press.

Dreyfus, H. L., and Rabinow, P. (1983). *Michel Foucault: Beyond Structuralism and Hermeneutics.* Chicago: University of Chicago Press.

Drucker, P. (1966). *The Effective Executive.* New York: Harper & Row.

Drucker, P. (1988). The Coming of the New Organization. *Harvard Business Review,* 66(1), pp. 45–53.

Dubos, R. (1961). *The Dreams of Reason.* New York: Columbia University Press.

Dubrovsky, V. (1987). Social Exchange in Group Consensus Development: Face-to-Face Versus Electronic Mail. *Proceedings of the Human Factors Society* (Vol. 31). Santa Monica, CA: Human Factors Society, pp. 701–705.

Duffield, D. W. (1926). *Progressive Indexing and Filing for Schools.* Tonawanda, NY: Rand Kardex Bureau for Library Bureau.

Dumais, S., Kraut, R., and Koch, S. (1988). Computers' Impact on Productivity and Work Life. In Allen, R. B. (Ed.), *ACM Conference on Office Automation Systems.* New York: Association for Computing Machinery, pp. 88–95.

Duncan, H. (1962). *Communication and Social Order.* New York: Oxford University Press.

Dunlop, R. A. (1970). The Emerging Technology of Information Utilities. In Sackman, H., and Nie, N. (Eds.), *The Information Utility and Social Choice.* Montvale, NJ: AFIPS, pp. 25–50.

Dunkle, J. (1990). Working Well in a Work-Group Environment. *Computerworld,* June 4, pp. SR31–35.

Durfee, E. H., Lesser, V. R., and Corkill, D. D. (1989). Trends in Cooperative Problem Solving. *IEEE Transactions on Knowledge and Data Engineering,* 1(1), pp. 63–83.

Durkheim, E. (1933/1964). *The Division of Labor in Society.* New York: Free Press.

Dvorak, J. (1988). New Age Villainy. *PC Magazine,* 7(16), p. 71.

Dvorak, J., and Seymour, J. (1988). Bravos and Bashes for Workgroup Computing. *PC Computing,* 1(3), pp. 33–34.

Dyson, E. (1990a). Why Groupware Is Gaining Ground. *Datamation,* 36(5), pp. 52–56.

Dyson, E. (1990b). A Notable Order for Groupware. *Datamation,* 36(9), p. 51.

Dyson, E. (1990c). Not Just Another Spreadsheet. *Forbes,* February 5, p. 161.

Dyson, E. (1990d). The Orchestra Gets a Conductor. *Forbes,* May 18, p. 349.

Dyson, E. (1991). How to Computerize a Business Conference. *Forbes,* April 29, p. 143.

Easton, G. K., George, J. F., Nunamaker, J. F., and Pendergast, M. O. (1990). Using Two Different Electronic Meeting Tools for the Same Task: An Experimental Comparison. *Journal of Management Information Systems,* 7(1), pp. 85–100.

Eddy, W. B. (1965). *The Manager and the Working Group.* New York: Praeger.

Edge, D. (1979). Technological Metaphor and Social Control. In Bugliarello, G., and Doner, D. B. (Eds.), *The History and Philosophy of Technology,* Urbana, IL: University of Illinois Press, pp. 309–324.

Edgely, C., and Turner, R. (1975). Masks and Social Relations: An Essay on the Sources and Assumptions of Dramaturgical Social Psychology. *Humbolt Journal of Social Relations,* 3(1), pp. 4–12.

Edwards, R. (1979). *Contested Terrain: The Transformation of the Workplace in the Twentieth Century.* New York: Basic.

Egido, C. (1988). Video Conferencing as a Technology to Support Group Work: A Review of Its Failures. *Proceedings of the Second Conference on Computer-Supported Cooperative Work.* (Vol. 2). Portland, OR, September 26–28, pp. 13–24.

Egido, C. (1990). Teleconferencing as a Technology to Support Cooperative Work. In Galegher, J., Kraut, R. E., and Egido, C. (Eds.), *Intellectual Teamwork*. Hillsdale, NJ: Erlbaum, pp. 351–372.

Ehn, P. (1988). Playing the Language-Games of Design and Use. *ACM Conference on Office Automation Systems*. New York: Association for Computing Machinery, pp. 142–157.

Ehrlich, S. (1987). Strategies for Encouraging Successful Adoption of Office Communication Systems. *ACM Transactions on Office Automation Systems*, 5(4), pp. 340–357.

Eisenstein, E. (1969). The Advent of Printing and the Problem of the Renaissance. *Past & Present*, 45, pp. 19–89.

Eisenstein, E. (1979). *The Printing Press as an Agent of Change*. Cambridge University Press.

Electronic Messaging News (1995). Companies Using World Wide Web as Internal Publishing System, 7(16), pp. 1–2.

Ellis, C. A., Gibbs, S. J., and Rein, G. L. (1990). Design and Use of a Group Editor. In Cockton, G. (Ed.), *Engineering for Human–Computer Interaction*. Amsterdam: North-Holland, pp. 13–25.

Ellis, C. A., Gibbs, S. J., and Rein, G. L. (1991). Groupware: Some Issues and Experiences. *Communications of the ACM*, 34(1), pp. 38–58.

Ellis, C. A., Rein, G. L., and Jarvenpaa, S. L. (1989). Nick Experimentation: Selected Results Concerning Effectiveness of Meeting Support Technology. *Journal of Management Information Systems*, 6(3), pp. 7–24.

Ellul, J. (1964). *The Technological Society* (Wilkinson, J., Trans.). New York: Knopf.

Emerson, R. W. (1971). *The Collected Works of Ralph Waldo Emerson* (Spiller, R. E., and Ferguson, A. R., Eds.). Cambridge, MA: Harvard University Press.

Emerson, T. (1970). *The System of Freedom of Expression*. New York: Random House.

Engelbart, D. C. (1963). A Conceptual Framework for the Augmentation of Man's Intellect. In Howerton, P. W., and Weeks, D. (Eds.), *Vistas in Information Handling* (Vol. 1). Washington, DC: Spartan Books, pp. 1–29.

Engelbart, D. C. (1988). The Augmented Knowledge Workshop. In Goldberg, A. (Ed.), *A History of Personal Workstations*. New York: ACM Press, pp. 187–231.

Engelbart, D. C., and Engelbart, C. (1990). Bootstrapping and the Handbook Cycle. *Telematics and Informatics*, 7(1), pp. 27–32.

Engelbart, D. C., and Lehtman, H. (1988). Working Together. *Byte*, 13(13), pp. 245–252.

Engelbart, D. C., Watson, R. W., and Norton, J. C. (1973). The Augmented Knowledge Workshop. *AFIPS Conference Proceedings* (Vol. 42). Montvale, NJ: AFIPS Press, pp. 9–21.

Erickson, T. (1989). Interfaces for Cooperative Work: An Eclectic Look at CSCW '88. *SIGCHI Bulletin*, 21(1), pp. 56–64.

Erikson, K. T. (1976). *Everything in Its Path*. New York: Simon & Schuster.

Eriksson, I., and Kalmi, R. (1986). Interpretation of Large Information Systems as a Set of Personal Information Systems and Enriching the Users' Knowledge with this View. In Nissen, H.-E., and Sandstrom, G. (Eds.), *Quality of Work versus Quality of Information Systems: Report of the Ninth Scandinavian Research Seminar on Systemeering*. Lund: University of Lund, Department of Information and Computer Sciences.

Evans, C. (1981). *The Micro Revolution*. New York: Pocket Books.

Evans, G. W., and Eichelman, W. (1976). Preliminary Models of Linkages Among Proxemic Variables. *Environment and Behavior*, 8, pp. 87–116.

Eveland, J. D., and Bikson, T. K. (1987). Evolving Electronic Communication Networks: An Empirical Assessment. *Office: Technology and People*, 3(2), pp. 103–128.

Fader, S. S. (1990). Meeting Savvy. *Graduating Engineer,* December, pp. 38–40.

Fakes, A. (1991). How the EC Works. *IEEE Software,* 8(3), p. 104.

Falk, L. (1987). To Make the Right Mistake. In Falk, L., and Fischer, B. (Eds.), *The Event Horizon.* Toronto: Coach House Press, pp. 43–54.

Fano, R. (1985). Computer-Mediated Communication. *IEEE Technology and Society Magazine,* 4(1), pp. 3–6.

Fanon, F. (1965). *Studies in a Dying Colonialism.* London: Earthscan.

Feder, B. J. (1991). At Monsanto, Teamwork Works. *New York Times,* June 25, C1, C12.

Feigenbaum, E., and McCorduck, P. (1983). *The Fifth Generation: Artificial Intelligence and Japan's Computer Challenge to the World.* Reading, MA: Addison-Wesley.

Feinberg, W. (1975). *Reason and Rhetoric.* New York: Wiley.

Fern, E. F. (1982). The Use of Focus Groups for Idea Generation: The Effects of Group Size, Acquaintanceship, and Moderator on Response Quantity and Quality. *Journal of Marketing Research,* 19, pp. 1–13.

Festinger, L., Pepitone, A., and Newcomb, T. (1952). Some Consequences of Deindividuation in a Group. *Journal of Abnormal and Social Psychology,* 47, pp. 382–389.

Festinger, L., Schachter, S., and Riecken, H. R. (1956). *When Prophecy Fails.* New York: Harper Torchbooks.

Feyerabend, P. (1987). Creativity – A Dangerous Myth. *Critical Inquiry,* 13, pp. 700–711.

Fickel, L. (1991). Don't Look Now, but . . . *Infoworld,* May 13, pp. 50–55.

Finholt, T., Sproull, L., and Kiesler, S. (1990). Communication and Performance in Ad Hoc Task Groups. In Galegher, J., Kraut, R. E., and Egido, C. (Eds.), *Intellectual Teamwork.* Hillsdale, NJ: Erlbaum, pp. 291–326.

Finnegan, R. (1989). Communication and Technology. *Language and Communication,* 9(2–3), pp. 107–127.

Fish, R., Kraut, R., Leland, M., and Cohen, M. (1988). Quilt: A Collaborative Tool for Cooperative Writing. *ACM Conference on Office Automation Systems.* New York: Association for Computing Machinery, pp. 30–37.

Fish, S. (1983). A Reply to Eugene Goodheart. In Graubard, S. (Ed.), *Reading in the 1980's.* New York: Bowker, pp. 233–238.

Fisher, S. S. (1990). Virtual Environments: Personal Simulations and Telepresence. *Multimedia Review,* Summer, pp. 24–30.

Fisher, W. R. (1985). The Narrative Paradigm: In the Beginning. *Journal of Communication,* 35(4), pp. 74–87.

Fisher, W. R. (1987). *Human Communication as Narration: Toward a Philosophy of Reason, Value, and Action.* Columbia: University of South Carolina Press.

Fisher, W. R. (1989). Clarifying the Narrative Paradigm. *Communication Monographs,* 56(1), pp. 55–58.

Flaherty, D. H. (1989). *Protecting Privacy in Surveillance Societies.* Chapel Hill: University of North Carolina Press.

Flanagan, B. (1990). The Office That (Almost) Does the Work for You. *Working Woman,* October, pp. 112–115.

Fleck, L. (1935). *The Genesis and Development of a Scientific Fact.* Basel: Benno Schwabe. (Translation, 1979. Chicago: University of Chicago Press.)

Flexner, A. (1930). *Universities.* London: Oxford University Press.

Flores, F., Graves, M., Hartfield, B., and Winograd, T. (1988). Computer Systems and the Design of Organizational Interaction. *ACM Transactions on Office Information Systems,* 6(2), pp. 153–172.

Florman, S. C. (1981). *Blaming Technology.* New York: St. Martin's.

Fogarty, K. (1994). New Groupware Entries to Fill Market Voids. *Network World,* October 17, p. 4.

Foucault, M. (1977). *Discipline and Punish*. London: Allen Lane.

Foucault, M. (1980). *Power/Knowledge: Selected Interviews and Other Writings, 1972–1977*. Brighton: Harvester.

Foucault, M. (1982). The Subject and Power. *Critical Inquiry*, 8, pp. 777–795.

Fowler, R. (1977). *Linguistics and the Novel*. London: Methuen.

Fox, W. H. (1990). Anonymity and Other Keys to Successful Problem-Solving Meetings. *National Productivity Review*, 8(2), pp. 145–156.

Freiberger, P., and Swaine, M. (1984). *Fire in the Valley: The Making of the Personal Computer*. Berkeley, CA: McGraw-Hill.

Fryrear, J. L., and Stephens, B. C. (1988). Group Psychotherapy Using Masks and Video to Facilitate Intrapersonal Communication. *Arts-in-Psychotherapy*, 15(3), pp. 227–234.

Galegher, J., and Kraut, R. E. (1990). Technology for Intellectual Teamwork. In Galegher, J., Kraut, R. E., and Egido, C. (Eds.), *Intellectual Teamwork*. Hillsdale, NJ: Erlbaum, pp. 1–20.

Galloway, L. (1914). *Organization and Management*. New York: Alexander Hamilton Institute.

Gardner, H. (1985). *The Mind's New Science*. New York: Random House.

Gardner, J. W. (1961). *Excellence*. New York: Harper Colophon.

Garson, B. (1988). *The Electronic Sweatshop: How Computers are Transforming the Office of the Future into the Factory of the Past*. New York: Simon & Schuster.

Gattiker, E., Gutek, B., and Berger, D. (1988). Office Technology and Employee Attitudes. *Social Science Microcomputer Review*, 6(3), pp. 327–340.

Gavison, R. (1980). Privacy and the Limits of Law. *Yale Law Journal*, 89, pp. 425–440.

Geertz, C. (1973). *The Interpretation of Cultures*. New York: Basic.

Geertz, C. (1979). From the Native's Point of View: On the Nature of Anthropological Understanding. In Rabinow, P., and Sullivan, W. M. (Eds.), *Interpretive Social Science*. Berkeley, CA: University of California Press, pp. 225–241.

Geertz, C. (1983). *Local Knowledge: Further Studies in Interpretive Anthropology*. New York: Basic.

Genette, G. (1980). *Narrative Discourse*. Ithaca, NY: Cornell University Press.

Gere, A. R., and Abbott, R. D. (1985). Talking About Writing: The Language of Writing Groups. *Research in the Teaching of English*, 19(4), pp. 362–381.

Gergen, K. J. (1982). *Toward Transformation in Social Knowledge*. New York: Springer-Verlag.

Gergen, K. J. (1985). The Social Constructionist Movement in Social Psychology. *American Psychologist*, 40(3), pp. 266–275.

Gergen, K. (1986). *If Persons Are Texts*. New Brunswick, NJ: Rutgers University Press.

Gergen, K. J. (1989). Warranting Voice and the Elaboration. In Shotter, J., and Gergen, K. (Eds.), *Texts of Identity*. London: Sage, pp. 70–81.

Gergen, K. J., and Gergen, M. M. (1984). *Historical Social Psychology*. Hillsdale, NJ: Erlbaum.

Gergen, K. J., and Gergen, M. M. (1986). Narrative Form and the Construction of Psychological Science. In Sarbin, T. R. (Ed.), *Narrative Psychology: The Storied Nature of Human Conduct*. New York: Praeger.

Gersick, C. J. G. (1988). Time and Transition in Work Teams: Toward a New Model of Group Development. *Academy of Management Journal*, 31(1), pp. 9–41.

Gersick, C. J. G. (1989). Marking Time: Predictable Transitions in Task Groups. *Academy of Management Journal*, 32(2), pp. 274–309.

Gerson, E. (1976). On "Quality of Life." *American Sociological Review*, 4, pp. 793–806.

Gerson, E., and Star, S. (1981). Analyzing Due Process in the Workplace. *SIGOIS Bulletin,* 7(2–3), pp. 70–78.

Gibbons, F. (1989). Groupware to Disappear. *Software Magazine,* May, p. 8.

Gibbs, J. P. (1990). Control as Sociology's Central Notion. *Social Science Journal,* 27(1), pp. 1–27.

Gibbs, S. J. (1989). LIZA: An Extensible Groupware Toolkit. *Proceedings of the ACM SIGCHI Conference on Human Factors in Computing Systems.* New York: ACM.

Gide, A. (1931). *The Counterfeiters* (Bussy, D. Trans.). New York: Modern Library.

Gilbert, G., and Heath, C. (1985). *Social Action and Artificial Intelligence.* London: Gower.

Gilbreth, L. M. (1914/1973). *The Psychology of Management.* Easton, PA: Hive. (Originally published in 1914.)

Gillin, P. (1990). Group(ware) Therapy: Tips for Success. *Computerworld,* 24(44), pp. 109–111.

Ginsberg, B. (1986). *The Captive Public: How Mass Opinion Promotes State Power.* New York: Basic.

Good, L. R., and Nelson, D. A. (1971). Effects of Person–Group and Intra-Group Attitude Similarity on Perceived Group Attractiveness and Cohesiveness. *Psychometric Science,* 25, pp. 215–217.

Goffman, E. (1959). *The Presentation of Self in Everyday Life.* Garden City, NJ: Doubleday.

Goffman, E. (1961). *Asylums.* Garden City, NJ: Doubleday.

Goffman, E. (1963). *Behavior in Public Places.* New York: Free Press.

Goffman, E. (1967). *Interaction Ritual.* Garden City, NJ: Doubleday.

Goffman, E. (1971). *Relations in Public: Microstudies of the Public Order.* New York: Basic.

Goffman, E. (1974). *Frame Analysis.* New York: Harper & Row.

Goodell, R. (1977). *The Visible Scientists.* Boston: Little, Brown.

Goodheart, E. (1983). The Text and the Interpretive Community. In Graubard, S. (Ed.), *Reading in the 1980's.* New York: Bowker, pp. 215–232.

Goodman, G., and Abel, M. (1987). Communication and Collaboration: Facilitating Cooperative Work Through Communication. *Office: Technology and People,* 3(2), pp. 129–146.

Gould, C. C. (1989). Access, Consent, and the Informed Community. In Gould, C. C. (Ed.), *The Information Web.* Boulder, CO: Westview, pp. 1–36.

Gould, S. J. (1981). *The Mismeasure of Man.* New York: Norton.

Graebner, W. (1987). *The Engineering of Consent.* Madison: University of Wisconsin Press.

Grailla, P. (1988). Lotus Notes. *PC Computing,* 1(3), pp. 83–84.

Gray, P. (1981). The SMU Decision Room Project. *Transactions of the First International Conference on Decision Support Systems,* (Vol. 1), Atlanta, June, pp. 122–129.

Gray, P. (1988). Group Decision Support Systems. *Decision Support Systems,* 3(3), pp. 233–242.

Green, M. K. (1986). A Kantian Evaluation of Taylorism in the Workplace. *Journal of Business Ethics,* 5, pp. 165–169.

Greenbaum, J. (1988). In Search of Cooperation: An Historical Analysis of Work Organization and Management Strategies. *Proceedings of the Second Conference on Computer-Supported Cooperative Work* (Vol. 2). Portland, September 26–28, pp. 102–114.

Greenfield, M. (1987). Privacy and the Undressed. *Newsweek,* October 19, p. 100.

Greenwood, E. (1957). Attributes of a Profession. *Social Work,* July, pp. 45–55.

Gregory, S. W. (1983). A Quantitative Analysis of Temporal Symmetry in Microsocial Relations. *American Sociological Review,* 48, pp. 129–135.

Greif, I. (1988a). From the Conference Chair. *Proceedings of the Second Conference on Computer-Supported Cooperative Work,* Portland, OR, pp. 3–4.

Greif, I. (1988b). *Computer-Supported Cooperative Work: A Book of Readings.* San Mateo, CA: Morgan Kauffman.

Greif, I., and Ellis, C. (1987). Editorial: Introduction to the Special Issue. *ACM Transactions on Office Automation Systems,* 5(2), pp. 113–114.

Greif, I., and Sarin, S. (1987). Data Sharing in Group Work. *ACM Transactions on Office Information Systems,* 5(2), pp. 187–211.

Grisso, T. (1981). *Juveniles' Waver of Rights: Legal and Psychological Competence.* New York: Plenum.

Griswold, A. W. (1959). *Liberal Education and the Democratic Ideal and Other Essays.* New Haven, CN: Yale University Press.

Gross, A. G. (1989). The Rhetorical Invention of Scientific Invention: The Emergence and Transformation of a Social Norm. In Simons, H. (Ed.), *Rhetoric in the Human Sciences.* Newbury Park, CA: Sage, pp. 89–108.

Grudin, J. (1988). Perils and Pitfalls. *Byte,* 13(13), pp. 261–264.

Grudin, J. (1989a). Why Groupware Applications Fail: Problems in Design and Evaluation. *Office: Technology and People,* 4(3), pp. 245–264.

Grudin, J. (1989b). CSCW'88: Report on the Conference and Review of the Proceedings. *SIGCHI Bulletin,* 20(4), pp. 80–84.

Grudin, J. (1990). Groupware and Cooperative Work: Problems and Prospects. In Laurel, B. (Ed.), *The Art of Human–Computer Interface Design.* Menlo Park, CA: Addison-Wesley, pp. 171–186.

Grudin, J. (1991). Interactive Systems: Bridging the Gaps Between Developers and Users. *Computer,* 24(4), pp. 59–69.

Grudin, J. (1994). Groupware and Social Dynamics: Eight Challenges for Developers. *Communications of the ACM,* 37(1), pp. 92–105.

Gruman, G. (1991). The Beginnings of Collaboration Technology. *IEEE Software,* 8(3), pp. 106–107, 118.

Gutek, B. A. (1990). Work Group Structure and Information Technology: A Structural Contingency Approach. In Galegher, J., Kraut, R. E., and Egido, C. (Eds.), *Intellectual Teamwork.* Hillsdale, NJ: Erlbaum, pp. 63–78.

Habermas, J. (1971). *Knowledge and Human Interests.* Boston: Beacon.

Habermas, J. (1973). Wahrheitstheorien. In Fahrenbach, H. (Ed.), *Wirklichkeit und Reflexion.* Neske: Pfulligen, pp. 211–265.

Hacking, I. (1984). Winner Take Less: The Evolution of Cooperation. *New York Review of Books,* June 28, pp. 17–21.

Haight, T. (1990). The Enemy Is Us. *Communications Week,* October 22, p. 46.

Halasz, F. (1988). Reflections on NoteCards. *Communications of the ACM,* 31(7), pp. 836–853.

Hall, R. (1975). *Occupations and the Social Structure.* Engelwood Cliffs, NJ: Prentice-Hall.

Hall, S. C. (1991). The Four Stages of NREN Growth. *EDUCOM Review,* 26(1), pp. 18–25.

Halonen, D., Horton, M., Kass, R., and Scott, P. (1990). Shared Hardware: A Novel Technology for Computer Support of Face-to-Face Meetings. *SIGOIS Bulletin,* 11(2–3), pp. 163–168.

Hamilton, R. (1992). Notes Productivity Claims Eyed. *Computerworld,* 26(24), p. 4.

Hamm, R. M. (1989). *The Need to Consider Modes of Cognition in Designing Systems That Require Distributed Decision Making.* IEEE International Conference on Systems, Man, and Cybernetics. New York: IEEE Press, pp. 482–483.

Hammer, M., and Champy, J. (1993). *Reengineering the Corporation.* New York: Harper Business.

Hammonds, K. H. (1990). Software: It's A New Game. *Business Week,* June 4, pp. 102–110.

Harasim, L. M., and Winkelmans, T. (1990). Computer-Mediated Scholarly Collaboration. *Knowledge: Creation, Diffusion, Utilization,* 11(4), pp. 382–409.

Hardin, G. (1982). *Naked Emperors: Essays of a Taboo Stalker.* Los Altos, CA: William Kaufmann.

Hardwig, J. (1985). Epistemic Dependence. *Journal of Philosophy,* 7, pp. 335–349.

Harre, R. (1981). Psychological Variety. In Heelas, P., and Lock, A. (Eds.), *Indigenous Psychologies: The Anthropology of the Self.* London: Academic Press, pp. 79–103.

Harre, R. (1983). *Personal Being.* Oxford: Basil Blackwell.

Harre, R. (1987). Enlarging the Paradigm. *New Ideas in Psychology,* 5(1), pp. 3–12.

Harre, R. (1989). Language Games and Texts of Identity. In Shotter, J., and Gergen, K. (Eds.), *Texts of Identity.* London: Sage, pp. 20–35.

Harris, R. (1989). How Does Writing Restructure Thought? *Language and Communication,* 9(2–3), pp. 99–106.

Harrison, B. (1984). *Framework: An Introduction.* Culver City, CA: Ashton-Tate.

Harrison, S., Minneman, S., Stults, B., and Weber, K. (1990). Video: A Design Medium. *SIGCHI Bulletin,* 21(3), pp. 86–90.

Hartman, J. J. (1981). Group Cohesion and the Regulation of Self-Esteem. In Kellerman, H. (Ed.), *Group Cohesion: Theoretical and Clinical Perspectives.* New York: Grune & Stratton, pp. 254–267.

Havelock, E. A. (1963). *Preface to Plato.* Cambridge, MA: Harvard University Press.

Hawthorn, J. (Ed.) (1985). *Narrative: From Malory to Motion Pictures.* London: Edward Arnold.

Haynes, W. L. (1989). Shifting Media, Shifting Paradigms, and the Growing Utility of Narrative as Metaphor. *Communication Studies,* 40(2), pp. 109–126.

Hayward, R. G., and Tate, G. (1986). *Personal Computing Contagion and Control – An Extension of Nolan's Stage Hypothesis.* Massey Computer Science Report, 86/8. Massey University, New Zealand.

Hearn, G. (1957). Leadership and the Spatial Factor in Small Groups. *Journal of Abnormal and Social Psychology,* 54, pp. 269–272.

Heeter, C. (1992). Being There: The Subjective Experience of Presence. *Presence,* 1(21), pp. 262–271.

Heidegger, M. (1962). *Being and Time.* New York: Harper & Row.

Heim, M. (1987). *Electric Language: A Philosophical Study of Word Processing.* New Haven, CN: Yale University Press.

Helmer, O. (1970). *Social Technology.* New York: Basic.

Hesse, B. W., Werner, C., and Altman, I. (1988). Temporal Aspects of Computer-Mediated Communication. *Computers in Human Behavior,* 4(2), pp. 147–165.

Hettinger, E. C. (1989). Justifying Intellectual Property. *Philosophy & Public Affairs,* 18(1), pp. 31–52.

HEW (U.S. Department of Health, Education and Welfare) (1973). *Records, Computers and the Rights of Citizens.* Cambridge, MA: MIT Press.

Hewitt, C. (1986). Offices Are Open Systems. *ACM Transactions on Office Information Systems,* 4(3), pp. 270–287.

Hewitt, C. (1989). Quotation in "Offices Need No AI." *Software Magazine,* October, p. 32.

Hewitt, J. P. (1989). *Dilemmas of the American Self.* Philadelphia: Temple University Press.

Heydebrand, W. V. (1989). New Organizational Forms. *Work and Occupations,* 16(3), pp. 323–357.

Hiemstra, G. (1982). Teleconferencing, Concern for Face, and Organizational Culture. In Burgoon, M. (Ed.), *Communication Yearbook 6.* Beverly Hills, CA: Sage, pp. 874–904.

Hill, W. C. (1989). The Mind at AI: Horseless Carriage to Clock. *AI Magazine,* 10(2), pp. 28–42.

Hilton, J. L., and Darley, J. M. (1985). Constructing Other Persons: A Limit on the Effect. *Journal of Experimental Social Psychology,* 21, pp. 1–18.

Hilts, P. J. (1982). *Scientific Temperaments.* New York: Simon & Schuster.

Hiltz, S. R. (1984). *On-Line Communities: A Case Study of the Office of the Future.* Norwood, NJ: Ablex.

Hiltz, S. R. (1986). The Virtual Classroom: Using Computer-Mediated Communication for University Teaching. *Journal of Communication,* 36(2), pp. 95–104.

Hiltz, S. R. (1988). Productivity Enhancement from Computer-Mediated Communication: A Systems Contingency Approach. *Communications of the ACM,* 31(12), pp. 1438–1454.

Hiltz, S. R. (1989). Experiments in Group Decision Making: Disinhibition, Deindividuation, and Group Process in Pen Name and Real Name Computer Conferences. *Decision Support Systems,* 5(2), pp. 217–232.

Hiltz, S. R. (1990). Collaborative Learning: The Virtual Classroom Approach. *THE Journal,* 17(10), pp. 59–65.

Hiltz, S. R., and Turoff, M. (1978). *The Network Nation: Human Communication via Computer.* Reading, MA: Addison-Wesley.

Hiltz, S. R., and Turoff, M. (1985). Structuring Computer-Mediated Communication Systems to Avoid Information Overload. *Communications of the ACM,* 28(7), pp. 680–689.

Hiltz, S. R., and Turoff, M. (1990). Teaching Computers and Society in a Virtual Classroom. *Proceedings of the Conference on Computers and the Quality of Life. SIGCAS Bulletin,* 20(3), pp. 69–72.

Hiltz, S. R., Turoff, M., and Johnson, K. (1989). Experiments in Group Decision Making: Part 3, Disinhibition, Deindividuation, and Group Process in Pen Name and Real Name Computer Conferences. *Decision Support Systems,* 5, pp. 217–232.

Hirscheim, R. A. (1985). *Office Automation: Social and Organizational Perspective.* New York: Wiley.

Hirschheim, R., and Newman, M. (1988). Information Systems and User Resistance: Theory and Practice. *Computer Journal,* 31(5), pp. 398–408.

Hirschhorn, L. (1989). Professionals, Authority, and Group Life: A Case Study of a Law Firm. *Human Resource Management,* 28(2), pp. 235–252.

Holland, K. (1995). What Every Virtual Mall Needs. *Business Week,* June 26, p. 101.

Holland, N. N. (1978). Human Identity. *Critical Inquiry,* 4(3), pp. 451–469.

Holpp, L. (1992). Making Choices: Self-Directed Teams or Total Quality Management? *Training,* 29(5), pp. 69–77.

Holt, A. W. (1988). Diplans: A New Language for the Study and Implementation of Coordination. *ACM Transactions on Office Automation Systems,* 6(2), pp. 109–125.

Holt, A. W. (1989a). Organizing Computer Use in the Context of Networks. *Proceedings of COMPCON (IEEE)* (Vol. 34). San Francisco, CA, February, pp. 201–207.

Holt, A. W. (1989b). True to Groupware. *Software Magazine,* August, p. 8.

Holt, A. W., Ramsey, H. R., and Grimes, J. D. (1983). Coordination Systems Technology as the Basis for a Programming Environment. *Electrical Communication,* 57, pp. 307–314.

Homans, G. (1961). *Social Behavior: Its Elementary Forms.* New York: Harcourt, Brace, & World.

Home, S. (1989). To Tell the Truth. *Lightworks,* 19, pp. 30–32.

Hooper, K. (1986). Architectural Design: An Analogy. In Norman, D. A., and Draper, S. W. (Eds.), *User-Centered System Design.* Hillsdale, NJ: Erlbaum, pp. 9–23.

Hooper, S. R., and Hannafin, M. J. (1989). The Effects of Aptitude Composition on Achievement During Small Group Learning. *Journal of Computer-Based Instruction,* 16(3), pp. 102–109.

Hopkins, E. E. (1977). Using Hand Calculators in Schools: Is Their Introduction Inevitable? *Education Digest,* 42(6), pp. 44–45.

Horowitz, I. L. (1986). *Communicating Ideas.* New York: Oxford University Press.

Horton, F. W. (1979). *Information Resources Management: Concept and Cases.* Cleveland, OH: Association for Systems Management.

Horton, M., Elwart-Keys, M., and Kass, R. (1989). Video as an Enabling Technology for Computer-Supported Cooperative Work. *SIGCHI Bulletin,* 21(2), pp. 96–99.

Horton, S. (1992). Team Effort: A Shift to Self-Directed Teams Helped This In-Plant to Boost Morale and Improve the Quality of Work. *American Printer,* 209(3), pp. 30–33.

House, J. S., Landis, K. R., and Umberson, D. (1988). Social Relationships and Health. *Science,* 241, pp. 540–545.

Howard, G. (1985). The Role of Values in the Science of Psychology. *American Psychologist,* 40(3), pp. 255–265.

Howard, R. (1985). *Brave New Workplace.* New York: Penguin.

Howard, R. (1987). Systems Design and Social Responsibility. *Office Technology and People,* 3(2), pp. 175–187.

Huber, G. (1984). Issues in the Design of Group Decision Support Systems. *MIS Quarterly,* 8(3), pp. 195–204.

Hughes, T. P. (1987). The Evolution of Large Technological Systems. In Bijker, W. E., Hughes, T. P., and Pinch, T. J. (Eds.), *The Social Construction of Technological Systems.* Cambridge, MA: MIT Press, pp. 51–82.

Hurwicz, M. (1990). Personality Plus the Network. *Computerworld,* June 11, pp. 53–57.

Hutchins, E. (1990). The Technology of Team Navigation. In Galegher, J., Kraut, R. E., and Egido, C. (Eds.), *Intellectual Teamwork.* Hillsdale, NJ: Erlbaum, pp. 191–220.

Hymowitz, C. (1988). A Survival Guide to the Office Meeting. *Wall Street Journal,* June 21, p. 35.

IEEE Spectrum (1983). Next Generation Impacts (Guterl, F., Ed.), 20(11), pp. 111–117.

Iizuka, A. (1982). The Spirit of Harmonious Cooperation. *Technology Review,* 85, pp. 53–54.

Illich, I. (1971). *Deschooling Society.* New York: Harper & Row.

Illich, I. (1973). *Tools for Conviviality.* New York: Harper & Row.

Information Week (1990a). Unearthing Solutions, February 26, p. 59.

Information Week (1990b). Notes on Networks, 273 (June 4), p. 80.

Infoworld (1991). Talking Head Aids Mac Users. July 1, p. 18.

Ishii, H. (1989). Trends of Groupware Technology. *Information Processing Society of Japan*, 30(12), pp. 1502–1508.

Ishii, H., and Miyake, N. (1991). Toward an Open Shared Workspace: Computer and Video Fusion Approach of TeamWorkstation. *Communications of the ACM*, 34, pp. 36–50.

Ives, H. E. (1930). Two-way Television. *Bell Labs Record*, 8.

Jackson, C. I., and Dalle Mura, S. L. (1988). Updating Science Ethics. *Issues in Science and Technology*, 4(3), pp. 28–30.

Jackson, L. (1987). Computers and the Social Psychology of Work. *Computers in Human Behavior*, 3(3–4), pp. 251–262.

Jackson, M. (1983). *Systems Development*. London: Prentice-Hall.

Jacobsen, L. (1989). The Group as an Object in the Cultural Field. *International Journal of Group Psychotherapy*, 39(4), pp. 475–497.

James, H. (1893). *The Wheel of Time: Collaboration* (Owen Wingrove, Ed.). New York: Harper & Bros.

James, J. (1951). A Preliminary Study of the Size Determinant in Small Group Interaction. *American Sociological Review*, 17(June), pp. 261–268.

James, W. (1892). *Psychology*. London: Macmillan.

James, W. (1907). *Varieties of Religious Experience*. New York: Longmans, Green.

James, W. (1967). *The Writings of William James: A Comprehensive Edition*. New York: Random House.

Janis, I. (1972). *Victims of Groupthink*. Boston: Houghton Mifflin.

Janis, I. (1982). *Groupthink: Psychological Studies of Policy Decisions and Fiascos* (Second Edition). Boston: Houghton Mifflin.

Janis, I., and Mann, L. (1977). *Decision Making: A Psychological Analysis of Conflict, Choice and Commitment*. New York: Free Press.

Janlert, L.-E. (1987). The Computer as a Person. *Journal for the Theory of Social Behaviour*, 17, pp. 321–341.

Jaschik, S. (1991). Education Department Rethinks Its Position on Privacy Protection Law. *Chronicle of Higher Education*, May 29, pp. A16–A17.

Jennings, D. M., Landweber, L. H., Fuchs, I. H., Farber, D. J., and Adrion, W. R. (1986). Computer Networking for Scientists. *Science*, 231, pp. 943–950.

Jennings, E. M. (1990). Paperless Writing Revisited. *Computers and the Humanities*, 24, pp. 43–48.

Jequier, N., and Blanc, G. (1979). *Appropriate Technology Directory*. Paris: OECD.

Jessup, L. M., Connolly, T., and Galegher, J. (1988). *The Effects of Anonymity on GDSS Group Process in an Idea Generating Task*. Unpublished manuscript, University of Arizona.

Johansen, R. (1988). *Groupware: Computer Support for Business Teams*. New York: Free Press.

Johnson, D. (1984). Mapping Ordinary Morals onto the Computer Society: A Philosophical Perspective. *Journal of Social Issues*, 40(3), pp. 63–76.

Johnson, D. (1985). *Computer Ethics*. Englewood Cliffs, NJ: Prentice-Hall.

Johnson, D. (1989). The Public–Private Status of Transactions in Computer Networks. In Gould, C. C. (Ed.), *The Information Web*. Boulder, CO: Westview, pp. 37–56.

Johnson, D., and Snapper, J. W. (1985). *Ethical Issues in the Use of Computers*. Belmont, CA: Wadsworth.

Johnson, H. (1960). *Sociology: A Systematic Introduction*. New York: Harcourt, Brace.

Johnston, S. (1990). Multimedia: Myth vs. Reality. *Infoworld,* 12(8), pp. 47–52.

Jorges, B. (1990). Images of Technology in Society: Computer as Butterfly and Bat. *Technology and Culture,* 31, pp. 203–227.

Jungerman, H. (1980). Speculations About Decision-Theoretic Aids for Personal Decision-Making. *Acta Psychologica,* 45, pp. 7–34.

Kain, C. J., Downs, J. C., and Black, D. D. (1988). Social Skills in the School Curriculum: A Systematic Approach. *NASSP Bulletin,* January, pp. 107–110.

Kafka, F. (1969). *The Castle.* New York: Modern Library.

Kanter, R. M. (1977). *Men and Women of the Corporation.* New York: Basic.

Kanter, R. M. (1983). *The ChangeMasters.* New York: Simon & Schuster.

Kaplan, F. S. (1981). Privies, Privacy, and Political Process: Some Thoughts on Bathroom Graffiti and Group Identity. In Kellerman, H. (Ed.), *Group Cohesion.* New York: Grune & Stratton, pp. 392–411.

Karlgaard, R. (1993). ASAP Interview: Tom Peters. *Forbes ASAP,* March 29, pp. 69–76.

Karraker, R. (1991). Highways of the Mind. *Whole Earth Review,* 70, pp. 4–11.

Katz, E., and Lazarsfeld, P. F. (1955). *Personal Influence: The Part Played by People in the Flow of Mass Communication.* Glencoe, IL: Free Press.

Katz, J. (1991). Science Funding: Letter to the Editor. *Science,* 252(5005), p. 490.

Katz, J. E., and Graveman, R. F. (1991). Privacy Issues of a National Research and Education Network. *Telematics and Informatics,* 8(1–2), pp. 71–120.

Kaufman, F. (1963). *The Forest Ranger.* New York: Free Press.

Kay, A. (1984). Computer Software. *Scientific American,* September, pp. 52–59.

Kay, A. (1990). User Interface: A Personal View. In Laurel, B. (Ed.), *The Art of Computer Interface Design.* Menlo Park, CA: Addison-Wesley, pp. 191–208.

Kay, S. (1990). Player-Managed Teams Score Very Well. *Computerworld,* November 26, p. 65.

Kaysen, C. (1967). Data Banks and Dossiers. *Public Interest,* 7, pp. 52–60.

Keen, P. G. W., and Scott Morton, M. (1978). *Decision Support Systems.* Reading, MA: Addison-Wesley.

Keizer, G. (1991). As Good as There. *Omni,* 13(7), pp. 39, 84–85.

Keller, J. J. (1990a). AT&T Jumps into Highly Competitive Network Applications Software Market. *Wall Street Journal,* March 28, p. B4.

Keller, J. J. (1990b). Motorola to Unveil Technology Today for Wireless Office Computer Systems. *Wall Street Journal,* October 23, p. B6.

Kellerman, H. (Ed.) (1981). *Group Cohesion.* New York: Grune & Stratton.

Kelly, K. (1985). Digital Retouching: The End of Photography as Evidence of Anything. *Whole Earth Review,* 47(July), pp. 42–50.

Kemeny, J. (1990). Computers in Education: Progress at a Snail's Pace. *EDUCOM Review,* 25(3), pp. 44–47.

Kennedy, N. (1989). *The Industrialization of Intelligence.* London: Unwin Hyman.

Kerr, C. (1964). *The Uses of the University.* Cambridge, MA: Harvard University Press.

Kerr, M. E. (1988). Chronic Anxiety and Defining a Self. *Atlantic Monthly,* 262(3), pp. 35–58.

Kibel, A. C. (1983). The Canonical Text. In Graubard, S. (Ed.), *Reading in the 1980's.* New York: Bowker, pp. 239–254.

Kidder, T. (1981). *The Soul of a New Machine.* Boston: Little, Brown.

Kiesler, S. (1986). The Hidden Messages in Computer Networks. *Harvard Business Review,* 64(1), pp. 46–60.

Kiesler, S., Siegel, J., and McGuire, T. (1984). Social Psychological Aspects of Computer-Mediated Communication. *American Psychologist,* 39(10), pp. 1123–1134.

Kiesler, S., and Sproull, L. (Eds.). (1987). *Computing and Change on Campus.* Cambridge University Press.

Kiesler, S., Zubrow, D., Moses, A., and Geller, V. (1985). Affect in Computer-Mediated Communication. *Human–Computer Interaction,* 1, 77–104.

Kira, A. (1970). The Bathroom. In Proshansky, H. M., Ittleson, W. H., and Rivlin, L. G. (Eds.), *Environmental Psychology.* New York: Holt, Rinehart, & Winston, pp. 269–275.

Kirkpatrick, D. (1992). Here Comes the Payoff from PCs. *Fortune,* 125(6), pp. 93–100.

Kirschner, B. J., Dies, R. R., and Brown, R. A. (1978). Effects of Experimental Manipulation of Self-Disclosure on Group Cohesiveness. *Journal of Consulting and Clinical Psychology,* 46, pp. 1171–1177.

Kitzinger, C. (1989). The Regulation of Lesbian Identities. In Shotter, J., and Gergen, K. (Eds.), *Texts of Identity.* Newbury Park, CA: Sage, pp. 82–98.

Klein, C. B. (1985). Group Work: 1985 and 2001. *Journal of Specialists in Group Work,* 10, pp. 88–91.

Klein, M. (1990). *Conflict Resolution in Cooperative Design.* Department of Computer Science, University of Illinois at Urbana-Champaign, Report No. UIUCDCS-R-89-1557.

Kling, R. (1980). Social Analyses of Computing: Theoretical Perspectives in Recent Empirical Research. *ACM Computing Surveys,* 12(1), pp. 61–110.

Kling, R. (1990). Reading "All About" Computerization: Five Common Genres of Social Analysis. In Schuler, D. (Ed.), *Proceedings of the 1990 Conference on Directions and Implications of Advanced Computing.* Palo Alto, CA: Computer Professionals for Social Responsibility.

Koestenbaum, W. (1989). *Double Talk.* New York: Routledge.

Kohn, A. (1986). *No Contest.* Boston: Houghton Mifflin.

Konsynski, B. R. (1986). *The University of Arizona's Planning Laboratory.* Department of Management Information Systems Document, College of Business and Public Administration, University of Arizona, Tucson.

Koohang, A. A., and Honeycutt, T. L. (1990). A Study of End-User Computing Within Organizations. *Proceedings of the 1990 Annual National Conference for the Association of Computer Educators.* Minneapolis, October 4–6, pp. 60–63.

Kovel, R., and Kovel, T. (1993). Before Computers, Lap Desks Ruled. *Oshkosh Northwestern,* August 15, p. E3.

Kraemer, K. L. (1982). Telecommunications/Transportation Substitution and Energy Conservation (Part 1). *Telecommunications Policy,* March, pp. 39–59.

Kraemer, K. L., and King, J. L. (1988). Computer-Based Systems for Cooperative Work and Group Decision Making. *ACM Computer Surveys,* 20(2), pp. 115–146.

Kraemer, K. L., King, J. L., Dunkle, D. E., and Lane, J. P. (1989). *Change and Control in Organizational Computing.* San Francisco: Jossey-Bass.

Kraft, P. (1977). *Programmers and Managers: The Routinization of Computer Programming in the United States.* New York: Springer-Verlag.

Kraut, R. E., and Dumais, S. (1990). Computerization and the Quality of Working Life: The Role of Control. *SIGOIS Bulletin,* 11(2–3), pp. 56–68.

Kraut, R. E., Egido, C., and Galegher, J. (1990). Patterns of Contact and Communication in Scientific Research Collaboration. In Galegher, J., Kraut, R. E., and Egido, C. (Eds.), *Intellectual Teamwork.* Hillsdale, NJ: Erlbaum, pp. 149–171.

Kraut, R. E., Galegher, J., and Egido, C. (1988). Relationships and Tasks in Scientific Collaboration. *Human–Computer Interaction,* 3, pp. 31–58.

Krech, D. (1962). *Individual in Society*. New York: McGraw-Hill.

Kreifelts, T. (1993). CSCW Shell in Preparation: Natural Cooperation Serves as Model. *ERCIM News*, 15(December), p. 21.

Krueger, M. (1983). *Artificial Reality*. Reading, MA: Addison-Wesley.

Krueger, M. (1991). *Artificial Reality II*. Reading, MA: Addison-Wesley.

Kuhn, T. (1970). *The Structure of Scientific Revolutions* (Second Edition). Chicago: University of Chicago Press.

Kull, D. (1982). Group Decisions: Can a Computer Help? *Computer Decisions*, 14(5), pp. 64–70.

Kurtzman, H. S. (1987). Deconstruction and Psychology. *New Ideas in Psychology*, 5(1), pp. 3–12.

LaFrance, M. (1990). Stories Knowledge Engineers Tell About Expert Systems. *Social Science Computer Review*, 8(1), pp. 13–23.

Lakin, F. (1990). Visual Languages for Cooperation: A Performing Medium Approach to Systems for Cooperative Work. In Galegher, J., Kraut, R. E., and Egido, C. (Eds.), *Intellectual Teamwork*. Hillsdale, NJ: Erlbaum, pp. 453–488.

Lakin, M. (1972). *Interpersonal Encounter: Theory and Practice in Sensitivity Training*. New York: McGraw-Hill.

Landow, G. P. (1987). Relationally Encoded Links and the Rhetoric of Hypertext. In Smith, J. (Ed.), *Hypertext 87*. Chapel Hill: University of North Carolina Dept. of Computer Science, pp. 331–344.

Landow, G. P. (1990). Hypertext and Collaborative Work. In Galegher, J., Kraut, R. E., and Egido, C. (Eds.), *Intellectual Teamwork*. Hillsdale, NJ: Erlbaum, pp. 407–428.

Lapidus, I. R. (1989). Ethics and the Practice of Science in a Computer Networked Environment. In Gould, C. C., *The Information Web*. Boulder, CO: Westview, pp. 119–146.

LaPlante, A. (1990). PC Generalist: A Thing of the Past. *Computerworld*, November 26, pp. 53–57.

Lapp, R. E. (1973). *The New Priesthood: The Scientific Elite and the Uses of Power*. New York: Harper & Row.

Larijani, L. (1993). *The Virtual Reality Primer*. New York: McGraw-Hill.

Lasch, C. (1978). *The Culture of Narcissism*. New York: Basic.

Latane, B., and Darley, J. M. (1970). *The Unresponsive Bystander: Why Doesn't He Help?* New York: Appleton-Century-Crofts.

Latane, B., Williams, K., and Harkins, S. (1979). Many Hands Make Light the Work: The Causes and Consequences of Social Loafing. *Journal of Personality and Social Psychology*, 37, pp. 822–832.

Latour, B., and Woolgar, S. (1979). *Laboratory Life: The Construction of Scientific Facts*. London: Sage.

Laurel, B. (1986). Interface as Mimesis. In Norman, D. A., and Draper, S. (Eds.), *User-Centered System Design*. Hillsdale, NJ: Erlbaum, pp. 67–85.

Laurel, B. (1990). POSTSCRIPT: On Visions, Monsters, and Artificial Life. In Laurel, B. (Ed.), *The Art of Human–Computer Interface Design*. Menlo Park, CA: Addison-Wesley, pp. 481–483.

Laurie, E. J. (1979). *Computers, Automation, and Society*. Homewood, IL: Irwin.

Lauriston, R. (1990). Work-Group Software Worth Waiting For. *PC World*, 8(6), pp. 122–137.

Lawler, E. E., and Mohrman, S. A. (1985). Quality Circles: After the Fad. *Harvard Business Review*, 85, pp. 65–71.

Leana, C. R. (1985). A Partial Test of Janis' Groupthink Model: Effects of Group Cohesiveness and Leader Behavior on Defective Decision Making. *Journal of Management*, 11(1), pp. 5–17.

Leary, T. (1990). The Interpersonal, Interactive, Interdimensional Interface. In Laurel, B. (Ed.), *The Art of Human–Computer Interface Design*. Menlo Park, CA: Addison-Wesley, pp. 229–234.

LeBon, G. (1895/1960). *The Crowd*. New York: Viking.

Lederberg, J., and Uncapher, K. (1989). *Towards a National Collaboratory*. Report of an Invitational Workshop at the Rockefeller University, March 17–18, 1989.

Ledgard, H. (1986). Programming Teams. *Abacus*, 3(3), pp. 8–15, 86.

Lee, J. A. (1982). The Social Science Bias in Management Research. *Business Horizons*, 25, pp. 1–31.

Lee, Y. (1989). Diverse Groupware Packages Struggle to Find an Identity. *Infoworld*, May 22, p. 24.

Leffingwell, W. H. (1925). *Office Management: Principles and Practice*. New York: Shaw.

Leibs, S. (1990). Electronic Publishing Software Marches Toward Groupware: Crowd Control. *Information Week*, August 6, pp. 27–30.

Leland, M., Fish, R., and Kraut, R. (1988). Collaborative Document Production Using Quilt. *Proceedings of the Second Conference on Computer-Supported Cooperative Work* (Vol. 2), September 26–28, pp. 206–215.

Lentini, L. (1991). Private Worlds and the Technology of the Imaginary. *Leonardo*, September, pp. 333–339.

Lerner, D. (1952). The Radir Project: A Reappraisal. *Meetings of the Political Science Association*, p. 14, cited in Bennis, W. (1956).

Lester, D. (1977). The Use of the Telephone in Counseling and Crisis Intervention. In Pool, I. de S. (Ed.), *The Social Impact of the Telephone*. Cambridge, MA: MIT Press, pp. 454–472.

Levinson, P. (1989). Intelligent Writing: The Electronic Liberation of Text. *Technology in Society*, 11, pp. 387–400.

Lewin, K. (1935). *A Dynamic Theory of Personality*. New York: McGraw-Hill.

Lewis, L. (1982). Facilitator: A Microcomputer Decision Support System for Small Groups. Unpublished Ph.D. dissertation, University of Louisville.

Licklider, J. C. R. (1970). Social Prospects of Information Utilities. In Sackman, H., and Nie, N. (Eds.), *The Information Utility and Social Choice*. Montvale, NJ: AFIPS Press, pp. 3–24.

Licklider, J. C. R., Taylor, R., and Herbert, E. (1968). The Computer as a Communication Device. *International Science and Technology*, April, pp. 21–32.

Lieberman, M. A. (1990). Understanding How Groups Work. *International Journal of Group Psychotherapy*, 40(1), pp. 31–52.

Lieberman, M. A., Yalom, I. D., and Miles, M. S. (1973). *Encounter Groups: First Facts*. New York: Basic.

Lieberstein, S. H. (1979). *Who Owns What Is in Your Head? Trade Secrets and the Mobile Employee*. New York: Hawthorn.

Lim, L. H., Raman, K. S., Wei, K. K. (1990). Does GDSS Promote More Democratic Decision-Making? The Singapore Experiment. *Proceedings of the Twenty-Third Annual Hawaii International Conference on System Sciences*, Vol. 3, pp. 59–60.

Littlewood, J. E. (1953). *A Mathematician's Miscellany*. London: Methuen.

Loehr, L. (1991). Between Silence and Voice: Communicating in Cross-Functional Project Teams. *IEEE Transactions on Professional Communication*, 34(1), pp. 51–56.

Long, J. W. (1984). The Wilderness Lab. *Training and Development Journal,* 38(5), pp. 58–69.

Longley, J., and Pruitt, D. G. (1980). Groupthink: A Critique of Janis' Theory. In Wheeler, L. (Ed.), *Review of Personality and Social Psychology* (Vol. 1). Beverly Hills, CA: Sage, pp. 74–93.

Lotus Quarterly (1990). Lotus Notes: The Information Pipeline, 3(1), pp. 9–16.

Lunsford, A., and Ede, L. (1986). Why Write . . . Together: A Research Update. *Rhetoric Review,* 5(1), pp. 71–81.

Luscher, K. (1990). The Social Reality of Perspectives: On G. H. Mead's Potential Relevance for the Analysis of Contemporary Societies. *Symbolic Interaction,* 13(1), pp. 1–18.

Lyytinen, K., and Auramaki, E. (1987). Collaborative Work: Survey and Bibliography. *SIGOIS Bulletin,* 8(4), pp. 24–28.

Machanick, P. (1988). *Design of Medical Education Software as Appropriate Technology Using Artificial Intelligence and Software Engineering.* Computer Science Department Technical Report, 1988-03, University of the Witswatersrand, Johannesburg.

Machlup, F. (1962). *The Production and Distribution of Knowledge in the United States.* Princeton, NJ: Princeton University Press.

MacIntyre, A. C. (1981). *After Virtue: A Study in Moral Theory.* Notre Dame: University of Notre Dame Press.

MacIver, R. (1947/1970). *On Community, Society, and Power.* (Bramson, L., Ed.) Chicago: University of Chicago Press.

Mackay, W. E. (1988). More Than Just a Communication System: Diversity in the Use of Electronic Mail. *Proceedings of the Second Conference on Computer-Supported Cooperative Work* (Vol. 2). Portland, OR, September 26–28, pp. 344–353.

Madsen, K. H. (1988). *Breakthrough by Breakdown: Metaphors and Structured Domains.* Aahrus University, Computer Science Department, Working Paper DAIMI PB-243.

Magner, D. K. (1991). Probing the Imbalance Between Individual Rights, Community Needs. *Chronicle of Higher Education,* February 15, p. A–3.

Mahmood, M. (1989). Review: A Research Center for Augmenting Human Intellect. *Computing Reviews,* 30(7), pp. 377–378.

Malone, T. W. (1988). *What Is Coordination Theory?* Paper presented at National Science Foundation Coordination Workshop, MIT, February 19.

Malone, T., and Crowston, K. (1990). What is Coordination Theory and How Can It Help Design Cooperative Work Systems? *Proceedings of the Third Conference on Computer-Supported Cooperative Work.* Los Angeles, CA, October 8–10. New York: ACM, pp. 357–370.

Malone, T., Yates, J., and Benjamin, R. (1987). Electronic Markets and Electronic Hierarchies. *Communications of the ACM,* 30(6), pp. 484–497.

Manasse, M. S. (1990). Complete Factorization of the Ninth Fermat Number. Electronic message (June 15), cited in Sproull and Kiesler (1991).

Maranhao, T. (1986). *Therapeutic Discourse and Socratic Dialogue: A Cultural Critique.* Madison: University of Wisconsin Press.

March, J. G., and Olsen, J. P. (1976). *The Technology of Foolishness: Ambiguity and Choice in Organizations.* Bergen: Universitetsforlaget, pp. 69–81.

March, J. G., and Simon, H. (1978). *Organizations.* New York: Wiley.

Margulis, S. T. (1977). Conceptions of Privacy: Current Status and Next Steps. *Journal of Social Issues,* 33, pp. 5–21.

Markoff, J. (1989). Spreadsheet Rivalry Heats Up. *New York Times,* January 17, p. 25.

Markoff, J. (1990). Creating a Giant Computer Highway. *New York Times,* September 2, p. 3–1, 3–6.

Marks, S. R. (1977). Multiple Roles and Role Strain: Some Notes on Human Energy, Time, and Commitment. *American Sociological Review,* 42, pp. 921–936.

Markus, M. L. (1989). Electronic Mail as the Medium of Managerial Choice. Anderson Graduate School of Management (UCLA) Working Paper #4-89.

Marrow, A. J. (1969). *The Practical Theorist: The Life and Work of Kurt Lewin.* New York: Basic.

Marshak, D. S. (1990). Filters: Separating the Wheat from the Chaff. *Patricia Seybold's Office Computing Report,* 13(11), pp. 1–16.

Martin, J. (1977). *Telematic Society.* Englewood Cliffs, NJ: Prentice-Hall.

Martin, J., Feldman, M. S., Hatch, M. J., and Sitkin, S. B. (1980). The Uniqueness Paradox in Organizational Stories. *Administrative Science Quarterly,* 28, pp. 438–453.

Marx, G. (1985). I'll Be Watching You: The New Surveillance. *Dissent,* Winter, pp. 26–34.

Marx, G., and Reichman, N. (1984). Routinizing the Discovery of Secrets: Computers as Informants. *American Behavioral Scientist,* 27(4), pp. 423–452.

Masuda, Y. (1980). *Managing in the Information Society.* Oxford: Basil Blackwell.

Matheson, K., and Zanna, M. (1988). The Impact of Computer-Mediated Behavior on Self-Awareness. *Computers in Human Behavior,* 4(3), pp. 221–234.

Matheson, K., and Zanna, M. (1990). Computer-Mediated Communications: The Focus Is on Me. *Social Science Computer Review,* 8(1), pp. 1–12.

May, R. (1975). *The Courage to Create.* New York: Norton.

Mayo, E. (1937). What Every Village Knows. *Survey Graphic,* 26, pp. 695–698.

Mayo, E. (1945). *Social Problems of an Industrial Civilization.* Cambridge, MA: Harvard University Press.

McCarthy, J. (1984). Some Expert Systems Need Common Sense. In Pagels, H. R. (Ed.), *Computer Culture.* New York: New York Academy of Sciences, pp. 129–137.

McCarthy, R. (1989). The Advantages of Using a Network. *Electronic Learning,* September, pp. 32–35.

McCauley, C. (1989). The Nature of Social Influence in Groupthink: Compliance and Internalization. *Journal of Personality and Social Psychology,* 57(2), pp. 250–260.

McClelland, K. (1985). *On the Social Significance of Interactional Synchrony.* Unpublished paper, Department of Sociology, Grinnell College.

McCorduck, P. (1985). *The Universal Machine: Confessions of a Technological Optimist.* New York: McGraw-Hill.

McCroskey, J. C. (1977). Oral Communication Apprehension: A Summary of Recent Theory and Research. *Human Communication Research,* 4, pp. 78–96.

McDowell, J. M., and Melvin, M. (1983). The Determinants of Co-Authorship. *Review of Economics and Statistics,* 65, pp. 155–160.

McGee, M. K. (1990). Education Networks Sprout. *Computer Systems News,* 473, p. 27.

McGoff, C., Hunt, A., Vogel, D., and Nunamaker, J. (1990). IBM's Experiences with GroupSystems. *Interfaces,* 20(6), pp. 39–52.

McGrath, J. E. (1990). Time Matters in Groups. In Galegher, J., Kraut, R., and Egido, C. (Eds.), *Intellectual Teamwork.* Hillsdale, NJ: Erlbaum, pp. 23–61.

McIsaac, D., and Wanless, D. (1985). Simulated Experiments in School Administration. *Educational Administration Quarterly,* 21(3), pp. 223–233.

McKnight, R. (1984). Spirituality in the Workplace. In Adams, John D. (Ed.), *Transforming Work.* Alexandria, VA: Miles River Press, pp. 138–153.

McLuhan, M. (1964). *Understanding Media*. New York: McGraw-Hill.

McLuhan, M., and Nevitt, B. (1972). *Take Today: The Executive as Dropout*. New York: Harcourt, Brace, Jovanovich.

McMahon, C. (1989). Promising and Coordination. *American Philosophical Quarterly*, 26(3), pp. 239–247.

McMullen, J. (1990). Microsoft in the Age of Networks. *Datamation*, May 1, pp. 36–39.

McMurdo, G. (1989). *Electronic Mail, Information Management and Organizational Culture*. IEE Colloquium Human Factors in Electronic Mail and Conferencing Systems. London: IEE, pp. 1–6.

McPartlin, J. P. (1990a). The Terrors of Technostress. *Information Week*, July 30, pp. 30–33.

McPartlin, J. P. (1990b). Taking Notes on Networks. *Information Week*, 273, p. 80.

Mead, G. H. (1934). *Mind, Self, and Society*. Chicago: University of Chicago Press.

Mead, G. H. (1964). The Objective Reality of Perspectives. In Reck, A. J. (Ed.), *Selected Writings*. Indianapolis, IN: Bobbs-Merrill, pp. 306–319.

Mehrabian, A. (1976). *Public Places and Private Spaces*. New York: Basic.

Merton, R. K. (1957). *Social Theory and Social Structure*. Glencoe, IL: Free Press.

Merton, R. K. (1968). The Matthew Effect in Science. *Science*, 159, pp. 56–63.

Merton, R. K. (1973). *The Sociology of Science*. Chicago: University of Chicago Press.

Merton, T. (1960). *Disputed Questions*. New York: Farrar, Straus, & Giroux.

Metz, C. (1974). *Language and Cinema*. The Hague: Mouton.

Meyer, J. W., and Rowan, B. (1977). Institutionalized Organizations: Formal Structure as Myth and Ceremony. *American Journal of Sociology*, 83(2), pp. 340–363.

Meyers, J. A. (1983). A Letter from the Publisher. *Time*, 121(1), p. 3.

Meyrowitz, J. (1985). *No Sense of Place*. New York: Oxford University Press.

Miao, X., Luh, P. B., Kleinman, D. L., and Burton, G. (1989). A Normative-Descriptive Study of Distributed Team Resource Allocation. *IEEE International Conference on Systems, Man, and Cybernetics*. New York: IEEE Press, pp. 474–479.

Michael, D. (1967). Social Engineering and the Future Environment. *American Psychologist*, 40, pp. 888–892.

Michael, D. (1968). *The Unprepared Society: Planning for a Precarious Future*. New York: Harper & Row.

Mill, J. S. (1864). *On Liberty*. 3rd edition. London: Longman, Green, Longman, Roberts, & Green.

Miller, B. D. (1979). "Culture" or "Culturing"? *Journal of Cultural and Educational Futures* (University of Minnesota), 1(1), pp. 7–12.

Miller, H. L. (1980). Hard Realities and Soft Social Science. *Public Interest*, 59, pp. 67–82.

Miller, M. W. (1991). Lawmakers Begin to Heed Calls to Protect Privacy and Civil Liberties as Computer Usage Explodes. *Wall Street Journal*, April 11, p. A-16.

Miller, R. J. (1983). The Human: Alien in the Robotic Environment. *Annals of the American Academy of Political and Social Science*, 470, pp. 11–15.

Minch, R. P. (1989). Research Issues Involving Hypertext in Decision Support Systems. *Proceedings of the Twenty-Second Hawaii International Conference on Systems Sciences*, Vol. 2, pp. 630–637.

Minsky, M. (1984). The Problems and the Promise. In Winston, P. H., and Prendergast, K. A., *The AI Business: The Commercial Uses of Artificial Intelligence*. Cambridge, MA: MIT Press, pp. 243–254.

Minsky, M. (1987). *The Society of Mind*. New York: Simon & Schuster.

Mintzberg, H. (1973). *The Nature of Managerial Work*. New York: Harper & Row.

Mitcham, C. (1986). Introduction: Information Technology and Computers as Themes in the Philosophy of Technology. In Mitcham, C., and Huning, A. (Eds.), *Philosophy and Technology: Vol. 2. Information Technology and Computers in Theory and Practice*. Boston: Reidel, pp. 1–14.

Mitcham, C., and Huning, A. (Eds.) (1986). *Philosophy and Technology: Vol. 2. Information Technology and Computers in Theory and Practice*. Boston: Reidel.

Mitroff, I., and Pauchant, T. (1990). *We're So Big and Powerful Nothing Bad Can Happen to Us*. New York: Carol.

Miyata, Y., and Norman, D. A. (1986). Psychological Issues in Support of Multiple Activities. In Norman, D. A., and Draper, S. W. (Eds.), *User-Centered System Design*. Hillsdale, NY: Erlbaum, pp. 265–284.

Moor, J. H. (1985). Are There Decisions Computers Should Never Make? *Ethical Issues in the Use of Computers*. Belmont, CA: Wadsworth, pp. 120–130.

Moore, B., Jr. (1984). *Privacy: Studies in Social and Cultural History*. Armonk, NY: Sharpe.

Moore, G. (1990). The 1st Amendment Is Safe at Prodigy. *New York Times*, December 16.

Moore, W. (1951). *Industrial Relations and the Social Order*. New York: Macmillan.

Moorhead, G. (1982). Groupthink: Hypothesis in Need of Testing. *Group and Organization Studies*, 7(4), pp. 429–444.

Moravec, H. P. (1988). *Mind Children*. Cambridge, MA: Harvard University Press.

Morgan, D. L., and Schwalbe, M. L. (1990). Mind and Self in Society: Linking Social Structure and Social Cognition. *Social Psychology Quarterly*, 53(2), pp. 148–164.

Morgan, D. L., and Spanish, M. T. (1984). Focus Groups: A New Tool for Qualitative Research. *Qualitative Sociology*, 7(3), pp. 253–270.

Morrell, K. (1988). Teaching with Hypercard. Perseus Project Department of Classics, Working Paper No. 3. Cambridge, MA: Harvard University Press.

Morris, J. H. (1989). Our Global City. *Communications of the ACM*, 32(6), pp. 661–662.

Mosco, V. (1982). *Pushbutton Fantasies: Critical Perspectives on Videotex and Information Technology*. Norwood, NJ: Ablex.

Moscovici, S., and Mugny, G. (1983). Minority Influence. In Paulus, P. (Ed.), *Basic Group Processes*. New York: Springer-Verlag, pp. 41–64.

Mosvick, R. K., and Nelson, R. B. (1987). *We've Got to Start Meeting Like This*. New York: Scott, Foresman.

Mowshowitz, A. (1976). *The Conquest of Will: Information Processing in Human Affairs*. Reading, MA: Addison-Wesley.

Muir, B. M. (1987). Trust Between Humans and Machines, and the Design of Decision Aids. *International Journal of Man–Machine Studies*, 27, pp. 527–539.

Mullen, B., and Hu, L. (1986). *Group Composition, the Self, and Religious Experience*. Paper Presented at the British Psychological Society's International Conference on Eastern Approaches to Self and Mind. Cardiff, Wales, July.

Muller, M. J., Smith, J. G., Shoher, J. Z., and Goldberg, H. (1991). Privacy, Anonymity, and Interpersonal Competition Issues Identified During Participatory Design of Project Management Groupware. *SIGCHI Bulletin*, 23(1), pp. 82–87.

Mundy, A. (1989). Unwilling Players in the Name Game. *U.S. News and World Report*, 106(17), pp. 52–54.

Myers, D. (1987). "Anonymity Is Part of the Magic": Individual Manipulation of Computer-Mediated Communication Contexts. *Qualitative Sociology*, 10(3), pp. 251–266.

Myers, D. G. (1987). *Social Psychology* (Second Edition). New York: McGraw-Hill.

Myers, G. (1986). Reality, Consensus, and Reform in the Rhetoric of Composition Teaching. *College English,* 48(2), pp. 154–173.

Myers, G. (1990). *Writing Biology.* Madison: University of Wisconsin Press.

Myers, W. (1991). Five Plenary Addresses Highlight Compcon Spring 91. *Computer,* 24(5), pp. 102–106.

Nagasundsram, M. (1990a). Middle-Range Technology: Designing for Social Acceptability. *SIGOIS Bulletin,* 11(1), pp. 22–27.

Nagasundsram, M. (1990b). Style and Substance in Communications: Implications for Message Structuring Systems. *SIGOIS Bulletin,* 11(4), pp. 33–41.

Nasby, W. (1989). Private and Public Self-Consciousness and the Articulation of the Self-Schema. *Journal of Personality and Social Psychology,* 56(1), pp. 117–123.

Nash, J. (1990). E-Mail Lawsuit Cranks Open Privacy Rights Can of Worms. *Computerworld,* August 13, p. 7.

Negroponte, N. (1990). The Noticeable Difference (pp. 245–246) and Hospital Corners (pp. 347–354). Both in Laurel, B. (Ed.), *The Art of Human–Computer Interface Design.* Menlo Park, CA: Addison-Wesley.

Negroponte, N. (1995). *Being Digital.* New York: Knopf.

Nelson, T. H. (1987). All for One and One for All. In Smith, J. (Ed.), *Hypertext 87.* Chapel Hill: University of North Carolina Dept. of Computer Science, pp. v–viii.

Nelson, T. H. (1981). *Literary Machines.* Swarthmore, PA: Nelson.

Nelson, T. H. (1990). The Right Way to Think About Software Design. In Laurel, B. (Ed.), *The Art of Human–Computer Interface Design.* Menlo Park, CA: Addison-Wesley, pp. 235–243.

Neuberg, S. L. (1989). The Goal of Forming Accurate Impressions During Social Interactions: Attenuating the Impact of Negative Expectancies. *Journal of Personality and Social Psychology,* 56(3), pp. 374–386.

Newell, A., Shaw, J. C., and Simon, H. A. (1958). Elements of a Theory of Human Problem Solving. *Psychological Review,* 65, pp. 151–166.

Newman, W. J. (1961). *The Futilitarian Society.* New York: Braziller.

Nickel, J. W. (1989). Computer Networks and Normative Change. In Gould, C. C. (Ed.), *The Information Web.* Boulder, CO: Westview, pp. 161–176.

Nixon, R. M. (1974). Quotation in the *Congressional Record,* January 30, p. H372.

Noble, D. F. (1977). *America by Design: Science, Technology, and the Rise of Corporate Capitalism.* New York: Knopf.

Noddings, N. (1984). *Caring: A Feminine Approach to Ethics and Moral Education.* Berkeley: University of California Press.

Norman, C. (1990). Science Indicators Healthy . . . For Now. *Science,* 247, p. 803.

Norman, D. (1992). *Turn Signals Are the Facial Expressions of Automobiles.* Reading, MA: Addison-Wesley.

Norman, D. A., and Draper, S. W. (1986). *User-Centered System Design.* Hillsdale, NJ: Erlbaum.

Nunamaker, J. (1991). Electronic Meeting Systems to Support Group Work. *Communications of the ACM,* 34, pp. 40–61.

Nunamaker, J., Dennis, A., and Valacich, J. (1991). Electronic Meeting Systems to Support Group Work. *Communications of the ACM,* 34(July), pp. 40–61.

Nurminen, M. (1982). *Human-Scale Information Systems.* Technical Report I.821. Bergen: Institutt for Informasjonsvitenskap, Universitetet i Bergen.

Nussbaum, K. (1989). Computer Monitoring: A Threat to the Right to Privacy? *The CPSR Newsletter,* 7(4), pp. 1–5.

O'Hara, M. H., and Wood, J. K. (1983). Patterns of Awareness: Consciousness and the Group Mind. *Gestalt Journal,* 6(2), pp. 103–116.

Oden, T. C. (1972). *The Intensive Group Experience.* Philadelphia: Westminster.

Ohkubo, M., and Ishii, H. (1990). Design and Implementation of a Shared Workspace by Integrating Individual Workspaces. *SIGOIS Bulletin,* 11(2–3), pp. 142–146.

Oldenburg, H. (1965–1973). *The Correspondence of Henry Oldenburg* (Hall, M. B., and Hall, R. Eds.). Madison: University of Wisconsin Press.

Olson, D. R. (1988). Mind and Media: The Epistemic Functions of Literacy. *Journal of Communication,* 38(3), pp. 27–36.

Olson, M. (1971). *The Logic of Collective Action: Public Goods and the Theory of Groups.* Cambridge, MA: Harvard University Press.

Olson, M. H., and Bly, S. A. (1991). The Portland Experience: A Report on a Distributed Research Group. *International Journal of Man–Machine Studies,* 34, pp. 211–228.

Ong, W. J. (1982). *Orality and Literacy: The Technologizing of the Word.* London: Methuen.

Opper, S. (1988). A Groupware Toolbox. *Byte,* 13(13), pp. 275–282.

Opt, S. K. (1987). Popular Discourse on Expert Systems. Unpublished Ph.D. dissertation, Ohio State University.

Oravec, J. (1982). The Future for Computer Professionals. *Wisconsin Vocational Educator,* 6, Winter, pp. 16–23.

Oravec, J. (1988a). Dependence Upon Computer Systems: The Dangers of the Computer as an Intellectual Crutch. *Proceedings of the Directions and Implications of Advanced Computing Conference.* Palo Alto: Computer Professionals for Social Responsibility, pp. 33–46.

Oravec, J. (1988b). Expert Systems as a Vehicle for the Transfer of Research to Practice. *Proceedings of the Seventh Annual Midwest Research-to-Practice Conference,* University of Wisconsin-Madison, School of Education, October 21–22.

Oravec, J. (1989a). *Issues in the Implementation of Expert Systems: A Scenario Approach.* Technological Literacy Conference No. 4, National Association for Science, Technology, and Society, Washington, DC, February 3–5.

Oravec, J. (1989b). *Computer System Design as Social Experimentation: Some Ethical Issues Involved in "Groupware" Design and Implementation.* Fourth International Conference on Computers and Philosophy, Carnegie-Mellon University, August 9–12.

Oravec, J. (1990a). *Interactions in Science and Society.* Bloomington, IN: Agency for Instructional Technology.

Oravec, J. (1990b). Some Social and Ethical Dimensions of the Use of Groupware in Educational Administration. *Proceedings of the Conference of the Association of Computer Educators.* Minneapolis, October 4–6, pp. 311–317.

Oravec, J. (1990c). CPSR Privacy Work in Madison. *CPSR Newsletter,* 8(4), pp. 22–23.

Oravec, J. (1990d). Groupware and Not-for-Profit Institutions: Cooperative Harmony or Culture Shock? *Computers and Society,* 20(3).

Oravec, J. (1992). "If We Could Do It Over, We'd . . .": Learning from Expert System Projects That Failed to Meet Expectations. *Journal of Systems and Software,* October, pp. 113–122.

Oravec, J. (1993). Secret Sharers: Consensual and Participatory Surveillance Concerns in the Context of Network-Based Systems. *SIGOIS Bulletin,* 14(1), pp. 32–40.

Oravec, J. (in press). The Camera Never Lies: Social Construction of Self and Group in Video, Film, and Photography. *Journal of Value Inquiry.*

Oravec, J. (1996). A Portrait of the Author as an Interacting Group. In Rada, R. (Ed.) *Groupware and Authoring*. Academic Press.

Oren, T. (1987). The Architecture of Static Hypertexts. In Smith, J. (Ed.), *Hypertext 87*. Chapel Hill: University of North Carolina Dept. of Computer Science, pp. 310–324.

Orr, J. (1986). Narratives at Work – Story Telling as Cooperative Diagnostic Activity. *Proceedings of the First Conference on Computer-Supported Cooperative Work*, Austin, TX, December 3–5, pp. 62–72.

Osigweh, C. A. B. (1988). The Challenge of Responsibilities: Confronting the Revolution in Workplace Rights in Modern Organizations. *Employee Responsibilities and Rights Journal*, 1(1), pp. 5–24.

Osmond, H. (1957). Function as a Basis of Psychiatric Ward Design. *Mental Hospitals*, 8, pp. 23–29.

[OTA] Office of Technology Assessment, U.S. Congress. (1986). *Federal Government Information Technology: Electronic Record Systems and Individual Privacy*. Washington, DC: OTA.

[OTA] Office of Technology Assessment, U.S. Congress. (1987). *The Electronic Supervisor*. Washington, DC: OTA.

Ouchi, W. G. (1981). *Theory Z*. Reading, MA: Addison-Wesley.

Over, R. (1982). Collaborative Research and Publication in Psychology. *American Psychologist*, 37, pp. 996–1001.

Overhage, C. F. J., and Harman, R. J. (1967). The On-Line Intellectual Community and the Information Transfer System at MIT in 1975. In Kochen, M. (Ed.), *The Growth of Knowledge*. New York: Wiley, pp. 77–96.

Owen, W. F. (1985). Metaphor Analysis of Cohesiveness in Small Discussion Groups. *Small Group Behavior*, 16(3), pp. 415–424.

Papa, M. J. (1990). Communication Network Patterns and Employee Performance with New Technology. *Communication Research*, 17(3), pp. 344–368.

Parker, D. K. (1979). *Ethical Conflicts in Computer Science and Technology*. Menlo Park, CA: SRI International.

Parker, G. (1990). *Team Players and Teamwork*. San Francisco, CA: Jossey-Bass.

Parker, K. C. H. (1988). Speaking Turns in Small Group Interaction: A Context Sensitive Model. *Journal of Personality and Social Psychology*, 54(6), pp. 965–971.

Parker Follett, M. (1941). *Dynamic Administration: The Collected Papers of Mary Parker Follett*. New York: Harper.

Parks, M. R. (1982). Ideology in Interpersonal Communication: Off the Couch and Into the World. In Burgoon, M. (Ed.), *Communication Yearbook 5*. New Brunswick, NJ: Transaction Books, pp. 79–107.

Parsons, T. (1937). *The Structure of Social Action: A Study in Social Theory*. New York: McGraw-Hill.

Pattison, R. (1982). *On Literacy*. New York: Oxford University Press.

Paulus, P. B. (1989). An Overview and Evaluation of Group Influence. In Paulus, P. B. (Ed.), *Psychology of Group Influence* (Second Edition). Hillsdale, NJ: Erlbaum, pp. 1–12.

PC Computing (1994). Lotus Notes Advertisement, 7(10), p. 145.

PC Week (1989). Editorial: PC Revolution Won, Real Work Begins, December 18, p. 79.

Pea, R. D. (1985). Beyond Amplification: Using the Computer to Reorganize Mental Functioning. *Educational Psychologist*, 20(4), pp. 167–182.

Penzias, A. (1989). *Ideas and Information*. New York: Simon & Schuster.

Perelman, C. (1979). *The New Rhetoric and the Humanities*. Boston, MA: Reidel.

Perelman, L. (1986). The Context of Classroom Writing. *College English,* 48(5), pp. 471–79.

Perin, C. (1989). *Electronic Social Fields in Bureaucracies.* American Anthropological Association Conference, Washington, DC, November 15.

Perrolle, J. (1987). *Computers and Social Change.* Belmont, CA: Wadsworth.

Perrow, C. (1979). *Complex Organizations* (Second Edition). Glenview, IL: Scott, Foresman.

Perry, R. B. (1949). *Characteristically American.* New York: Knopf.

Perry, T. (1994). The Media Event: Hype Helps and Hinders Virtual Reality. *IEEE Spectrum,* 31(1), p. 21.

Peters, T. J. (1987). *Thriving on Chaos.* New York: Knopf.

Peters, T. J. (1992). *Liberation Management.* New York: Knopf.

Peters, T. J., and Waterman, R. H. (1982). *In Search of Excellence.* New York: Harper & Row.

Petitti, G. I. (1989). Video as an Externalizing Object in Drama Therapy. *Arts in Psychotherapy,* 16(2), pp. 121–125.

Pinch, T. J., and Bijker, W. E. (1987). The Social Construction of Facts and Artifacts: Or How Sociology of Science and the Sociology of Technology Might Benefit Each Other. In Bijker, W. E., Hughes, T. P., and Pinch, T. J. (Eds.), *The Social Construction of Technological Systems.* Cambridge, MA: MIT Press, pp. 17–50.

Pirsig, R. (1974). *Zen and the Art of Motorcycle Maintenance.* New York: Morrow.

Planalp, S., and Hewes, D. E. (1982). Cognitive Approach to Communication Theory. In Burgoon, M. (Ed.), *Communication Yearbook 5.* New Brunswick, NJ: Transaction Books, pp. 49–77.

Plant, J. (1930). Some Psychiatric Aspects of Crowded Living Conditions. *American Journal of Psychiatry,* 9, pp. 849–860.

Pliskin, N., Ball, L. D., and Curley, K. F. (1989). Impediments to the Proliferation of Electronic Mail: A Study from the User's Perspective. *Human Systems Management,* 8, pp. 233–241.

Polanyi, L. (1989). *Telling the American Story: A Structural and Cultural Analysis of Conversational Storytelling.* Cambridge, MA: MIT Press.

Polanyi, M. (1959). *The Study of Man.* Chicago: University of Chicago Press.

Pool, I. de S. (Ed.) (1977). *The Social Impact of the Telephone.* Cambridge, MA: MIT Press.

Pool, R. (1989). Strange Bedfellows. *Science,* 245(August 18), pp. 700–703.

Poole, M. S. (1983a). Decision Development in Small Groups II: A Study of Multiple Sequences of Decision-Making. *Communication Monographs,* 50, pp. 206–232.

Poole, M. S. (1983b). Decision Development in Small Groups III: A Multiple Sequence Model of Group Decision Development. *Communication Monographs,* 50, pp. 321–341.

Poole, M. S., and DeSanctis, G. (1990). Understanding the Use of Group Decision Support Systems: The Theory of Adaptive Structuration. In Fulk, J., and Steinfeld, C. (Eds.) *Organizations and Communication Technology.* Newbury Park, CA: Sage, pp. 173–193.

Porat, M. U. (1977). *The Information Economy.* Washington, DC: Department of Commerce, Office of Telecommunications.

Post, R. C. (1989). The Social Foundations of Privacy: Community and Self in Common Law Tort. *California Law Review,* 77(5), pp. 957–1010.

Powell, D. (1989). Videoconferencing: A Wise Strategy. *Networking Management,* 7(12), pp. 28–38.

Prentice-Dunn, S., and Rogers, R. W. (1989). Deindividuation and the Self-Regulation of

Behavior. In Paulus, P. B. (Ed.), *Psychology of Group Influence* (Second Edition). Hillsdale, NJ: Erlbaum, pp. 87–109.

Price, D. K. (1963). *Big Science, Little Science*. New York: Columbia University Press.

Price, J. (1988). Creating a Style for On-Line Help. In Barrett, E. (Ed.), *Text, ConText, and HyperText*. Cambridge, MA: MIT Press, pp. 329–342.

Propst, R. (1968). *The Office – A Facility Based on Change*. Elmhurst, IL: Business Press.

Pye, D. (1978). *The Nature and Aesthetics of Design*. New York: Van Nostrand Rheinhold.

Pylyshyn, Z. (1984). *Computation and Cognition*. Montgomery, VT: Bradford.

Ralston, A. (1987). Let Them Use Calculators. *Technology Review*, 90, pp. 30–31.

Rao, U., and Turoff, M. (1990). Hypertext Functionality: A Theoretical Framework. *International Journal of Human–Computer Interaction*, 2(4), pp. 333–357.

Rapoport, A. (1961). *Fights, Games and Debates*. Ann Arbor: University of Michigan Press.

Rash, W. R., Jr. (1990). The Growth of Groupware. *Byte*, 15(November).

Raskin, J. (1987). The Hype in Hypertext: A Critique. In Smith, J. (Ed.), *Hypertext 87*. Chapel Hill: University of North Carolina Dept. of Computer Science, pp. 325–330.

Rawlins, C. (1990). The Impact of Teleconferencing on the Leadership of Small Decision-Making Groups. *Journal of Organizational Behavior Management*, 10(2), pp. 37–52.

Rawls, A. W. (1989). Interaction Order or Interaction Ritual: Comment on Collins. *Symbolic Interaction*, 12(1), pp. 103–109.

Raymond, J., and Yee, C. (1900). The Collaborative Process and Professional Ethics. *IEEE Transactions on Professional Communication*, 33(2), pp. 77–81.

Reddy, S. (1991). Automatic Office. *LAN Magazine*, July, pp. 75–80.

Reder, S., and Schwab, R. (1988). The Communicative Economy of the Workgroup: Multi-Channel Genres of Communication. *Proceedings of the Second Conference on Computer-Supported Cooperative Work*, September 26–28, pp. 354–368.

Reed, S. (1990). From the Editor. *Connect*, 3(3), p. 3.

Regan, P. (1990). Protecting Privacy and Controlling Bureaucracies. *Governance*, 3(1), pp. 33–54.

Reich, C. A. (1970). *The Greening of America*. New York: Bantam.

Reich, R. B. (1987). Entrepreneurship Reconsidered: The Team as Hero. *Harvard Business Review*, 65(3), 77–83.

Rein, G. L., and Ellis, C. A. (1989). The Nick Experiment Reinterpreted: Implications for Developers and Evaluators of Groupware. *Office: Technology and People*, 5(1), pp. 47–75.

Reither, J. A., and Vipond, D. (1989). Writing as Collaboration. *College English*, 51(8), pp. 855–865.

Rescher, N. (1984). *The Limits of Science*. Berkeley: University of California Press.

Reynolds, C. (1990). Letter of the Law. *Personal Computer World*, 13(5), pp. 208–213.

Rheingold, H. (1985). *Tools for Thought*. New York: Simon & Schuster.

Rheingold, H. (1991). *Virtual Reality*. New York: Simon & Schuster.

Rice, R. E., and Barnett, G. A. (1985). Group Communication Networking in an Information Environment: Applying Metric Multidimensional Scaling. *Communication Yearbook 7*. New Brunswick, NJ: International Communication Association, pp. 315–338.

Richards, R. E. (1988). Breaking Out of Conceptual Methodological Traps: A Case Study from Research on the Computer-Mediated Classroom. *Proceedings of the Human Factors Society*, Vol. 32, pp. 1305–1306.

Richman, L. S. (1987). Software Catches the Team Spirit. *Fortune*. June 8, 1987, pp. 125–136.

Ridgeway, C., and Johnson, C. (1990). What Is the Relationship Between Socioemotional Behavior and Status in Task Groups? *American Journal of Sociology*, 95(5), pp. 1189–1212.

Riesman, D. (1961). *The Lonely Crowd*. New Haven, CT: Yale University Press.

Riesman, D., and Glazer, N. (1951). *Faces in the Crowd: Individual Studies in Character and Politics*. New Haven, CT: Yale University Press.

Ritchie, L. D. (1991). Another Turn of the Information Revolution. *Communication Research*, 18(3), pp. 412–427.

Robinson, K. (1993). ELO: The Elusive Office. *ERCIM News*, 15(December), p. 14.

Robinson, P. (1983). From Suttee to Baseball to Cockfight. *New York Times Book Review*, September 25, pp. 11, 35.

Roethlisberger, F. J., and Dickson, W. J. (1939). *Management and the Worker*. Cambridge, MA: Harvard University Press.

Romanyshyn, R. D. (1989). *Technology as Symptom and Dream*. New York: Routledge.

Root, R. W. (1988). Design of a Multi-Media Vehicle for Social Browsing. *Proceedings of the Second Conference on Computer-Supported Cooperative Work* (Vol. 2), Portland, OR, September 26–28, pp. 25–38.

Rorty, R. (1978). *Philosophy and the Mirror of Nature*. Oxford: Basil Blackwell.

Rose, N. (1989). Individualizing Psychology. In Shotter, J., and Gergen, K. (Eds.), *Texts of Identity*. Newbury Park, CA: Sage, pp. 119–132.

Rose, P. (1989). Literary Warhol. *Yale Review*, 79(1), pp. 21–31.

Rosenbrock, H. (1991). *Machines with a Purpose*. Oxford University Press.

Rosenfeld, L. B. (1979). Self-Disclosure Avoidance: Why I Am Afraid to Tell You Who I Am. *Communication Monographs*, 46, pp. 63–74.

Rothenberg, M. (1993). *TeamAgenda* Keeps Groups in Line. *MacWeek*, January 25, p. 6.

Rothrock, A. M. (1953). Supervising and Training for Teamwork. In Bush, G. P., and Hattery, L. H. (Eds.), *Teamwork in Research*. Washington, DC: American University Press, pp. 82–92.

Rowland, W. (1984). Deconstructing American Communications Policy. *Critical Studies in Mass Communication*, 1(4), pp. 423–435.

Rubinyi, R. M. (1989). Computers and Community: The Organizational Impact. *Journal of Communication*, 39(3), pp. 110–123.

Rule, J. (1973). *Private Lives and Public Surveillance*. London: Allen Lane.

Rule, J., McAdam, D., Sterns, L., and Uglow, D. (1980). *The Politics of Privacy*. New York: New American Library.

Rushby, N. (1990). The Learning Credit Card. *Interactive Learning International*, 6(1), pp. 43–44.

Rutan, J. S., and Groves, J. E. (1989). Presidential Address. *International Journal of Group Psychotherapy*, 39(1), pp. 3–15.

Ryle, G. (1962). *Dilemmas*. Cambridge University Press.

Sackman, H. (1969). The Information Utility, Science, and Society. In Sackman, H., and Nie, N. (Eds.), *The Information Utility and Social Choice*. Montvale, NJ: AFIPS Press, pp. 143–166.

Safayeni, F., MacGregor, J., Lee, E., and Bavelas, A. (1987). Social and Task-Related Impacts of Office Automation: An Exploratory Field Study of a Conceptual Model of the Office. *Human Systems Management*, 7(2), pp. 103–114.

Saffo, P. (1991). Future Conference Room Furniture: Personal Workstations. *Infoworld*, April 29, p. 50.

Safire, W. (1994). Is It Live? Techs Tinkering with Talent. *Milwaukee Journal,* January 4, p. A-11.

Sakane, I. (1991). Recovering the Wholeness of Art: Information Versus Material. *Leonardo,* 24(3), pp. 259–261.

Sampson, E. E. (1977). Psychology and the American Ideal. *Journal of Personality and Social Psychology,* 35, pp. 767–782.

Sampson, E. E. (1985). The Decentralization of Identity: Towards a Revised Concept of Personal and Social Order. *American Psychologist,* 40, pp. 1203–1211.

Sampson, E. E. (1988). The Debate on Individualism. *American Psychologist,* 43, pp. 15–22.

Sampson, E. E. (1989). The Deconstruction of the Self. In Shotter, J., and Gergen, K. J. (Eds.), *Texts of Identity.* Newbury Park, CA: Sage, pp. 1–19.

Samuelson, P. (1991). Is Information Property? *Communications of the ACM,* 34(3), pp. 15–18.

Sanders, B. D. (1990). Making Work Groups Work. *Computerworld,* March 5, pp. 85–89.

Sapolsky, H. M. (1972). *The Polaris System Development: Bureaucratic and Programmatic Success in Government.* Cambridge, MA: Harvard University Press.

Sarbin, T. (1982). *The Social Context of Conduct: Psychological Writings of Theodore Sarbin* (Allen, V. L. and Scheibe, K. E., Eds.). New York: Praeger.

Sarton, G. (1935). Query no. 53, "Standing on the Shoulders of Giants." *Isis,* 24, pp. 107–109.

Savage, C. M. (1990). *Fifth Generation Management.* Bedford, MA: Digital Press.

Sayre, N. (1975). *Rosalind Franklin and DNA.* New York: Norton.

Schaef, A. W., and Fassel, D. (1988). *The Addictive Organization.* San Francisco: Harper & Row.

Schanze, H. (1987). Writing, Literacy and Word-Processing: Changes in the Concept of Literature in the Framework of New Media. *Literacy and Linguistic Computing,* 2(1), pp. 25–28.

Schelling, T. (1969). Some Thoughts on the Relevance of Game Theory to the Analysis of Ethical Systems. In Buchler, I. R., and Nutini, H. G. (Eds.), *Game Theory and the Behavioral Sciences.* Pittsburgh: University of Pittsburgh Press, pp. 45–60.

Schelling, T. (1984). *Choice and Consequence.* Cambridge, MA: Harvard University Press.

Schirmacher, W. (1986). Privacy as an Ethical Problem in the Computer Society. In Mitcham, C., and Huning, A. (Eds.), *Philosophy and Technology: Vol. 2. Information Technology and Computers in Theory and Practice.* Boston: Reidel, pp. 257–267.

Schnechtman, M. (1990). Personhood and Personal Identity. *Journal of Philosophy,* 87, pp. 71–92.

Schneider, L. (1982). Words, Words, Only Words: How Word Processing Vendors Sell Their Wares in Norway. Trondheim: SINTEF.

Schrage, M. (1990). *Shared Minds: The New Technologies of Collaboration.* New York: Random House.

Schuler, D. (1994). Community Networks: Building a New Participatory Medium. *Communications of the ACM,* 37(1), pp. 38–51.

Schumacher, E. F. (1973). *Small Is Beautiful.* New York: Harper & Row.

Schur, E. (1976). *The Awareness Trap: Self-Absorption Instead of Social Change.* New York: Quadrangle-New York Times.

Schwalbe, M. (1988). Role Taking Reconsidered: Linking Competence and Performance to Social Structure. *Journal for the Theory of Social Behaviour,* 18(4), pp. 411–436.

Schwartz, B. (1968). The Social Psychology of Privacy. *American Journal of Sociology,* 73, pp. 741–752.

Schwartz, J. (1989). Back to the Source. *American Demographics,* 11(1), pp. 22–26.

Schwartz, T. (1981). *Media: The Second God.* New York: Random House.

Schweiger, D. M., Sandberg, W. R., and Rechner, P. L. (1989). Experimental Effects of Dialectical Inquiry, Devil's Advocacy, and Consensus Approaches to Strategic Decision Making. *Academy of Management Journal,* 32(4), pp. 745–772.

Schweser, C. (1983). The Economics of Academic Publishing. *Journal of Economic Education,* 14, pp. 60–64.

Scott Morton, M. S. (Ed.). (1991). *The Corporation of the 1990's: Information Technology and Organizational Transformation.* New York: Oxford University Press.

Searle, J. R. (1969). *Speech Acts.* Cambridge University Press.

Seidman, H. (1980). *Politics, Position, and Power.* New York: Oxford University Press.

Seipp, D. J. (1981). *The Right to Privacy in American History.* Cambridge, MA: Harvard University, Center for Information Policy Research.

Selznick, P. (1982). *Law and Society in Transition.* New York: Harper & Row.

Sennett, R. (1977). *The Fall of Public Man.* New York: Vintage.

Seta, J. J., Crisson, J. E., Seta, C. E., and Wang, M. A. (1989). Task Performance and Perceptions of Anxiety. *Journal of Personality and Social Psychology,* 56(3), pp. 387–396.

Seybold, P. (1987). Collective Force: Tools for Group Productivity. *Computerworld,* 21(48A), pp. 35–38.

Seymour, J. (1988). The Coordinator. *PC Computing,* 1(3), pp. 82–83.

Shaiken, H. (1986). *Work Transformed: Automation and Labor in the Computer Age.* Lexington, MA: Lexington Books.

Shamberg, M. (1971). *Guerrilla Television.* New York: Holt, Rinehart, & Winston.

Shapiro, M. A. (1991). Memory and Decision Processes in the Construction of Social Reality. *Communication Research,* 18(1), pp. 3–24.

Shaw, M. (1981). *Group Dynamics: The Psychology of Small Group Behavior* (Third Edition). New York: McGraw-Hill.

Shenkar, O., and Ronen, S. (1987). The Cultural Context of Negotiations: The Implications of Chinese Interpersonal Norms. *Journal of Applied Behavioral Science,* 23(2), pp. 263–275.

Shepard, P. (1987). Telephone Therapy: An Alternative to Isolation. *Clinical Social Work,* 15(Spring), pp. 56–65.

Shibutani, T. (1955). Reference Groups as Perspectives. *American Journal of Sociology,* 60, pp. 562–569.

Shils, E. (1966). Privacy: Its Constitution and Vicissitudes. *Law and Contemporary Problems,* 73, pp. 741–752.

Shimamura, K. (1991). Developed Image Transmission Network Service – Groupware: A New Horizon of TV Conference. *Journal of Instructional Television Engineering Japan,* 45(1), pp. 34–37.

Shneiderman, B. (1987). *Designing the User Interface.* Reading, MA: Addison-Wesley.

Shneiderman, B. (1990a). Human Values and the Future of Technology: A Declaration of Empowerment. *Computers & Society,* 20(3), pp. 1–6.

Shneiderman, B. (1990b). Future Directions for Human–Computer Interaction. *International Journal of Human–Computer Interaction,* 2(1), pp. 73–90.

Short, J., Williams, E., and Christie, B. (1976). *The Social Psychology of Telecommunications.* London: Wiley.

Shotter, J. (1986). Realism and Relativism, Rules and Intentionality, Theories and Accounts: A Response to Morse. *New Ideas in Psychology,* 4, pp. 71–84.

Shotter, J. (1989). Social Accountability and the Social Construction of "You." In Shotter, J., and Gergen, K. (Eds.), *Texts of Identity*, Newbury Park, CA: Sage, pp. 133–151.

Shotter, J., and Gergen, K. J. (Eds.). (1989). *Texts of Identity*. Newbury Park, CA: Sage.

Sibley, H. (1918). The Shop Paper as an Aid to Management. *Factory*, 10(April) (cited in Yates, 1989.)

Siegel, J., Dubrovsky, V., Kiesler, S., and McGuire, T. (1986). Group Processes in Computer-Mediated Communication. *Organizational Behavior and Human Processes*, 37, pp. 157–187.

Silverman, R. J. (1982). Marketing Scholarship: Strategies of Persuasion. *Knowledge: Creation, Diffusion, Utilization*, 3(4), pp. 503–520.

Simmel, G. (1950). *The Sociology of Georg Simmel* (Wolff, K. H., Ed. and Trans.). New York: Free Press.

Simon, B. (1991). Tracking the Minutes that Groups Spend on a Project. *PC Magazine*, 10(14), p. 50.

Simon, H. A. (1957). *Administrative Behavior*. New York: Free Press.

Simon, H. A. (1963/1981). *The Sciences of the Artificial* (First Edition/Second Edition). Cambridge, MA: MIT Press.

Simon, H. A. (1977). *The New Science of Management Decision*. Englewood Cliffs, NJ: Prentice-Hall.

Simon, H. A. (1983). *Reason in Human Affairs*. Stanford, CA: Stanford University Press.

Simons, H. W. (1989). Distinguishing the Rhetorical from the Real: The Case of Psychotherapeutic Placebos. In Simons, H. W. (Ed.), *Rhetoric in the Human Sciences*. Newbury Park, CA: Sage, pp. 109–118.

Sindermann, C. (1982). *Winning the Games Scientists Play*. New York: Plenum.

Sine, S. (1990). Rethinking the Organization. *Enterprise*, 4(1), pp. 24–27.

Singh, B. (1988). Invited Talk on Coordination Systems at the Organizational Computing Conference, Austin TX, November 13–14 (cited in Ellis et al., 1991).

Skafte, D. (1987). Video in Groups: Implications for a Social Theory of the Self. *International Journal of Group Psychotherapy*, 37(3), pp. 389–402.

Slater, S. W. (1989). Computer Support for the Authoring of Documents. *Information Media and Technology*, 23(3), pp. 109–111.

Slavin, R. E. (1983). *Cooperative Learning*. New York: Longman.

Sloman, A. (1978). *The Computer Revolution in Philosophy*. Hassocks: Harvester.

Smeaton, A. F. (1990). Hypertext: The Past, the Present, and Our Future. Dublin City University, Glasnevin, Dublin. Working Paper CA-0290.

Smith, D. (1990). *The Conceptual Practices of Power*. Boston, MA: Northeastern University Press.

Smith, G. (1995). Call It Palpable Progress. *Business Week*, October 9, pp. 93–96.

Smith, H. W. (1980). The CB Handle: An Announcement of Adult Identity. *Symbolic Interaction*, 3(2), pp. 95–108.

Smith, J. B., Weiss, S. F., and Ferguson, G. J. (1987). A Hypertext Writing Environment and Its Cognitive Basis. In Smith, J. (Ed.), *Hypertext 87*. Chapel Hill: University of North Carolina Dept. of Computer Science, pp. 195–214.

Smith, R. E. (1979). *Privacy: How to Protect What's Left of It*. Garden City, NY: Doubleday.

Smith, T. (1990). Study: Client/Server Computing on a Roll. *Network World*, November 19, pp. 17–18.

Smith, T., and Barstow, K. (1988). The Impact of Personality Factors in the Use of Computer-Based Group Collaboration Systems. *TIMS/ORSA*, October 23–26, Denver, CO.

Solomon-Godeau, A. (1986). Who Is Speaking Thus? Some Questions About Documentary Photography. In Falk, L., and Fischer, B. (Eds.), *The Event Horizon*. Toronto: Coach House, pp. 193–214.

Solzhenistsyn, A. I. (1969). *Cancer Ward*. New York: Modern Library.

Sommer, R. (1969). *Personal Space: The Behavioral Basis of Design*. Englewood Cliffs, NJ: Prentice-Hall.

Sorgaard, P. (1987). A Cooperative Work Perspective on Use and Development of Artifacts. Aarhus University, Computer Science Department, Working Paper DAIMI PB-234.

Spence, J. T. (1985). Achievement American Style. *American Psychologist*, 40(12), pp. 1285–1295.

Sprat, T. (1667). *The History of the Royal Society of London*. London.

Sproull, L. S., and Kiesler, S. (1986). Reducing Social Context Cues: The Case of Electronic Mail. *Management Science*, 32, pp. 1492–1511.

Sproull, L. S., and Kiesler, S. (1991). *Connections*. Cambridge, MA: MIT Press.

Srivastva, S., and Barrett, F. J. (1988). The Transforming Nature of Metaphors in Group Development: A Study in Group Theory. *Human Relations*, 41(1), pp. 31–64.

Stamper, R. (1985). Knowledge as Action: A Logic of Social Norms and Individual Affordances. In Gilbert, G. N., and Heath, C. (Eds.), *Social Action and Artificial Intelligence*. Brookfield, VT: Gower, pp. 172–191.

Stasser, G. (1988). Computer Simulation as a Research Tool: The DISCUSS Model of Group Decision Making. *Journal of Experimental Social Psychology*, 24, pp. 393–422.

Steeb, R., and Johnson, R. C. (1981). A Computer-Based Interactive System for Group Decisionmaking. *IEEE Transactions on Systems, Man, and Cybernetics*, SMC-11(8), pp. 554–552.

Stefik, M., Bobrow, D. G., Foster, G., Lanning, S., and Tatar D. (1987). WYSIWIS Revised: Early Experiences with Multi-User Interfaces. *ACM Transactions on Office Information Systems*, 5(2), pp. 147–165.

Steier, D. (1990). Creating a Scientific Community at the Interface Between Engineering Design and AI. *AI Magazine*, 11, pp. 18–22.

Stein, M. R. (1960). *The Eclipse of Community*. Princeton, NJ: Princeton University Press.

Steiner, I. D. (1966). Models for Inferring Relationships Between Group Size and Potential Group Productivity. *Behavioral Science*, 11, pp. 273–283.

Steiner, I. D. (1982). Heuristic Models of Groupthink. In Brandstatter, H., Davis, J. H., and Stocker-Kreichgauer, G. (Eds.), *Group Decision Making*. New York: Academic Press, pp. 503–524.

Steiner, I. D. (1983). Whatever Happened to the Touted Revival of the Group? In Blumberg, H., Hare, A., Kent, V., and Davies, M. (Eds.), *Small Groups and Social Interaction* (Volume 2). New York: Wiley, pp. 539–548.

Steinfield, C. A. (1986). Computer-Mediated Communication in an Organizational Setting: Explaining Task-Related and Socioemotional Uses. In McLaughlin, M. L. (Ed.), *Communication Yearbook 9*. Beverly Hills, CA: Sage, pp. 777–804.

Steinzor, B. (1950). The Spatial Factor in Face to Face Discussion Groups. *Journal of Abnormal and Social Psychology*, 45, pp. 552–555.

Stephenson, G. M., Clark, N. K., and Wade, G. S. (1986). Meetings Make Evidence? An Experimental Study of Collaborative and Individual Recall of a Simulated Police Investigation. *Journal of Personality and Social Psychology*, 50, pp. 113–122.

Sterling, T. D. (1974). Guidelines for Humanizing Computerized Information Systems: A Report from Stanley House. *Communications of the ACM*, 17(11), pp. 609–613.

Stern, G. (1967). *McLuhan: Hot and Cool.* New York: New American Library.

Stern, R. (1986). Penned In. *Critical Inquiry,* 13(1).

Stewart, A. (1986). Appropriate Educational Technology: Does "Appropriateness" Have Implications for the Theoretical Framework of Educational Technology? *ECTJ,* 33(1), pp. 58–65.

Stoller, F. H. (1967). Group Psychotherapy on Television: An Innovation with Hospitalized Patients. *American Psychologist,* 22, pp. 158–162.

Stone, R. T. H. (1989). Inadequacy of Privacy: *Hunter v. Southam* and the Meaning of "Unreasonable." *McGill Law Journal,* 34, pp. 685–704.

Storer, N. W. (1973). Introduction. In Storer, N. (Ed.), *The Sociology of Science* (Robert K. Merton). Chicago: University of Chicago Press.

Storms, M. (1973). Videotape and the Attribution Process: Reversing Actors' and Observers' Points of View. *Journal of Personality and Social Psychology,* 27(2), pp. 165–175.

Stoutland, F. (1990). Self and Society in the Claims of Individualism. *Studies in Philosophy and Education,* 10, pp. 105–127.

Strassman, P. A. (1985). *Information Payoff: The Transformation of Work in the Electronic Age.* New York: Free Press.

Stratton, C. R. (1989). Collaborative Writing in the Workplace. *IEEE Transactions on Professional Communication,* 32(3), pp. 178–182.

Straub, D., and Beauclair, R. (1988). Current and Future Uses of Group Decision Support System Technology: Report of a Recent Empirical Study. *Journal of Management Information Systems,* 5(1), pp. 101–116.

Stroup, A. (1990). *A Company of Scientists: Botany, Patronage, and Community at the Seventeenth-Century Parisian Royal Academy of Sciences.* Berkeley, CA: University of California Press.

Struch, N., and Schwartz, S. H. (1989). Intergroup Aggression: Its Predictors and Distinctness from In-Group Bias. *Journal of Personality and Social Psychology,* 56(3), pp. 364–373.

Suchman, L. (1988a). From the Program Chair. *Proceedings of the Second Conference on Computer-Supported Cooperative Work,* Portland, OR, September 26–29, pp. v–vi.

Suchman, L. (1988b). Representing Practice in Cognitive Science. *Human Studies,* 11, pp. 305–325.

Sundstrom, E., DeMeuse, K. P., and Futrell, D. (1990). Work Teams: Applications and Effectiveness. *American Psychologist,* 45(2), pp. 120–137.

Sundstrom, E., Herbert, R. K., and Brown, D. W. (1982). Privacy and Communication in an Open Plan Office: A Case Study. *Environment and Behavior,* 14(5), pp. 543–559.

Sundstrom, E., and Sundstrom M. G. (1986). *Workplaces: The Psychology of the Physical Environment in Offices and Factories.* Cambridge University Press.

Sutherland, I. E. (1965). The Ultimate Display. *Proceedings of the International Federation of Information Processing (IFIP) Congress 65,* p. 506.

Sutherland, I. E. (1968). A Head-Mounted Three Dimensional Display. *Proceedings of the AFIPS Fall Joint Computer Conference.* Washington, DC: Thompson Books, pp. 757–64.

Szasz, T. (1961). *The Myth of Mental Illness.* New York: Dell.

Tamblyn, C. (1991). Image Processing in Chicago Video Art, 1970–1980. *Leonardo,* 24(3), pp. 303–310.

Tannenbaum, A. (1962). Control in Organizations. *Administrative Science Quarterly,* 7, pp. 236–257.

Tart, C. (1990). Multiple Personality, Altered States, and Virtual Reality: The World

Simulation Process Approach. *Dissociation: Progress in the Dissociative Disorders,* 3(4), pp. 222–233.

Taylor, F. W. (1911/1947). *Scientific Management.* New York: Harper Brothers.

Taylor, G. S., and Davis, J. S. (1989). Individual Privacy and Computer-Based Human Resource Information Systems. *Journal of Business Ethics,* 8, pp. 569–576.

Taylor, J. R. (1988). Are New Technologies Really Reshaping Our Organizations? *Computer Communications,* 11(5), pp. 245–252.

Tenner, E. (1990). From Slip to Chip: How Evolving Techniques of Information Gathering, Storage and Retrieval Have Shaped the Way We Do Mental Work. *Princeton Alumni Weekly,* November 21, pp. 9–14.

Terdoslavich, W. (1990). PCs Reach Out. *Computer Systems News,* 467, p. 33.

Teubner, G. (1989). How the Law Thinks: Toward a Constructivist Epistemology of Law. *Law and Society Review,* 23(5), pp. 727–757.

Thagard, P. (1988). *Computational Philosophy of Science.* Cambridge, MA: MIT Press.

Thelen, H. A. (1954). *Dynamics of Groups at Work.* Chicago: University of Chicago Press.

Thibaut, J. W., and Kelly, H. H. (1959). *The Social Psychology of Groups.* New York: Wiley.

Thomson, A. (1993). *Virtual Girl.* New York: Ace Books.

Thompson, G. B. (1975). An Assessment Methodology for Evaluating Communications Innovations. *IEEE Transactions on Communications,* 23, pp. 1045–1054.

Thompson, L., Sarbaugh-McCall, M., and Norris, D. F. (1989). The Social Impacts of Computing: Control in Organizations. *Social Science Computer Review,* 7(4), pp. 407–417.

Thordsen, M. L., and Klein, G. A. (1989). Cognitive Processes of the Team Mind. *IEEE International Conference on Systems, Man, and Cybernetics.* New York: IEEE Press, pp. 46–49.

Tjosvold, D. (1984). Cooperation Theory and Organizations. *Human Relations,* 37(9), pp. 743–767.

Tjosvold, D. (1986). *Working Together to Get Things Done.* Lexington, MA: Lexington Books.

Tjosvold, D., and McNeely, L. T. (1988). Innovation Through Communication in an Educational Bureaucracy. *Communication Research,* 15(5), pp. 568–581.

Todorov, T. (1990). *Genres in Discourse.* Cambridge University Press.

Tondl, L. (1989). Systems Analysis of Rational Actions and the Delegation Problems. *Systems Research,* 6(4), pp. 321–329.

Toolan, M. J. (1988). *Narrative: A Critical Linguistic Introduction.* London: Routledge.

Traub, D. C. (1990). Simulated World as Classroom: The Potential for Designed Learning Within Virtual Environments. *Multimedia Review,* Summer, pp. 18–23.

Trigg, R., and Irish, P. M. (1987). Hypertext Habitats: Experiences of Writers in Note-Cards. In Smith, J. (Ed.), *Hypertext 87.* Chapel Hill: University of North Carolina Dept. of Computer Science, pp. 89–108.

Trigg, R., Suchman, L., and Halasz, F. (1986). Supporting Collaboration in NoteCards. *Proceedings of the First Conference on Computer-Supported Cooperative Work,* Austin, TX, December 3–5.

Trimbur, J. (1989). Consensus and Difference in Collaborative Learning. *College English,* 51(6), pp. 602–618.

Triplett, N. (1898). The Dynamogenic Factors in Pacemaking and Competition. *American Journal of Psychology,* 9, pp. 507–533.

Tuckman, B. (1965). Developmental Sequence in Small Groups. *Psychological Bulletin,* 63, pp. 384–399.

Tuckman, B., and Jensen, M. (1977). Stages of Small Group Development. *Group and Organizational Studies,* 2, pp. 419–427.

Turkle, S. (1984). *The Second Self: Computers and the Human Spirit.* New York: Simon & Schuster.

Turner, F. J. (1920). The Significance of the Frontier in American History. In Turner, F. J. (Ed.), *The Frontier in American History.* New York: Holt, pp. 1–28.

Turner, J. C., and Oakes, P. J. (1989). Self-Categorization Theory and Social Influence. In Paulus, P. B. (Ed.), *Psychology of Group Influence* (Second Edition). Hillsdale, NJ: Erlbaum, pp. 223–278.

Turoff, M. (1989). The Anatomy of a Computer Application Innovation: Computer Mediated Communications (CMC). *Technological Forecasting and Social Change,* 36, pp. 107–122.

Turoff, M., and Hiltz, S. R. (1982). Computer Support for Group Versus Individual Decisions. *IEEE Transactions on Communications,* COM 30(1), pp. 82–90.

Twain, M. (1869/1984). *The Innocents Abroad, Roughing It.* New York: The Library of America.

Unger, R. (1975). *Knowledge and Politics.* New York: Free Press.

Uppal, G. (1984). *Narratives in Conversation.* Unpublished M.A. thesis, University of Singapore.

Vainio-Larsson, A. (1988). *Hypermedia and Human–Computer Interaction.* Technical Report LiU-LIBLAB-R-1988:1, Department of Computer and Information Science. Linkoping, Sweden: Linkoping University.

Vallee, J. (1982). *The Network Revolution: Confessions of a Computer Scientist.* Berkeley, CA: And/Or Press.

Van, J. (1990). Computers Taking a Seat at Meetings. *Chicago Tribune,* December 31, pp. 1, 4 (Business Section).

Vanden Heuvel, M. (1991). *Performing Drama: Dramatizing Performance.* Ann Arbor: University of Michigan Press.

Vansina, J. (1985). *Oral Tradition as History.* Madison, WI: University of Wisconsin Press.

Vian, K., and Johansen, R. (1983). Knowledge Synthesis and Computer-Based Communication Systems: Changing Behaviors and Concepts. In Ward, S. A., and Reed, L. J. (Eds.), *Knowledge Structure and Use: Implications for Synthesis and Interpretation.* Philadelphia: Temple University Press, pp. 487–514.

Vogel, D. R., and Nunamaker, J. F. (1990). Design and Assessment of a Group Decision Support System. In Galegher, J., Kraut, R. E., and Egido, C. (Eds.), *Intellectual Teamwork,* Hillsdale, NJ: Erlbaum, pp. 511–528.

Vogel, D. R., Nunamaker, J. F., Martz, W. B., Grohowski, R., and McGoff, C. (1989). Electronic Meeting System Experience at IBM. *Journal of Management Information Systems,* 6(3), pp. 25–43.

Volonino, L. (1989). A Synthesis of Group Dynamic Processes and GDSS Designs to Foster Innovative Organizational Decisions. *Proceedings of the Twenty-Second Annual Hawaii International Conference on System Sciences,* Vol. 22, pp. 504–511.

von Biel, V. (1991). Groupware Grows Up. *MacUser,* 7(6), pp. 207–212.

Von Simson, C. (1990). Burger, Fries, and Project Management. *Computerworld,* April 2, p. 39.

Wall Street Journal (1990). Electronic Mail: Is It for Your Eyes Only? August 6, B-1.

Ware, W. H. (1982). *A Taxonomy for Privacy.* Report on the National Symposium on Personal Privacy and Information Technology, American Bar Association.

Warren, S., and Brandeis, L. (1890). The Right of Privacy. *Harvard Law Review*, 4, p. 193.

Waters, J. A., and Bird, F. (1987). The Moral Dimension of Organizational Culture. *Journal of Business Ethics*, 6, pp. 15–22.

Watkins, J. W. N. (1973). Historical Explanation in the Social Sciences. In O'Neill, J. (Ed.), *Modes of Individualism and Collectivism*. Exeter, NH: Heinemann, pp. 166–178.

Watson, J. (1968). *The Double Helix: A Personal Account of the Discovery of the Structure of DNA*. New York: Atheneum.

Watson, R., DeSanctis, G., and Poole, M. S. (1988). Using a GDSS to Facilitate Group Consensus: Some Intended and Unintended Consequences. *MIS Quarterly*, 12(3), pp. 463–477.

Watzlawick, P., Beavin, J. H., and Jackson, D. D. (1967). *Pragmatics of Human Communication*. New York: Norton, 1967.

Webb, N. W. (1987). Peer Interaction and Learning with Computers in Small Groups. *Computers in Human Behavior*, 3(3–4), pp. 193–209.

Weber, M. (1956/1978). *Economy and Society*. Berkeley: University of California Press.

Weber, M. (1958). *The Protestant Ethic and the Spirit of Capitalism*. New York: Scribner.

Wegner, P. (1991). *Perspectives on Object-Oriented Design*. Department of Computer Science, Brown University, Technical Report CS-91-01.

Weick, K. E. (1979). *The Social Psychology of Organizing*. Reading, MA: Addison-Wesley.

Weick, K. E. (1989). Organized Improvisation: 20 Years of Organizing. *Communication Studies*, 40(4), pp. 241–248.

Weinberg, A. M. (1970). Scientific Teams and Scientific Laboratories. *Daedalus*, 99(4), pp. 1056–1075.

Weinberg, G. (1971). *The Psychology of Computer Programming*. New York: Van Nostrand Reinhold.

Weizenbaum, J. (1979). *Computer Power and Human Reason: From Judgment to Calculation*. San Francisco: Freeman.

Wellens, A. R., and Ergener, D. (1988). The C.I.T.I.E.S. Game: A Computer-Based Situation Assessment Task for Studying Distributed Decision Making. *Simulation and Games*, 19, pp. 304–327.

Wellner, P., Mackay, W., and Gold, R. (1993). Computer-Augmented Environments: Back to the Real World. *Communications of the ACM*, 36(7), pp. 24–26.

Westin, A. (1970). *Privacy and Freedom*. New York: Atheneum.

Westin, A. (1972). *Databanks in a Free Society*. (Project on Computer Databanks, National Academy of Sciences.) New York: Quadrangle Books.

Westin, A. (1982). Home Information Systems: The Privacy Debate. *Datamation*, 28(1), pp. 100–114.

Weston, R. E. (1962). Modest Proposal. *Physics Today*, 15, pp. 79–80.

Wexelblat, A. (1993). *Virtual Reality: Applications and Explorations*. Boston: Academic Publishing.

Wheelis, A. (1958). *The Quest for Identity*. New York: Norton.

White, J. B. (1991). GM Struggles to Get Saturn Car on Track After Rough Launch. *Wall Street Journal*, May 24, p. A1, A12.

White, J. R. (1991). President's Letter: Privacy. *Communications of the ACM*, 34(4), pp. 11–12.

Whiteside, J., and Wixon, D. (1988). Contextualism as a World Hypothesis for the Reformation of Meetings. *Proceedings of the Second Conference on Computer-Supported Cooperative Group Work* (Vol. 2), Portland, OR, September 26–28.

Whitley, R. D. (1972). Black Boxism and the Sociology of Science. In Halmos, P. (Ed.), *The Sociology of Science*. Keele: University of Keele, pp. 62–92.

Whittaker, A. (1991). Let My PCs Go. *Byte,* 16(4), April, p. 394.

Whittock, T. (1990). *Metaphor and Film*. Cambridge University Press.

Whyte, W. H. (1956). *The Organization Man*. New York: Doubleday.

Wicklund, R. A. (1989). The Appropriation of Ideas. In Paulus, P. B. (Ed.), *Psychology of Group Influence*. Hillsdale, NJ: Erlbaum, pp. 393–420.

Wiener, N. (1948). *Cybernetics*. Cambridge, MA: MIT Press.

Wiener, N. (1954/1967). *The Human Use of Human Beings*. New York: Doubleday.

Wiil, U. K. (1993). Experiences with HyperBase: A Hypertext Database Supporting Cooperative Work. *SIGMOD Record,* 22(4), pp. 19–25.

Wilde, O. (1984). *Teleny: A Novel Attributed to Oscar Wilde*. San Francisco: Gay Sunshine Press.

Wilensky, H. L. (1964). The Professionalization of Everyone? *American Journal of Sociology,* September, pp. 138–158.

Wilke, J. R. (1993). Computer Links Erode Hierarchical Nature of Workplace Culture. *Wall Street Journal,* December 9, p. 1.

Wilkinson, R. (1988). *The Pursuit of American Character*. New York: Harper & Row.

Williams, B. (1989). Setting the User Free (Letters). *PC Computing,* 2(1).

Williams, D. (1990). New Technologies for Coordinating Work. *Datamation,* May 15, pp. 92–96.

Williams, E. (1977). Experimental Comparisons of Face-to-Face and Mediated Communication: A Review. *Psychological Bulletin,* 84, pp. 963–976.

Williams, G. (1992). Coming to Grips with the Non-Teamplayer. *Supervisory Management,* 37(5), p. 5.

Williams, R. (1974). *Television: Technology and Cultural Form*. Glasgow: Fontana/ Collins.

Williams, R. M. (1960). *American Society*. New York: Knopf.

Williams, W. H. (1910). *Railroad Correspondence File* (Revised by John L. Hanna.) New York: Devinne-Hallenbeck Co.

Wilson, K. G. (1988). *Technologies of Control: The New Interactive Media for the Home*. Madison: University of Wisconsin Press.

Winner, L. (1977). *Autonomous Technology*. Cambridge, MA: MIT Press.

Winnicott, D. W. (1951/1974). *Playing and Reality*. Harmondsworth: Penguin.

Winnicott, D. W. (1971). *Therapeutic Consultations in Child Psychiatry*. New York: Basic.

Winograd, T. (1988a). Guest Editor's Introduction to the Issue: Special Issue on the Language/Action Perspective. *ACM Transactions on Office Automation Systems,* 6(2), pp. 83–86.

Winograd, T. (1988b). Where the Action Is. *Byte,* 13(13), 256–258.

Winograd, T. (1989). Groupware: The Next Wave or Just Another Advertising Slogan? *Proceedings of COMPCON* (IEEE) (Vol. 34). San Francisco, CA, February, pp. 198–200.

Winograd, T., and Flores, F. (1986). *Understanding Computers and Cognition*. New York: Ablex.

Wittgenstein, L. (1968). *Philosophical Investigations*. London: Basil Blackwell.

Wolfe, J., and Box, T. M. (1988). Team Cohesion Effects on Business Game Performance. *Simulation & Games,* 19, pp. 82–98.

Wollen, P. (1969). *Signs and Meaning in the Cinema*. London: Secker & Warburg.

Woolf, V. (1929). *A Room of One's Own*. New York: Harcourt, Brace.

Woolgar, S. (1985). Why Not a Sociology of Machines? The Case of Sociology and Artificial Intelligence. *Sociology*, 19, pp. 557–572.

Woolgar, S. (1987). Reconstructing Man and Machine: A Note on Sociological Critiques of Cognitivism. In Bijker, W. E., Hughes, T. P., and Pinch, T. J. (Eds.), *The Social Construction of Technological Systems*. Cambridge, MA: MIT Press, pp. 311–328.

Wrong, D. H. (1961). The Oversocialized Conception of Man in Modern Sociology. *American Sociological Review*, 26(2), pp. 183–193.

Wrong, D. H. (1966). The Idea of "Community": A Critique. *Dissent*, 13, pp. 290–297.

Yalom, I. D. (1975). *The Theory and Practice of Group Psychotherapy* (Second Edition). New York: Basic.

Yamgishi, T., and Sato, K. (1986). Motivational Bases of the Public-Goods Problem. *Journal of Personality and Social Psychology*, 50, pp. 67–73.

Yankelovich, N., Landow, G., and Cody, D. (1985). Reading and Writing the Electronic Book. *IEEE Computer*, 18, pp. 15–30.

Yates, J. (1989). *Control Through Communication: The Rise of System in American Management*. Baltimore, MD: Johns Hopkins University Press.

Young, K. (1989). Narrative Embodiments: Enclaves of the Self in the Realm of Medicine. In Shotter, J., and Gergen, K. J. (Eds.), *Texts of Identity*. Newbury Park, CA: Sage, pp. 152–165.

Youngblood, G. (1987). Art and Ontology: Electronic Visualization in Chicago. In Falk, L., and Fischer, B. (Eds.), *The Event Horizon*. Toronto: Coach House, pp. 323–346.

Zachary, G. P. (1990). "Artificial Reality" Gets Taken Seriously in Tokyo (Technology). *Wall Street Journal*, October 11, B-1.

Ziman, J. (1968). *Public Knowledge: An Essay Concerning the Social Dimension of Science*. Cambridge University Press.

Ziman, J. (1976). *The Force of Knowledge*. Cambridge University Press.

Zimbardo, P. G. (1970). The Human Choice: Individuation, Reason, and Order Versus Deindividuation, Impulse, and Chaos. In Arnold, W. J., and Levine, D. (Eds.), *Nebraska Symposium on Motivation*. Lincoln: University of Nebraska Press, pp. 237–307.

Zimbardo, P. G. (1977). *Shyness: What It Is and What to Do About It*. Reading, MA: Addison-Wesley.

Zimmer, L., and Cornell, P. (1990). An Examination of Flexible Group Work Spaces in the Open Office. *Proceedings of the Human Factors Society 34th Annual Meeting*, pp. 542–546.

Zinn, K. L. (1977). Computer Facilitation of Communication Within Professional Communities. *Behavioral Research Methods and Instrumentation*, 9(2), pp. 96–107.

Zuboff, S. (1988). *The Age of the Smart Machine*. New York: Random House.

Zuckerman, H. A. (1968). Patterns of Name Ordering Among Authors of Scientific Papers: A Study of Social Symbolism and Its Ambiguity. *American Journal of Sociology*, pp. 276–291.

Zuckerman, S. (1984). Medical Malpractice Claims, Legal Costs, and the Practice of Defensive Medicine. *Health Affairs*, 3(3), pp. 128–134.

Author index

Subject index

374